Benjamin Fiore, S.J., is president and professor of religious studies at Campion College at the University of Regina (Canada).

THE PASTORAL EPISTLES

First Timothy
Second Timothy
Titus

Sacra Pagina Series

Volume 12

The Pastoral Epistles

First Timothy
Second Timothy
Titus

Benjamin Fiore, S.J.

Daniel J. Harrington, S.J.
Editor

A Michael Glazier Book

LITURGICAL PRESS
Collegeville, Minnesota

www.litpress.org

A Michael Glazier Book published by Liturgical Press.

Unless otherwise stated, Scripture translation is the author's.

1 2 3 4 5 6 7 8 9

Library of Congress Cataloging-in-Publication Data

Fiore, Benjamin, 1943–
The Pastoral Epistles : First Timothy, Second Timothy, Titus / Benjamin Fiore, Daniel J. Harrington, editor.
p. cm. — (Sacra pagina series ; v. 12)
"A Michael Glazier book."
Includes bibliographical references and indexes.
ISBN-13: 978-0-8146-5814-7
ISBN-10: 0-8146-5814-8
1. Bible. N.T. Pastoral Epistles—Criticism, interpretation, etc.
I. Harrington, Daniel, J. II. Title.

BS2735.52.F56 2007
227'.83077—dc22

2006036755

Dedicated with thanks to

the Jesuits of the New York and Upper Canada Provinces and to

my colleagues at Canisius and Campion Colleges

CONTENTS

FIRST TIMOTHY, SECOND TIMOTHY, TITUS

1 TIMOTHY

2 TIMOTHY

TITUS

Translation, Notes, Interpretation

Indexes

EDITOR'S PREFACE

Sacra Pagina is a multi-volume commentary on the books of the New Testament. The expression *Sacra Pagina* ("Sacred Page") originally referred to the text of Scripture. In the Middle Ages it also described the study of Scripture to which the interpreter brought the tools of grammar, rhetoric, dialectic, and philosophy. Thus *Sacra Pagina* encompasses both the text to be studied and the activity of interpretation.

This series presents fresh translations and modern expositions of all the books of the New Testament. Written by an international team of Catholic biblical scholars, it is intended for biblical professionals, graduate students, theologians, clergy, and religious educators. The volumes present basic introductory information and close exposition. They self-consciously adopt specific methodological perspectives, but maintain a focus on the issues raised by the New Testament compositions themselves. The goal of *Sacra Pagina* is to provide sound critical analysis without any loss of sensitivity to religious meaning. This series is therefore catholic in two senses of the word: inclusive in its methods and perspectives, and shaped by the context of the Catholic tradition.

The Second Vatican Council described the study of the "sacred page" as the "very soul of sacred theology" (*Dei Verbum* 24). The volumes in this series illustrate how Catholic scholars contribute to the council's call to provide access to Sacred Scripture for all the Christian faithful. Rather than pretending to say the final word on any text, these volumes seek to open up the riches of the New Testament and to invite as many people as possible to study seriously the "sacred page."

Daniel J. Harrington, s.j.

ABBREVIATIONS

Biblical Books and Apocrypha

Gen	Nah	1-2-3-4 Kgdms	John
Exod	Hab	Add Esth	Acts
Lev	Zeph	Bar	Rom
Num	Hag	Bel	1-2 Cor
Deut	Zech	1-2 Esdr	Gal
Josh	Mal	4 Ezra	Eph
Judg	Ps (*pl.*: Pss)	Jdt	Phil
1-2 Sam	Job	Ep Jer	Col
1-2 Kgs	Prov	1-2-3-4 Macc	1-2 Thess
Isa	Ruth	Pr Azar	1-2 Tim
Jer	Cant	Pr Man	Titus
Ezek	Eccl (*or* Qoh)	Sir	Phlm
Hos	Lam	Sus	Heb
Joel	Esth	Tob	Jas
Amos	Dan	Wis	1-2 Pet
Obad	Ezra	Matt	1-2-3 John
Jonah	Neh	Mark	Jude
Mic	1-2 Chr	Luke	Rev

Other Ancient Texts

Aelian, *Var. hist.*	*Varia historia*
Aeschines, *Tim.*	*In Timarchum*
Aeschylus, *Choeph.*	*Choephori*
Anth. graec.	*Anthologia graeca*
Apuleius	
Apol.	*Apologia*
Metam.	*Metamorphoses*
Aristotle	
Eth. nic.	*Ethica nichomachea*
Pol.	*Politica*

Cicero	
Amic	*De Amicitia*
Att.	*Epistulae ad Atticum*
Cael.	*Pro Caelio*
Fam.	*Epistulae ad familiares*
Off.	*De Officiis*
Rosc. Amer.	*Pro Sexto Roscio Amerino*
Verr.	*In Verrem*
Corp. herm.	*Corpus Hermeticum*
Demophilus, *Sim.*	*Similitudines*
Demosthenes, *Or.*	*Orationes*
Dio Cassius, *Rom. Hist.*	*Roman History*
Dio Chrysostom	
Alex.	*Or. 32 Ad Alexandrinos*
Charid.	*Or. 30 Charidemus*
Nicom.	*Or. 38 Ad Nicomedienses*
1 Tars.	*Or. 33 Tarsica prior*
Diog. L.	Diogenes Laertius, *De clarorum philosophorum vitis*
Dionysius of Halicarnassus	
Ant. rom.	*Antiquitates Romanae*
Thuc.	*De Thucydide*
Ep. Aristippus	*Epistle of Aristippus* (*Cynic Epistles*)
Ep. Diogenes	*Epistle of Diogenes* (*Cynic Epistles*)
Ep. Socrates	*Epistle of Socrates* (*Cynic epistles*)
Epictetus	
Diatr.	*Diatribae* (*Dissertationes*)
Ench.	*Enchiridion*
Gnom.	*Gnomologium*
Euripides, *El.*	Euripides, *Electra*
Horace	
Carm.	*Carmina*
Ep.	*Epistulae*
Juvenal, *Sat.*	*Satirae*
Libanius	
Decl.	*Declamationes*
Loc.	*Loci communes*
Livy, *Hist.*	Livy, *Ab Urbe Condita* (*Historia Romae*)
Lucian	
Cal.	*Calumniae non temere credendum*
Cat.	*Cataplus*
Demon.	*Demonax*
Dial. d.	*Dialogi deorum*
Dial. Mort.	*Dialogi mortuorum*
Imag.	*Imagines*
Iupp. Trag.	*Iuppiter tragoedus*
Musc. laud.	*Muscae laudation*
Pereg.	*De Morte Peregrini*

Pisc.	*Piscator*
Vit. auct.	*Vitarum auctio*
Marcus Aurelius, *Ant.*	*Eis heauton*
Martial, *Ep.*	*Epigrammates*
Maximus of Tyre, *Or.*	*Orationes*
Musonius Rufus	
fr.	*Fragment*
Or.	*Orationes*
Ovid	
Ars	*Ars amatoria*
Metam.	*Metamorphoses*
Tristia	*Tristia ex Ponto*
Philemon, *fr.*	Philemon, *fragment*
Philodemus, *fr.*	Philodemus, *Fragment* in *On Frank Speech*
Plato	
Leg.	*Leges*
Phaed.	*Phaedo*
Phaedr.	*Phaedrus*
Tim.	*Timaeus*
Plautus, *Curc.*	Plautus, *Curculio*
Pliny, *Nat.*	Pliny (the Elder), *Naturalis historia*
Pliny, *Ep.*	Pliny (the Younger), *Epistulae*
Plutarch	
Adol. poet. aud.	*Quomodo adolescens poetas audire debeat*
Adul.amic.	*Quomodo adulator ab amico internoscatur*
Comp. Lyc. Num	*Comparatio Lycurgi et Numae*
Conj. praec.	*Conjugalia Praecepta*
Cupid. divit.	*De cupiditate divitiarum*
De esu	*De esu cranium*
Ti. C. Gracch.	*Tiberius et Caius Gracchus*
Inim. util.	*De capienda ex inimicis utilitate*
Is. Os.	*De Iside et Osiride*
Mor.	*Moralia*
Oth.	*Otho*
Pel.	*Pelopidas*
Rect. rat. aud.	*De recta ratione audiendi*
Virt. mor.	*De virtute morali*
Virt. Prof.	*Quomodo quis suos in virtute sentiat profectus*
Poll.	Pollianus
Polybius, *Hist.*	*Historia*
Pseudo-Aelius Aristides, *Rhet.*	*Rhetorica*
Pseudo-Isocrates, *Or.*	*Orationes*
Pseudo-Phocylidesa, *Sent.*	*Sententiae*
Pseudo-Plato, *Def.*	*Definitiones*
Pseudo-Plutarch	
Lib. ed.	*De liberis educandis*
Vit. Hom.	*De vita et poesi Homeri*

Quintilian, *Inst.*	*Institutio Oratoria*
Sallust, *Bell. Cat.*	*Bellum catilinae*
Seneca	
Ben.	*De beneficiis*
Ep.	*Epistulae morales*
Tranq.	*De tranquillitate animi*
Prov.	*De providentia*
Sextus Empiricus, *Math.*	*Adversus mathematicos*
Simplicius, *Epict.*	*In Epictetum commentaria*
Stobaeus	
Eth.	*Ethica*
fr.	*fragment*
Strabo, *Geogr.*	*Geographica*
Terence, *Heaut.*	*Heauton timoroumenos*
Themistius, *Or.*	*Orationes*
Theon, *Rhet.*	*Rhetorica*
Vit. Pyth.	Iamblichus, *De Vita Pythagorica*

Jewish Texts

Jos.As.	Joseph and Asenath
Josephus	
C. Ap.	*Against Apion*
Ant.	*Jewish Antiquities*
Bell.	*Jewish War*
Old Testament Pseudepigrapha	
2 Bar.	*2 Baruch*
Ep. Arist.	*Letter of Aristaeus*
Pss. Sol.	*Psalms of Solomon*
3–4 Macc.	*3–4 Maccabees*
T. Mos.	*Testament of Moses*
Testaments of the 12 Patriarchs	
T. Dan.	*Testament of Dan*
T. Iss.	*Testament of Issachar*
T. Jud.	*Testament of Judah*
T. Levi	*Testament of Levi*
T. Naph.	*Testament of Naphtali*
T. Reu.	*Testament of Reuben*
T. Sim.	*Testament of Simeon*
Old Testament Versions	
MT	Masoretic Text
LXX	*Septuagint*
Philo	
Abraham	*On the Life of Abraham*
Agriculture	*On Agriculture*
Alleg. Interp.	*Allegorical Interpretation*

Creation	*On the Creation of the World*
Curses	*On Curses*
Decalogue	*On the Decalogue*
Dreams	*On Dreams*
Embassy	*On the Embassy to Gaius*
Eternity	*On the Eternity of the World*
Flight	*On Flight and Finding*
Giants	*On Giants*
Heir	*Who Is the Heir?*
Life	*The Life*
Moses	*On the Life of Moses*
Prelim. Studies	*On the Preliminary Studies*
Rewards	*On Rewards and Punishments*
QE	*Questions and Answers on Exodus*
QG	*Questions and Answers on Genesis*
Sacrifices	*On the Sacrifices of Cain and Abel*
Spec. Leg.	*On the Special Laws*
Unchangeable	*That God Is Unchangeable*
Worse	*That the Worse Attacks the Better*
Rabbinic Works	
Abot. R. Nat.	*ʾAbot de Rabbi Nathan*
Deut. Rab.	*Deuteronomy Rabbah*
Gen. Rab.	*Genesis Rabbah*
Mek. Exod.	*Mekilta on Exodus*
Num R	*Numbers Rabbah*
Pesiq. Rab.	*Pesiqta Rabbati*
Pirqe R. El.	*Pirqe Rabbi Eliezer*
Tanḥ	*Tanḥuma*
Yalq. Schim. Ber.	*Yalqut Schim. Berešit*
Talmud	
b. Sotah	*Babylonian Talmud Sotah*
y. Sotah	*Jerusalem Talmud Sotah*
Targums	
Tg. Jer.	*Targum Jeremiah*

Early Christian and Patristic Texts

ACD	Augustine. *On Christian Doctrine*. Indianapolis: Bobbs-Merrill, 1958
ANF	*Ante-Nicene Fathers*. Reprint, Peabody, MA: Hendrickson, 1994
Apostolic Fathers	
Barn.	*Barnabas*
1-2 Clem.	*1–2 Clement*
Did.	*Didachē*

Diogn.	*Diognetus*
Herm. *Mand.*	Shepherd of Hermas, *Mandate*
Herm. *Sim.*	Shepherd of Hermas, *Similitude*
Herm. *Vis.*	Shepherd of Hermas, *Vision*
Ign. *Eph.*	Ignatius, *To the Ephesians*
Ign. *Magn.*	Ignatius, *To the Magnesians*
Ign. *Phld.*	Ignatius, *To the Philadelphians*
Ign. *Pol.*	Ignatius, *To Polycarp*
Ign. *Smyrn.*	Ignatius, *To the Smyrnaeans*
Ign. *Trall.*	Ignatius, *To the Trallians*
Mart. Pol.	*Martyrdom of Polycarp*
Pol. *Phil.*	Polycarp, *To the Philippians*
Athenagoras, *Leg.*	*Legatio pro Christianis*
Augustine	
Civ.	*The City of God*
Conf.	*Confessions*
Enchir.	*Enchiridion on faith, hope, and love*
Serm.	*Sermons*
Trin.	*The Trinity*
Basil, *Bapt.*	*On Baptism*
CMFL	John Chrysostom. *On Marriage and Family Life*. Crestwood, NY: St. Vladimir's Press, 1986
COP	John Chrysostom. *Six Books on the Priesthood*. Crestwood, NY: St. Vladimir's Press, 1984
CSEL	*Corpus Scriptorum Ecclesiasticorum Latinorum*. Vienna, 1866
Epiphanius, *Pan.*	*Refutation of All Heresies*
Eusebius, *Hist. Eccl.*	*Ecclesiastical History*
FC	*Fathers of the Church*. Washington, DC: Catholic University Press, 1947
Hippolytus, *Haer.*	*Refutation of All Heresies*
HOG	Bede the Venerable. *Homilies on the Gospels*. Kalamazoo: Cistercian Publications, 1991
Irenaeus, *Haer.*	*Against Heresies*
Jerome, *Epist.*	*Letters*
JMD	*Selections from Justin Martyr's Diologue with Trypho, a Jew*. London: Lutterworth, 1963
John Chrysostom	
Catech.	*Catechesis*
Hom. 1 Cor.	*Homilies on 1 Corinthians*
Hom. 1 Tim.	*Homilies on the First Epistle to Timothy*
Hom. 2 Tim	*Homilies on the Second Epistle to Timothy*
Hom. Tit.	*Homilies on the Epistle to Titus*
Stat.	*To the Antiochenes about Statues*
Justin	
Apol.	*Apology*
Dial.	*Dialogue with Trypho*

LCC	*The Library of Christian Classics*. Philadelphia: Westminster, 1953–1966
NPNF	*A Select Library of the Nicene and Post-Nicene Fathers of the Christian Church*. Reprint. Grand Rapids: Eerdmans, 1952–1956
NT Apocrypha	
Acts Pet.	*Acts of Peter*
Acts Pil.	*Acts of Pilate*
Acts Thom.	*Acts of Thomas*
Prot. Jas.	*Protevangelium of James*
OAC	Origen. *Contra Celsum*. Cambridge: Cambridge University Press, 1953
Origen, *Cels.*	*Against Celsus*
OSW	*Origen. Selected Writings*. Mahwah, NJ: Paulist, 1979
PE	The Pastoral Epistles
PG	*Patrologia Graeca*. Paris: Migne, 1857–1886
PL	*Patrologia Latina*. Paris: Migne, 1844–1864
Q	*Quelle*, a hypothesized NT sayings source
TEM	*Theodori episcopi Mopsuesteni: In epistolas b. Pauli commentarii*. Cambridge: Cambridge University Press, 1880–1882
Tertullian	
Apol.	*Apology*
Marc.	*Against Marcion*
Praescr.	*Prescription Against Heretics*
Virg.	*The Veiling of Virgins*
WSA	*The Works of St. Augustine: A Translation for the Twenty-first Century*. Brooklyn: New City Press, 1991

Periodicals, Reference Works, and Serials

ABD	*Anchor Bible Dictionary*
AJA	*American Journal of Archaeology*
AnBib	Analecta biblica
ANRW	*Aufstieg und Niedergang der römischen Welt*
Arch	*Archaeology*
BA	*Biblical Archaeologist*
BAGD	Bauer, Arndt, Gingrich, and Danker, *A Greek-English Lexicon of the New Testament*
BDF	Friedrich Blass and Albert Debrunner. *A Greek Grammar of the New Testament and other Early Christian Literature*. Trans. and rev. by Robert W. Funk. Chicago: University of Chicago Press, 1974
BeO	*Bibbia e Oriente*
BGU	*Aegyptische Urkunden aus den Königlichen Staatlichen Museen zu Berlin, Griechische Urkunden*. 15 vols. Berlin, 1895–1983
Bib	*Biblica*

BL	*Bibel und Liturgie*
BSac	*Bibliotheca Sacra*
BT	*The Bible Translator*
BTB	*Biblical Theology Bulletin*
BJRL	*Bulletin of the John Rylands Library*
BZ	*Biblische Zeitschrift*
BZNW	Beihefte zur Zeitschrift für die neutestamentliche Wissenschaft
CBQ	*Catholic Biblical Quarterly*
CH	*Church History*
ConBNT	Coniectanea biblica neotestamentica
CTSA	Catholic Theological Society of America, *Proceedings*
EDNT	*Exegetical Dictionary of the New Testament*
EvQ	*Evangelical Quarterly*
EvT	*Evangelische Theologie*
ExpTim	*Expository Times*
FoiVie	*Foi et Vie*
Greg	*Gregorianum*
GNS	Good News Studies
HTR	*Harvard Theological Review*
HUCA	*Hebrew Union College Annual*
HUT	Hermeneutische Untersuchungen zur Theologie
IKZ	*Internazionale kirchliche Zeitschrift*
Int	*Interpretation*
JAC	*Jahrbuch für Antike und Christentum*
JBL	*Journal of Biblical Literature*
JETS	*Journal of the Evangelical Theological Society*
JJP	*Journal of Juristic Papyrology*
JSNT	*Journal for the Study of the New Testament*
JSNTSup	Journal for the Study of the New Testament: Supplement Series
JTS	*Journal of Theological Studies*
LB	*Linguistica biblica*
LQ	*Lutheran Quarterly*
LSJ	Liddell-Scott-Jones, *Greek-English Lexicon*
LTQ	*Lexington Theological Quarterly*
MM	James H. Moulton and George Milligan, eds. *The Vocabulary of the Greek Testament: Illustrated from the Papyri and other Non-Literary Sources*. Grand Rapids: Eerdmans, 1974
MTZ	*Münchener theologische Zeitschrift*
NAB	New American Bible
NTS	*New Testament Studies*
NovT	*Novum Testamentum*
NovTSup	Novum Testamentum Supplements
PIBA	*Proceedings of the Irish Biblical Association*
RB	*Revue Biblique*
RivB	*Rivista biblica*
RivBSup	Supplements to *Rivista biblica*
SANT	Studien zum Alten und Neuen Testament

SBLDS	Society of Biblical Literature Dissertation Series
SBLMS	Society of Biblical Literature Monograph Series
SecCent	*Second Century*
SNTSMS	Society for New Testament Studies Monograph Series
SNTSU	Studien zum Neuen Testament und seiner Umwelt
TBT	*The Bible Today*
TDNT	*Theological Dictionary of the New Testament*
TS	*Theological Studies*
TynBul	*Tyndale Bulletin*
TZ	*Theologische Zeitschrift*
VC	*Vigiliae Christianae*
ZKT	*Zeitschrift für katholische Theologie*
ZNW	*Zeitschrift für die neutestamentliche Wissenschaft*

First Timothy, Second Timothy, Titus

AUTHOR'S PREFACE

My study of the New Testament in general and the Pastoral Epistles in particular has allowed me to expand my interest in Latin and Greek literature and culture into the area of biblical studies. Under the guidance of Abraham J. Malherbe at Yale, the classical training I received under the Jesuits from high school through university was focused on the world of the Greco-Roman moralists and rhetoricians and on how the New Testament writings, particularly the Pauline correspondence, reflected these. Working groups of like-minded colleagues in the regional and national Society of Biblical Literature and Catholic Biblical Association helped me to pursue these studies. This commentary is a product of that interest.

As a priest in the Society of Jesus, I complement my academic work with church ministry. The Pastoral Epistles offer opportunities for exploration in both areas. Clearly there is material in the Pastoral Epistles that no longer corresponds to realities in the church today. Nonetheless, a particular challenge is to find in these letters teachings and directives of relevance beyond their original context and applicable to church audiences of any age. I have tried to be faithful to this task in the explanations and interpretations of the text of the letters.

The translation of the epistles, unless otherwise noted, is my own and in doing the translation I tried to stay as close to the Greek text as possible. The division of each section of Translation Notes and Interpretation does not correspond to the outlines in the Introduction to each letter. Those outlines intend to indicate the flow of thought in each letter, while the divisions aim to break up the text into manageable portions for interpretation.

I am indebted to the series editor, Daniel Harrington, S.J., for his guidance and patience in the production of this commentary. I also am grateful to the support of the Jesuit communities where I did the research and writing, in Buffalo, Toronto, and Regina. The interest and assistance of my colleagues at Canisius College in Buffalo and Campion College in Regina have been fundamental to the success of this work. The encouragement of my family and friends has been a mainstay throughout the project. It goes without saying that the vision of Michael Glazier in conceiving and launching this series has resulted in a great benefit for those who use the volumes and for the persons they touch in their teaching, preaching, and direction.

Benjamin Fiore, s.j.
Campion College, Regina, Saskatchewan
July 2006

INTRODUCTION

I. METHODOLOGY AND INTERPRETIVE APPROACH

Paul ordinarily wrote his letters to Christian communities in a particular city or region. Even the letter to Philemon includes other named individuals and the entire house church among the addressees. The Pastoral Epistles stand out as exceptions in that they are addressed to individual recipients: Timothy, for two letters, and Titus. Moreover, the recipients have the same relationship to the sender. They are his dear children in the faith, and they are given the responsibility of organizing and supervising Christians across a large geographic area (Crete) or metropolitan region (Ephesus). As such, these relatively young church leaders have doctrinal and jurisdictional authority unlike the authority of the church leaders identified in Paul's other letters, and even of Timothy himself in those letters.

The close relationship among these three letters and their divergence from the other letters of Paul is also apparent in their content and style. The conflict over the Jewish Law does not center on the efficacy of required actions for justification, the issue that split Paul's churches from those tied to the Jerusalem leadership. Rather the problem is that of quibbling over the interpretation of the Law, an exaggerated asceticism, and esoteric speculation. The letters promote good works without hesitation. The *parousia* is still awaited, but not with Paul's original urgency. The long-term doctrinal stability and social standing of the community are the Pastoral Epistles' concerns. Faith, as understood here, combines Paul's trust in God to save with a knowledge of the truth.

The three letters weave credal summaries and excerpts of other materials into the text. The explicit attention given to these, and the allusions to community officers and ecclesial procedures, suggest a level of organization and a history of Christian tradition that go beyond that evidenced by the other letters of Paul. These letters urge direct confrontation with false teachers as well as excommunication. With an eye on the opinion of outsiders, the letters call for upright behavior from all segments of the community, and they see good reputation as a qualification for potential officeholders. In view of these similarities among the three Pastoral Epistles and the differences between them and the other Pauline letters, this commentary treats the letters as a unity within the Pauline correspondence. The PE also provide a glimpse of the situation of the church that is like that in the epistles of Peter, Jude, and James. The delayed *parousia* and the identification of contemporary heretical teachers with the false teachers foreseen in the final days, the focus on organizational matters in the church and in the members' households, and the use of the names of the original apostolic founders of the Christian movement are some of the features that link these letters.

While echoing Pauline themes and concerns, the PE give their treatment of them a twist that is characteristic of Pauline communities at a later stage of their development. Nonetheless, they carry the name of Paul and his associates, known from his letters and the Acts of the Apostles, to affirm a relationship and link as well as to draw on the authority of the community's founding figure. These observations and others detailed below identify the PE as pseudonymous when compared with the letters of undisputed Pauline authorship, referred to as the Pauline *homologoumena*.

The PE refer to First Testament scriptures as well as to later Jewish writings, and this reflects the Jewish roots of the community. This is consistent with their relationship to Paul. Nonetheless, the social and cultural environment of the places associated with the PE, Ephesus and Crete, was Greco-Roman. The epistles not only quote from Greek literature but they employ Greco-Roman hortatory strategies and devices that were taught in the schools and exercised in public and private life. The PE incorporate Greco-Roman moral teachings and presume the applicability of prevailing sociocultural values to life in the Christian households and house churches. This commentary makes use of Greco-Roman materials to illuminate the connections between the PE and their context.

In the PE Paul presents himself as a model of a converted and saved sinner as well as an apostle in word and action. He expects his addressees, Timothy and Titus, to play a similar exemplary role for their church communities. Individuals in the community as well as the community in its entirety are also expected to model ideal belief and behavior to those outside the community and thereby win their esteem for the community's members and its belief system. A study of the use of example in Greek and Roman exhortation epistles, such as the Cynic epistles under the name of Socrates and the Socratics, broadens our understanding of the hortatory strategy of the PE. Such a study also provides a rationale for the trio of letters in the name of Paul as a sketch of the expectations of the Christian life derived from the inspiration of the primary apostolic promoter, from the PE community's standpoint.

Readers of the PE have commented on the relative paucity of teaching content, especially in view of the atmosphere of doctrinal crisis occasioned by the false teachers. Actually, there is a good deal of teaching material in the letters, but attention to their Greco-Roman background reveals that the principal purpose of the PE is not to teach but to exhort. Reference to the tactics of the paraenetic literature of their day reveals that the PE, like other paraenetic works, presume knowledge and acceptance of commonly held beliefs and practices and do not elaborate them. Rather, they remind readers of the need to uphold these in the face of those who do not.

One of the distinctive features of the content of the PE is their view of faith as knowledge of the truth. A study of Greco-Roman literature, as noted below, helps explain the divergence of this understanding of faith from the usage in Paul's letters. In this regard the letters parallel the Greco-Roman idea of the salvific effects of knowledge and the actions that flow from it.

The use and interpretation of the PE during the formation of the New Testament canon is instructive, since these represent the first reflections and applications of the PE. With their hortatory character, the PE lend themselves to patristic-era moral interpretations. The church order material is read backward through the lens of contemporary ecclesiastical structures toward which the PE are moving. This commentary selects patristic interpretations that offer abiding moral and spiritual applications. The patristic interpretations are easily found in *Colossians, 1–2 Thessalonians, 1–2 Timothy, Titus,* in the Ancient Christian Commentary on Scripture, New Testament IX, edited by Peter Gorday (Downers Grove: InterVarsity Press, 2000).

Since the PE speak clearly about what leadership positions in the church require and also about the specific duties of community members, they offer an appealing source for contemporary Christians who wish to lead the Christian life as guided by the New Testament. This commentary takes a cautious approach to this effort to determine how to apply the letters' requirements. It tries to assess the regulations within the historical context from which they arise and to find themes and lines of action for today that are consistent with the perspective in the texts.

Beyond the specific regulations, the PE express an ecclesiastical focus that has characterized Catholic Christianity through the centuries. The concern with preserving and handing on the tradition of teaching as it has been received has guided the church's concern to formulate beliefs carefully and to reject those that have shown themselves to be inadequate. Consistent with this effort and with the idea of faith as knowledge of the truth is the intellectual tradition that characterizes Catholic Christianity and embraces not just theology but all areas of human learning. The insistence on works as a demonstration of saving faith has also been a hallmark of Catholic Christianity, especially since the Reformation controversies. Thus the commentary tries to indicate places where the PE have particular relevance to the faith life of contemporary Christians.

II. LITERARY CHARACTER OF THE LETTERS

In his commentary on 1 Timothy, Thomas Aquinas referred to it as "a rule, so to speak, for pastors." At the dawn of the formation of the list of New Testament books, the Muratorian canon (ca. 170 C.E.) described the letters written by Paul, including "one to Titus, and two to Timothy, in simple personal affection and love indeed; but yet these are hallowed in the esteem of the Catholic Church, *and* in the regulation of ecclesiastical discipline." The recognition of the pastoral dimension of the two letters to Timothy and the one to Titus has led to the more recent characterization of Titus (by D. N. Berdot in 1703) and subsequently all three (by Paul Anton in 1726) as the Pastoral Epistles. While the three letters exhibit great similarities in style and content, there is a clear difference between the testamentary 2 Timothy and the church order documents 1 Timothy and Titus.

1. *Testamentary Letters*

To understand 2 Timothy as Paul's "last will and testament" in letter form to his associate and designated head of the Ephesian church (1 Tim 3:1; see also 2 Tim 4:19), it is helpful to see what Luke has done with the notion of Paul's testament in the prose narrative of Paul's farewell discourse to the Ephesian elders at Acts 20:17-38. The passage in Acts follows the typical pattern of a testament already in use in the apocryphal *Testament of the Twelve Patriarchs*, as Lewis R. Donelson makes clear. There one finds (1) the statement of impending death of the patriarch to those gathered about him, and (2) a recollection of his life as paradigm for the listeners/readers, with both positive and negative aspects to follow and avoid. (3) Following this are predictions about future occurrences, with warnings and exhortations on how to deal with that future.

In Acts one finds (1) Paul presenting himself as a paradigm for imitation, but with only positive virtues detailed. He is the type of the faithful church leader who did not shrink back even when faced with persecution (Acts 20:18-20, 26-27). (2) Paul passes his authority to the Ephesian elders, who are to be guardians/overseers in their care for the community (20:28). This feature, natural to a testament, is distinctive in Acts and is not part of the classic testamentary pattern. (3) Paul then warns of coming "wolves" within the church who will draw some of the faithful after them (20:29-30). (4) Paul promises them God's sustenance and ultimate reward (20:32), and (5) alludes to his imminent death (20:22-25, 38), but foresees completing the course of his mission (20:24). The specifics of the prediction and exhortation here fit the situation of the church as it engages in heterodoxy/orthodoxy discussions. The transfer of authority provides an authoritative link for current church leaders with their predecessor Paul.

Similarly in 2 Timothy: (1) Paul is a direct paradigm at 2 Tim 1:13 and 3:10-12, and the example is amplified by autobiographical references (1:11-12; 2:8-10; 3:10-11; 4:6-18). In these reminiscences Paul emerges as the suffering apostle, abandoned and attacked by fellow Christians but faithful to his kerygmatic duty. (2) Paul enjoins Timothy to select those who will carry on the ministry Paul entrusts to him (2:2-3). They are to be unashamed guardians of the tradition (1:8, 14), soldiers, and capable of teaching others (2:1-7). They carry forward the tradition, undeflected by new ideas (3:14) in their work of preaching and correcting (4:1-2). (3) The appearance and success of heretics is predicted (2:20–3:9), but Paul promises that God will sustain the faithful elders as he did Paul in his trials (1:12; 4:8, 16-18). (4) God's firm (2:19) guardianship of the tradition (1:12) ends with God awarding the faithful the crown of righteousness and punishing the faithless (2:11-13; 4:8). (5) Paul declares his death to be near in this farewell (1:8, 17; 2:9; 4:6-8, 16-18) and summons a gathering of his associates (4:9-21). Like Acts 20:17-38, 2 Timothy uses Paul's last will and testament to address the community situation of conflict between orthodoxy and heresy. The letter aims to embolden the audience to cling fast to the Pauline tradition in thought and action against those Paul "predicted" would deviate from it.

Noticing the testamentary character of 2 Timothy helps the reader situate its biographical and hortatory features in a larger context of form and purpose. It might also help in understanding the three Pastoral Epistles as a collection within the Pauline corpus. In the collection of pseudonymous Cynic epistles of Socrates and the Socratics, Socrates' *Epistle 6* and Aristippus' *Epistle 27* both employ features characteristic of testamentary letters of Greek philosophers such as Epicurus and Plato. The two letters echo the Cynic outlook and exhortation strategy in the letter corpus as a whole. The alleged writers of these letters, in addition to being models of incorporating Cynic virtue into their lives, also stand as models of the careful handing on of the tradition of virtue taught and lived. One might see the same rhetorical strategy at work among the three Pastoral Epistles, and even extend this observation to understand the relation of these letters to the larger Pauline corpus to which it was added.

2. *Church Order Epistles*

In addition to the testamentary letter, the Pastoral Epistles include two "church order" epistles, 1 Timothy and Titus. From a technical viewpoint these letters resemble official memoranda given in classical antiquity to subordinate officials on their assumption of a new position, such as the Egyptian Tebtunis papyrus 703. The memoranda outline duties, delimit prerogatives, and summarize what was discussed between the official and the subordinate before the latter's departure to his post. 𝔓Tebt 703 even outlines qualities of outstanding rule and its opposite, and calls on the official to be a model ruler in the pattern of his superior. His public manifestation of good rule engenders respect for the law among his subjects. In addition to specific duties, it also includes exhortations accompanied by vice and virtue lists, examples, and the promise of reward for faithful service. Similar memoranda or "appointment charters" (e.g., BGU VIII 1768) carry the requirement that they be published. Reference to this sort of official memorandum letter or appointment charter helps readers of the Pastoral Epistles make sense of the anomaly that the letters contain commands and duties that presumably would have been covered by Paul in meetings with Timothy and Titus before he left them in charge at Ephesus and Crete respectively.

Like the official memoranda or "appointment charters," 1 Timothy and Titus share a focus on matters of community behavior in traditional household codes and community organization, although the organizational patterns are not consistent. When examined together, as Gordon D. Fee finds, the "church order" material (1 Tim 3:1-16; 4:6–6:2, 11-16, 20a; Titus 1:5-9; 2:1-10) consists of qualifications rather than duties, and presents paradigms of behavior and attitude rather than definitions of proper thought and required action. These sections of the letters suggest that the church is well along in its development as a structured community, but there is no organizational chart for this structure here, nor is there even consistency in titles between the two letters. Hence, in the organizational structure at Ephesus, 1 Timothy refers to overseers/bishops (3:1-7); assistants/deacons (3:8-13); widows (5:3, 9-15); elders/presbyters/presiders (5:17-20). On Crete, by contrast, Titus mentions presbyters/elders-overseers/bishops (1:5-9). Within or near the church organization sections of both letters, however, the reader finds warnings against and exhortations about taking effective measures to deal with false teachers (1 Tim 4:1-4; 5:13; 6:3-10, 20b-21; Titus 1:10-16). The "church order" sections thus serve the general purpose of the letters, which is to exhort church leaders to confront and refute false teachers while at the same time defending and advancing the true Pauline tradition.

As Joseph A. Fitzmyer notes, the notion of "church" (*ekklēsia*) in the Pastoral Epistles differs markedly from that in the undisputed Pauline letters and in the other deutero-Pauline letters. There are only three occurrences of the term in 1 Timothy (5:16, "the church"; 3:5, "church of God"; 3:15, "the household of God . . . church of the living God, pillar and bulwark of the truth") and none in 2 Timothy and Titus, unlike its frequent use in the other Pauline writings. The church as "body of Christ" from 1 Cor 12:27-28 and then in Col 2:17; Eph 4:12 gives way in the Pastoral Epistles to the church as the assembly of Christians who are to be properly overseen in the interests of preserving sound teaching. Timothy and Titus are the primary trustees of this oversight ministry as Paul's delegates, and they are to pass on the ministry to persons they deem qualified. Their responsibilities are wide. One task is teaching (1 Tim 4:13, 16; 5:17) the true and sound doctrine (1 Tim 1:10; 4:6; Titus 1:9, 14; 2:10; 2 Tim 4:3) originally entrusted to Paul (1 Tim 1:11) over against false doctrine (1 Tim 1:3-4; 6:3), vain speculations, and blasphemy (1 Tim 1:4, 20; 4:7; Titus 1:11). Another is preaching the Christian message (1 Tim 5:17; 2 Tim 4:2, 5) and exhorting to the Christian way of life (1 Tim 4:13; 5:1; 6:2). They must guard what has been entrusted to them (1 Tim 6:20; 2 Tim 1:14) and see to the correct reading of scripture (1 Tim 4:13). The letters are concerned with their proper exercise of authority (1 Tim 2:12; 3:1; 5:17) and with the community's prayer (1 Tim 2:1-2, 8, although no mention of the Eucharist can be found).

As mentioned above, the ministries within the church are differentiated under several official titles. Only Paul has the title apostle and herald (1 Tim 4:6), and he shares the teaching function, although not the title, with other officeholders. Timothy and Titus are ministers in the general sense. Timothy received his authority in a ceremony of laying on of hands by presbyters (1 Tim 4:14) and by Paul (2 Tim 1:6). Titus has authority similar to Timothy's (Titus 1:5; 2:15). No investiture ceremony is noted, but it may be implied. The origins of the overseer/bishop title (1 Tim 3:1-7; Titus 1:7) are in question, with the administrative overseer in the Greek world, the overseers of the Jerusalem Temple, and the Qumran community superior all proposed as the source. Paul uses the overseer/bishop title along with assistant/deacon (but not elder/presbyter) in Phil 1:1, and he recognizes those who are over others in 1 Thess 5:12. Thus it is not surprising to find the title overseer/bishop in the Pastorals. The chief duty is that of teaching (1 Tim 3:2).

Elder/presbyter (1 Tim 5:17, 19; Titus 1:5) was a title for an official in the Greek world, and in the Jewish milieu it designated a member of a local council (Josh 20:4; Ruth 4:2) or part of the Sanhedrin. The Christians appear to have taken it over from the Jewish context (Acts 11:30; 21:18). In Titus the description of the elders'/presbyters' qualifications blends with those of the bishop/overseer, and the letter seems to be talking about one person with two different titles. Exhorting with sound teaching is the responsibility of the bishop, together with refuting opponents (1:9). Teaching, along with preaching and presiding, are also ascribed to presbyters in 1 Tim 5:17. This might indicate that in the still fluid situation of officeholders some who presided might have chosen to preach, others to teach, and others to do both. In another place (3:2) teaching ability is an overseer/bishop's qualification, with no mention of presiding. With elders/presbyters and overseers/bishops along with the assistants/deacons, three roles are differentiated in 1 Timothy. Titus names only two, elders/presbyters and overseer/bishop, but he may be describing only one. The roles become stabilized by the time Polycarp (Pol. *Phil.* 5:3) and Ignatius (Ign. *Eph.* 4.1; Ign. *Magn.* 6.1; Ign. *Trall.* 2.1-2; 3.1; Ign. *Smyrn.* 8.1; 9.1) write their letters (ca. 110 C.E.) and the *Didachē* (15:1-2) finds it way into circulation (ca. 100 C.E.).

As for the assistants/deacons, their qualifications at 1 Tim 3:8-13 give no clear picture of what they actually did and whom they assisted. Fitzmyer sees them as participating in the work of evangelization. For this he takes a hint from the seven deacons in Acts 6, who replaced the Twelve in their service at tables (6:2, distributing food and necessary goods or perhaps even alms as financial officers at the community tables/money counters) but were also engaged in preaching (Stephen and Philip). This conception of a broader ministry also receives support from the application of the title "deacon" and its function to Timothy at 1 Tim 4:6 and 2 Tim 4:5. First Timothy 3:11 seems to introduce women as assistants/deacons along with men.

The last category of officials identified is the widows at 1 Tim 5:3, 9-16. What they were expected to do in practice is not spelled out. As steward of God's household (Titus 1:7), the overseer/bishop is at the top of the administrative pyramid, however the rest of the offices are lined up.

3. *Exhortation Letters*

The nature and aim of the Pastoral Epistles are somewhat clarified by reference to testamentary letters and also to official memoranda or "appointment charters," which expressed both prescriptions and exhortations in circular letter form and used examples to make the expectations more concrete. Literary, hortatory epistles in classical antiquity provide more comprehensive parallels to the Pastoral Epistles, as they blend hortatory content with epistolary form. The teaching letter developed from the dialogue in philosophical schools and subsequently became a surrogate for the dialogue between the heads of the schools and their far-flung pupils. The letter exhorted as well as taught, and the exhortation was both to philosophy and to a corresponding ethical life. In adopting the letter form over the public lecture some teachers deliberately set the exhortation within a more familiar setting, where the letter stands for the presence of the writer in the ongoing conversation. The tone of the letter is that of quiet persuasion by a friend who is acquitting himself of the friendly task of exhorting, entreating, advising, and correcting through prescriptions and personal examples (Seneca, *Ep.* 38.1; 75.1; 16.1-2; 27.1; 40.1; Cicero, *Fam.* 5.17.3; 5.13.3-4; *Am.* 13.44; *Off.* 1.17.58; Pliny, *Ep.* 1.14.3-4; 1.12.11-12; 4.17.4-9). The Cynic Epistles of Socrates and the Socratics employ the letter form and a broad range of hortatory devices to moderate the tendencies of exaggerated and harsh Cynicism, advancing a milder form. These pseudonymous letters employ the example of Socrates, titular founder of Cynicism, and prominent followers in the Cynic school of philosophy to propose and substantiate their philosophical perspectives for their readers.

Beyond the testamentary and "church order" material in the Pastoral Epistles, they all share a common concern with exhorting their readers to adhere to the traditional true faith and act in accordance with it. They also oppose deviations from the knowledge and teaching of the truth and highlight the moral decline associated with those errors. In this respect the Pastoral Epistles can be understood as exhortation epistles. In carrying out their aim, they employ the full range of hortatory devices as taught in the rhetorical schools and put to use in the literary exhortation letters by other real or pseudonymous authors of their day.

Thus Abraham J. Malherbe finds that the epistle to Titus, while addressing church order material in chapter 1, devotes the rest of its length to the faith and conduct of the church members and of Titus himself. Moreover, even in chapter 1, beyond the matters of church organization at 1:5-9, the letter addresses the true faith (1:1-4) and advises on how to deal with those who repudiate it (1:10-16). Friendship language in the mode of father and son sets the paraenetic tone in the salutation (1:4; see 1 Tim 1:2, 18; 2 Tim 1:2; 2:1), which is the basis of much of the paraenetic writing in the period of the Pastoral Epistles. Other typical paraenetic devices appear in the letter to Titus. Titus is to judge the qualifications of aspiring officials (1:6-9), oppose false teachers (1:13), teach soundly (2:1; 3:1), exhort the community (2:6), be a model of good works (2:7), and isolate heretics (3:9-11). Imperatives abound in the letter (1:13; 2:1, 6, 15; 3:1; see 1:5, 7, 9, 11), and there are vice and virtue lists and a concern with good deeds (1:16; 2:7, 14; 3:1, 8, 14) as well as with living a pious life (2:12). As one of many antitheses in the letter, Titus is to model the true path of faith and action (2:7), while the false teachers present a model to be avoided (1:15-16). In all, the letter exhorts to what is beneficial (3:8) and warns away from what is useless and futile (3:9). The lists of vices, virtues, and household duties are conventional values and expectations of the day. The christological warrants (2:11-14; 3:4-8) for the paraenesis provide its root in the Christian faith of the community. The call to remind/remember long-held beliefs and practices (3:1-8; 1 Tim 1:3-7; 2 Tim 2:14; and see 1 Tim 1:16; 4:12; 2 Tim 3:10-14) is another typical paraenetic device.

The conceptual framework for the hortatory effort of all three of the Pastoral Epistles, in Malherbe's view, is expressed at Titus 2:11-14. Here the letter's author expresses the doctrine of God our savior (2:10) as a warrant for the letter's precepts. Christ's appearance is a saving one (2:11, 13; 3:4; see 2 Tim 1:10-13). Moreover, the Pastoral Epistles frequently link salvation with teaching (1 Tim 4:16; 2 Tim 3:14-17). The letters know that baptism was a saving event for those who received it (3:5) and that salvation is a free gift of God's grace (3:7). The letter to Titus, however, also states that the saving grace of God is "training us to reject godless ways and worldly desires and to live temperately . . ." (NAB 2:11-14; see 2 Tim 3:16, where divinely inspired scriptures teach wisdom for salvation). The saving role of education derives from Hellenistic moral philosophy (Dio Chrysostom, *Or.* 32,15-16), for education cures the irrational soul of the natural illness of the human condition (Dio Chrysostom, *Or.* 13,31-32; Plutarch, *Adul. Poet. aud.* 42C). This philosophical education is practical and concerns itself with household and conjugal duties (Seneca, *Ep.* 94,1; Ps-Plutarch, *Lib. ed.* 7D-F), a connection Titus makes with the household code at 2:1-10. Of course, the Pastoral Epistles differ from the Hellenistic moralists in that the cognitive element derives from apostolic tradition and Scripture (2 Tim 3:14-17; Titus 1:9; see 1 Tim 6:3) and not simply human reason. The letters' audience gains understanding by reflecting on the apostolic tradition (2 Tim 2:7-13). The Pastoral Epistles are unique in the New Testament in proposing a cognitive notion of salvation akin to that of the Hellenistic moral philosophers. This insight appears to be the contribution of the author of the Pastoral Epistles, as they propose that the grace of God saves but also educates the believers to pursue lives that are morally sound.

III. HISTORICAL BACKGROUND

1. *Jewish/Jewish-Christian Opponents*

While the doctrines advanced by the false teachers in the Pastoral Epistles are not clearly delineated, the danger they pose is significant. The threat of their teaching to the true, traditional belief and their personal ruin receive mention in each of the letters (1 Tim 1:3-7, 18b-20; 4:1-3; 6:3-10, 20-21; 2 Tim 2:14-18, 23-26; 3:1-9; 4:3-4; Titus 1:10-16; 3:9-11), and the letters paint them in apocalyptic colors (1 Tim 4:1; 2 Tim 3:1; 4:3). One consistent characteristic of the false teaching is its Jewish (Titus 1:10) and, in particular, Pharisaic connections. The author of the Pastoral Epistles exhibits knowledge of Jewish legal and apocryphal traditions (e.g., Jannes and Jambres at 2 Tim 3:8). According to Klaus Berger, the opponents might be diaspora Pharisees or Pharisaical Jewish-Christians. The author of the Pastoral Epistles wants to keep the lines clear between them and the Pauline Christian communities for whom the letters are written. Thus the Pastoral Epistles reject the opponents' explanation of the Law (1 Tim 1:7), to which they oppose their own understanding of it (1 Tim 1:8-11); they also advance an instruction that aims at "love from a pure heart" (NAB 1 Tim 1:5), a fundamental view of Paul (1 Cor 13:4-7; Gal 5:14; Rom 13:8-10) and basic to the gospel tradition (Mark 12:31, *parr.*; John 13:34). Moreover, the Pastoral Epistles refer to their opponents' legal teaching as promoting human laws (Titus 1:4), which was a critique of the Pharisees in the controversies with Jesus (Mark 7:8-9). The critique of the opponents as hypocritical (1 Tim 4:2; Titus 1:16) echoes a gospel critique of Pharisees (Matt 23:25). The letters reject the opponents' ascetical teachings (1 Tim 4:3; Titus 1:14-15), another anti-Pharisee tradition from the gospels (Mark 7:19; Rom 14:2, 21; see Matt 19:12 for Jesus' measured advancement of sexual abstinence). Resurrection is a distinctively Pharisaic belief. The opponents' erroneous teaching that the resurrection has already taken place (2 Tim 2:18) need not refer to a Gnostic belief but might well refer to baptism (John 5:24; Rom 6:4; Col 2:12), conversion (Col 2:11), asceticism (Col 2:18), or a metaphorical resurrection (Jos.As. 8:9). The myths, genealogies, and Jewish fables (1 Tim 1:4; 4:7; 2 Tim 4:4; Titus 1:14; 3:9) suggest to Berger the book of *Jubilees'* retelling of scriptural history. The identity of the opponents remains an open question. Furthermore, while the Pastoral Epistles try to deal with the threat they pose, they also use the false teachers as examples that serve as a negative foil to the positive examples in the letters. As such they have a place in the repertory of hortatory devices used by the letter to promote fidelity to tradition through correct knowledge and action.

For Reference and Further Study

Berger, Klaus. "Jesus als Pharisäer und frühe Christen als Pharisäer," *NovT* 30 (1988) 231–62.

Donelson, Lewis R. "Cult Histories and the Sources of Acts," *Bib* 68 (1987) 1–21.

Fee, Gordon D. "Reflections on Church Order in the Pastoral Epistles, with Further Reflection on the Hermeneutics of *Ad Hoc* Documents," *JETS* 28 (1985) 141–51.

Fiore, Benjamin. *The Function of Personal Example in the Socratic and Pastoral Epistles.* AnBib 105. Rome: Biblical Institute Press, 1986, 79–126, 161–63.

Fitzmyer, Joseph A. "The Structured Ministry of the Church in the Pastoral Epistles," *CBQ* 66 (2004) 582–96.

Juel, Donald. "*Episkopē* in the New Testament," *LQ* 2 (1988) 343–55.

Malherbe, Abraham J. "Paraenesis in the Epistle to Titus," in James Starr and Troels Engberg-Pedersen, eds., *Early Christian Paraenesis in Context*. BZNW 125. Berlin and New York: Walter de Gruyter, 2004, 297–317.

Martin, Sean Charles. *Pauli Testamentum: 2 Timothy and the Last Words of Moses*. Tesi Gregoriana, Serie Teologia 18. Rome: Pontificia Università Gregoriana, 1997.

Quinn, Jerome D., and William C. Wacker. *The First and Second Letters to Timothy: A New Translation with Notes and Commentary*. Grand Rapids: Eerdmans, 2000.

2. *Authorship*

The authenticity of the Pastoral Epistles has long been in dispute, and it is not surprising that the issue has been approached in many ways. Some, like the French Dominican Ceslas Spicq, argue for Pauline authorship.

Others, like Gordon D. Fee, regard them as written by a follower of Paul but under Paul's authority in the '50s or '60s. Walter Bauer saw them as not by Paul and as written later, against Marcion. Similarly, Martin Dibelius and Percy N. Harrison placed them in the early second century.

Supporters of the letters' pseudonymity, such as J. L. Houlden, survey a wide range of content, vocabulary, style, and form. We may say in summary that an analysis of the structure of examples from the authentic Pauline letters and in the Pastoral Epistles reveals sufficient differences in the presentation of the material to support the view that the Pastoral Epistles are pseudonymous. Although their author might not have been Paul, the Pastoral Epistles decidedly place themselves within the Pauline tradition, albeit with alterations that make accommodations to the situation of a more developed church structure and a more complex relationship with the larger society.

A characteristic feature of Paul's exhortation in his letters is the call to the imitation of examples he proposes. He appeals to his own example as a model for imitation at Gal 4:12; 1 Thess 1:5-6 and 2:14-16; Phil 3:17; 1 Cor 4:16 and 11:1. Paul also names persons from his own mission team (Timothy at Phil 2:22), from his churches (Epaphroditus at 2:29-30), and entire church communities (Gal 4:14) to illustrate desired attitudes or actions. Scripture (Abraham at Rom 4:3) and midrash (1 Cor 10:6-11) supply other examples. Illustrative persons (a potter at Rom 9:20) and natural objects (the body at 1 Cor 12:14-21, a branch at Rom 11:17) serve a similar purpose. Human behavior (1 Cor 12:23-24), typical situations (1 Thess 5:2-4, 7), or human occupations (building at 1 Cor 3:10-15) expand the store of examples in Paul. The primary example is Christ himself (Phil 2:5 and Rom 14:15) and Paul as he follows Christ's example (1 Cor 11:1). The practical strategy behind his summoning of examples finds an illustration in the second chapter of the letter to the Philippians, where he proposes a succession of models of self-sacrifice after which he wants the community to pattern their thoughts and actions (2:1-5). These paradigmatic figures are Christ (2:6-11), himself (2:12-18), Timothy (2:19-24), and Epaphroditus (2:25-30). They present the ideal that stands against the pattern of the self-promoting rival teachers (1:15-17).

The Pastoral Epistles use the same hortatory device of the call to imitate Paul at 1 Tim 1:3-20; 2 Tim 1:3-18; 3:1–4:8. Moreover, the addressees Timothy and Titus are also supposed to be models for the community (1 Tim 4:12; Titus 2:7-8), as Timothy's mother and grandmother are for him (2 Tim 1:5). The community should be models of blameless lives, giving authenticity to the teaching of the letters and validating the criticism of the false teachers' failings (1 Tim 5:14; 6:14; 6:1). Example is an essential feature of the hortatory strategy of the Pastoral Epistles.

In the rhetorical exercise of the *chreia*, described by ancient rhetoricians as a multipart exercise in the development of a theme, the following elements are typical: (1) encomium of the author of the saying or *chreia;* (2) paraphrase or restatement of the saying; (3) argument from the opposite side; (4) justification or proof; (5) historical example (personal); (6) analogy from nature; (7) testimony of the ancients; (8) epilogue. This rhetorical exercise became the tool of moral philosophers, such as Seneca in his *Epistle 104* and the author of the Socratic Epistles, in their effort to promote their moral perspective. This form of discourse also found its way into the writings of Christian rhetoricians and moralists such as Origen. In practice the hortatory elements in the sections where a *chreia* is developed follow the rhetorical exercise books and include the statement, a comparison, admonition, negative example, positive example, antithetical analogies, proofs, gnomic sayings and appeal to authority, exhortation, and restatement.

In the three "example" passages from the Pastoral Epistles noted above, the hortatory elements and their structure echo that of the development of a *chreia*. In 1 Tim 1:3-20, for instance, one finds the statement of the obligation and its explanation (1:3-5), negative examples (1:6-7), antithetical explanation (1:8-10), appeal to gospel authority (1:11), positive example (1:12), antithesis (1:13-14), authoritative saying in gnomic form (1:15), restatement of opening prescription expanded with the fighting metaphor (1:18-19a), and contrasting examples that include the nautical image (1:19b-20).

Similarly, at 2 Tim 1:3-18 a friendly remembrance and encomium of Timothy with corroboration in the examples of his mother and grandmother (1:3-5) prepares for the exhortation (1:6). This statement is explained in antithetical form (1:7) and then is restated in negative and positive terms (1:8) and explained with reference to the authoritative witness of Jesus and the Gospel (1:9-10). The delineation of the example of Paul (1:11-12a) gets support from the banking image of the "deposit" (1:12b) and leads to the explicit reference to it (1:13), further specified by imperatives (1:13-14), contrasted with named apostates (1:15) and faithful followers (1:16-18). The next chapter repeats and expands on the exhortation.

The third example passage at 2 Tim 3:1–4:8 starts with a negative example (3:1) that is specified by a vice list (3:2-5a) and an exhortation (3:5b). The negative example is further described in these persons' tactics (3:6-7) and by analogy to apocryphal scriptural figures (3:8). The positive examples of Paul and his sufferings (3:10-11) and Timothy's faithful following of them contrasts with the negative example of the false teachers and those duped by them (3:12-13). The statement of the exhortation (3:14a), justified (3:14b) and supported by reference to Scripture (3:15-17), finds an echo in a second exhortation (4:1-2), bolstered by negative and positive examples (4:3-4) and the example of Paul (4:6-8) that frame a restatement of the exhortation (4:5).

In the undisputed Pauline letters noted above, 1 Thessalonians and Galatians use a variety of hortatory devices in the example passages. These include antithesis, comparison, prescription, and appeal to scriptural authority, but they lack the broad range of such devices employed in the Pastoral Epistles and the Greco-Roman popular philosophical works. Philippians 3, on the other hand, does resemble the latter works in its elaboration of its exhortation with the cluster of devices specified in the elaboration of the *chreia* (negative example, Paul's example, racing metaphor, statement of correct attitude, promise of its proof, restatement, command, contrast, gnomic saying and elaboration, concluding command). The aim of the passage, however, is not purely hortatory; it is a polemic and Paul's apologia for his authority. More consistently hortatory is 1 Cor 8:1–11:1, where the range of devices matches that of the developed *chreia*. The development over three chapters, however, is more diffuse than what has been encountered in the Pastoral Epistles or the popular philosophical works. Only 2 Thessalonians 3 employs the pattern of devices (statement, proof, restatement, command, example, authority, negative example, and concluding commands) in a concise hortatory section. Like the Pastoral Epistles, 2 Thessalonians is considered by many not to have been written by Paul.

For Reference and Further Study

Brox, Norbert. "Lukas als Verfasser der Pastoralbriefe," *JAC* 13 (1970) 76–94.

Collins, Raymond F. *Letters That Paul Did Not Write: The Epistle to the Hebrews and the Pauline Pseudepigrapha*. Wilmington: Michael Glazier, 1988.

de Boer, Martinus C. "Images of Paul in the Post-Apostolic Period," *CBQ* 42 (1980) 359–79.

Dibelius, Martin, and Hans Conzelmann. *The Pastoral Epistles*. Trans. Philip Buttolph and Adela Yarbro. Hermeneia. Philadelphia: Fortress Press, 1972.

Donelson, Lewis R. *Pseudepigraphy and Ethical Argument in the Pastoral Epistles*. HUT 22. Tübingen: J.C.B Mohr [Paul Siebeck], 1986.

Harrison, Percy N. "The Authorship of the Pastoral Epistles," *ExpTim* 67 (1955) 77–81.

Houlden, James Leslie. *The Pastoral Epistles: I and II Timothy, Titus*. Harmondsworth: Penguin, 1976.

Maloney, Elliott C. "Biblical Authorship and the Pastoral Letters," *TBT* 24 (1986) 119–23.

Michaelis, Wilhelm. *Pastoralbriefe und Gefangenschaftsbriefe: Zur Echtheitsfrage der Pastoralbriefe*. Neutestamentliche Forschungen, Paulusstudien 1, 6. Gütersloh: Bertelsmann, 1930.

Moule, C.F.D. "The Problem of the Pastoral Epistles: A Reappraisal," *BJRL* 47 (1965) 430–52.

Nauck, Wolfgang. "Die Herkunft des Verfassers der Pastoralbriefe, ein Beitrag zur Auslegung der Pastoralbriefe." Diss. Göttingen, 1950.

Wegscheider, Julius A. *Der erste Briefe des Apostels Paulus an den Timotheus, neu übersetzt und erklärt, mit Beziehung auf die neuesten Untersuchungen über die Authentie desselben*. Göttingen: Johann F. Röwer, 1810.

Zmijewski, Josef. "Apostolische Paradosis und Pseudepigraphie im Neuen Testament 'Durch Erinnerung wachhalten' [2 Petr 1,13; 3,1]," *BZ* n.s. 2 (1979) 161–71.

3. *Date*

The differentiated official functions outlined in 1 Timothy and Titus and the qualifications offered to guide the selection of candidates for office suggest a later stage of development than that in the undisputed Pauline letters. In specifying details of qualifications and responsibilities of bishop/overseer, presbyter/elder, deacon/assistant, widow, as well as evangelist/admonitor/authoritative supervisor of all the Christians in Ephesus or on the island of Crete, the letters suggest a situation closer to that of the church in *1 Clement* or the letters of Ignatius. The position of Timothy and Titus as apostolic delegates over local church communities points to a second-generation, post-apostolic supervisory system (ca. 80–90 C.E. for the Pastoral Epistles). Resistance to this arrangement in practice is suggested in Paul's admonition to the model leader Titus at 2:15 not to let anyone look down on him, and in his admonition to Timothy at 1 Tim 4:12 not to let anyone treat him with contempt because of his age. At 2 Tim 1:6 Timothy is similarly encouraged to rely on the charism of his position in the face of opposition, the "gift of God having come to him by the imposition of hands." Noteworthy is the fact that the Pastoral Epistles refer at 2 Tim 1:6 and 1 Tim 4:14 to a process for transmitting official authority through the imposition of hands that has already become an accepted practice. Moreover, the collective body of presbyters are the ones who impose hands. As for the other officeholders described in the letters, it is telling that one qualification is that candidates not include "new converts" (1 Tim 3:6), which might imply that time has moved on from Paul's first organization of house church communities.

That said, however, the community functions in the Pastoral Epistles do not include the clear authority, liturgical priority, or consistency in title and hierarchy that are found attached to the offices in *1 Clement* (ca. 96–97 C.E.) and Ignatius (ca. 110–115 C.E.); for example, *1 Clement* 47 mentions elders/presbyters and their functions as community leaders (1, 14, 21) and as overseers/bishops (42). In the latter position they exercise the liturgical function of offering gifts at the Eucharist (44). While the duties are more clearly expressed, the tripartite division of offices,—overseer/bishop, elder/presbyter, assistant/deacon—is not yet fixed. In Ignatius' letters, on the other hand, the situation has changed. There is a single bishop in charge of a region and the bishop exercises a presiding role that legitimates the community eucharistic liturgy (Ign. *Smyrn.* 8). With the bishop is a presbyteral council, analogous to the college of apostles (Ign. *Eph.* 2, 20; Ign. *Magn.* 2, 6, 7, 13; Ign. *Trall.* 3, 13). Like the apostles, they seem to perform the apostolic work of evangelism, preaching, and teaching, in addition to consulting with the overseer/bishop as a body in matters of government and discipline. They are assisted by deacons. Deacons accompany Ignatius (Ign. *Phld.* 11; Ign. *Smyrn.* 10; Ign. *Eph.* 2), serve as scribes (Ign. *Smyrn.* 12), act as messengers (Ign. *Phld.* 10), and are subordinate to the incumbents of the other two ranks. They administer alms, assist the sick, feed the hungry, and act as agents of the bishop in his ministry (Ign. *Magn.* 2, 6; Ign. *Phld.* 4; Ign. *Smyrn.* 12). Since Ignatius is at pains to support the monoepiscopacy (Ign. *Trall.* 3.1-2), the institution and the tripartite division of offices seems to be at its beginning stages. The contemporaneous letter of Polycarp *To the Philippians* does not mention a bishop, but he does ascribe the bishop's disciplinary and pastoral responsibilities to the elders/presbyters. He mentions assistants/deacons as well. The ecclesiastical development in Asia Minor has not yet traveled to church communities farther west. These historical observations on the development of ecclesiastical structures would locate the Pastoral Epistles around 80–90 C.E., between Paul's death in the mid-60's and the mid-nineties (the date of *1 Clement*) and the early 100's when Ignatius flourished and was martyred.

For Reference and Further Study

Barrett, C. K. "Pauline Controversies in the Post-Pauline Period," *NTS* 20 (1974) 229–45.

Bauer, Walter. *Orthodoxy and Heresy in Earliest Christianity*. Philadelphia: Fortress Press, 1979.

Brown, Raymond E. "*Episkopē* and *Episkopos*: The New Testament Evidence," *TS* 41 (1980) 322–38.

Collins, Raymond F. "Pastoral Ministry: Timothy and Titus," *Church* (1987) 20–24.

Fee, Gordon D. *1 and 2 Timothy, Titus*. NIBC. Peabody, MA: Hendrickson, 1984.

Fiore, Benjamin. *Personal Example*, 42–44, 98–100.

________. "Paul, Exemplification, and Imitation," in J. Paul Sampley, ed., *Paul in the Greco-Roman World: A Handbook*. Harrisburg, London, and New York: Trinity Press International, 2003, 228–57.

Harrison, Percy N. *Paulines and Pastorals*. London: Villiers, 1964.

Hock, Ronald F., and Edward N. O'Neil, trans. and ed. *The Chreia and Ancient Rhetoric: Classroom Exercises*. Writings from the Greco-Roman World, 2. Atlanta: Society of Biblical Literature, 2002.

Jay, Eric G. "From Presbyters-Bishops to Bishops and Presbyters," *SecCent* 1 (1981) 125–62.

Kennedy, George A., tr. & ed. *Progymnasmata: Greek Textbooks of Prose Composition and Rhetoric*. Writings from the Greco-Roman World 10. Atlanta: Society of Biblical Literature, 2003.

Lemaire, André. "Pastoral Epistles: Redaction and Theology," *BTB* 2 (1972) 25–42.

Schürmann, Heinz. "Haben die paulinischen Wertungen und Weisungen Modell-charakter?" *Greg* 56 (1975) 237–71.

Spiq, Ceslas. *Saint Paul: Les Épîtres pastorales*. 2 vols. 4th rev. ed. Paris: Gabalda, 1969.
Wolbert, Werner. "Vorbild und paränetische Autorität," *MTZ* 32 (1981) 249–70.

IV. HORTATORY STRATEGY AND CONTENT

1. *Exemplary Figures*

The three Pastoral Epistles were written under the name of Paul and their addressees were his coworkers. This commentary accepts the arguments that favor the position that all three Pastoral Epistles were composed by a member of the Pauline community, writing in his name and most likely after his death. Nonetheless, references in the commentary are made to Paul's statements in the letters, as if he were the writer. This serves to retain, to some extent, the aura of Pauline authorship created by the letter writer. It also makes the comments less cumbersome. As the author of the Pastoral Epistles is not Paul, so too the addressees Timothy and Titus might well be fictitious. What the epistles present to the reader and to the church community that accepts them as scriptural is a formulation of the Pauline tradition for a later generation, as it meets challenges that arise from the growth of the church community and from conflicts in interpretation and teaching. The founding figures of the community become examples for those who succeeded them, and the policies described in the letters set the pattern for ecclesiastical structures developed over time.

2. *Christology*

Along with the exemplary figures of Paul, founding father of the community, and of Timothy and Titus his beloved sons, associates, and successors, the Pastoral Epistles incorporate statements of the true teaching. Most of these record the community's understanding of Jesus. Thus they remind the addressees and the wider audience of Jesus' human existence, death, resurrection, and glorification (1 Tim 3:16). Mention of Jesus' testimony to Pontius Pilate (1 Tim 6:13) is an allusion to the gospel story unique in the Pauline correspondence. His expected return on the day appointed by God, on the other hand, is thoroughly Pauline (see 1 Cor 15:24-28), but the affirmation of Jesus as end-time judge (2 Tim 4:8) finds clear expression only at 2 Thess 2:12. Jesus' pre-existence, suggested at 1 Tim 3:16, has an even stronger affirmation at 2 Tim 1:9-10, where God's salvation is acknowledged as effected in Christ Jesus before time began. The same passage goes on to note the earthly life of Jesus as well as his victory over death in his resurrection. In addition, the passage asserts the fundamental Pauline insight that salvation comes to humanity not through human works but through the divine design and grace (and see Titus 3:4-7). This salvation includes the manifestation of life and immortality to those who hear the Gospel.

Echoing the gospel admonition to profess Jesus' words unashamedly and to take up one's cross in following Jesus and gaining life by losing it (Mark 8:34-38 *parr.*), 2 Tim 2:11-13 urges the faithful to persevere and die with Christ in order to live and reign with him. Passing from death to life finds another expression in the reference at Titus 3:4-7, which is also consistent with Paul, to rebirth in baptism and renewal by the Holy Spirit (see Rom 5:5; 6:3-4). Once again the justification is accomplished by God's grace and not by righteous deeds. Pauline, too, is the declaration that this merciful justification makes its recipients heirs of eternal life (Gal 3:26-29; 4:6-7).

Jesus' role is that of the unique mediator between the savior God and humanity, whom the human Jesus ransomed by his death (1 Tim 2:5-6). Nonetheless, Jesus also receives the title Lord and is mentioned in parallel with God (1 Tim 1:1, 12; 6:3, 14; 2 Tim 1:2, 18; 4:8) and as savior (2 Tim 1:10; Titus 1:4; 2:13; 3:6; see also Jesus as the one whom widows serve and please: 1 Tim 5: 4-6, 11, and as the end-time judge, 2 Tim 4:1, 8).

3. *Soteriology*

The Pastoral Epistles speak of Jesus Christ as the one "who saved us" (2 Tim 1:9-10). He did this by destroying death and bringing life and immortality to light through the Gospel. He appointed Paul to be preacher, apostle, and teacher of this Gospel. Connecting salvation with Paul's preaching makes clear who the recipients of this salvation are, since that preaching aimed at reaching the ears of all peoples (2 Tim 4:17; cf. Rom 15:14-21). While 2 Timothy 2:19 echoes the conviction in the Hebrew Scriptures that the Israelites are God's own people, the passage breaks through borders by referring to all who call on the Lord's name. This includes those peoples who have heard and accepted the Gospel message and keep away from doing evil. This message constitutes the tradition that started with Paul and then passes on to Timothy and Titus, who preserve and teach the traditional faith (1 Tim 1:18; 4:6-16; 6:11-16, 20; 2 Tim 3:10–4:5; Titus 2:1, 15; 3:8). These, in turn, appoint others as teachers, who will appoint still other teachers (1 Tim 3:2; Titus 1:9; 2 Tim 2:1-2). It is not surprising that the letter to Titus takes issue with Jewish Christians and 1 Timothy contests the false teachers' interpretation of the Law (1 Tim 1:7) and ascetical requirements (1 Tim 4:1-5). God has made a new people for himself by cleansing them and making them his own through baptism (Titus 2:14; 3:5).

The Pastoral Epistles, therefore, speak of God's will that everyone be saved. They also refer to Jesus' mediation between God and humanity and the fact that he gave himself as a ransom for all (1 Tim 2:4). This is the Gospel message Paul and his successors proclaim to the Gentile world (1 Tim 3:16).

The salvation willed by God for all becomes effective in those who believe (1 Tim 4:10) and who come to the knowledge of the truth (1 Tim 2:4). In view of this the Pastoral Epistles stress the preservation and propagation of true belief. In addition to preaching and teaching, exemplary action and progress in virtue also serve the same end by leading all those who see them to salvation (1 Tim 4:16). Finally, there is the expectation that those who accept the true tradition will live virtuously and devote themselves to good works (Titus 2:14).

While there are references in the Pastoral Epistles to Paul's mission to the Gentiles and his successors' responsibility to preach the word (2 Tim 4:2), the overall focus is on teaching and maintaining the tradition of faith within the geographical areas with which the letters are identified, Ephesus and Crete. It appears that the aim is to make the Gospel message penetrate more deeply into these areas rather than to spread it widely over many regions, as Paul's ministry accomplished. In practical terms, then, the Pastoral Epistles look to bring the Gospel message of salvation to all their neighbors rather than to all people in the world. Once again the strategy is twofold: teaching the true tradition and demonstrating it in virtuous action.

GENERAL BIBLIOGRAPHY

Balch, David, and Carolyn Osiek. *Families in the New Testament World: Households and House Churches*. Louisville: Westminster John Knox, 2003.

Borse, Udo. *1. und 2. Timotheusbrief, Titusbrief*. Stuttgarter Kleiner Kommentar, Neues Testament 13. Stuttgart: Katholisches Bibelwerk, 1985.

Brox, Norbert. *Die Pastoralbriefe: übersezt und erklärt*. Regensburg: Pustet, 1969.

Dewey. Joanna. "1 Timothy," in Carol A. Newsom and Sharon H. Ringe, eds., *The Women's Bible Commentary*. London: SPCK; Louisville: Westminster John Knox, 1992; expanded ed. 1998, 444–49.

Dibelius, Martin, and Hans Conzelmann. *The Pastoral Epistles*. Trans. Philip Buttolph and Adela Yarbro. Hermeneia. Philadelphia: Fortress Press, 1972.

Fee, Gordon D. *1 and 2 Timothy, Titus*. New International Bible Commentary. Peabody, MA: Hendrickson, 1984.

Fiore, Benjamin, S.J. *The Function of Personal Example in the Socratic and Pastoral Epistles*. AnBib 105. Rome: Biblical Institute Press, 1986.

Giles, Kevin. *Patterns of Ministry Among the First Christians*. Melbourne: CollinsDove, 1989.

Gorday, Peter, ed. *Colossians, 1–2 Thessalonians, 1–2 Timothy, Titus*, Ancient Christian Commentary on Scripture, New Testament IX. Downers Grove: InterVarsity Press, 2000.

Hanson, Anthony Tyrrell. *Studies in the Pastoral Epistles*. London: SPCK, 1968.

Houlden, J. L. *The Pastoral Epistles: I and II Timothy, Titus*. Harmondsworth: Penguin, 1976.

Knight, George W. III. *The Faithful Sayings in the Pastoral Letters.* Grand Rapids: Baker Book House, 1979.

Malherbe, Abraham J. *Paul and the Popular Philosophers*. Minneapolis: Fortress Press, 1989.

Quinn, Jerome D., and William C. Wacker. *The First and Second Letters to Timothy: A New Translation with Notes and Commentary*. Grand Rapids: Eerdmans, 2000.

Towner, Philip H. *The Goal of Our Instruction: The Structure of Theology and Ethics in the Pastoral Epistles*. JSNTSup 34. Sheffield: Sheffield Academic Press, 1989.

Spicq, Ceslas O.P. *Saint Paul: Les Épîtres pastorales*. 2 vols. 4th rev. ed. Paris: Gabalda, 1969.

Torjesen, Karen Jo. *When Women Were Priests: Women's Leadership in the Early Church and the Scandal of their Subordination in the Rise of Christianity*. San Francisco: HarperSanFrancisco, 1993.

Verner, David C. *The Household of God: The Social World of the Pastoral Epistles*. SBLDS 71. Chico: Scholars Press, 1983.

1 Timothy

1 TIMOTHY

INTRODUCTION

The addressee of the first letter, Timothy, was one of Paul's most effective and respected coworkers. Thus he represents Paul at 1 Cor 4:17, 16:10; Phil 2:19-24; 1 Thess 3:2, 6; and he is listed among those who send greetings with Paul at 2 Cor 1:1, 19; Phil 1:1; Col 1:1; 1 Thess 1:1; 2 Thess 1:1; Phlm 1; Rom 16:21 (see also Acts 16:1; 17:14-15; 18:5; 19:22; 20:4). In this letter he receives a reminder of his commission to supervise the appointment of officials for the church communities in Ephesus, to see to the establishment of proper relationships among community members, and to spearhead the defense of Pauline tradition against harmful deviations. These three concerns form the strands that are woven into the letter. To accomplish his tasks Timothy has authority over the several Ephesian house church communities. This expands the ministry of Pauline emissary that he exercises in Paul's letters and in Acts.

After the greeting (1:1-2) the letter introduces, in the guise of a reminder of an oral commission, Timothy's principal task and the main concern of the letter, which is to counter those proposing false doctrine and fanciful speculations. Here the dispute is over the interpretation and application of traditional Jewish Law (the Decalogue, 1:3-11). Paul's progress from ignorant unbelief to being a minister of the true teaching stands as an example of the effects of Jesus' merciful salvation (1:12-17). Timothy receives the task to resist the faithless and is reminded of a ceremony of installation in the past. His antagonists are also named, which serves as a counterexample to his (1:18-20).

The letter then launches into procedures and rules for the local church. The conduct and purpose of community prayer includes prayer for secular authority (2:1-7). The true belief that Jesus died for all people supports this perspective. The church rule about prayer flows into household regulations (2:8-15) for men (prayer) and women (behavior).

Church regulations resume (3:1-13) with qualifications for officials. Teaching ability (for overseers/bishops) and good reputation (for both overseers/bishops and assistants/deacons) are particularly important. Personal virtues and household management abilities round out the list.

A capsule summary of the true teaching about Jesus' incarnation and the universal reach of the Christian proclamation (3:14-16) leads into a characterization of false teaching, with an emphasis on misguided asceticism (4:1-5). The charge to Timothy to uphold sound teaching by word and example concludes with another reminder of the gift he received previously at an "ordination" ceremony to the presbyterate (4:6-16).

Household rules enter again (5:1-8, 16), but the rules for widows allow for the insertion of regulations for church "widows" who serve with monetary compensation (5:9-15). Once again maintaining the community's reputation figures in the restrictions on accepting widows onto the official church rolls. The regulations continue with rules for dealing with presbyters/elders, their pay and modes of public correction (5:17-22). Again publicity, bad and good, is part of the rules' motivation, as Timothy is reminded to look to his health and set himself apart from sinful people (5:23-25). The section ends with rules for slaves and addresses apparent dissatisfaction at their having to continue in servitude even with believing masters (6:1-2).

Reference to misguided teaching and its effects (6:3-5) leads to a disquisition, perhaps a sermon fragment, on the pitfalls of desiring riches (6:6-19). The sermon is interrupted by another reminder to Timothy of his duty to pursue virtue and of the vocation ceremony in the past (6:11-16). This receives backing from a reference to Jesus' *parousia* or "second coming." Timothy is a model of the person who seeks what is of true value.

The letter ends with yet another charge to Timothy to guard the tradition and avoid the apostates' babbling (6:20-21a). The brevity and abruptness of the letter's close is not characteristic of the letters of Paul (6:21b).

Outline

1:1-2	Greeting
1:3-20	Challenges and Responsibilities
1:3-11	False and true teaching about the Law
1:12-17	Paul, model of forgiveness
1:18-20	Charge to Timothy
2:1–6:2	Church and Domestic Regulations
2:1-7	Church prayer
2:8-15	Domestic rules: men and women
3:1-13	Church officials: overseers/bishops and assistants/deacons
3:14–4:16	Church doctrine; erroneous teaching; Timothy's task
5:1-8	Domestic rules: elders, widows

- 5:9-15 Church officials: widows
- 5:16 Domestic rules: widows
- 5:17-25 Church rules: presbyters, public reprimand
- 6:1-2 Domestic rules: slaves

6:3-19 Proper View of Wealth

6:20-21 Concluding Charge to Timothy

TRANSLATION, NOTES, INTERPRETATION

1. *Greeting* (1:1-2)

1. Paul, apostle of Jesus Christ by command of God our savior and Christ Jesus our hope, 2. to Timothy, true child in faith: Favor, mercy, and peace from God the Father and Christ Jesus our Lord.

Notes

1. *Paul:* Paul wrote this from Laodicea according to a fifth-century manuscript and from Nicopolis according to a ninth-century manuscript. A fourth-century manuscript gives no point of origin.

Paul to Timothy, greetings: This is the typical formula for the opening of a Greek letter.

apostle: In the PE only Paul has the title "apostle." The Lukan (34x) and Pauline (34x, five of them in the PE) corpora account for most of the eighty NT uses. The term is generally used for "the Twelve," even by Luke, who refers it to Paul and Barnabas only in Acts 14:4, 14. Luke is careful to establish the continuity of tradition from Jesus to the Spirit-filled Twelve around whom the church of Jerusalem is centered and who are the source from which the Gospel spread (Acts 1:1-8). The single appearance in 3 Kings 14:6 (LXX), translating *sheluach,* identifies the divine emissary as the prophet Ahijah, and there is some evidence of late Palestinian Jewish use of *shaliach* for rabbinic emissaries. Luke might attest the connection of apostle and prophet in the Q passage Luke 11:49, or he might have read back into Q the meaning of *apostolos* as commissioned missionary, which was perhaps developed in Antioch by Paul, who alone uses the singular form of the word. Paul, "least of the apostles" (1 Cor 15:9), claims the title as witness of the risen Lord and recipient of a divine call (1 Cor 15:9-10; Gal 1:15-16). He distinguishes the "circle of the Twelve" from the larger number of primitive church apostles (1 Cor 15:5-6) and then from apostles of the congregation with their special tasks and missions (1 Cor 15:7; Phil 2:25; 2 Cor 8:23). Among these one finds Barnabas (Acts 13:1-3; 14:4, 14), Andronicus and Junia (Rom 16:7), but not Apollos (1 Cor 3:9), Timothy (1 Cor 4:17), and Titus (2 Cor 8:23). At least some of these apostles clearly preceded Paul in the Christian movement. To the PE, Paul is the apostle *par excellence*, apostle to the Gentiles by divine appointment (1 Tim 2:7), and without appeal to common apostolic tradition (1 Cor 15:3-4).

Christ Jesus our hope: This is the order of the name and title preferred in the PE (9 of 11 times in 1 Timothy, 12 of 13 times in 2 Timothy, 1 of 4 times in Titus). Neither "Jesus" nor "Christ" appears separately. The order "Jesus Christ" is used in a credal statement (2 Tim 2:8) and following the titles "Our Lord" (1 Tim 6:3, 14) and "our savior" (Titus 2:3), where the name thus separates two titles. Paul's earlier letters use "Jesus" and "Christ" separately, and vary the order freely when the two are combined. In the PE Christ Jesus or Jesus Christ appears to be the name of Jesus, with some implication of title still remaining and with the order providing some emphasis to Christ. The titles "Lord" and "Savior" (1 Tim 1:12; 2:5; 6:3, 14; 2 Tim 1:2, 10; Titus 1:4) and actions (1 Tim 6:3 in parallel with God the lifegiver) are attributed to him. Titus 2:13 connects "hope" with the appearance of the glory of God and of the savior Jesus. The same letter at 1:2 and 3:7 ties hope to eternal life promised by God for those justified by Jesus Christ the savior.

Savior: This word is rarely used of God (Luke 1:47, Jude 25) outside the PE and, whether of God or Christ, of the twenty-four NT usages, ten of them appear in the PE and eight in other late NT works associated with Asia Minor (Ephesians, 2 Peter, 1 John, Jude).

2. *Timothy, true child:* In Derbe, according to Acts 16:1, Paul chose Timothy, son of a Jewish mother who was a believer and a Greek father, to be a mission companion. Paul had him circumcised and took him along on his mission tour together with Silas, with whom he set out from Antioch. Paul and Silas alone are named in the Philippi episode, a "we" section (Acts 16:11-42). Still in eclipse behind Paul and Silas in further travels (Acts 17:1-13), Timothy resurfaces at Acts 17:14, where he remains in Beroea with Silas. Summoned by Paul (Acts 17:15), he and Silas join Paul in Corinth (Acts 18:5), travel with him to Ephesus, whence he is dispatched with Erastus back to Macedonia (Acts 19:22), where Paul rejoins him later with a company of associates. Timothy then precedes Paul to Troas (Acts 20:4). Paul's traveling party, the "we" of Acts, seems not to include Timothy, and "we" leave and go on to Mytilene, Miletus, and eventually to Jerusalem, while Timothy is no longer mentioned. His name appears in all of the Pauline letters but Galatians, Ephesians, and Titus. While in Acts he and Erastus are called "assistants" (*diakonountōn*), Paul himself calls him "coworker" (*synergos*, Rom 16:21; 1 Thess 3:12), "brother" (*adelphos*, 2 Cor 1:1; Col 1:1; 1 Thess 3:2; Phlm 1), "slave" of Christ Jesus (*doulos*, Phil 1:1), and, as here, "child" (*teknon*, 1 Cor 4:17 and 1 Tim 1:18; 2 Tim 1:2). In addition to preaching (2 Cor 1:19), he is a coauthor with Paul of some of the letters (2 Cor 1:1; Phil 1:1; Col 1:1; 1 Thess 1:1; 2 Thess 1:1; Phlm 1) and functions as Paul's trusted representative to troubled communities (1 Cor 4:17; 16:10; Phil 2:19). Since Paul uses "child" (*teknon*) for his converts (the Corinthians, 1 Cor 4:17; the Galatians, Gal 4:19; Onesimus, Phlm 10; the Philippians, Phil 2:22; and Timothy), it would have been on his first journey through Lystra (Acts 13:8-20) that he converted Timothy. With community commendation garnered over the intervening time,

Paul chose him to become his assistant in place of the unreliable John Mark, whom he rejected at the start of this second mission tour (Acts 15:38). The favor he won in Paul's eyes is based on his reliable and selfless dedication to Paul in the work of the Gospel (Phil 2:19-22; 1 Cor 4:17b).

favor, mercy, and peace: A common expression in Pauline epistolary greetings, *charis* ("favor") looks ahead to 1 Tim 1:14, where Paul gives thanks for the divine favor occasioning his conversion. An addition to the more usual Pauline pair "grace . . . peace" (Rom 1:7; 1 Cor 1:3; 2 Cor 1:2; Gal 1:3; Eph 1:2; Phil 1:2; Col 1:2; 1 Thess 1:1; 2 Thess 1:2; Phlm 3; Titus 1:4; but see also 2 Tim 1:2), it introduces a soteriological note that reappears at 1 Tim 1:13, 16 and 2 Tim 1:16, 18; Titus 3:5. With "peace" added to the greeting formula, Paul preserves a characteristic peculiar to Semitic letter writing. Moreover, his use of *charis* ("grace") presents a Christian play on the Greek *chairein* ("greetings") of the standard Greek formula. The formula "grace and peace" is analogous to the opening blessing "peace and mercy" found in certain Near Eastern letters. It is equivalent in Greek to a religious health wish (White, p. 437). The addition of "from God . . . and Christ Jesus" further Christianizes the formula. As with "favor" (Rom 1:7), *eleos* ("mercy"), a staple of Pauline epistolary greetings, looks ahead to 1 Tim 1:13 and 16 and Paul's reception of mercy and divine forbearance (and see 2 Tim 1:2, 16, 18; Titus 3:5).

Lord: This title is used in all the NT books except Titus (but see the variants to 1:4) and 1-3 John. It appears twenty-two times in 1 and 2 Timothy. In 1 Timothy, of six uses only 6:15 seems to refer not to Jesus but to God (Fitzmyer, *EDNT*, refers it to Jesus there). Second Timothy refers it most often to Jesus, except at 2 Tim 1:18; 2:19a, b and perhaps 2:22 and 24. Its application to Jesus raises him above the human level and it is normally used of the risen Jesus and Jesus in his *parousia*. While not attested as a direct translation of YHWH until the fifth-century LXX manuscripts (earlier Greek versions retained YHWH in the text), the last two centuries B.C.E. saw Palestinian usage of the Aramaic *mareh/marya*, the Hebrew *adon*, and even the Greek *kyrios* for YHWH, thus preparing the way for the NT use of the title. The NT usage is traceable to the early Palestinian church, as evidenced by the Aramaic liturgical acclamation *maranatha* ("Come, O Lord," 1 Cor 16:22). Paul quotes the early confession "Jesus Christ is Lord" (1 Cor 12:3 and Rom 10:9), and the hymn of Phil 2:6-11 accords Jesus the title and adoration equivalent to that given YHWH in Isa 45:23. The title/name thus exalts Jesus to a level on a par with YHWH, though he is not entirely identified with YHWH.

Interpretation

The first letter to Timothy, like the letter to Titus, is concerned with "church order" issues. It lists the qualifications of church ministers. The problem of apostates and false teachers also receives attention. The recurrent insistence on dealing with the false teachers suggests that this is the context for the letter. Thus the addressee is warned to ensure correct teaching, avoid the wayward, and even estrange them from the community. The letter also highlights the possibility of conversion, even for these false teachers, by noting the example of Paul's own conversion. Direct advice to the addressee complements an exhortation on the misguided pursuit of riches.

The earliest commentators discerned a variety of purposes for the letter. Thus John Chrysostom saw Paul instructing his convert and disciple Timothy as pastor and teacher for the church. Theodore noted that the instructions on worship, governance, and teaching are meant for the churches in Ephesus and in all of Asia, but also for every bishop as capable overseer of the church. Theodoret (PG 82:787C-788C) saw Paul strengthening Timothy for the refutation of heresy and the governance of the church, while Ambrosiaster (CSEL 81, 3:252) observed it to be a message to Paul's convert from Judaism on how to be an effective leader and evangelist, especially in the face of Judaizing heresies.

This pseudonymous "official" letter presents the readers with two models: the addressee Timothy and the sender Paul. It also sketches official and communal responsibilities for belief and action. Attention is directed toward outsiders as this and the other two Pastoral Epistles work to establish and maintain the Christians' reputation in the community at large. Paul, as the sender, lists his name first, in accordance with Greek epistolary usage, "Paul to X, greetings." Paul designates himself as "apostle," as is the case in other Pauline letters, except Philippians, 1 and 2 Thessalonians, and Philemon, where others are named as co-senders with Paul. Paul's apostolic status rests on the divine command (1:1) and empowerment (1:12). Reference to his former hostility to Christianity (1:13) underlines the saving mercy of God, of which he is a prime example for all believers (1:16). He is also a model of obedience in accepting and living out the ministry of service enjoined on him (*epitagē*, 1:1 and 1:11-12). In his exercise of authority he issues commands and lays down behavioral policy over a wide area of church life (3:15), and he expects it to be acted on. This exercise of authority echoes Paul's practice in the *homologoumena* or Pauline letters of undisputed authorship (1 Cor 4:14-17; 5:3-5; 2 Cor 13:10; Phil 1:27-28; Phlm 8-9).

God, who is called "savior" at 1:1, receives that title at 1 Tim 2:3; 4:10; Titus 1:3; 2:10; 3:4, following Hellenistic Jewish usage. The salvation of sinners is attributed to Christ Jesus at 1:15, and Jesus is also given the title at 2 Tim 1:10; Titus 1:4; 2:13; 3:6, and is associated with salvation at 2 Tim 2:10; 3:15-16. The earliest reference to this in the undisputedly authentic letters of Paul is Phil 3:20. It was already a fixed title for Jesus by the time of the PE and becomes dogmatically fixed by 2 Pet 1:1, 11; 2:20; 3:2, 18. Its use is associated with language related to the imperial cult (*epiphaneia*, 1 Tim 6:14; 2 Tim 1:10; 4:1, 8; Titus 2:11; *megas theos*, Titus 2:13; *philanthropia*, Titus 3:4).

Similarly, Paul notes that mercy was shown him by Christ (1:16), while he sees in both "God the Father and Christ Jesus our Lord" the common source of mercy at 1:2. Even the command to be an apostle, which comes from God at 1:1, is attributed to Christ Jesus at 1:12. The letter ascribes the lofty title "Lord" to Jesus at 1:2, 12. Moreover, Jesus exercises patience (*makrothymia*) at 1:16. This is a characteristic of God in the Hebrew Scriptures and the Septuagint. Nonetheless, despite a parallelism of function, the traditional ways of identifying God restrain the author from collapsing all the categories, and God "the Father" remains the "King of the ages, the imperishable, unseen, only God" (1:17; and see 6:15). Jesus is the earthly revelation of the heavenly God.

Paul's reference to Jesus as "our hope" expresses an eschatological expectation that runs throughout the PE and counterbalances the letters' stress on the establishment of church structures, on preserving and transmitting the content of faith, and on ethical uprightness as a means to win approval from outside the Christian community. Titus 1:2; 2:13; and 3:7 express the object of hope: the expectation of Jesus' second coming and the inauguration of eternal life (see 2 Tim 4:8). While Jesus is identified with hope at 1 Tim 1:1, God the universal savior is the object of hope at 1 Tim 4:10 (and see 1 Tim 5:5 and 6:17).

Timothy, Paul's associate since his second mission journey (Acts 16:1, and see 2 Cor 1:19) and his trusted emissary to handle community problems (1 Cor 4:17; Phil 2:19; 1 Thess 3:2), is often mentioned elsewhere as sending greetings (Rom 16:21) or sending the letter itself along with Paul (2 Cor 1:1; Phil 1:1; Col 1:1; Phlm 1) and Silvanus (1 Thess 1:1; 2 Thess 1:1). In those instances he is called "brother" (2 Cor 1:1; Col 1:1; Phlm 1; and see Heb 13:23), "coworker" (Rom 16:21), "slave" (Phil 1:1), and, as here, "child" (Phil 2:22; 1 Cor 4:17). The responsibility enjoyed in association with Paul in the Pauline tradition provides the foundation for the supervisory role in which the PE cast Timothy. His subordinate status as Paul's emissary carries over into his task in 1 and 2 Timothy of seeing to the stability of the Ephesian community. The backing of Pauline authority and the encouragement given the younger Timothy by Paul's commendations in the face of potential opposition (1 Cor 16:10-11; Phil 2:20-23) carried into the PE (1 Tim 4:12; 2 Tim 1:6-8). The collaborative relationship between Paul and Timothy, and Paul's repeated reliance on Timothy to serve as his surrogate in handling community difficulties, provide the setting on which the PE rest. The effort of the letters to maintain the integrity of Pauline tradition in the face of inauthentic developments, and to advance that tradition to cover developments in the thought and practice of the Pauline community, relies on the memory of the relationship between Paul and Timothy. In calling Timothy "true" (*gnēsios*) child in faith, Paul anticipates the criticism of teachers of false doctrine at v. 3. This is also one of the tasks assigned to Timothy. As in Philippians 2, Timothy presents an example of fidelity to Paul in true service to the community and its authentic tradition. Timothy demonstrates the aim of Paul's instruction (1 Tim 1:5), which includes "a faith free of wickedness."

In the context of a collaborative ministry, familiar from the earlier letters of Paul and the Acts of the Apostles, the first letter to Timothy records Paul's instructions, already given orally to his representative. The rhetorical situation of the letter, as a written memorandum, makes sense of the otherwise anomalous situation of a letter detailing instructions that should have been covered orally and only recently. Such a procedure would be known to the audience from secular practice of official, widely circulated letters containing the instructions (*entolai*) given newly appointed subordinate officials, detailing the general obligations of the office and the policies to be pursued.

Timothy's official position is not identical with any of those outlined in the "church order" sections. Although he passes on the Pauline doctrine (1 Tim 3:15; 4:6) and participates in the commissioning of presbyters (1 Tim 5:22), he is not to be thought of as a (proto-)monarchical bishop as that office emerges in the letters of Ignatius. He is given no liturgical preeminence in the Eucharist, nor is there any mention of subordination of presbyters, deacons, widows, and/or overseers to him by virtue of such an office. If anything, he is to be an example of Christian living for all to observe and follow (1 Tim 4:12-16). The authority envisioned in the letter derives from his relationship to Paul (1 Tim 3:14-15), to whom he is subordinated (1 Tim 4:13).

The epistolary situation is one of apostasy (1:3, 6; 4:1) and associated irreligious behavior (1:5, and see 2 Tim 2:14-17; Titus 1:16). The letter does not describe the doctrine of the false teachers beyond suggesting a Jewish and legal cast to their teaching (*nomodidaskaloi*, 1:7, and see Titus 1:10, 14), myths (1:4; 4:7), and speculations (1:4). They promote ascetical practices (4:3, 8, and Titus 1:15) and profess a knowledge that runs counter to the Pauline tradition (6:20-21). Second Timothy 2:18 adds that they teach that the resurrection has already taken place, an over-spiritualized and over-realized eschatology. From the credal summaries, doxologies, and statements about the true teaching one can also conclude through "mirror reading" that the false teaching misconstrues and perhaps restricts the availability of salvation, which is declared universal (1 Tim 2:4, 6; 4:10; see 2 Tim 4:17; Titus 2:11). The teaching also seems to devalue the redemptive death of the incarnate Jesus (1 Tim 1:15; 2:5-6; 3:16; 6:13; see 2 Tim 1:8, 10; 2:8; Titus 2:14; 3:4) and to ignore the *parousia* and its significance for the individual's eternal life (6:14-16, 19 and 2 Tim 2:11-13; 4:1, 8, 18; Titus 2:12-13; 3:7).

Thus the pseudonymous letters were written to confront a real situation of conflict over the valid representation of Pauline tradition and its authentic development. The letters indicate the critical nature of the situation. It is described as the eschatological conflict (1 Tim 4:1; 2 Tim 3:1; 4:3-4) foretold by

God's spirit. The apostates are enjoying success (2 Tim 3:9) and are winning individuals over (2 Tim 2:18; 3:6). The exemplary leader Timothy himself seems to falter in relying on the power of the gift of God and is inclined to be ashamed of the Gospel (2 Tim 1:6-8). He is reminded to share in the suffering of defending the teaching (2 Tim 1:8; 2:3; 4:5). Persecution is said to be the lot of all believers (2 Tim 2:11; 3:12). Paul himself is a paradigm of endurance in suffering (2 Tim 4:6, 14, 17-18) and abandonment (2 Tim 1:15; 4:16-18) for the beleaguered community.

The situation in Crete seems less severe. Although the many rebellious false teachers overturn the faith of whole households (Titus 1:11), it seems possible to silence them (1:11) or, after several warnings, to break contact with them (3:10).

The "favor" (*charis*) in Paul's conventional greeting finds amplification at 1:14, where Paul recalls his own reception of abundant favor from Jesus. Inasmuch as Paul is the prime "example" (*hypotypōsis*) of a sinner who found divine forbearance and mercy, it is fitting that he wish this same benefit for his emissary, who in turn will work to bring both the promise and the experience of it to the Ephesian community (4:16). The salvation of all people by God through Jesus Christ is a central belief in 1 Timothy (1:14, 20; 2:5; 4:10; see 2 Tim 1:19; 2:25; Titus 2:11; 3:3-7).

"God our Father and Christ Jesus our Lord" is a formula common to the Pauline epistles (Rom 1:7; 1 Cor 1:3; 8:6; 2 Cor 1:2; Eph 1:2; 6:23; 1 Thess 1:1; 3:4; 2 Thess 1:1, 2; 2:16; Phlm 3; see Rom 15:6; 2 Cor 1:3; 11:31; Eph 1:3, 17; 5:20; Col 1:3; Phil 2:11; 1 Thess 3:13). In the OT, God is the father of the Israelite nation as a whole, creating them as his people in the Exodus and giving them nurture and instruction (Deut 32:5-11; Jer 31:9). Recognition of God as father came to be linked with knowledge of God's truth, the "hidden counsels" (Wis 3:13-24; 1QH[a] 9:35-36), and the righteous called out to God the Father for protection against the wicked of the world (Sir 51:10-14). The title establishes the patriarchal perspective of the PE (1 Tim 3:15; 2 Tim 2:19-21). The letters stress God as Father of a household rather than the Greeks' god of the cosmos. The preeminence of God the Father remains, even with the addition of "Christ Jesus our Lord." As source with the Father of favor, mercy, and peace, Christ Jesus explains the transmission of these divine gifts to humans.

Paul, like a good parent, chastises the troublesome Corinthians in 1 Cor 4: 15-16 but offers himself as a good example to follow. He has a special relationship with them as the community's founder, their father in Christ. At 1 Thess 2:11-12 he uses the exhorting father image once again, and to a community that imitates his example (1:6) and of which he feels bereft in his separation from them (2:17). He nurses (2:7) and feeds baby food (1 Cor 3:1-4) to his converts until they mature and can digest meatier teaching. Paul demonstrates a pattern of leadership whose bonds with the faithful are not just authoritative or juridical. Even when exasperated with his converts' waywardness (Gal 4:19-20), he admonishes them with a view to their improvement (*nouthetōn*, 1 Cor 4:14; "in travail until Christ be formed in you," Gal 4:19) and not to shame them. Paul uses the terms "father" and "son," language of "fictive kinship" to express his relationship with Timothy. Paul had a particularly close relationship with Timothy, Titus, and Onesimus (1 Cor 4:17; Phil 2:22; 1 Tim 1:2, 18; 2 Tim 1:2; 2:1; Titus 1:4; Phlm 10). Bonds of affection express the human side of Paul's mission with his associates. Family language rings hollow and unconvincing without evidence of mutual warmth and cooperation.

For Reference and Further Study

Agnew, Francis. "On the Origin of the Term Apostolos," *CBQ* 38 (1976) 49–53.

Bahr, Gordon J. "Paul and Letter Writing in the First Century," *CBQ* 28 (1966) 465–77.

Balz, Horst, and Gerhard Schneider, eds. *Exegetical Dictionary of the New Testament*. 3 vols. Grand Rapids: Eerdmans, 1990, 1991, 1993.

Bartlett, David. *Ministry in the New Testament*. Minneapolis: Fortress Press, 1993.

Borse, Udo. *1. und 2. Timotheusbrief, Titusbrief*. Stuttgarter Kleiner Kommentar, Neues Testament 13. Stuttgart: Katholisches Bibelwerk, 1985, 23.

Cohen, Shaye J. D. "Was Timothy Jewish (Acts 16:1-3)? Patristic Exegesis, Rabbinic Law, and Matrilineal Descent," *JBL* 105 (1986) 251–68.

Cuss, Dominique. *Imperial Cult and Honorary Terms in the* NT. Paradosis, Contributions to the History of Early Christian Literature and Theology 23. Fribourg: Fribourg University Press, 1974.

Danker, Frederick William, ed. *A Greek-English Lexicon of the New Testament and other Early Christian Literature*. 3rd ed. Chicago and London: University of Chicago Press, 2000.

de Boer, Martinus. "Images of Paul in the Post-Apostolic Period," *CBQ* 42 (1980) 359–80.

Fiore, Benjamin. *The Function of Personal Example in the Socratic and Pastoral Epistles*. AnBib 105. Rome: Biblical Institute Press, 1986, 79–84.

Fox, Robin Lane. *Pagans and Christians*. San Francisco: Harper & Row, 1988, 39–41.

Giles, Kevin. *Patterns of Ministry among the First Christians*. Melbourne: Collins Dove, 1989, 151–72.

Gorday, Peter, ed. *Colossians, 1–2 Thessalonians, 1–2 Timothy, Titus, Philemon*. Ancient Christian Commentary on Scriptures: New Testament IX. Downers Grove: InterVarsity Press, 2000.

Hasler, Victor. "Epiphanie und Christologie in den Pastoralbriefen," *TZ* 33 (1977) 193–209.

Howard, George. "The Tetragram and the NT," *JBL* 96 (1977) 63–83.

Knight, George W. III. *The Faithful Sayings in the Pastoral Letters*. Grand Rapids: Baker, 1979, see 1:15 and also pp. 32–35.

Mitchell, Margaret M. "New Testament Envoys in the Context of Greco-Roman Diplomatic and Epistolary Conventions: The Example of Timothy and Titus," *JBL* 111 (1992) 641–62.

Moda, Aldo. "Le Lettere pastorali e la bibliografia di Paolo. Saggio biblografico," *BeO* 27 (1985) 149–61.

Nolland, John. "Grace as Power," *NovT* 28 (1986) 26–31.

________. "Luke's Use of *charis*," *NTS* 32 (1986) 614–20.

Reverdin, Olivier. *Le Culte des souverains dans l'Empire romain.* Entreteins sur l'Antiquité classique de la Fondation Hardt 19. Paris: Klincksied, 1973.

Ross, James Thomas. "The Conception of *sōteria* in the New Testament." Diss., University of Chicago, 1947.

Stowers, Stanley K. *Letter Writing in Greco-Roman Antiquity*. Philadelphia: Westminster, 1989.

Strack, Hermann L., and Paul Billerbeck, *Kommentar zum Neuen Testament aus Talmud und Midrasch.* 6 vols. 6th ed. Munich: Beck, 1974–1975, 3:594.

Tarocchi, Stefano. *Il Dio Longanime. La longanimità nell'epistolario paolino*. RivBSup 28. Bologna: Edizioni Dehoniane, 1993.

White, John L. "Saint Paul and the Apostolic Letter Tradition," *CBQ* 45 (1983) 433–44.

Wild, Robert A. "The Image of Paul in the Pastoral Letters," *TBT* 23 (1985) 239–45.

________. "Portraits of Paul Created by His Early Christian Admirers," *Chicago Studies* 24 (1985) 273–89.

2. *Reminder and Appeal; False Teachers* (1:3-11)

3. My appeal is just the same as when I, upon setting out for Macedonia, called on you to stay on at Ephesus to instruct certain persons not to spread a different teaching, 4. or to give attention to myths and endless genealogies that put forth speculations instead of God's order in faith. 5. Now the aim of the command is love proceeding from a pure heart, a good conscience, and a faith free of wickedness. 6. When certain people strayed from these, they turned aside toward futile chatter. 7. Although they would like to be teachers of the law, they do not understand the teaching, which they are maintaining and about which they are making firm assertions.

8. Yes, we know that the law is good, if one applies it legitimately, 9. aware that law is not directed at a just person but at those who are lawbreakers and disobedient, impious sinners, unholy and godless, killers of their fathers and mothers, murderers, 10. sexually immoral, men who lie with men, kidnappers, liars, perjurers, and whatever else opposes the sound teaching 11. in accordance with the gospel of the glory of the blessed God, with which I have been entrusted.

Notes

3. *just the same as:* The conclusion of the opening sentence, referred to by this comparative conjunction, is unexpressed. "So carry out my instructions" must be supplied by the reader. This elliptical form of expression is found in papyrus letters of instruction, as is the particle *kathōs* ("so") with the full idea expressed (*MM* 314). The usage here gives 1 Timothy the character of an *aide memoire,* a letter-summary of instructions from a superior to a delegate outlining the latter's duties.

Macedonia: Acts 19:22 records just the opposite situation, with Paul sending Timothy and Erastus to Macedonia while he remained at Ephesus, leaving for Macedonia only after that (Acts 20:1) and joining Timothy (Acts 20:4). The itinerary here can only with great difficulty, if at all, be harmonized with what we know from the other Pauline letters and Acts.

called on: The work of exhorting is often ascribed to Christian prophets. Paul and Barnabas are called prophets at Acts 13:1. Paul sees exhorting as the work of a prophet at 1 Cor 14:1-5, where he also notes their "building up the church." Exhortation is Paul's work at 1 Thess 2:3. He gives Timothy that task at 1 Thess 3:2 (and see 1 Tim 5:6; 6:2; 2 Tim 4:2; Titus 2:6, 15). The overall aim of building the church is clear at 2 Cor 13:10 and 1 Tim 3:15. The appeal to Timothy is expressed with a milder word than the instruction Timothy is to give to members of the Ephesian community. This coincides with the collaborative relationship between Timothy and Paul in the Pauline letters (see pp. 32–33 above). On the other hand, Timothy's authoritative role vis-à-vis the false teachers is cast as stronger than in the Pauline letters, where in 1 Cor 4:17 he is to "remind" the Corinthians, who are directed not to be causes of "fear" for him (1 Cor 16:10), and in Phil 2:19, where he is to serve ostensibly as a news gatherer, as he is at 1 Thess 3:2 in addition to encouraging the Thessalonians.

Ephesus: The principal city of the Roman province of Asia and cult center of the goddess Artemis (Diana), Ephesus was a center of Paul's mission efforts for two years. On his second mission journey he was "prevented by the Holy Spirit" from going to Asia (Acts 16:6), as he seems to have planned, and eventually he went on to Macedonia. He reached Ephesus for a brief stay only after his initial work in Corinth (Acts 18:19-21). He returned to Ephesus on his third journey (Acts 19:1–20:1) and stayed for over two years, during which he suffered affliction (1 Cor 15:32; 2 Cor 1:8), but he had great success as well. Asia and its capital Ephesus were also home to Johannine (Rev 1:4–3:22) and Petrine Christian communities (1 Pet 1:1; 2 Pet 3:1), and they appear to have been a destination for Jewish-Christian refugees before, and even more after the collapse of the Jewish revolt of 66–73 B.C.E. Eusebius, *Hist. Eccl.* 3.4 lists Timothy as the first bishop of Ephesus.

spread a different teaching: Literally "to teach otherwise"; the Christian verb, found only in 1 Timothy (and see Ign. *Pol.* 3:1), implies heretical teaching in contrast with the sound teaching of the PE. The idea is comparable to Paul's "other gospel" (Gal 1:6).

4. *myths and endless genealogies:* In the NT only in the PE and 2 Peter. The word there is negative, the opposite of truth (2 Tim 4:4; Titus 1:14). Myths are described as "godless" (1 Tim 4:7) and "clever" (2 Pet 1:16). This echoes Jewish usage (Philo, *Curses* 162; Josephus, *C. Ap.* 2.37), but the juxtaposition of truth to myth was already made by Plato (*Tim.* 26E; *Phaed.* 61B) and Epictetus (*Diatr.* 3.24.18). *Second Clement* 13:3 associates the adjective "deceptive" (*planos*) with myth. The genealogies probably refer to the OT, Essene or rabbinic lists or lineage and tradition rather than to Gnostic lists of aeons and archons. The latter were documented only in the second century and later (Tertullian *Praescr.* 14.7, 33 [ANF 3:246, 259]; Irenaeus *Haer.* 1.1 [LCC 1:358]), after the writing of the PE. The tales and genealogies seem to refer to tales of "births of founders" (*MM*) or perhaps to lines of tradition of teachers. Hebrews 7:3, 6 establishes Jesus' preeminence over the OT priesthood (Gen 14:17-20 and Ps 110:4) and thus the irrelevance of genealogical data, unlike Matthew and Luke who both provide (different) genealogies for Jesus. The christological summaries of the PE unequivocally assert the human Jesus' relationship with God the Father as part of the fundamental (Pauline) faith tradition (1 Tim 1:15; 3:16; 2 Tim 1:8; Titus 2:5, 13; 3:4-7). Polybius IX 2, 1-3 uses the phrase in reference to colonization, the founding of cities, and the relationships of people. Strabo, *Geogr.* XI 5, 3 distinguishes fables from historical accounts.

   God's order: Some patristic usage attests the meaning "instruction in the faith," but the predominant patristic uses, the ordinary meaning of the word (*oikonomia*), the household imagery throughout the letter, and the recurrent theme of universal salvation in God's eschatological plan all weigh in favor of the translation proposed here (contra BAGD, *EDNT*). The speculations of the alternative teachings stand in contrast to the letter's expressions of the true teaching about God and the eschatological plan for salvation.

5. *love proceeding from a pure heart:* In the PE the word "love" (*agapē*) is never used by itself as it is in the undisputedly authentic Pauline letters, never in the triad "faith, hope, and love" found in 1 Corinthians 13 (see also 1 Thess 1:3; 5:8; Col 1:4-5), and not as the highest gift (Gal 5:6; Phil 1:9; 1 Cor 13:13). Rather, it is one quality among others that describes the Christian. While the undisputed Pauline letters stress that love is a gift and not a work, the usage here suggests it is one of the results of the instructions that follow. The word denotes a deliberate choice of its object, as opposed to "physical attraction" (*eros*) and "a warm fellow feeling or fondness" (*philia*), and thus "esteem." In religious usage it is a calculated disposition of regard and pious inclination toward God and one's fellows. "Pure" suggests being cleansed of sin and at 2 Tim 2:22 associates the heart with calling on the Lord (a liturgical usage found in LXX Deut 4:29; 10:12; 11:13). Paul used "heart" (*kardia*) in the Hebrew sense of the whole inner person: mind, emotion, and will. He also makes use of the Hellenistic terms "mind" (*nous*) or "intellect" (*dianoia*), used by Philo and Josephus in place of "heart" (*kardia*). The PE follow this usage.

   good conscience and a faith free of wickedness: While in the undisputed letters written by Paul conscience looked to the past in reaction to deeds done, the use with "good" (*agathē*) here implies that it is an organ of decision according to an approved standard (compare 1 Pet 3:16). The phrase appears again at 1 Tim 1:18. The false teachers, by implication here and expressly at 1 Tim 4:2 and also Titus 1:15, fall into wicked conduct because their consciences are corrupted by their rejection of authentic faith (and see Rom 1:18-23). "Faith" is not merely another quality of Christian existence, but rather retains the Pauline sense of the individual believer's relationship of trust in and reliance on God, as mediated by Jesus Christ. Faith often appears with love, at times in a pair (1 Tim 1:14; 2 Tim 1:13) or together with other qualities (1 Tim 2:15; 4:12; 2 Tim 2:22). The adjective "free of wickedness" (*anypokritou*) sets up the contrast with the baseless pretensions of the false teachers that follow (1 Tim 1:6-7, 18-20; 4:1-3; 6:3-5, 20-21). The term "hypocrite" in Jewish-Greek literature refers to a form of wrongdoing, with no suggestion of presenting a good appearance to disguise the true character. Opposition to God and law, rather than "hypocrisy," is at issue (see Matt 6:2; 15:7; 16:3; 23:13, 23; 24:51; Luke 13:15; as well as 2 Pet 2:2, 21; *1 Clem*. 35:5; Herm. *Vis*. 3.7.1; Jude 11; *Barn*. 11:7; Herm. *Mand*. 6:1.2-4). See also Herm. *Sim*. 9.19.2, "hypocrites and teachers of wickedness"; *Sim*. 9.18.3, "wicked blasphemers and hypocrites."

6. *strayed:* The image of leaving the path of true teaching, a typical description of the false teachers and their fellows in the PE (1 Tim 1:19; 4:1; 6:10, 21; 2 Tim 1:15, 18; 3:14; 4:4), suggests the rabbinic "two ways" teaching and recalls early Christian identification as "the way" (*hodos*) in Acts (9:2; 19:23; 22:4; 24:14, 22).

7. *teachers of the law:* The false teachers betray some links with Jewish tradition in their promotion of rabbinic legal teaching (see Titus 1:14-15). Their extreme asceticism, decried at 4:3, separates them from the traditional Jewish and Christian mainstreams. Quintilian, *Inst*. I 1, 8 decried the teachers who teach even though they are inadequately learned themselves.

8. *the law is good:* This is only apparently a non-Pauline assessment of the Law (Gal 3:24). While Paul criticized as futile the attempts to find righteousness by observing the Law's regulations (Gal 5:4 and Rom 7:9-10), he went on to declare the Law to be holy (Rom 7:12) but ineffective to promote holiness and life in the believer. Only the Spirit can do that (Rom 8:13; Gal 5:5) and thereby guide the believer into fulfilling the Law in love (Gal 5:14-18 and 6:2). Unlike the view expressed in Gal 3:19-22, he declares the Law to be good here and, in fact, engages in hortatory teaching rather than kerygmatic proclamation. He encourages the addressee Timothy to do the same (4:11).

9. *just person:* Another apparently non-Pauline usage. The immediate context leans toward the secular Greek meaning of one who satisfies ordinary legal norms, and therefore implies the idea of becoming just by one's law-abiding actions (1 Tim 1:11; Titus 1:8, where it is one of a list of virtues, and 2 Tim 2:22; 3:16, where one pursues "righteousness" [*dikaiosynē*]). The crown of righteousness Paul looks forward to, however, comes from Jesus (2 Tim 4:8), and Titus (3:4-7) expresses the Pauline tradition that one is justified by grace and not by righteous deeds. The autobiographical sketch at 1 Tim 1:12-17 makes a similar point, although with different terminology. The PE may thus endorse freedom from the Law for the just person analogously to Gal 5:18. In any case, this dispute over the Law indicates the ties of the Christian community of the PE to their Jewish

roots and the continued viability of the Law. Lucian, *Demon.* 59, takes a more cynical view when he notes that laws do no good whether for good or evil persons, since the good do not need them and the evil will not be improved.

disobedient: Subjection is an important attitude in the PE. It is a standard requirement in the household and church codes at 1 Tim 2:11; 3:4; Titus 1:6; 2:5, 9 (and cf. Rom 13:1, 5; 1 Cor 14:32, 34; Eph 5:21, 24; Col 3:18). The lawlessness and sin noted here of the disobedient echo the Pauline letters of undisputed authorship (Rom 8:7; 10:3; 2 Cor 9:13), as do disobedience and association with idle chatter (1:6; see Titus 1:10 and Rom 8:20). The eschatological dimension of judgment and salvation expressed here (1:16) and elsewhere (4:7-10; 2 Tim 2:11-13; 4:7-8; Titus 2:11-14; 3:3-7) rests on submission to God and its expression in appropriate behavior. Submission itself is a frequently mentioned characteristic of the end-time order in the Pauline letters of undisputed authorship (1 Cor 15:27-28; Phil 3:21; Eph 1:22; see Heb 2:8). Paul follows the "command" (*epitagē*, 1:1) of God and thus is the opposite of the disobedient here. The misinformed teachings about the Law have somehow misrepresented it in such a way that the apostates' disciples end by violating the commandments. Their over-realized eschatology (2 Tim 2:18), misunderstanding of the basis of salvation (note the letters' counter-stress on the historical redemptive actions of Jesus Christ), intellectualized but misguided faith (e.g., "speculations" 1 Tim 1:4; "investigations," "disputes over words," 6:4; 2 Tim 3:5), and the defective piety of their Christian way of life (2 Tim 3:5) all contribute to their transgressions.

impious sinners . . . godless: A hendiadys. In the LXX both words render the Hebrew *rašaʿ*. While "impious" (*asebēs*) is more frequent in the LXX, the NT prefers "sinner" (*hamartōlos*). Hellenistic Judaism expanded the notion of impiety to include impious behavior generally, which offends against God. The word "godless" (*bebēlois*) is found in the NT only four times. More than "secular, accessible to everyone," as in the classical sense, it describes distance from salvation. The PE echoes Hellenistic Jewish usage (3 Macc 4:16 = 1 Tim 6:20; 2 Tim 2:16; 3 Macc 2:2 = 1 Tim 1:9; see also 1 Tim 4:7; 3 Macc 2:14; Heb 12:16 = Philo, *Spec. Leg.* 1.102).

killers of their fathers and mothers: The offense is surely an exaggerated violation of the command to honor parents, although none of the other vices are extreme violations of their respective commandments. Perhaps the letter has in mind the abandonment of widows to the mercy of the church (5:4, 8, 16). This accords with the intent of the fourth commandment ("Honor your father and your mother"), which prohibits abandonment of one's elderly parents. As mentioned in the next note, this list of offenses seems to be based on a version of the Decalogue in Philo, where the commandment to honor one's parents is the fifth commandment on the first of the two tablets.

10. *men who lie with men:* Since both Jewish and Greco-Roman antiquity applied sexual labels on the basis of acts rather than orientation or affective preference, and since male sexuality in classical and Roman antiquity was polyvalent, with various options pursued, even simultaneously, one described a man sexually by describing his acts. The term here excludes homosexuals (a modern designation) who are celibate, and female homosexuals. It does include heterosexual males who engage in homosexual acts. Its association here with a fornicator or

sexually immoral person (*pornois*, Sir 23:17; Philo, *Alleg. Interp.* 8; see 1 Cor 5:1-13; 6:12-20) suggests activity with females and males respectively that departs from ordinary marital sexual relations within a family. The offenses are only from the male perspective.

kidnappers: The offense of kidnapping or slave trading seems to interrupt the Decalogue order of the list. Rabbinic exposition (*Mek. Exod.* 77b on 20:15) distinguishes between theft of things and kidnapping and refers the seventh commandment to kidnapping (*EDNT*). Kidnapping of an Israelite has been considered by some to be the subject of the original commandment. The entire vice list might have been constructed on the basis of the two tablets of the Decalogue. The first tablet ends with honoring one's parents as the fifth commandment in late Jewish tradition (Philo, *Decalogue* 51, and also Josephus, *Ant.* 3.90-92). All the first-tablet vices are joined on the list with "and" (*kai*) and refer to general transgressions but not to specific commandments, except for the fifth (and see Philo, *Decalogue* 121; *Spec. Leg.* 2.225 for inclusion of parents with God). The list ends with an "etcetera" before listing sins against covetousness.

sound: This metaphorical description of the Christian teaching (*didaskalia*) is found only in the PE in the NT (see also 2 Tim 4:3; Titus 1:9; 2:1; cf. 1 Tim 6:3; 2 Tim 1:13 with "words," and Titus 1:13; 2:2 with "[in] the faith," as well as the adjective "sound" at Titus 2:8). The PE defend the teaching as correct and appealing to sound intelligence. This Hellenistic metaphor (Plutarch, *Mor.* 20 E-F; Philo, *Abraham* 223; Josephus, *C. Ap.* 1.222; Epictetus, *Diatr.* 3.9.2, 4-6) and other medical images were used by moralists, especially Cynics and Stoics, to describe the process and aim of their instruction as well as to argue against their opponents.

The expression "sound teaching" (*hygiainousę̄ didaskalią*) is hortatory and has a strong antithetical cast to it. The teaching is sound inasmuch as it conforms to Pauline teaching. While sound teaching issues in morally upright behavior, the opposite is true of false teaching. This is the basic perception behind the PE's polemical use of the medical imagery. (*Ou*)*ch hygiaineis* ("You are not in your senses," *Menandrea* 77.220) captures the sense of the PE usage and accords with other pejorative characterizations of the false teachers (compare Titus 1:15 and 1 Tim 1:6; Titus 1:10; 3:9).

11. *the blessed God: Blessed* is an attribute ascribed to the gods by the Greeks inasmuch as they live above earthly sufferings and labors, and so it is more than "happy" (*eudaimōn*, Epicurus in *Diog. L.* X.123 [27]). Similarly Philo ascribes blessedness to God (*Abraham* 202; *Unchangeable* 55.161; *Sacrifices* 101, 40, 95, 147; *Spec. Leg.* 1.329; 2.53) as proper to the divine nature (*Deus.* 108; *Dreams* I.94; *Spec. Leg.* 3.178; 4.48 and 123). In the Bible only the PE here and at 1 Tim 6:15 describe the blessed transcendence of God above earthly suffering and corruption with the word *makarios* ("blessed"; Titus 2:13 so describes the Christian hope, which belongs to God's incorruptible sphere). The word appropriately separates not only God, but also Paul and those who uphold the Gospel and sound teaching from the corrupt sphere of the false teachers.

I have been entrusted: The root of the Greek verb "entrust" (*pist-*) relates it to "faith" (*pistis*), a key concern in this chapter (1:2, 4, 5, 11, 12, 13, 14, 15, 16, 19), and the PE generally. Paul's own path of faith, outlined in the next verses (12-17), led him from "non-faith" (*apistia*) to "faith" (*pistis*). Paul makes no reference to his faith as a Jew, but considers faith and the lack of it only from a Christian perspective. His remark here looks ahead to that exposition and back to the false teachers, their heterodox teaching, and their opposition to sound teaching. The Gospel he received in trust contrasts with that, as the clear identity of God contrasts with the unsure foundation of the false teachers' declarations (v. 7). The origin in God of Paul's mission for the Gospel echoes v. 1 and underlines his apostolic authority.

Interpretation

The thanksgiving and example (1:12-17) stand sandwiched between parallel descriptions of the false teachers (1:3-11 and 18-20). The addressee and the Pauline community are thus presented with contrasting examples of approaches to the Christian life and teachings. The negative examples come first. It was a common paraenetic device to propose the option to be rejected first. This built up a positive expectation for the preferred alternative. The Epicureans, for example, employed this strategy. The initially unnamed (*tines*) heterodox teachers stray not just in content (1:3-4, 6-7) but also in conduct (1:9-10). Verse 5, at the center of the first description of the negative example, puts the focus on exhortation to moral virtue in accord with true faith and doctrine. Thus the section is vague on the doctrinal errors of the teachers (1:4, 7). The implication of v. 5 is that the opponents' faith is wicked and contrary to God's laws, although they profess to be legal specialists (1:7). Consequently their speculations are said to be blind to the divine order of things (1:4). The letter's extensive paraenesis is concerned with the practical consequences of this undisciplined faith, especially to forestall its influence in the Ephesian church.

The practical side of faith also receives mention in v. 5 (and see v. 18); i.e., "pure heart" (*katharas kardias*) and "good conscience" (*syneidēseos agathēs*). The letters encourage and lay down guidelines for proper activity in accord with faith. The considerate reactions of the believers' hearts and the decision of their consciences are expected to produce upright actions. The false teachers and their followers are incapable of such choices and actions as long as their faith perspective is wayward.

This implication in v. 5 is carried forward in the second half of the description of the apostate teachers. While they do not know about the law they teach, the letter claims such knowledge for Paul and the addressee ("we know," *oidamen*). Moreover, since the false teachers have abandoned the sound teaching they are inclined to the vice and sin outlined. The nature of the list is paraenetic, as indicated by the commonplace, not context-specific content, its stock form (compare 1 Cor 6:9-10; Rom 1:24-32; Pollux,

Onomasticon VI.151), the contrast between good and bad, and the generic conclusion ("whatever else"). Consequently, one cannot read the vice list as a historical description; it is a rhetorical characterization to denigrate the opponents.

Despite the fact that the false teachers are self-styled "teachers of the law," they are not like the Judaizers of Paul's mission. The applicability of the Law to the Gentiles is not an issue in the PE, nor are Paul's apostolic credentials in question. Rather, the struggle is over the true interpretation of the Pauline tradition, and issues of conduct among the women and slaves seem to have been raised by an inappropriate exercise of Pauline freedom. Furthermore, end-time resurrection, ascetical practices, and mythical/genealogical speculation are at issue. In this respect the controversy resembles that of Colossians or 1 Corinthians and not that of Galatians. The question of the universality of or limits to salvation turns not on actions in conformity with Jewish Law, for the PE encourage lawful activity (1:8; 2:14). The opponents seem to limit salvation on the basis of knowledge (6:20; see Titus 1:16) and theological/christological speculations (6:4; 2 Tim 2:23; Titus 3:9). This esoteric teaching goes on to draw ascetical lessons from the law that apply to the "just." Thus the practice of faith is a particular concern of this letter.

John Chrysostom in his *Hom. 1 Tim.* (NPNF 1, 13:410) asks, "What is enabled by faith?" To this he answers: the reception of God's mercies that we may become better persons, to doubt and dispute of nothing, but to repose in confidence. This confidence thus arises from an acknowledgment of God's mercy. This accompanies an acceptance of traditional teaching. While theological speculations can deepen and update the understanding of the tradition, they can also lead to confusion if they are set against that teaching. Seeing the mystery of God's mercy as the universal reference point provides the necessary perspective for human speculation. Put another way, Augustine, *De Disciplina Christiana* 1.35.39-1.36.41 (ACD 30-31) declares that the end of all divine scriptures is love for the being in which we should all rejoice. He refers to 2 Tim 2:14 when he describes the Law as profitable for edification if one uses it lawfully. For the end of the Law "is love out of a pure heart, and a good conscience and faith unfeigned" (see his *Conf.* 12:18 [LCC 7:284], *Trin.* 8.4.6 [LCC 8:44]). Further on at *De Disciplina Christiana* 1.40.44 (ACD 33) he notes that unfeigned faith and a pure heart lead us to love nothing but what should be loved. We are not to love money or honors or pleasures, but rather God himself and the ones he serves. The PE, with their perspective on a proper interpretation of the Law, encourage the readers to take the Decalogue seriously and to find the contemporary relevance to the ancient laws that are the ever-abiding will of God. Clearly the care of the elderly and marital and sexual morality are of great social concern today. Enslavement and abuse of migrant workers, of women in the sex trade, and of children in sweatshops are known to all. The kidnapping of children for armed conflict and of hostages for political ends remains a problem. Perjury in political life and falsifying reports in the business and financial world corrupt society. The ignoring and belittling of church teaching and hostility to church ministers and teachers is commonplace.

For Reference and Further Study

Bauer, Walter. *Orthodoxy and Heresy in Earliest Christianity*. Philadelphia: Fortress Press, 1971, 86–87.

Boswell, John. *Christianity, Social Tolerance and Homosexuality: Gay People in Western Europe from the Beginning of the Christian Era to the Fourteenth Century*. Chicago and London: University of Chicago Press, 1980.

Brox, Norbert. *Die Pastoralbriefe: übersezt und erklärt*. Regensburg: Pustet, 1969, 100–101, 107–108.

Collins, Raymond F. *Christian Morality: Biblical Foundations*. Notre Dame: University of Notre Dame Press, 1986, 55–57, 59–60.

Dover, Kenneth James. *Greek Homosexuality*. London and Cambridge, MA: Harvard University Press, 1978, 1989.

Fiore, Benjamin. *Personal Example*, 79–84.

Jewett, Robert. *Paul's Anthropological Terms: A Study of Their Use in Conflict Settings*. Leiden: Brill, 1971, 305–33, 402–46.

Johnson, Marshall D. *The Purpose of Biblical Genealogies with Special Reference to the Setting of the Genealogies of Jesus*. SNTSMS 8. Cambridge and New York: Cambridge University Press, 1969.

Lilja, Saara. *Homosexuality in Republican and Augustan Rome*. Commentationes Humanorum Litteratum 74. Helsinki: Societas Scientium Fennica, 1983.

Malherbe, Abraham J., ed. *Moral Exhortation: A Greco-Roman Sourcebook*. Library of Early Christianity 4. Philadelphia: Westminster, 1986.

________. "Medical Imagery in the Pastoral Epistles," in idem, *Paul and the Popular Philosophers*. Minneapolis: Fortress Press, 1989, 19–35.

McEleney, Neil J. "The Vice Lists of the Pastoral Epistles," *CBQ* 36 (1974) 203–19.

Osborne, H. "*Syneidēsis*," *JTS o.s.* 32 (1930–1931) 167–79.

Petersen, William L. "Can *ARSENOKOITAI* Be Translated by 'Homosexuals'? (1 Cor. 6.9; 1 Tim. 1.10)," *VC* 40 (1986) 187–91.

Pierce, Claude Anthony. *Conscience in the New Testament*. London: SCM, 1955.

Reumann, John. *The Use of* oikonomia *and related Terms in Greek Sources to about A.D. 100 as a Background for Patristic Applications*. Dissertation: University of Pennsylvania, 1957.

Thrall, Margaret E. "The Pauline Use of *Syneidēsis*," *NTS* 14 (1967–1968) 118–26.

Tooley, Wilfred. "Stewards of God: An Examination of the Terms *oikonomos* and *oikonomia* in the NT," *SJT* 19 (1966) 74–86.

Towner, Philip H. *The Goal of Our Instruction: The Structure of Theology and Ethics in the Pastoral Epistles*. JSNTSup 34. Sheffield: Sheffield Academic Press, 1989, 154–59.

Turner, Nigel. "Hypocrisy," in idem, ed., *Christian Words*. Edinburgh: T&T Clark, 1980, 219–20.

Wright, David F. "Homosexuals or Prostitutes. The Meaning of *ARSENOKOITAI* (I Cor 6:9, 1 Tim 1:10)," *VC* 38 (1984) 125–53.

———. "Translating *Arsenokoitai* (1 Cor 6:9; 1 Tim 1:10)," *VC* 41 (1987) 396–98.

3. *Thanksgiving; Mercy; Timothy's Task* (1:12-20)

12. I am grateful to Christ Jesus, our Lord, who strengthened me, that he considered me trustworthy inasmuch as he appointed me for service, 13. even though I once was a blasphemer, a persecutor, and an insolent man. Nevertheless, I was shown mercy because in my unbelief I acted without knowledge. 14. Yes, the favor of our Lord was all the more abundant with the faith and love that are in Christ Jesus. 15. This saying is trustworthy and deserving of full acceptance, "Christ Jesus came into the world to save sinners," and of these I am the most prominent. 16. For this purpose, however, I was shown mercy, so that in me, as the most prominent, Christ Jesus might demonstrate his total forbearance to provide a prototype of those who are going to believe in him for eternal life. 17. And so, to the king of the ages, the immortal, invisible, only God, honor and glory for ages of ages. Amen. 18. This instruction I entrust to you, Timothy, my child, in accord with the preceding prophecies about you, that in light of them you engage in the noble campaign, 19. keeping faith and good conscience. Certain persons by repudiating conscience have suffered shipwreck in matters of faith. 20. Among these are Hymenaeos and Alexander, whom I gave over to Satan to be disciplined not to blaspheme.

Notes

12. *I am grateful:* The thanksgiving is the final letter opening convention in 1 Timothy. The parallels in Hellenistic correspondence are expressions of thanks to the deity for rescue from some danger. The senders thereby thank the providers of their welfare and safety. Paul reverses this pattern and gives thanks for the recipients' well-being. In that way he stresses the spiritual and Christian side of their welfare. Paul also adds a prayer for God's help in continuing his well-being and thus announces his expectations for the community. First Timothy returns to Hellenistic usage in giving thanks for divine rescue from ignorance, faithlessness, and consequent evildoing. Like earlier Pauline letters, however, this thanksgiving focuses on the faith and action desired of the addressees and even of the opponents.

who strengthened: This strengthening receives amplification in the autobiographical 2 Timothy (2:1; 4:17; compare "strength," *dynamis* at 1:7, 8; 3:5; and "is able," *dynatos* at 1:12). There we learn that the power received is directed toward fearless testimony in the face of opposition. The gift is not Paul's alone but has come to Timothy (2:1) and to all believers (1:7; 3:5) and is critical to Timothy's fighting the good fight (1 Tim 1:19) and to his enduring the hardship of his labor for the Gospel (Titus 2:3).

trustworthy . . . appointed me for service: The word "trustworthy" (*piston*) expresses reliability with reference to his "service" (*diakonia*) and echoes the notion of trustworthiness behind "I have been entrusted" (*episteuthēn*, v. 11). As such it highlights a key quality the letter encourages in the addressee and the Ephesian church, while it decries its absence among the apostates. "Service" (*diakonia*) indicates ministry in a general sense as opposed to the functions of a specific office as outlined at 3:8-13. Timothy's task is described with the same word at 2 Tim 4:5 (and compare 4:11 for Mark), and he is called "assistant" (*diakonos*) at 1 Tim 4:6 (see also 2 Tim 1:18 for Onesiphoros).

13. *blasphemer, persecutor, and insolent man:* While in secular Greek the word refers to one who uses injurious or frivolous speech that belittles the sacredness of the gods, the word in Judaism and Christianity denotes an egregious sinner. Herm. *Sim.* IX.19.1, 3 held it impossible for blasphemers to repent. This echoes the LXX at Matt 26:65 and Sir 3:16 (and see 2 Macc 9:28; 10:4 for Antiochus, and also Isa 52:5). Revelation applies the term to "the beast" in the end-time struggle in the context of the ruler cult, where claiming divine veneration for the Roman emperors and the application of divine predicates (Lord and God, Savior) to them are blasphemies of the name of God (Rev 1:3, 5, 6; 17:3; see 2 Tim 3:2). The blasphemy of Paul (see Acts 26:11 and 13:45; 18:6) differs from that of the apostates. Paul was saved by divine favor from his blasphemy but, as he said, he acted in ignorance. The false teachers, however, are in a more dangerous situation because they have rejected and thereby offended (blasphemed) the God they knew (see Herm. *Sim.* IX.19.1 and 3 above). In general Paul of the PE makes little reference to his Jewish past (except 2 Tim 1:3). Even here the faults he admits are typical of Gentile sinners "caught in their ignorance" (Rom 1:21-22). Thus he is a paradigm of Gentile repentance and conversion in an increasingly Gentile Christian church. This matches the PE's emphasis on universal salvation and Paul's mission to all peoples. Moreover, the Gentile church has deep theological roots in the Law (1:8) and Scripture (2:15) of Judaism and Jewish Christianity. To be "insolent" (*hybristēs*) is one of the vices of the Gentiles at Rom 1:30. While Paul admitted persecuting the church in Phil 3:6 (and see 1 Cor 15:9; Gal 1:13, 23; Acts 9:4; 22:4, 19), he says he did that "in zeal" (*kata zēlos*) in defense of God and not as blasphemous and insolent. Nonetheless, in Acts 9:5 Paul refers to himself as "kicking against the goad" prior to his conversion.

I was shown mercy: The mercy of God (vv. 13 and 16) is highlighted by repetition, by strong contrast ("but," *alla*) to the sinner's initial opposition, by the magnitude of the opposition ("most prominent," *prōtos*, v. 15), and by the christological affirmation (v. 15) and theological doxology (v. 17).

in my unbelief I acted without knowledge: Paul's faithlessness associates his example with the shipwrecked faith of the apostate teachers who blaspheme as he did (v. 20). The negative examples are thereby effectively neutralized and shown to move in a direction opposite to the design of God. Paul's ignorance parallels that of the false teachers (v. 7). Overlooking godless acts as done in ignorance by Jews (Acts 3:17) and Gentiles (Acts 17:30) was a theme in early Christian preaching. Overlooking what was done in ignorance there, as here, serves the call to repentance (see also Eph 4:18; 1 Pet 1:14; compare Rom 1:22, 28).

14. *faith and love:* "In Christ Jesus" expresses Paul's association with Jesus who strengthened him and gave him his Gospel ministry (v. 12, and for the phrase "in Christ" see 3:13; 2 Tim 1:1). "Faith" (*pisteōs*) describes Paul's new relationship to God, transformed from his former unbelief. "Love" (*agapēs*), on the other hand, characterizes his new relationship to humankind, especially Christians to whom he was formerly persecutor and insolent (v. 13).

15. *This saying is trustworthy:* This formula is found only in the PE (see also 1:15; 3:1; 4:9; 2 Tim 2:11; Titus 3:8; compare Titus 1:9) with loose and inconclusive parallels in Jewish literature. Knight identifies it as a citation formula, which also serves to emphasize the saying (note the initial position of "trustworthy"). The formula precedes the saying that concludes at "to save," which is last in the Greek word order. A late and poorly attested variant for *trustworthy*, i.e., "human" (*anthrōpinos*), appears to have been transferred here from 3:1 where the same reading appears, according to Westcott and Hort. The phrase following the formula goes on to commend the saying for wide acceptance. The phrase is common in later Greek authors (*MM*). A similar phrase at 1 Tim 6:1 (and compare Acts 24:3) suggests that "full" (*pasēs*) is primarily intensive rather than extensive in meaning (thus "full" rather than "by all"). The context and the saying itself sustain the extensive meaning as a secondary emphasis. The formula precedes the saying, which concludes the verse.

Christ came into the world to save sinners: Recitative "that" (*hoti*) introduces a quotation (BDF 397 and 470). The aorist tense indicates a completed action. The reference is to the historical Jesus' ministry. Johannine use of the phrase "came into the world" (see John 1:9; 3:17; 12:46-47; 16:28; and see 1 Tim 3:16) suggests Jesus' preexistence and incarnation for a salvific end, which the saying here declares. The earlier Pauline letters and Pauline Christianity (see 1 Cor 8:6; 2 Cor 8:9; Rom 8:3, 29-30; Phil 2:6-8; Col 1:15-20) maintain views similar to the one expressed here (see also 2 Tim 1:9). The "world" (*kosmon*) refers to a physical as well as a moral and spiritual environment (compare John 1:10). Salvation was accomplished in Christ once and for all (the sense of the aorist). Jesus' coming to save sinners is declared also at Matt 9:13 *parr.*; John 3:17; 12:47.

the most prominent: While proud of his Pharisaic observance and righteousness under Judaism (Phil 3:4-6), Paul came to understand that all are sinners (Rom 3:9; 5:19). With this admission here, the universality of sinfulness is affirmed and with it the universal need for salvation. Paul's characterization of himself as the foremost of sinners echoes his description as "least of the apostles" and hardly worthy of the title in view of his persecution of the church (1 Cor 15:9; and see also Eph 3:8, where Paul is "the least of the holy ones" [NAB]).

16. *forbearance:* This is an attribute of God and, as here, of Jesus. The LXX stressed God's forbearance rather than continue the emphasis on divine wrath in the

MT (see LXX Psalm 7; Job 7:15-16; Isa 57:15). In early Judaism (already in the LXX Sir 5:4 and 4 Ezra 7:34; 2 Bar. 21:20; 59:6; *Ep. Aris.* 188) forbearance is largely characteristic of the interim period during which God withholds wrath in order to allow sinners to repent. This is the meaning here, where Jesus Christ exhibits divine forbearance to the sinner Paul and, presumably, to the other sinners for whose repentance Paul's conversion is the prototype (*EDNT*).

prototype: Paul's example manifests the divine mercy and forbearance. The lived manifestation of beliefs is a prime concern of the PE. As a further consequence of this demonstration by Paul and others, the letters hope to attract the apostates and nonbelievers to the true faith as well. Paul, the primary example, is referred to directly again at 2 Tim 3:10-11. Timothy and Titus are to be examples too (1 Tim 4:12; 2 Tim 1:13; Titus 2:7; and see 2 Tim 2:15). The community members also demonstrate the validity of the faith by their actions (1 Tim 3: 2, 7, 10; 5:14; 6:1, 14; Titus 2:5, 9-10, 15). Related to this is the visible manifestation of God's salvation and favor in Jesus' life (1 Tim 3:16; 2 Tim 1:10; 4:1, 8; Titus 1:3; 3:4) and in the future (1 Tim 6:14; Titus 2:13). Also related is the call for good works consistent with the Christians' faith claims (1 Tim 2:10; 5:10, 25; 6:18; 2 Tim 3:17; Titus 2:7, 14; 3:1, 8, 14), just as misdeeds point to faithlessness (Titus 1:16). Similarly the "testimony" (*martyrion*) given by Jesus (1 Tim 2:6; 2 Tim 1:8) includes not just a declaration but the act of redemptive self-offering. This inspires similar action in Paul, which he urges on Timothy (2 Tim 1:8-13, where it is characterized as *hypotypōsin*) and the community (2 Tim 3:12).

for eternal life: The end-time expectation of the PE is constant ("on that day," 2 Tim 1:12, 18; 4:8; the second coming, 1 Tim 6:14, 15; 2 Tim 4:1; Titus 2:13; final judgment, 2 Tim 2:12). While the letters manifest a concern for establishing church structures and defending the integrity of the teaching, this is related to the present as a time of salvation through divine forbearance. The present age is the final days (1 Tim 4:1; 2 Tim 3:1; compare Acts 2:17; Heb 1:2; 1 Pet 1:20; 1 John 2:18; 1 Cor 10:11) and the false teachers are agents of the end-time forces of evil (Mark 13:22; 2 Thess 2:3; Rev 13:5). So admonitions are given to those "in the present age" (*tǭ nyn aiōni*, 1 Tim 6:17-18) to prepare them for the age to come (1 Tim 6:15-16, 19) and to help them live out the salvation that has been made present by Jesus (1 Tim 4:8). The believers are able to face final judgment in confidence because of the help received through Jesus' first epiphany (2 Tim 1:10; Titus 2:11; 3:4), which is described as a saving appearance, as it is at 1 Tim 1:15.

17. *King of the ages . . . Amen:* For the title see Jer 10:10 and Sir 36:22. The immortality of God is declared in Greco-Roman literature, such as Philo, *Opif.* 12; Plutarch, *Mor.* 420 A-B; *Ep. Aris.* 6, 3; Sextus Empiricus, *Math.* IX 33; *Diog. L.* 10. 123. The doxology uses attributes of God applied elsewhere in the NT (king, John 12:13; eternal, Rom 1:23; unseen, Rom 1:20; Col 1:15; John 1:18; only, Rom 16:27; John 5:44). The PE present Jesus Christ as the earthly manifestation of God.

18. *prophecies:* Acts 13:2 describes a worship setting in which a prophetic oracle is uttered in conjunction with a commissioning service in which the Spirit-prompted oracle selected Barnabas and Saul for their mission. The prophets and teachers then finished their prayer and fasting, imposed hands, and sent them off. A similar circumstance seems to have occurred at Ephesus, resulting

in Timothy's commissioning. At 2 Tim 1:6 Paul is described as taking part in that event as prophet and apostle. The oracle and commissioning (see also 4:1) by prophets suggests a loose ecclesiastical structure akin to that of Acts. Timothy is given the task of service of the Gospel (see 2 Tim 4:5). Timothy entrusts duties to others with a similar gesture of laying on of hands (5:22; compare 2 Cor 8:19; Acts 6:6; 14:23).

the noble campaign: The military image reappears at 2 Tim 2:3-4. At 2 Cor 10:4 and 1 Cor 9:7 the image refers to the apostle's defense of the Gospel against opposition. The weapons mentioned in 2 Corinthians 10 were spoken of at 2 Cor 6:7 as weapons of righteousness to advance the "day of salvation," an eschatological note (and see Rom 6:13 and 13:12; Eph 6:10-17). The battle might lead to suffering (2 Tim 1:8; 2:9; 4:5). Likewise the battle imagery here is associated with Timothy's confrontation with the false teachers where the latter, in turn, are given eschatological significance (4:1; 2 Tim 3:1-8). Maximus of Tyre, 13, 4 speaks of life as a battle with God as general and the human as the combatant.

19. *faith and good conscience:* The aim of the instruction (v. 5) is recalled here. Faith describes the individual's alignment with Christ and the Christian teaching. At 1:5 "conscience" (*syneidēseōs*) links correct belief with the conduct corresponding to it (see also 1 Tim 3:8-9, where the deacons' conduct stands in relation to their faith under good conscience). Thus the false teachers, by repudiating conscience and countenancing inappropriate behavior (1:6-10) that opposes the Gospel, have ruined their faith. Proper conduct in good conscience expresses faith and supports it. This view is consistent with the promotion of direct and indirect examples in the letter (see "prototype" above). *Syneidēsis*, meaning "conscience," first appears in Wis 17:11. Prior to that in the Hebrew Bible the word refers to knowing and the function of conscience was laid to the heart.

shipwreck: The Stoic-Cynic text *Cebetis Tabula* 24, 1-2 uses the shipwreck image to describe the result for those who live worthless and laborious lives and end up "going astray" (*planōntai*). Philo, *Dreams* 2.147 sees shipwreck as the end of lives where carnal impulses win out over reason. First Timothy uses this analysis in terms of the life of faith and the practical consequences of a misguided conscience.

20. *Hymenaeos and Alexander I gave over . . . to be disciplined:* Hymenaeos is not otherwise known (see 2 Tim 2:17). Alexander, an Ephesian Jew, was named as part of the crowd in the chaotic incident of the silversmiths. He was shouted down, and so it is not clear what position he represented (Acts 19:33), although it might have been to defend Paul. Perhaps he is the same Alexander. Second Timothy mentions both Hymenaeos at 2:27 and Alexander at 4:14. The offenders are excluded from the community, a move that sets a practical example for Timothy and designated community leaders for dealing with apostates (and see 1 Cor 5: 5, 13; Matt 18:17). The exclusion of blasphemers here is less drastic than at Herm. *Sim.* IX.18.3, for it is reversible, and that is also the hope implied in the example of Paul at 1:13-14. In a humiliating reversal, the erstwhile teachers of the Law must themselves be trained or disciplined. Divine discipline that leads to repentance is mentioned at *1 Clem.* 56.3-7, 16 (paraphrasing Ps 118:18 and Job 5:17-26). Cyril of Scythia (37.23 and 73.3) mentions discipline by the

daimōn (similar to this verse). The presbyters administer corrective discipline at *1 Clem.* 57.1 to prevent being cast out from the hope of Christ (and compare 1 Cor 11:32).

Interpretation

The negative example is reiterated more briefly at 1:19-20. Here (1:20) the false teachers are named. Again, bad conscience and its destructive consequences for faith (1:19b), a negative echo of v. 5, are at issue. The advice to Timothy at 1:18-19a functions as v. 5 does and establishes the positive counterpart to the negative example. It looks to the positive alternative to the false teachers, i.e., Paul and his personal recollection of being saved at 1:12-17. While the apostate false teachers have gone from knowledge and faith to ignorance and unbelief, Paul's progress is in the opposite direction (1:13-14). Paul's transformation from hostility to service of God results from divine mercy working itself out in Christ Jesus' display of forbearance for his blasphemy and saving him from the consequences of his sins. Strengthened by Jesus, Paul finds an abundance of faith and love where blasphemy, persecution, and insolence once ruled (compare Rom 5:20). Paul's newfound faith is dogmatic (he is no longer "without knowledge," *agnoōn*, 13) and personal (to believe "in him," *ep' autǭ*, 16).

Paul exemplifies what can result from this instruction (1:5), which is "love from a pure heart, a good conscience, and a sincere faith" (NAB). Thus he calls attention to the abundant faith and love in Christ Jesus (1:14) and the good conscience of one saved from sin (1:13). Paul's ministry has its origins in God and Christ Jesus our Lord (1:1 and 1:11-12) and does not arise from his own wishes as does that of the false teachers (1:7). As such he, rather than they, is an example for Timothy, who receives a charge from Paul and according to "prophetic words" about him (1:18). Paul, once a first-class sinner (1:13, 15-16), but transformed by Jesus' forbearance, has become an example of the possibility of conversion and salvation from sinfulness to belief for everlasting life (1:15-16). The salvation is, therefore, both a present reality and a future hope. The righteous life of the present flows from the faith of the person saved, displays this to all observers, and looks toward eternal life. The saying itself, "Jesus came into the world to save sinners," has resonances in the Synoptic (Mark 2:17; Luke 5:32; 19:10; Matt 9:13) and Johannine (3:17; 12:47) traditions. Verbal and conceptual variations, however, prevent identifying either as a source for 1 Tim 1:15 (the order of "Christ Jesus" is proper to the PE; coming to save sinners is not a synoptic formula and neither is coming into the world; "sinner" in John does not have the same meaning as in the PE, nor do the PE have the Johannine idea of being sent). The saying might well be a liturgical formula based on several traditions.

The incarnation of Jesus is a magnificent gesture of divine condescension and a key tenet of Christian faith and Gospel witness. The Incarnation, however, finds its completion in the Passion, death, and resurrection of the Incarnate One, with the effect of offering the possibility of reconciliation of sinners with God. The Pauline gospel of the cross (1 Cor 1:18-30) finds a clear and concise reiteration here.

The reversal effected by Jesus' mercy receives emphasis from its repetition and the use of the strong adversative *alla* ("nevertheless") at 1:13, 16. This example speaks first to the false teachers, specifically Hymenaeos and Alexander. They are excommunicated in order to be instructed (1:20), a reversal of their teaching pretensions. This echoes Paul's being brought out of his ignorance (1:13), and so they are far from being given up as lost. In all of this the initiative is the Lord's, whose forbearance (1:10), abundant grace, faith, love (1:14), and power (1:12) effect the salvific change toward true faith and actions in harmony with it. Paul (1:20) and Timothy (1:3, 18) present a challenge to the wayward to open up the process of change. The eschatological framework of the process ("for eternal life," *eis zoēn aiōnion*, 16) is reiterated in the doxology ("for ages of ages," *eis tous aiōnas tōn aiōnōn*, 17).

The sinner is not considered lost, but rather is capable of repenting and returning to God. Excommunication protects the community and also might jolt the sinner to repentance. The eternal consequences of infidelity justify severe corrective measures.

Although the *parousia* appears to be far off, the faithful are encouraged to see aspects of the end-time conflict in the opposition to true faith experienced in the present. Our time provides us with the challenge to confront error and evil deeds lest these overtake the truth and snuff out justice. This is the one-time and final struggle in each believer's time-bound life, with no rerun of the struggle once life is over. The conduct of the resistance to evil and the result serve to encourage others now and in the future as they face similar testing until the universal final day.

John Chrysostom, *Stat*. 12.1 (NPNF 1 9:418), agrees with 1 Timothy and says to remind the sinner to receive pardon, give thanks, but not forget the sin. Don't fret over it, but use it as a lesson not to relapse. This example will encourage others in despair to be comforted and stand tall. Augustine, *Serm*. 278 1.2 (WSA 3/8:50-51) declares God to be the only medicine that cures the soul. The soul is capable of injuring itself, but not of curing itself.

For Reference and Further Study

Aune, David E. *Prophecy in Early Christianity and the Ancient Mediterranean World*. Grand Rapids: Eerdmans, 1983, 266.

Blank, Sheldon H. "The Curse, the Blasphemy, the Spell, and the Oath," *HUCA* 23 (1950/51) 73–95.

Brockhaus, Ulrich. *Charisma und Amt: die paulinische Charismenlehre auf dem Hintergrund der frühchristliche Gemeindefunktionen*. Wuppertal: Brockhaus, 1972.

Collins, Adela Y. "The Function of 'Excommunication' in Paul," *HTR* 73 (1980) 251–67.

de Boer, Martinus. "Images of Paul in the Post-Pauline Period," *CBQ* 42 (1980) 359–80.

Dixon, Suzanne. *The Roman Family*. Baltimore: Johns Hopkins University Press, 1992, 61–97.

Donelson, Lewis R. "The Structure of Ethical Argument in the Pastorals," *BTB* 18 (1988) 108–13.

Ellis, E. Earle. "The Role of the Christian Prophets in Acts," in W. Ward Gasque and Ralph P. Martin, eds., *Apostolic History and the Gospel*. Grand Rapids: Eerdmans, 1970, 55–67.

Fiore, Benjamin. *Personal Example*, 22, 198–216.

Hainz, Josef. "Amt und Amstvermittlung bei Paulus," in idem, ed., *Kirche im Werden*. Paderborn: Schöningh, 1976, 109–22.

Jervis, L. Ann. "Paul the Poet in First Timothy 1:11-17; 2:3b-7; 3:14-16," *CBQ* 61 (1999) 695–712.

Knight, *Faithful Sayings*, 1–49.

Lee, Edwin K. "Words Denoting 'Pattern' in the New Testament," *NTS* 8 (1961–62) 166–73.

Moulton, J. H. *A Grammar of New Testament Greek. III, Syntax*. Ed. Nigel Turner. Edinburgh: T&T Clark, 1963, 225.

Osiek, Carolyn, and David L. Balch. *Families in the New Testament World: Households and House Churches*. Louisville: Westminster John Knox, 2003, 118–23.

Schubert, Paul. *Form and Function of the Pauline Thanksgivings*. BZNW 20. Berlin: Töpelmann, 1939, 158–79.

Swete, Henry B. "The Faithful Sayings," *JTS* 18 (1916) 1–7.

Towner, Philip H. "The Present Age in the Eschatology of the Pastoral Epistles," *NTS* 32 (1986) 427–48.

________. *Goal of Our Instruction*, chapters 5 and 7.

Turner, Nigel. "Blasphemy," in *Christian Words*, 46–48.

Van Unnik, Willem C. "The Teaching of Good Works in 1 Peter," *NTS* 1 (1954–55) 92–110.

Verner, David C. *The Household of God: The Social World of the Pastoral Epistles*. SBLDS 71. Chico: Scholars, 1983, 83–111.

Wolter, Michael. "Paulus, der Bekehrte Gottesfeind, zum Verständnis von 1 Tim 1:13," *NovT* 31 (1989) 48–66.

4. *Church Order: Community Prayer* (2:1-7)

1. First of all, therefore, I urge entreaties, prayers, intercessions, thanksgivings to be offered for all people, 2. for kings and all who are in places of prominence, that we might lead tranquil and quiet lives in all piety and probity. 3. This is good and pleasing in the sight of God our savior, 4. who wishes that all people be saved and come to knowledge of the truth.

> 5. There is, after all, one God, and there is also one mediator between God and humans, a human, Christ Jesus.
>
> 6. He is the one who gave himself as ransom for all; this was the testimony at the proper time.

7. For this I was appointed preacher and apostle (I am telling the truth, I am not lying), a teacher of the nations in faith and truth.

Notes

1. *entreaties:* These "entreaties" (*deēseis*), mentioned first in the list "entreaties, prayers, intercessions, thanksgivings," are a more specific type of prayers to God, as distinguished from the more general "prayer" (*proseuchē*; for the pair see Eph 6:18 and 1 Tim 5:5). While "entreaty" is based on LXX usage and peculiar to Christian writings, "prayer" is a widely used Greco-Roman word. It and its cognates are more frequent in the NT. Luke uses "entreaty" to characterize the piety of those associated with Jesus and the early Christian community (Luke 1:13; 2:37; 5:33; and see "entreaty" at Luke 10:2; 21:36; 22:32 and Acts 4:31; 8:24; 10:2). Paul uses the noun at Rom 10:1; 2 Cor 1:11; 9:14; Phil 1:4, 19; and see 2 Tim 1:3; 1 Pet 3:12; Jas 5:16, and the verb at Rom 1:10; 1 Thess 3:10. At Eph 6:18 prayer is recommended in the context of eschatological battle, while at Phil 4:6 Paul urges prayer, entreaty, and thanksgiving in declaring that the Lord is near (4:5) and alluding to end-time struggle and hope (3:18-21 and 4:3).

   for all people: The universality of the prayer in light of God's will to save all (2:3, which restates 1:15) turns the addressees' attention outward to nonbelievers. This missionary concern will recur as an undercurrent throughout the letters. The spiritual efficacy of believers for the good of unbelievers was already voiced by Paul in 1 Cor 7:14; compare Acts 8:6. Perhaps there is a polemic concern here to distance the Pastorals community from the false teachers, who might well think that some are beyond salvation. This letter, on the other hand, looks to universal salvation (3:16; 5:10), even that of the opponents (2 Tim 2:25-26; Titus 2:11).

2. *for kings:* The hybridized church order and household code at 1 Pet 2:11–3:12 provides a good parallel for the church order section and household code material in 1 Timothy. The concern in 1 Peter is to maintain good conduct in order to avoid slanderous criticism (2:15) and perhaps even win over some in the wider community by being seen as people who do good (2:12). Key in this is remaining subject to human institutions, starting with the sovereign (2:13) and extending to all (2:17). So, too, 1 Timothy calls for prayer for the good of all while singling out kings and prominent persons whose opinion carries political

and social influence. (Paul himself urged honor and subjection to authorities and political structures at Rom 13:1-7.) Prayer for chiefs of state in Hellenistic Judaism is found in Jeremiah 36 LXX; Ezra 6:6-12; *1 Bar* 1:1–3:8; *Ep. Aris.* 45; 1 Macc 7:33; Josephus, *Ant.* 12.402; *Bell.* II.197. Like 1 Tim 2:2, *1 Clem.* 60:2-4 and 61:1-2 have a prayer for Roman rulers that they may govern well and that all on earth may have peace (compare 1 Pet 2:13-17; Rom 13:1-7; Titus 3:1). Tertullian, *Apol.* 31.1-2 (FC 10:87) points to this text to show the detractors of Christianity that Christians have an interest in the emperor's welfare, with prayer publicly enjoined on them (and see Origen, *Cels.* 8.73 [OAC 509]). First Timothy adds the intention of their and everyone else's salvation.

tranquil and quiet lives: This is not a call to a life similar to the Epicureans' withdrawal from public affairs, since the community leaders and members are expected to have good public reputations (e.g., 3:7; 5:14; Titus 1:6; 2:8). Rather, the exhortation looks to the reasonable expectation that the Christian community will escape public interference if it does not arouse public and official condemnation by reason of behavior that upsets traditional social values.

Bede, *Homilies on the Gospels* 1.6 (*HOG* 1:52), reminds us that the mediator's intervention, i.e., Jesus' birth, was through a divinely arranged plan "that in a calm among the storm of wars a singular tranquility of unusual peace should cover the whole world" (and see *Diogn.* 9.1-2). The prayer for universal peace is always appropriate. Since faith in action is an undercurrent of the PE, working for peace and reconciliation can also be seen as an imperative for the Christian faithful.

New religions were greeted with suspicion in the traditional society of the late Roman republic and early empire. These religions were accused of threatening the established social order (Tacitus, *Historiae* 5.5), introduced outlandish superstitions and odd rituals often carried out in secret (Plutarch, *Conj. praec.* 140D), and were linked with sexual immorality (Apuleius, *Metam.* IX.14; Juvenal, *Sat.* 6). Christians were objects of disdain (Lucian, *Peregr.* 13; Pliny, *Ep.* 96).

Furthermore, the extreme behavior encouraged (e.g., asceticism, 1 Tim 4:3) or tolerated (emancipation of slaves, 1 Tim 6:1-2, and of women, 1 Tim 2:11-15; 5:8, 11-13), the disturbance caused within the community by heterodox teaching (see 1 Tim 1:4-7; 6:3-5; 2 Tim 2:16-18; 3:1-9; 4:3-4; Titus 3:9), and the danger to the moral fabric of the community (e.g., 1 Tim 1:9-10; 6:3-5, 9-10; 2 Tim 3:2-5; Titus 1:15-16) could be a cause for the low esteem for and even prejudice against the church (compare 1 Thess 4:11).

The prayer for a tranquil and peaceful life, therefore, is not surprising. It also echoes the type of life prized in Greco-Roman writers such as Plutarch, *Mor.* 1033 C-D; *Otho* 4,4; Epictetus, *Diatr.* 1.10.2; Cicero, *De Senectute* 22; *Pro Sestio* 23; and even as a school exercise in Theon, *Rhet.* 12.247-248, 251. As mentioned above, however, 1 Timothy is not to be understood as the Epicurean withdrawal from public activity some of its contemporaries promote.

quiet: This word and its cognate "be quiet" (*hēsychazō*) appears elsewhere in the NT to indicate cessation from argument and objections (Acts 11:18; 21:14; 22:2) and tranquility associated with minding one's own affairs (1 Thess 4:11; 2 Thess 3:12). This certainly proposes a positive alternative to the false teachers' speculations and contestations and the community uproar resulting from them. Its use in 1 Thessalonians 4 indicates that this community ideal is not opposed to an eschatological expectation.

piety: Except for Acts 3:12, all other NT uses of the word *eusebeia* are in the PE (10x) and 2 Peter (4x). The same is true for the cognates "act piously" (*eusebeō*, Acts 17:23 and 1 Tim 5:4), "pious" (*eusebēs*, Acts 10:27; 2 Pet 2:9), "piously" (*eusebōs*, 2 Tim 3:12; Titus 2:12). While rare in the LXX, it is relatively frequent in the Apocrypha, especially *4 Maccabees*. The Greek concept originally referred to the externals of the cult and later came to mean religious piety. The word in the PE has been associated with the letters' "bourgeois" outlook in conjunction with the church's readjustment to the delay of the *parousia*. This claim of eschatological tepidity in the PE is questionable; so too is the interpretation of their promotion of piety. In the terminology of the Greek popular philosophers, "piety" came to mean "knowledge of divine worship" (*epistēmē theōn therapeias*, Sextus Empiricus, *Pros physikous* 1.123 p. 242 [Kern]; *Diog. L.* 7.119), and compare "impiety" or *asebeia* as "ignorance of divine worship" (*agnoia theōn therapeias*, Stobaeus, *Eth.* II.68; Pseudo-Plato, *Def.* 412e), and in Gnostic texts "piety with knowledge" (*hē meta gnōseos eusebeia*, *Corp. herm.* VI.5; X.19). This echoes the diaspora Jewish usage in the LXX, where piety translates "fear of the Lord" or "reverential awe" in texts where it is associated with knowledge of God (Isa 11:2; 33:6; Prov 1:7). The accusation at 2 Tim 3:5 that the false teachers have only the appearance of piety but not its power rests on the preceding charge (3:4b) that they are lovers of pleasure rather than of God, and this is backed up by the vice list in 3:2-4a. Similarly, Titus 1:16 notes that false teachers "claim to know God but deny him by their deeds." Thus the false teachers hold their knowledge of God to be piety (and see 1 Tim 6:3, 5 and 20), but their actions are not guided by it (whether they divorce ethics from theology or their misguided theology leads to immoral behavior). Therefore it cannot be true. The implication is clear; true piety is manifested in deeds. Thus 1 Tim 2:2 calls for a tranquil way of living, with piety and probity, while 1 Tim 4:8 recommends piety based on present salvation and eternal life in the future as opposed to asceticism on the basis of erroneous myths. The misconduct and sin of heterodox teachers at 1 Tim 6:3-5 are contrasted with the virtuous life of piety (1 Tim 6:6, 11-12). Similarly, 1 Tim 5:4 uses the verb in an application to family obligations, and the adverb at 2 Tim 3:12 contrasts the new life of those who accept Jesus with the depravity of the deceivers and deceived, while at Titus 2:12-14 a link is made between the present devout life in this age, rendered pure of lawlessness, with the hope of the *parousia* (see also 1 Tim 3:15-16). The recognition of truth in hope of eternal life can also be found at Titus 1:1. It thus appears that piety includes the intellectual side of faith, that is, correct doctrine. At the same time it also looks to Christian life as a visible result of this correct knowledge of God. The saving action of Jesus makes this new life possible, and the new life looks ahead to the *parousia* and eternal life. The non-Pauline term thus meets the new challenge of the teachers, with their new knowledge of the truths of faith and its disruptive effects in the community (and see *1 Clem.* 15.1).

probity: The word *semnotēs* ("probity") and its cognate (*semnos*, "honorable") appears almost exclusively in the PE (except Phil 4:8). Probity is here expected of all in the community. This is made explicit for household masters at 1 Tim 3:4, for male deacons at 1 Tim 3:8, for female deacons at 1 Tim 3:11, for older women at Titus 2:2, and for Titus at Titus 2:7. A concern for the uprightness of the community in the eyes of outsiders runs throughout the letters (see Wis 8:7).

3. *savior:* See the Note on 1:1.

4. *that all people be saved:* This, together with the title "savior" (*sōtēr*) for God, underlines a key theological position of the PE (see 1 Tim 1:15; 4:10), probably in reaction to an understanding of salvation among the false teachers that is not as extensive and is linked to their esoteric knowledge (see piety above, and 1 Tim 1:6-7). The letters, therefore, reiterate "our" salvation (1 Tim 1:1; 2:3; 2 Tim 1:9-10; Titus 1:3, 4; 2:10; 3:4) as paradigmatic for that of all people who accept the truth of faith as God and Christ desire that all do.

   Salvation is from ignorance (1 Tim 2:4; Titus 4:10). Salvation is also from sin and leads to a new life of holiness (2 Tim 1:9; Titus 2:14; 3:4-7). This salvation and new life are both present and linked with the revelation and hope of an immortal future (2 Tim 1:9, 10; Titus 1:2-3). This is consonant with the idea of piety (see above). By his proclamation of the word of God, Paul mediates salvation to the elect (2 Tim 2:10 and see 1 Tim 4:16 for Timothy). The key event in the salvation process is the appearance on earth and redemptive death of Jesus (1 Tim 1:15; 2 Tim 1:10; Titus 3:4-5). This is a historical reality and not a mythical fabrication (1 Tim 1:4; 4:7; Titus 1:14), of which the false teachers are proponents (and compare 2 Pet 1:16).

   knowledge of the truth: Knowledge implies recognition of God, which is also effective in the conduct of the one who knows God. Biblical "truth" (*alētheia*) differs from secular truth or something simply genuine (Turner, *Christian Words*, 464–67). The LXX often applies the word to God as a quality (Gen 24:27; 32:10; 2 Kgs 2:6; 15:20; Pss 39 [40]:11; 42 [43]:3), and it also can involve behavior and speech, but the latter as other than correctness in information (Judg 9:16; 1 Kgs 12:24). The psalmist prays to be led in God's truth (Ps 24 [25]:5, LXX for God's "faithfulness," and see Gen 47:29; Josh 2:14; 2 Kgs 15:20; Neh 9:33). While Plutarch (*Is. Os.* 2) uses it to mean correct information about the gods as opposed to false propaganda, Philo (*Spec. Leg.* 4.178) ties it to Judaism and ultimate truth. In the letters undisputedly written by Paul and in the PE the truth seems to mean the Gospel preaching (2 Tim 2:15; 4:4; 2 Cor 6:7; Col 1:5; Eph 1:13) or a body of doctrine beyond the Gospel (Rom 1:18, 25; 3:7; 15:8; see Jas 5:19). For 1 Tim 3:15; 2 Tim 2:15 the truth appears to be an accepted body of doctrine. The phrase "knowledge of the truth" (*epignōsis alētheias*) is akin to a *terminus technicus* for accepting Christianity at 1 Tim 2:4; 2 Tim 2:25; 3:7; Titus 1:1, and for some this has signaled a narrowing of the understanding of Christian faith to its intellectual or dogmatic content. Titus 1:1 (and compare 1 Tim 2:7; 4:3), however, distinguishes "faith" from "knowledge of the truth" and adds the qualification "in accordance with piety." Thus, while the intellectual aspect of Christianity is stressed in light of the conflict with heterodox, apostate teachers, there is still a distinction between intellectual content and faith. Moreover, the knowledge of the truth is ineluctably connected with proper action, a connection already made at Rom 1:18, 25, 28; 2:20 (and see Col 1:6, 9-10). Surprisingly, 2 Thess 2:12-14 refers to belief with truth as its object, which the PE do not do. Therefore, while the undeniable stress on knowledge of the truth is understandable in light of the community situation, the PE do not restrict Christianity to its intellectual component.

5. *one God:* The fundamental theological insight carried over from Judaism (Mal 2:10) is reiterated throughout the NT (1 Cor 8:4; 12:5-6; Rom 3:30; Eph 4:5-6).

   mediator: Parallel with the credal affirmation about the one God at 1 Cor 8:6 is the affirmation of belief in the one Lord Jesus Christ. Here at 1 Tim 2:5 a similar double credal affirmation appears. The first is the affirmation of the oneness of God; the second is of Christ Jesus as a human being (see Rom 5:5) and mediator (see also Heb 8:6; 9:15-28; 12:24; and compare Gal 3:19-20 for Moses). The letter uses the word *anthrōpos*, the word for "human" as opposed to the male gender-specific *anēr*, which appears in v. 8 for the prayer instructions for men in the community. Secular Greek usage describes the mediator or arbitrator as one who mediates between two parties to remove a disagreement or reach a common goal. In Hellenistic Judaism (*T. Dan* 6:2) the mediator between God and humanity is the interceding angel. The primary mediator, however, is Moses (Philo, *Moses* 2.116; *Dreams* 1.143; *Heir* 206; Josephus, *Ant.* 7.193; *T. Mos.* 1:14; 3:12; *Deut. Rab.* 3 [201], referring to Exod 34:1; *Pesiq. Rab.* 45 on Exod 34:30). Whereas the concept of mediation in connection with Moses' mediation of the covenant is disparaged at Gal 3:19-20, in 1 Timothy it is Christianized and prized. Moses is the type of Jesus as mediator (1 Cor 10:2 and Rom 6:3), for Jesus' mediation brings into effect God's salvific will (1 Tim 2:4). The universality of this salvific aim (as opposed to the false teachers' view) and of Christianity (as distinct from Jewish particularism) is expressed with the words "humans," v. 5, and "all," v. 6. Jesus' humanity is stressed here (see 1 Tim 1:15 and Tertullian, *De Carne Christi* 15 [ANF 3:534], against the Gnostic Valentinus' spiritual flesh, specifies a human substance as Paul's only meaning) and his self-sacrificing and redemptive death is proclaimed (and compare Titus 2:14 as well as Rom 3:24; 5:18; 6:6-11). The identity of Jesus as mediator between God and humanity indicates the enduring presence of that redemptive mediation. Augustine, *Enchir.* 108.28 (LCC 7:404) explains that the mediator had to be a sinless human, and God as well, to heal humanity through divine humility. The salvific effects of his death in the past extend into the present, the now of salvation, by the Gospel, in expectation of life eternal (2 Tim 1:10; Titus 1:13; 2:11-12). A. T. Hanson suggests that at this point Timothy is using an outline of prayer for public worship, and he finds intriguing parallel phraseology at *1 Clem.* 59.2, 4; 60. 4; 61.1, 2, 3.

6. *ransom:* The fundamental christological and soteriological affirmation in v. 6a re-expresses Mark 10:45 with some stylistic alterations. Although the Messianic title "son of man" (*huios tou anthrōpou*) in the gospels would fit the role of the mediator, 1 Tim 2:5 uses "Christ" (*christos*). The Greek expression "himself" (*heautōn*) substitutes for the Hebrew "his life" (*tēn psychēn*, BDF 283.4). The prefix *anti-* added to *lytron* in the word *antilytron* ("ransom") reflects the PE's preference for compound words. "For all" (*hyper pantōn*) is the Greek equivalent of the Hebrew universal/indefinite "for many" (*anti pollōn*).

   The three Hebrew words behind the Greek *antilytron* ("ransom") suggest vicarious payment for the life of another in covering a fault or debt (*koper* in

Hebrew). *Mekilta on Exodus* 21:30 (93a) explains that the price of payment is the value of the guilty party if he were to be sold as a slave. The redemption is by the nearest relative, which came to mean God as "redeemer" (*goʾel*) of Israel, God's people; but the redemption can be accomplished by a nonfamily member (*podeh*) who makes payment. The payment is not inanimate, but rather life for life. While Hebrew thought first applied the idea of redemption to the release of the nation from bondage (Exod 6:6 and Isaiah 40–55), it came to be connected with sin as the life of faith came to be individualized (Ps 129:8; 144:10). This grew to include redemption from death and from the powers of the underworld (Ps 48:15; Job 19:25). There can be no self-redemption here; only God can redeem in the face of death.

Later Jewish thought expressed the idea of the atoning power of the wise man (Philo, *Sacr*. 121) and the righteous sufferer. Secular usage of *lytron* also denotes "payment" for release of prisoners, slaves, or persons under a bond. Infrequent cultic use refers to payment to a deity to whom a person is indebted (Lucian, *Dial. d*. 4.2; Aeschylus, *Choeph*. 48).

First Timothy 2:6 thus repeats a basic formula of Christian belief. Universal salvation is expressed by the redemption of Christ's self-offering. It is an offering of life for life, by one like and kin to the captives. Nonetheless, while human, Christ Jesus is more than human (see 1:2) and so can effect the payment that is more than self-redemption by humans. The issue raised later (e.g., by Anselm) as to who received the payment is not addressed. Romans 3:24-26 describes the redemption with cultic imagery. The redemption in Romans 3, Mark 10, and here is from the bondage of sin and opens access to eternal life (see also Titus 2:14).

testimony: This noun in the accusative is in apposition with v. 6a and is the object of the verb "give" (*dous*). While the relative clause in v. 7 identifies the testimony with the Gospel, the word also refers to the testimony of the paschal events (both Jesus' words and his actions) for Jesus' own day. First Timothy 6:13 recalls Jesus' testimony (*martyrēsantos*) before Pilate, to which Timothy's confession stands in parallel (see Titus 1:3). Second Timothy 1:8-11 calls attention to the moment of the manifestation of God's grace according to the prior design. This manifestation was made in the death of Christ the savior. The testimony of the Lord parallels Paul's, and both involve suffering and death (2:11; 4:6). The Gospel brings the saving effects of this into the current generation of believers.

7. *preacher:* Used only in the PE, the word points to the proclamation task that is yet to be accomplished, a missionary accent (see also 2 Tim 1:11 and cognates "preaching," *kērygma*, 2 Tim 4:17; Titus 1:3; "preach," *kēryssō*, 1 Tim 3:16; 2 Tim 4:2). For "apostle" see 1 Tim 1:1.

I am telling the truth: The Pauline phrase (Rom 9:1) alerts the audience in an oral reading context to the veracity of what follows.

teacher: Paul, who engages in teaching (1 Cor 4:17), does not use the title of himself, but he lists it along with other "gifts" (1 Cor 12:28-29). The function is critical for the PE in view of the doctrinal struggles at Ephesus. See 2 Tim 1:11 and contrast the unauthorized teachers at 2 Tim 4:3.

Interpretation

First Timothy 2:1–6:2 is at once the body of the letter and the PE's adaptation of the household or station code scheme. The household or station code in Greco-Roman moral instruction outlined the duties of members of households according to a standard pattern, usually husbands and wives, fathers and children, masters and slaves. Such a list is often referred to as a *Haustafel* or list of household duties. In the line of development from the *Haustafel* at Col 3:18–4:1; Eph 5:21–6:9 through the household code with the additional exhortations to community groups and officers at Pol. *Phil.* 4:2–6:1; Ign. *Pol.* 4:1–6:2, the PE also include qualifications for officials here and at Titus 1:5-9; 2:1-10; 3:1-11 and particular advice to the addressees. Material that is not part of the expanded schema also interrupts the station code here. In the body of the letter Paul gives advice and directives to the community in a setting in which the letter is the surrogate presence of the apostle.

In describing the intention of the community's prayer (2:2), Paul stresses supplication for quiet and tranquility with piety and reverence, an obvious contrast with the endless genealogies and speculation (1:4) of the false teachers. These teachers also lurk in the shadows of the description of God's will for all to be saved and come to know the truth. This sums up Paul's path (1:13, 15-16) and by way of contrast describes what the false teachers need. The same holds true for the qualities of piety and reverence, for the false teachers (1:9) are "irreverent" (*asebeis*) and "unruly" (*anypotaktoi*). The hierarchical focus on prayer for "kings and all in prominent places" relates both to the larger community toward which the letters turn a steady and cautious eye (3:7; 6:1; 2 Tim 1:8; 2:15; Titus 2:7-8) and to the community of the PE itself. The lawless and unruly false teachers resist the requirements of order, while the letters advance order in their focus on community officials described and designated (Titus 1:5), including Timothy (and Titus), easy targets of criticism because of their youth (e.g., 4:12; 2 Tim 2:22; Titus 2:15). The salvation willed by God (2:3) finds expression as accomplished by the historical event of Jesus' self-gift in ransom for all (2:5-6) which, again, recalls the universally applicable example of Paul (1:16). This divine will worked out in the unique mediation of Jesus between the one God and all humans clarifies the divine plan, ignored by the false teachers as they vainly research myths and genealogies (1:4).

Another aspect of the example of Paul from 1:12, 16 is his task of announcing and teaching this salvation to all nations. In this way Paul advances the part of Jesus' work that invited participation and emulation, that is, witness (2:16). Paul's apostolic proclamation and teaching aims at the "peoples" (*ethnōn*, and see Rom 15:7-24) and thus parallels Jesus' universal mediation between God and humanity. This carries forward the divine will that all be saved, for salvation is linked with coming to know the truth (2:4), and truth, along with faith, characterizes Paul's preaching/teaching (2:6).

In this chapter the letter turns from the allusion to sound teaching and warnings against the false teachers to "church order" material (compare Eph 5:22–6:9; Col 3:18–4:1; 1 Pet 2:13–3:7; Titus 2:2-10), which continues through 3:16. In this connection, at 3:15 the author identifies the church as the household of God. The church's growth necessitated organization and institutionalization and could no longer entrust itself to charismatic enthusiasm (Brox, *Pastoralbriefe*, 121). Paul details his hortatory prescriptions after the brief credal affirmation, which expresses the basis (Jesus' death and resurrection witness) and motivation (succeeding Jesus' witness to lead people to salvation) for his work. The PE thus locate the "church order" within the apostolic tradition of Paul.

For Reference and Further Study

Balch, David L. *Let Wives Be Submissive: The Domestic Code in 1 Peter*. SBLMS 26. Chico: Scholars Press, 1981, 73–74, 101–102.

Banks, Robert. *Paul's Idea of Community: The Early House Churches in Their Historical Setting*. Grand Rapids: Eerdmans, 1980.

Borse, Udo. *1. und 2. Timotheusbrief*, 37–38, 40.

Fee, Gordon D. "Reflections on Church Order in the Pastoral Epistles, with Further Reflection on the Hermeneutics of *ad hoc* Documents," *JETS* 28 (1985) 141–51.

Fiore, Benjamin. "Household Rules at Ephesus," in John T. Fitzgerald, Thomas H. Olbricht, and L. Michael White, eds., *Early Christianity and Classical Culture: Comparative Studies in Honor of Abraham J. Malherbe*. Leiden and Boston: Brill, 2003, 606–607.

Foerster, Werner. "*EYSEBEIA* in den Pastoralbriefen," *NTS* 5 (1958–1959) 213–18.

Grosheide, Frederik Willem. "The Pauline Epistles as Kerygma," in *Studia Paulina in honorem Johannis de Zwaan septuagenarii*. Haarlem: Bohn, 1953, 139–45.

Hahn, Ferdinand. "Die Schöpfungsmittlerschaft Christi bei Paulus und in der Deuteropaulinen," in Cesare Casale Marcheselli, ed., *Parola e Spirito, Studi in Onore di Settimio Cipriani*. Brescia: Paideia, 1982, 1:661–78.

Hanson, Anthony Tyrrell. *Studies in the Pastoral Epistles*. London: SPCK, 1968, 23, 56–77.

MacDonald, Dennis Ronald. *The Legend and the Apostle: The Battle for Paul in Story and Canon*. Philadelphia: Westminster, 1983, 54–72.

Modrzejewski, Joseph M. "Private Arbitration in Graeco-Roman Egypt," *JJP* 6 (1952) 247 n. 79.

Nilsson, Martin Persson. "The High God and the Mediator," *HTR* 56 (1963) 101–20.

Senior, Donald. *"Parousia," TBT* 25 (1987) 220–22.

Verner, David C. *Household of God*, 83–111, 166–71.

Veyne, Paul, ed. *A History of Private Life from Pagan Rome to Byzantium*. Trans. Arthur Goldhammer. Cambridge, MA: Harvard University Press, 1987, 210–14.

5. *Rules for Men and Women* (2:8-15)

8. I, therefore, want the men in every place to pray, lifting up holy hands without anger and disagreement. 9. Likewise, I also want women to dress themselves in respectable clothing with modesty and moderation, not in braids and with gold jewelry or pearls or rich clothes. 10. No, but, as fits women who lay claim to reverence for God, with good works. 11. Let a woman learn in silence in complete submission. 12. Yes, I do not permit a wife to teach or to take authority over her husband, but rather to be in silence. 13. The reason is that Adam was formed first, then Eve. 14. Moreover, Adam was not deceived but the woman, after being deceived, ended up in transgression. 15. Yet she will be saved through the bearing of children, if they continue in faith, love, and holiness with moderation.

Notes

8. *I want:* The word has imperative force resting on Paul's apostolic authority. It appears in the legislative decree of Antiochus III quoted in Josephus, *Ant.* 12.150 and in the official decree 𝔓 *Lond* 904.30 (*MM*). As such it lends 1 Timothy the character of an official memorandum.

in every place: The instruction refers to liturgical prayer that takes place in more than one household-church. The large room of some well-to-do hosts' houses could accommodate several hundred persons, but perhaps forty to fifty would be more usual in the public reception room of the moderately well-to-do. The phrase might also recall Mal 1:11 as a fulfillment of the prophecy of prayer everywhere and not just in the Temple. This echoes the universal salvation theme at 1 Tim 2:14.

lifting up holy hands without anger and disagreement: This was a common posture of prayer in the Greco-Roman as well as the Jewish worlds and was frequently associated with blessing (Lev 9:22-24; Sir 50:20; *Gen. Rab.* 60 (38b); and see Horace, *Ep.* 3.23.1-6; Ovid, *Metam.* IX.701, *Tristia* I 11,19-22; Livy, *Hist.* V.21,14-15; Seneca, *Ep.* 41,1-2). See Valerius Maximus II 2,8 and IV 4,2 for the specification of "holy hands." The "orans" figure in catacomb art attests the perdurance of the custom into Christian usage. These prayers correspond with the intention of 1 Tim 2:1. The instruction need not imply that only the men or husbands may pray, but rather suggests that the men might have been angry and quarrelsome. Perhaps this reflects the community dissensions occasioned by the false teachers. *Didachē* 14:2 has a similar instruction about reconciling quarrels before joining the worship meeting (and compare Matt 5:23; 1 Cor 11:20-22, 28-34). Similarly 1 Cor 14:26-33, 36-40 refers to curtailing the disruptive exhibition of gifts at worship and, like this passage, is associated with restrictions regarding women's or wives' (v. 35 refers to their husbands) active interventions at worship services (34-35). See also Sir 7:10.

Origen, *Prayer* (OSW 166) says that every place is suitable for prayer if a person prays well. Basil, *Bapt.* (FC 9:409) and John Chrysostom, *Hom. 1 Tim.* 8 (NPNF 1,

13:432-433) assert that this passage was meant to distinguish Christian prayer from Jewish sacrificial prayer confined to the Temple in Jerusalem. Basil specifies that prayer should be in a place consecrated to God, while Chrysostom focuses on the manner of prayer, pure of vice (as does Tertullian, *Prayer* 13 [ANF 3:685]). It must be remembered that Christians did not build churches until after the Edict of Toleration in 313 C.E. Before then Christian communal worship was held in private homes. Over time these homes were in part remodeled to accommodate the Christian community on a regular basis. The house-church in Dura Europos and the House of Peter in Capernaum are two examples of houses partially remodeled in the first centuries of Christianity. One of the challenges of liturgy today is to create a welcoming setting while still accommodating larger numbers than attended worship in primitive Christianity.

9. *women:* Women's (wives') roles in worship receive treatment parallel ("likewise," *hōsautōs*) to the men's (husbands'). First the letter addresses their overall bearing in prayer.

   moderation, not in braids: Plutarch, *Conj. praec.* 141E declares that it is not gold, jewels, or scarlet that make a wife decorous, but rather that which gives her "dignity" (*semnotēs*), "good behavior" (*eutaxia*), and "modesty" (*aidōs*). See also Livy, *Hist.* 34.7.10; Phintys, *On the Temperance of Women* 153.15-28; and Lucian, *Imag.* 11 ("worthy adornment," *dikaion kosmēma*; "virtue," *aretē*; "moderation," *sōphrosynē*; "gentleness," *epieikeia*; "benevolence," *philanthrōpia*); Aelian, *Var. Hist.* VII 9; Seneca, *Ad Helviam* 16,4. Plato, *Phaed.* 114d-115a speaks of virtues ("decency," *kosmos*; "moderation," *sōphrosynē*; "uprightness," *diakiosynē*; "fortitude," *andreia*; "freedom," *eleutheria*; "truth," *alētheia*) as the adornment of the soul as it enters the next life. Juvenal, *Sat.* 6.492 and Petronius, *Satyricon* 67 describe wealthy women's elaborate adornments at the time (see also Pollux, *Onomasticon* V.95-96; Terence, *Heaut.* II/3, 282-291; Horace, *Sat.* 2.97; Martial, *Ep.* 2.36). External adornment signals the condition of the soul in Josephus, *Bell.* 2.8.4; IV 561-562. It is disparaged by Polybius, *Hist.* XI 9, 6-7.

10. *with good works:* Piety (*eusebeia*), the external counterpart to faith claims, has been discussed above at 2:2. *Numbers Rabbah* 14 (176c) extols Sarah and Abraham for being full of good works and attracting proselytes. For a similar expectation elsewhere in Paul see Rom 2:7, 10; 2 Cor 9:8; Gal 6:9-10. Good works are not promoted as a way to gain salvation, since Christ bestowed justification according to his eternal plan and favor (2 Tim 1:9; Titus 3:5-7; and Gal 2:16; Rom 3:20, 28). Christ renders those saved in this way capable of doing good (Titus 2:14) and they are expected to move from capability to action (2 Tim 2:21; Titus 3:1, 8, 14; good works are the expression of true riches, 1 Tim 6:18). By way of contrast, the letters portray those who are faithless and in error as incapable of doing anything good (Titus 1:15-16, and see Rom 13:12; Eph 5:11). As prime examples for the community, the addressees, coworkers of Paul, must excel in good deeds (2 Tim 3:17; Titus 2:7). To present a convincing Christian message, members of the community have to be seen as living in a way that shows that their faith makes a practical difference in their lives. In addition to personal virtues, good deeds constitute an essential part of this practical evangelism. The strategy of the PE is echoed in Jas 2:14-18, 22, which expects claims of faith

to be demonstrated in deeds. Thus in the last century Mahatma Gandhi, while attracted to Christianity by its teachings, faulted Christians for not putting them into practice.

11. *a woman . . . in silence:* Switching to the singular and to the imperative, the letter commands women to learn in silence. Philo, *Spec. Leg.* 3.169, urges a life of seclusion at home, not meddling as a busybody, but surrounded by quiet, and in prayer. Similarly Plutarch, *Conj. praec.* 142D, urges women to keep silence in public (see also Aristotle, *Pol.* 1260a3), and to speak only to or through their husbands, who are to share their learning with them at home (145C-E). Juvenal satirizes women who debate with men on the basis of what they have studied (*Sat.* 6.398-412; 434-456). In its characterization of women the letter echoes the bias and concerns of the larger society. The instructions both to women on domesticity and to men on peacefulness coincide with opinion in the larger society from which the PE hope to gain approval, or at least to avoid condemnation.

The home was the women's domain and area of responsibility. They supervised domestic work arrangements, childrearing, and shopping, and were expected not to be away from home, even to visit neighbors (Cato, *Agriculture* 143). The Isis cult, despite its prominent roles for women and its appeal across social and gender lines, nonetheless extolled motherhood. In that respect it agreed with Augustus' efforts to promote marriage and childbearing (Dio Cassius, *Rom. Hist.* 56.1-10 [LCL 7.2-25]). The silence enjoined here reflects the women's share in maintaining a life of peace and quiet (2:2). The prohibition against speaking here appears to echo 1 Cor 14:34-35, which also deals with orderliness in worship. But 1 Corinthians is concerned with prophets, while 1 Timothy deals with correct instruction in an atmosphere of acceptance rather than contentiousness and disputation learned from false teachers (Titus 3:9-13). Alan Padgett suggests that the women's submission might be to their teachers and not to men in general. Restricting the place of women here and in other Paulinist writings (Col 3:18-19; Eph 5:22-33; Titus 2:4-5; and also 1 Cor 11:3-16 and 14:34-35, as well as 1 Pet 3:1-7) departs from the egalitarian statements (Gal 3:27-28; 1 Cor 7:2-5) and practices of Paul's churches, as suggested by the women house-church leaders (1 Cor 1:11; 16:19; Rom 16:3), coworkers (Rom 16:6-7; Phil 4:2-3), and assistants (Rom 16:1-2).

submission: Submission is behavior characteristically advanced in household codes (see 1 Tim 3:4; Titus 2:5, 9; 3:1; Rom 13:1, 5; Eph 5:21, 24; Col 3:18) and is in harmony with the obedience to God's command followed by Paul (1 Tim 1:1, 12; 2:7; 2 Tim 1:11) and violated by the false teachers (1 Tim 1:9; Titus 1:10; compare Titus 1:6).

12. *I do not permit a wife to teach or to take authority:* The subjects are normally persons who assume an official position (*EDNT*, and see John 19:38; Mark 10:4; Acts 21:39, 40; 26:1; 28:16). In earlier Pauline letters the verb *epitrepō* is used only in the disputed passage 1 Cor 14:34 and in reference to the Lord at 1 Cor 16:7. It is a strong word and makes explicit the implication of *boulomai* (v. 8). Some question whether the statement is prescriptive or merely descriptive. In the latter case it would not lay the grounds for excluding women from the teaching ministry. The reservation of the work of bishop/presbyter to men (1 Tim 3:1-7;

Titus 1:5-9), however, indicates the letters' exclusion of women from the work of teaching and the exercise of authority over men. The act receives so clear a prohibition that one is led to understand that women in the Ephesian church were teaching, most likely in consequence of the equality they derived from Paul's baptismal teaching (Gal 3:28). Similarly, Paul presumes equal access to spiritual gifts. Thus 1 Corinthians 12 speaks of the availability without gender distinction of Spirit gifts, one of which is "teacher," 1 Cor 12:29. Women in Paul's churches headed household churches, some with their husbands (Prisca and Aquila who taught Apollos, Acts 18:26, and see Rom 16:3; 1 Cor 16:19; 2 Tim 4:19; Junia and Andronicus, Rom 16:7; Lydia, Acts 16:15; Chloe, 1 Cor 1:11; and perhaps Phoebe, Rom 16:2). Since the leaders of households who are overseers and elders in the PE teach, one can assume that this was not uncommon (1 Tim 3:2; Titus 1:9). In addition to these women, others performed a wide range of tasks for which Paul acknowledges them (e.g., Rom 16:6, 12, 15, and Phil 4:2-3). The high profile of these female agents in the Pauline churches seems to have led some to adopt positions that appeared extreme to others. For example, the emancipatory "neither male and female" of Gal 3:28 might have led some women to see no need to procreate, or even to marry (1 Cor 7:28, 36) or to stay married (1 Cor 7: 5, 10-11). The false teachers' extreme asceticism (1 Tim 4:3) and over-spiritualized eschatology (2 Tim 2:18) would abet these emancipatory orientations.

The *Acts of Paul and Thecla* extols the extreme against which the PE are reacting: chastity, emancipation from a wife's role, ascetical abstinence, realized resurrection. Both Thecla and Paul advance these ideals. This text offers a possible glimpse into the nature of the disruption in the community over the true development and application of the Pauline tradition. In any case the women are excluded from the area of public speech, including teaching, which is the domain of male honor and political dominance (see Euripides, *El.* 930-937; Philemon, *fr.* 120 Kassel/Austin; Plautus, *Menaechmi* V/2, 792-797). They find themselves restricted to the area of private speech, where their shame or discreet timidity is properly expressed. In this regard the prohibition against all speech at 1 Cor 14:33-35 is more comprehensive than the regulation here in 1 Timothy (Brox, *Pastoralbriefe*, 134). Further expressions of this feminine shame or recognition of sexual vulnerability were her restrained public demeanor and unostentatious attire. The social strategy of the PE looks to restore the equilibrium of the church in the eyes of the larger community by bringing the behavior of church members into line with the expectations of Greco-Roman society and in keeping with Pauline tradition. Revelation 2:20 refers to a woman apostate teacher at Thyatira as "Jezebel." Moulton-Milligan relates the word "to take authority" (*authentein*) to "master," "autocrat" (*authentēs*), a secular meaning that explains the hapax cognate here. Thus the verb means "to act on one's own authority." The word might have an inceptive sense to describe initiating an action or taking an action on one's own prerogative, i.e., taking charge. The verb tense thereby introduces a note of unwarranted usurpation as part of the justification of the prohibition.

The restriction here reflects Plutarch's view that household activities demonstrate the husband's rule and choices (*Conj. praec.* 139D). Octavian's teacher and counselor Arius Didymus similarly held that the man has the rule over the house by nature (*Epitomē* 149.5-8, and see also Philo, *Spec. Leg.* 2.225-227; 3.169-171; *Decalogue* 165-167; Josephus, *C. Ap.* 2.199; Juvenal's satire of an imperious matron (6.206-274), and Martial, *Ep.* 8.12. Note Diodorus Siculus' accusation that the Isis cult led women to think they should exercise authority over their husbands (1.271-272) and also Tacitus, *Historiae* 5.5. Dionysius of Halicarnassus in like manner criticizes cults, *Ant. Rom.* 1.7.2; 2.19, and insists on the subordination of children, wives, and slaves, 2.24.3; 2.26.1; 2.27.4.

13. *first:* The allusion to Gen 2:7, 22 declares Adam's temporal priority to Eve in creation. A similar allusion at 1 Cor 11:8-9 is part of Paul's substantiation of his argument for the rules on head coverings during the community's worship there, based on "headship" of the husband over his wife. Using similar Jewish traditions here, the PE apply them to a more fundamental issue, akin to that treated at 1 Cor 14:34-35. Adam and Eve are representatives of humans in their respective genders. The first reason ("for," *gar*) for restricting women's teaching and exercise of authority rests on the order ("first . . . then," *prōtos . . . eita*) of human creation, and on the inferior status of women that results from this.

14. *the woman, after being deceived:* The second reason ("and," *kai*) is based on an allusion to Gen 3:6, 12-13 (see Sir 25:23), which is taken to demonstrate woman's innate gullibility (see also *Ep. Aris.* 250; Philo, *QG* 1.33, 47, and *Pirqe R. El.* 13). The PE see the deception of women as a problem at 2 Tim 3:7, and this agrees with the Greco Roman society's low estimation of female intelligence noted above. That same passage from 2 Timothy educes a second cultural bias, that is, women's susceptibility to sexual desires (*agomena epithymiais*). Juvenal satirizes the matron who indulges in sexual freedom in her preference for exotic and outlandish foreign religions (6.116-118, and see Suetonius, *Tiberius* 35-36, and Josephus, *Ant.* 18.65-80). The Romans lumped Judaism, the Isis and Dionysus cults all together and criticized them for seducing and defrauding wealthy women who tend to get entangled in them. Libanius, *Decl.* 40, 18 expresses the prevailing social prejudice about women being prone to deception and sexual seduction. This suspicion is not unexpected in a society (whether Jewish or Greco-Roman) where women are the (sexual) property of men. Thus any sort of intrusion by another male into the women's sphere of the household carried sexual overtones.

    The compound verb "deceived" (*exapatētheisa*) suggests sexual seduction. A haggadic tradition speculated that Eve was seduced by the serpent (*4 Macc.* 18:6-8; Philo, *Alleg. Interp.* 3.59-66, where Adam is "mind" (*nous*), Eve "feeling" (*aesthēsis*), and the serpent "pleasure" (*hēdonē*): *Life* 9-11, and compare John 8:44). Paul seems to be aware of the legend in 2 Cor 11:1-3, 14, where he contrasts the betrothal of a chaste virgin (the community) to Christ with Eve's deception by the serpent (and see later evidence in *Protevangelion Jas.* 3.1; *Acts Pil.* 2.3; *Diogn.* 12.8, and rabbinic sources *Gen. R.* 18; *m.Sota* 9b; *Jalk. Schim Ber.* 42). See also Slavic Enoch 30:11. The author thus uses a tradition known in the Pauline churches and suited to the prevailing social attitudes toward women and the effort to bring the community into conformity with social custom.

    Alan Padgett suggests that Eve functions as a type for the women of the Pastorals' community, the antitype who, like Eve, tend to listen to the snake or false teachers. Thus there is no general antifeminine bias in the analogy. Rather, the antitype evokes the corresponding element of susceptibility to deception in the type. In this connection Adam is a type of nondeception and probably is meant to focus on Timothy as the antitype. Romans 5:12-14, however, attributes the deception and its consequences to Adam, who is the type of the sinless Christ to come.

Motherhood, in the context of domestic submissiveness, is the women's way to salvation. Typology continues in the requirement of childbearing for salvation. Through her seed Eve was saved or at least would be saved from sin and from the wrath of God on followers of Satan. So women contemporary with the epistle, tainted by false teaching (1 Tim 4:3) and avoiding the marriage bed, will be saved by rejecting the snake or false teachers' instructions and returning to normal marital practice.

15. *bearing of children:* The pain of childbearing is the specific punishment in Gen 3:16 that God places upon the sinful woman, and presumably bearing the punishment is her way of atoning for her sin. In the PE childbearing by women within their own households, one of the wifely duties, will counter the temptation to be deceived/seduced and will lead to women's salvation. This is unlike Paul's views of marriage (as corresponding to one's gift, 1 Cor 7:7; a necessity for some to avoid immorality, 1 Cor 7:2, 9; with duties attached, 1 Cor 7:3, but not to produce children) and of salvation (given freely by God through Christ, Rom 3:21-26, and see 2 Tim 1:9; Titus 3:5). On the other hand, after characterizing women as inherently subordinate and gullible or open to seduction, and as insignificant and unreliable, removed from a public role in the church, the author of the letter had to assure women of a place of significance and holiness. This place for them was the home, in the fulfillment of socially expected domestic duties.

Epictetus (*Diatr.* 3.7.19-20), in criticizing the Epicureans, expressed the commonly held view that marriage, childbearing, the household, and the political order are all related (and see Plato, *Leg.* 6.773B; Aristotle, *Pol.* 1260b). The PE, in the instructions about women, restrain activities that threaten the social order and promote those that sustain it (note Titus 3:5). The household regulations here have broad implications, since the household is the microcosm of the whole state. The PE try to establish the Christian community clearly on the side of those who support rather than corrupt the social order, and they hope thereby to escape society's condemnation.

Interpretation

First the author addresses the men, and his prescription counters the destructive activity of men exemplified in the false teachers (1:6, 9-10) and the erstwhile Paul (1:13, 15). Just as he preaches to and teaches all nations/peoples (2:7), so he requires people everywhere (2:8) to pray, and he reiterates the need for quiet in the exclusion of anger and argument.

The insistence on prayer for a peaceful and upright context is not at all banal. The letter sees only such a context as productive and expressive of a grasp of the truth on which salvation rests. Although Christians today can establish churches in which to pray, contrary to the situation in the time of the PE, the spirit of Christian prayer is that it can be engaged in anywhere at all. Maximus of Turin, *Sermons* 38.3 (ACW 50:93), sees that the prayer gesture of uplifted hands describes a cross so that the one at prayer might confess with the stance of the body the Lord's suffering. John Chrysostom, *Catech. Ult.* 2.4 (NPNF 1 9:169-170), recalls Paul's words here but adds that the women should take off all ornament and place it in the hands of Christ through the poor.

In number, women receive the lion's share of the prescriptions. The aim is to advance conduct and deeds appropriate to their religious claims (2:9-10). Already at 1:9-10 actions and beliefs were shown to be linked in the case of the false teachers and negative examples. The requirement of a peaceful life, which was the aim (2:2) of men's prayer (2:7), falls more heavily on women than on men (the women are to be both in peace, vv. 11-12, and in submission). Silence and obedience are to characterize their learning and they are excluded from teaching or exercising authority over men (2:11-12). These are tasks given over to Paul and his addressees, Timothy and Titus, and assigned to men later in this letter and in the letter to Titus. The emphasis in this section on rules for the women's submission suggests that the letter is trying to reverse a practice common among women. Women appear to have played prominent roles in Paul's churches as house-church heads (Prisca, Rom 16:3; 1 Cor 16:9; Acts 18:2, 18, 26; Lydia, Acts 16:4, 40; Chloe, 1 Cor 1:11), assistants (Phoebe, Rom 16:1; Euodia and Syntyche, Phil 4:2; Apphia, Philemon 2; see also Rom 16:6, 12, 15) and prophets (1 Cor 11:5). Here in 1 Timothy the author introduces a change. God's plan, bypassed by the false teachers (1:4), substantiates Paul's position here. Two scriptural arguments support the prohibition against women teaching men. The priority of the creation of Adam suggests the man's social priority in the structure of authority according to God's plan. The priority of Eve in being deceived into transgressing God's design suggests the woman's fallible grasp of the truth, susceptibility to false teachers' blandishments, and consequent unsuitability to teach publicly.

While 1 Timothy follows a common exegesis of Gen 3:1-7, Augustine, *Civ.* 14.11.2, proposes an explanation of the Fall that finds guilt in both Adam and Eve, while at the same time maintaining the opinion that only Eve was deceived. In this understanding Adam's sin is even more deliberate than Eve's in that he sinned knowingly and deliberately. He chose to follow social convention and refused to be separated from his partner even in a union of sin. People can become accomplices in evil when they accept social conventions and structures they know to be against the laws of justice. This is particularly troubling in a world characterized by extreme disparity of economic resources and by social, racial, political, and gender disequillibrium.

Although the description of women's way to salvation through childbirth has been called "heretical" by some modern scholars (see Osiek and Balch, *Families in the New Testament World*, 121–23), first-century Greek moralists such as Maximus of Tyre (*Or.* 36.6b) note that marriage is for procreation and others cast a jaundiced eye on sexual pleasure even between spouses (Musonius Rufus, *fr.* 12, and Seneca, *De matrimonio fr.*). This would explain how the Pastorals, in their attempt to present the Christian community's best face toward the Graeco-Roman world, would stress childbearing within marriage. Furthermore, Philo and Josephus seem to follow the lead of Hellenistic moralists as they disparage pleasure in marriage. Later Jewish texts such as the *Testaments of the Twelve Patriarchs* (see *T. Iss.* 2.3), while denigrating sexual pleasure, stress the Law's emphasis on sexual relations to procreate offspring. Josephus (*C. Ap.* 2.22-30 and *Ant.* 18.1.5, where he describes the Essenes) makes a similar observation. At *T. Naph.* 8.8 (echoing Eccl 3:5 and 1 Cor 7:5) Naphthali says, "So there are two commandments, and if they are not done in their order, they bring sin." Sexual intercourse for the purpose of procreation is a way to avoid sin. If this view of procreation as fulfilling the expectations of the Law is fundamental to the Jewish view of marriage, then the prescription in 1 Tim 2:15 is not necessarily the invention of the author aping the Augustan moral reform efforts. It might well be an example of the letter's claim to know and follow the Law in its best aspects (1 Tim 1:8).

The plural "continue" (*meinōsin*, 2:15) could refer to the women when *gynē* (2:14) is understood as a collective noun. If so, then motherhood takes its place alongside the fundamental characteristics of faith, love, holiness, and prudence. These point to the women's relation to God ("faith," *pistis*) and human interrelations expressive of it. Or else it could refer to the children of the household, whom the women principally care for and whose conduct features in their father's qualifications for office (3:4). Domestic and maternal virtue thus counterbalances the precarious feminine grasp of the truth and anchors women in the hope of salvation. This letter (at 5:6, 11-13), like 2 Timothy (3:2-7) and Titus (2:5), documents the bias that women are easy victims of false teachers.

The regulations restricting women to domestic roles are influenced by cultural and traditional biases. As we have come to experience today, women are capable of exercising public as well as private roles. The level of education of women is on a par with that of men, and many of the private religious colleges in the United States are experiencing a ratio of women to men students that approaches 60/40. Moreover, the number of women in leadership positions in campus organizations often exceeds that of men. A similar observation can be made about women in parish organizations and on parish committees. A lesson here is to be careful to discern the degree to which our position on issues of the day might be skewed by cultural biases.

Another dimension of the problem with discerning bias is the current trend among some women in North America. There, the domestic role of women is finding an increased valuation among younger women who are not driven by the feminist struggle for equality as were women in the generation preceding them. The pull of motherhood and the challenge of raising children and running a home are leading many women to pursue traditional family roles in lieu of a career. Younger women are skeptical of the claim that they can "have it all," both a professional career and motherhood. While men are still slow to take on a share in the domestic work, men are more involved than previously in child rearing, home schooling, cooking, and the like.

For Reference and Further Study

Cantarella, Eva. *Pandora's Daughters: The Role and Status of Women in Greek and Roman Antiquity*. Baltimore and London: Johns Hopkins University Press, 1987.

Falk, Daniel K. "Women in the Greco-Roman World and Judaism," in Craig A. Evans and Stanley E. Porter, eds., *Dictionary of New Testament Background*. Downers Grove: InterVarsity Press, 2000, 1276–82.

Graham, Ronald W. "Women in the Pauline Churches: A Review Article," *LTQ* 11 (1976) 25–34.

Harris, Timothy J. "Why Did Paul Mention Eve's Deception? A Critique of P. W. Barnett's Interpretation of 1 Timothy 2," *EvQ* 61 (1989) 225–38.

Jonge, Marinus de. "Rachel's Virtuous Behavior in the *Testament of Issachar*," in David L. Balch, Everett Ferguson, and Wayne A. Meeks, eds., *Greeks, Romans and Christians: Essays in Honor of Abraham J. Malherbe*. Minneapolis: Fortress Press, 1990, 343–46.

Knight, George W. III. "*Authenteō* in Reference to Women in 1 Timothy 2.12," *NTS* 30 (1984) 143–57.

________. "The New Testament Teaching on the Role Relationship of Male and Female with Special Reference to the Teaching/Ruling Functions in the Church," *JETS* 18 (1975) 81–91.

________. *Faithful Sayings*, 68–73.

Levison, Jack. "Is Eve to Blame? A Contextual Analysis of Sirach 25:24," *CBQ* 47 (1985) 617–23.

Padgett, Alan. "Wealthy Women at Ephesus: 1 Timothy 2:8-15 in Social Context," *Int* 41 (1987) 19–31. For another view see H. Wayne House, "The Speaking of Women and the Prohibition of the Law," *BSac* 145 (1988) 301–318, especially 310–18.

Portefaix, Lilian. "'Good Citizenship' in the Household of God: Women's Position in the Pastorals Reconsidered in Light of Roman Rule," in Amy-Jill Levine with Marianne Blickenstaff, eds., *A Feminist Companion to the Deutero-Pauline Epistles*. Cleveland: Pilgrim Press, 2003, 147–58.

Redekop, Gloria N. "Let the Women Learn: 1 Timothy 2:1-15 Reconsidered," *Studies in Religion/Sciences Religieuses* (Waterloo) 19 (1990) 235–45.

Towner, Philip H. *Goal of Our Instruction*, 147–54.

van der Jagdt, K. A. "Women Are Saved through Childbearing (1 Timothy 2:11-15), *TBT* 39 (1988) 201–208.

Walker, William O. "The 'Theology of Woman's Place' and the 'Paulinist' Tradition," *Semeia* 28 (1983) 101–12.

6. *Qualities of Leadership Candidates: Overseer/Bishop* (3:1-7)

1. This saying is true: "If someone strives for the office of overseer, he desires a good occupation." 2. The overseer, therefore, has to be above reproach, married only once, clear-headed, self-controlled, respectable, hospitable, possessing teaching skills, 3. neither a heavy drinker nor violent. On the contrary, he must be kind, peaceable, not greedy, 4. supervising his own household appropriately, keeping his children under control, and with complete probity. 5. You see, if someone does not know how to supervise his own household, how will he take care of the church of God? 6. He must not be a recent convert, lest he become puffed up and stumble into the accuser's condemnation. 7. He also has to have a good reputation among the outsiders, lest he stumble into disgrace and the accuser's trap.

Notes

1. *This saying is true:* The saying is better understood to be what follows in 1b, which the letter goes on to elaborate. As is the case with other sayings, in the elaboration the author uses traditional material. No such saying has been found in secular Greek. Its origin with the author of the PE is unlikely because in the PE "desire" (*epithymia*) is a negative word, whereas it is positive here and elsewhere in the NT (Phil 1:23; 1 Thess 2:17). "Strives" (*oregetai*) and "good occupation" (*kalou ergou*) are likewise atypical for the PE. While "office of overseer" (*episkopē*) is rarely used anywhere in the NT (Luke 19:44; Acts 1:20; 1 Tim 3:1; 1 Pet 2:12), Paul uses *episkopos* (Phil 1:1; and see Acts 20:28; 1 Tim 3:2; Titus 1:7; 1 Pet 2:25). The saying could well have originated in the Pauline churches, where the office is unlike that of the civil or even religious overseer function. "Human" (*anthrōpinos*), the variant reading for "true" (*pistos*), has no support in the early Greek manuscripts and might have originated with a scribal distinction between the credal sayings elsewhere and this more mundane saying on official service.

   strives for the office of overseer: The verb "strives" (*oregetai*) suggests a heartfelt longing. That longing is emphasized by the verb "desires" (*epithymei*) in the next clause. The qualifications of being married only once (v. 2) and not a new convert (v. 6) indicate that this is an office and not just a personal honor. The word and its cognate "overseer" (*episkopos*) refer to protective guardianship or shepherding at 1 Pet 2:25; 5:1-5; Acts 20:28. This is particularly needed to confront assaults by false teachers (Titus 1:9-11; Acts 20:28; 1 Pet 5:1-5). "Elders" are related to "overseers" (Acts 20:17, 28; Titus 1:5, 7; 1 Pet 5:1, 2) and are those from whom "overseers" are chosen (implied at Titus 1:7). Thus the overseers exhort, refute, and admonish (Titus 1:9, 13) the wayward as well as taking care of the household of God and teaching (1 Tim 3:2, 5). It is unlikely that the references to a single overseer ("someone," *tis*) at 1 Tim 3:1 and to the overseer at Titus 1:7 refer to a monarchical bishop as in the letters of Ignatius. First, the hierarchical relationships receive no clear definition. Second, there is no stress on everyone's obedience to the bishop. Third, presiding at the Eucharist is not one of his functions. Fourth, 1 Timothy does not describe the assistants as *his* assistants (deacons). Fifth, 1 Peter, written perhaps about the same time, does not yet give evidence of knowing the institution. Sixth, it is not clear that the overseers preside over the council of presbyters/elders (1 Tim 4:4) and over the church. There could well be more than one overseer (and the later *1 Clem.* 47.6; 44.4-5; *Did.* 15.1 suggest a plurality of overseers as well). The functions of overseer and presbyter/elder generally overlap in 1 Timothy.

The overseers are, rather, part of the larger group of presbyters/elders and their task is to oversee, that is, to preach, teach, and admonish. The office originated in the Pauline household church structure and the Greco-Roman expectation that the wealthy would benefit others with their wealth. While mentioned at Phil 1:1, the office structures are not yet fixed. Paul singled out leaders, however, for respect and acknowledgment (1 Cor 16:6; 1 Thess 5:12-13; Rom 12:8; and see Acts 14:23). Leadership functions came to be more organized into official structures of bishops and deacons. Throughout the Pauline churches (Rome, *1 Clement* 52; Macedonia, Phil 1:1; Antioch, *Did.* 15.1; Ephesus and Crete, the PE) other functions such as those of prophets (*Didachē* 13; 1 Tim 4:14), presbyters (*1 Clem.* 57.1; Titus 1:5; 1 Tim 4:14), and widows (1 Tim 5:3) coexisted in a still-emerging hierarchy.

a good occupation: The good work is made possible by the salvific death of Christ (Titus 2:14, and see 3:14). Work also applies to Timothy's task as evangelist (2 Tim 4:5, and see 1 Thess 5:12-13 and Eph 4:12).

2. *overseer:* While this official is selected from among the household leaders, his task is not limited to a particular house church but rather has the "church of God" in general as its object. See 3:15 for a parallel use of "church of God" without a definite article for the church of God. There the totality of the Ephesian household churches was to be the object of Timothy's concern (and compare the pottery image at 2 Tim 2:20-21).

Presbyters (1 Tim 5:17, "elders in leadership roles," *proestotes presbyteroi*, a consolidation of a more general leadership role in Pauline churches as at Rom 12:8 and 1 Thess 5:12) seem to have supervised the individual household churches (in every place, 1 Tim 2:8; Priscilla and Aquila, 2 Tim 4:19, and compare Rom 9:3-5; Onesiphorus, 2 Tim 1:16-18 and 4:19).

The singular does not denote a unique, monarchical bishop (see the Introduction, pp. 11–12, 19–20). Rather it is generic, as its use here at the start of an office code suggests. Moreover, although "overseers" ("bishops"), "elders" ("presbyters"), and "assistants" ("deacons") are mentioned in 1 Timothy (Titus 1:5-9 mentions only overseers and elders), it might be unhistorical to think of a three-tiered hierarchy at this stage of the church's development. *Didachē* 15:1 refers to overseers and assistants alongside prophets, apostles, and teachers, without assigning a hierarchical order to them (contrast Ign. *Magn.* 13). The overseer has teaching expertise as one of his qualifications (3:2, and see Titus 1:9), and so the PE might be consolidating in the overseer the functions of the prophet and teacher. This would be an early indication of the consolidation of duties in the overseer (bishop's) office. There is no reference to liturgical oversight in the PE, a prominent feature in Ignatius (e.g., Ign. *Phld.* 4). The author of the PE seems to favor "elders" and might use the term "overseer" as found in the sources used to compile the directives found in these letters. No passage clearly explains the differences among the three ministries. The elders form a sort of *collegium* (1 Tim 4:14; see Titus 1:5, and compare Acts 11:30; 14:23; 15; 20:17; 21:18; 1 Pet 5:1; James 5:14) who impose hands and perform teaching and presiding functions 1 Tim 5:17-19), for which there is a set salary (Brox, *Pastoralbriefe*, 148–50). While the letters foresee some ministerial activity for women (deacons and widows), they present a conservative position on the place of women in the households.

has to be above reproach: The introduction to the list of the overseer's qualifications here and at Titus 1:7 and the first two qualifications, "blameless . . . married only once" (*anepilēmpton . . . mias gynaikos andra*, 1 Tim 3:2, and *anenklētos, mias gynaikos anēr*, Titus 1:6, and see 1:7), as well as a generally comparable, although somewhat rearranged list of other qualifications (1 Tim 3:2-7 and Titus 1:6-9), suggest that the author is using a traditional office code (see Onasander 1,1-4.8, where similar qualifications are listed for a general, i.e., "reserved," *sōphrona*; "self-controlled," *enkratē*; "discreet," *nēptēn*; "simple," *liton*; "hardworking," *diaponon*; "perceptive," *noeron*; "not greedy," *aphilargyron*; "neither young nor old," *mēte neon mēte presbyteron*; "perhaps even a father of children," *an tyche kai patera paidōn*; "a fluent speaker," *ikanon legein*; "of high repute," *endoxon*). The author adds to this material and thereby adjusts it to the particular circumstance. The general expectation of being "above reproach" receives specific contours in the list of vices at v. 3. Xenophon, *Cyropaedia* I 2,15, stresses blamelessness as the requirement to pass from the group of young boys to that of mature men, while Plutarch, *Mor.* 4 B-C, finds that to be a quality required of an effective teacher. It corresponds to v. 7 ("a good reputation," *martyrian kalēn*) and looks outside the community (*apo tōn exothen*). While this has been taken as an indication of the "bourgeois" moral outlook of the PE, it could better be seen in connection with the letters' view of the universality of salvation and their commitment to making an impression on the wider public good enough to win both respect and even conversion (see 1 Tim 5:14, 25; 6:1, 14; 2 Tim 2:15; Titus 2:5, 8, 10, and see also Paul's example of salvation, 1 Tim 1:15-16; the aim of prayer, 2:2; gospel testimony, 2:6; 2 Tim 2:8; the restrictions on women 2:9-15).

married only once: Various interpretations of this qualification have been proposed: (1) a requirement to marry; (2) a prohibition against polygamy; (3) a prohibition against divorce and remarriage; (4) a prohibition against remarriage after the death of a spouse; (5) a requirement of faithfulness in marriage; (6) a prohibition against remarriage. The first focuses on marital status (against 1 Cor 7:32) rather than character. The second lacks evidence of the practice of polygamy in the late first century. Moreover, the requirement of widows at 5:9 to be "married only once" (*henos andros gynē*) could not refer to polyandry, of which there is no evidence in Greco-Roman or Jewish societies. The third coordinates with the Gospel (Mark 10:11-12 and parallels, perhaps John 4:18; 1 Cor 7:11, and see Herm. *Mand.* 4.1.6) but is oddly indirect in not referring directly to divorce. Then too, while it covers the case of widows at 1 Tim 5:9, again it is not clear that divorce and not just remarriage in widowhood is meant (the honorific funerary title *univira* does not distinguish between widows and unmarried divorcees and may even simply designate women who predeceased their husbands). The fourth runs into objections that the PE are imposing an ascetical requirement of celibacy on widows and widowers, contrary to 1 Tim 4:3; it also contradicts the prohibition at 1 Tim 5:14. The fifth, while it also fits the rule for widows, is a less obvious rendering of the Greek, when more direct expressions such as "not an adulterer" were available. The last hews closely to the Greek, as opposed to (3) and (5), avoids the unsubstantiated cultural hypotheses of (1) and (2), and accommodates (4) and the implications of (3). It also expresses the fidelity of (5), but in a way appropriate to the time of the letter, when remarriage for the widowed was not forbidden but remaining unmarried brought honor to the Lord (Herm. *Mand.* 4.4.1-2, and see Athenagoras, *Leg.* 33.4-5 and Tertullian, *To His Wife* 1.7). The requirement here and at 5:14 indicates a degree of equality in the letter's view of the marriage partners. Udo Borse, *1 und 2 Timotheusbriefe*, 41-42, argues that the qualification against remarriage is meant to exclude adult former pagans, who might have been divorced and remarried before converting to Christianity. These would be excluded from positions of spiritual service and entrance into the enrolled widows. While Paul embraced the unmarried state for the sake of Christ, and urges imitation of himself in this regard (1 Cor 7:1, 7-8, 27, 32-35, 37-38, 40), the apostles were married (Matt 8:14; 1 Cor 9:5) and church practice in the earliest period did not adopt Paul's example, as is evidenced in this passage.

clear headed, etc.: A comparison of the list at 1 Tim 3:2-7 with that at Titus 1:6-9 reveals a similar order, with some rearrangement. This suggests the traditional nature of the lists.

1 Timothy 3:2-7	**Titus 1:6-9**
above reproach (*anepilēmptos*, 2)	irreproachable (*anegklētos*, 6,7)
married only once (*mias gynaikos anēr*, 2)	married only once (*mias gynaikos anēr*, 6)
hospitable (*philoxenos*, 2)	hospitable (*philoxenos*, 6)
respectable (*kosmios*, 2)	? loving what is good (*philagathos*, 8)
clear headed (*nēphalios*, 2)	? self-controlled (*enkratēs*, 8)
keeping his children under control (*tekna echōn en hypotagę̄*, 4)	with faithful children (*tekna echōn pista*, 6)
reserved (*sōphrōn*, 2)	reserved (*sōphrōn*, 8)
possessing teaching skills (*didaktikos*, 2)	holding fast to the trustworthy message (*antechomenos tou pistou logou*, 9)

———	just (*dikaios*, 8)
———	devout (*hosios*, 8)
kind (*epieikēs*, 3)	not self-willed (*mē authadēs*, 7)
peaceable (*amachos*, 3)	not irascible (*mē orgilos*, 7)
not a heavy drinker (*mē paroinos*, 3)	not addicted to wine (*mē paroinos*, 7)
not violent (*mē plēktēs*, 3)	not violent (*mē plēktēs*, 7)
not greedy (*aphilargyros*, 3)	not greedy (*mē aischrokerdēs*, 7)
to supervise his own household (*tou idiou oikou proistamenos*, 5)	with faithful children who are not liable to a charge of debauchery nor disobedient (*tekna echōn pista, mē en kategorią asotias ē anypotakta*, 6)
not a new convert (*mē neophytos*, 6)	———

The lists employ terms that echo virtue and vice lists from popular moral philosophers. Kingship treatise authors (e.g., Dio Chrysostom and Plutarch) use them to depict exemplary types to be pursued and avoided (Seneca, *Ep.* 95. 65-67). The virtues and vices are not exclusive to leaders but are attributable to the common public. Thus the church leaders here are expected to exemplify characteristics for the church at large. "Self-controlled" and "respectable" (*sōphrōn and kosmion*), for example, match the requirements of women in the church (1 Tim 2:9), and "nonbelligerent" (*amachon*) mirrors an expectation of the men to be "without anger" (*chōris orgēs*, 1 Tim 2:8), while "not greedy" (*aphilargyron*) and "with . . . probity" (*meta . . . semnotētos*) refer to the community generally (1 Tim 2:2 and 6:7).

hospitable, possessing teaching skills: Since this qualification is in a generic list it is not clear whether teaching is a distinctive responsibility of overseers. The rephrased mention of this task at Titus 1:9 shows the author's hand and thus the specificity of teaching as a task proper to the overseers (see also *Did.* 15:1; Ign. *Phld.* 8:2). The expectation of showing hospitality (see also 5:10 for the same expectation of widows) was a commonplace from the early church (see Rom 12:13; Heb 13:2; 1 Pet 4:9) and onward through the centuries.

4. *his own household:* The church's growth finds verification in the fact that a number of household masters are potential officials and a "recent convert" (v. 6) can be put off for later (contrast Acts 16:15). The household was a social-economic unit composed of the immediate family, slaves, former slaves turned current clients, hired laborers, and sometimes tenants and business associates in a relationship of subordination rather than kinship. The PE accept this institution as their model for the church (1 Tim 3:15; 2 Tim 2:20-26; Titus 1:7) and this ecclesiological image underlies their adoption of household code material. The continuity between household and house church in terms of rules of behavior and interaction among members and techniques of exercising authority by the leaders demonstrates the reality of the interconnection between secular life and the life of faith in the Christian community. Household management ability is valued as an indication of supervisory skill in general. It is not sought as a skill that corresponds

to the specific church function of running a household church, which was the task of the presbyter.

In secular society the household was the image of the state, and public officials first had to be trained and become practiced in household management (Aeschines, *Tim.* 30; Polybius, X 22,5; Philo, *Flight* 38-39; *Spec. Leg.* 1.169-171; Plutarch, *Mor.* 144 B-C; Libanius, *Decl.* 38,43; Cicero, *Att.* X 9,6; Seneca, *De Clementia* I 10).

This exclusion of new converts and its explanation, and the reiteration and explanation of the need for good repute, are all added to the traditional code material and relate it to the situation at Ephesus. The community's reputation needs shoring up in light of the damaging circumstances of wrangling and disruptive apostates and socially unacceptable excesses of women and slaves. Proven skill by mature leaders offers the best promise of success in this effort at damage control.

While authority structures and the path to officeholding in the church have changed significantly over the centuries since the PE were written, the household still provides a standard of suitability. Specifically, the qualities behind the art of being a good parent are still viable today as indicators of responsible ministerial and leadership capabilities. Indeed, the traditional title "father" maintains the ideal. Applicants for ordination and for membership in religious congregations are expected to be persons whose personal qualities would suit them just as well for the role of parents. Like parents, effective church officials look to the well-being of the faithful first and foremost, nurturing growth to maturity in faith and service.

6. *become puffed up:* Peculiar to the PE, the word refers to the false teachers at 1 Tim 6:4 and 2 Tim 3:4. The restriction against converts who might become conceited suggests that false teaching impresses only the inexperienced. This is a subtle refutation of the false teaching.

   the accuser: The women assistants at 1 Tim 3:11 and older women at Titus 2:3 are told not to be slanderers (and see 2 Tim 3:3 for a reference to slanderers at the end-time). The meaning "slanderer" would fit the concern over good reputation and accusations (vv. 2, 6, 7) of the context. Second Timothy 2:26 seems, however, to refer to the devil (an alternate translation of *diabolos*), who lays a snare and works his will (the same image appears at 1 Tim 3:7). Here, too, the condemnation by the accuser of the conceited overseer could take place before God's throne in the final days (*EDNT*). Satan was already mentioned at 1:20, and the eschatological undercurrent runs throughout the letters. Thus while the trap might be accusers in the wider community who catch the Christians in disgraceful behavior, like the false teachers (2 Tim 2:23), these are merely the henchmen of the ultimate accuser, the devil.

7. *good reputation . . . lest he stumble into disgrace:* For a similar concern for reputation see 1 Tim 5:10. The word for reputation here (*martyria*) and its cognates more often refer to testimony: to the Cretans' deception, Titus 1:13; to the charge against presbyters, 1 Tim 5:19; to Timothy's confession of faith, 1 Tim 6:12; to Jesus' witness before Pilate, 1 Tim 6:13; or more generally to the testimony of Jesus' self-sacrifice and redemptive suffering (1 Tim 2:6; 2 Tim 1:8) and Paul's

suffering in accomplishing his work of preaching, 2 Tim 1:8. The witnesses at 2 Tim 2:2 seem to be transmitters of Paul's teaching. Open and public character links both the Gospel proclamation and the virtuous life of its proponents. The inept service of the new convert-overseer would lead to popular contempt and push him into the devil's snare.

Interpretation

The second unit of the body of the letter (3:1-13) proposes another aspect of the expanded station code, that is, qualifications for two offices in the community. Like the behavior expected of women (2:10), the position of overseer is a good work. Men (3:2) who desire and aspire to it (3:1) must possess blameless personal and social qualities. Fidelity (an implication of the restriction to one wife), self-control, and peacefulness (3:2-3, and see Titus 3:2) recall the context where truth can be taught and maintained (2:2-4, 8) and set the authorized overseer teachers against their counterfeits in the community (1:19-20). The emphasis on management skills, reputation, and maturity (3:4-7) reveals a community jealous of its standing in society at large. The repeated "lest he stumble" (*hina mē . . . empesę̄*, 3:6-7) suggests a certain lack of confidence in untested leaders in light of bad past experience, while the household image and commonplace virtues imply a community that has adopted social structures and norms of the larger community. The latter strategy thus sanctions embracing moral, social, economic, and political criteria of society, both to protect the community from attack and to attract outsiders to it (see also 2:8-15).

Throughout both testaments the relationship of God and his people and of Christ and the church has found expression in the image of husband and wife (e.g., Eph 5:23 and the bridegroom parables). Fidelity is one of the principal attributes of God in the Hebrew Bible, and it is reiterated in the New Testament (Ps 25:10 and John 1:17). Adultery and prostitution symbolize infidelity (Hosea, and Rev 2:14, 20). The regulation that officials be married only once might be inspired by the divine virtues. As such, the officeholder's fidelity is not just during life but continues unbroken even after death. The restored diaconate after Vatican II reinstated the expectation that deacons not remarry after the death of a spouse, thus bringing the sign of fidelity into the present.

For Reference and Further Study

Bartlett, David L. *Ministry in the New Testament*. Minneapolis: Fortress Press, 1993, 168–69, 176–78.

Brox, Norbert. *Pastoralbriefe*, 141–46, 154–55, 160–66.

Collins, Raymond F. "Pastoral Ministry: Timothy and Titus," *Church* (Summer 1987) 20–24.

Creehy, J. "The Qumran MEBAQQER and the Christian EPISKOPOS," *PIBA* 2 (1977) 29–36.

Fiore, Benjamin. *Personal Example*, 73–76, 187–88, 196.

Giles, Kevin. *Patterns of Ministry*, 28–88.

Glasscock, Ed. "The 'Husband of One Wife' Requirement in 1 Timothy 3:2," *BSac* 140 (1983) 244–58.

Hanson, Anthony Tyrrell. *Studies in the Pastoral Epistles*. London: SPCK, 1968, 5–28.

Jay, Eric G. "From Presbyters-Bishops to Bishops and Presbyters," *SecCen* 1 (1981) 125–62.

Klauck, Hans-Josef. "Die Hausgemeinde als Lebensform im Urchristentum," *MTZ* 32 (1981) 1–15.

Knight, George W. III. *Faithful Sayings*, 50–61.

Meeks, Wayne A. *The First Urban Christians: The Social World of the Apostle Paul*. New Haven: Yale University Press, 1983, 29–30, 75–77.

Oden, Amy G., ed. *And You Welcomed Me: A Sourcebook on Hospitality in Early Christianity*. Nashville: Abingdon Press, 2003.

Thiering, Barbara E. "*Mebaqqer* and *Episkopos* in the Light of the Temple Scroll," *JBL* 100 (1981) 59–74.

Verner, David C. *Household of God*, 70–72, 103–106, 128–31.

7. *Qualities of Leadership Candidates: Assistants/Deacons* (3:8-13)

> 8. Similarly, assistants have to be honorable, not insincere, not addicted to a lot of wine, not greedy for dishonest money, 9. holding on to the mystery of faith with a clean conscience. 10. In addition, these should be examined first. After that, if they prove to be irreproachable, let them engage in service. 11. Likewise, the women have to be honorable, not slanderous, clear-headed, faithful in every respect. 12. Assistants may be married only once, supervising their children and their own households well. 13. You see, the ones who do the work of assistant well gain for themselves a good standing and wide-ranging confidence in the faith in Christ Jesus.

Notes

8. *assistants:* "Assistants" (*diakonoi*) are a second office for which, again, a traditional list of virtues and vices serves to specify the qualifications. As an indication of the as-yet-unsettled terminology in the PE, the function of assisting or ministering (*diakonia*) is applied to Paul (1 Tim 1:12), Timothy (2 Tim 4:5, and he is called "assistant" at 1 Tim 4:6), Mark, and Paul (2 Tim 4:11), while Onesiphorus ministered (*diakoneō*, 2 Tim 1:18). This follows the usage in the Pauline letters, where Paul refers to his work (Rom 11:13; 2 Cor 4:1) and that of special servants

(1 Cor 16:15) and of all Christians (1 Cor 12:15; Rom 12:7). Paul also uses the term more distinctly (Phil 1:11 and Rom 16:1), as it is used here. First Timothy refers to an official function here, since a test of worthiness precedes admission into the service (v. 10).

The assistant's functions are equally indeterminate. First Peter 4:10-11 sees two functions: service of the word of God and other service. Sincerity ("not slanderers," v. 11) and orthodoxy (vv. 8-9) are unique to the list in 1 Timothy, as well as being faithful (v. 11), if one includes the women's qualifications. Teaching is not explicitly mentioned and is not necessarily implied by the insistence that they hold to the mystery of faith. Thus the office might have developed into a strictly service and caritative function (Acts 6:1-4), with teaching (known to 1 Pet 4:10 and Acts 8) left to the overseers and presbyters.

9. *mystery of faith with a clean conscience:* In non-Christian Greek the word *mystērion* refers to the esoteric rite of the Eleusinian Mysteries and teaching about it (Aristophanes, *Frogs* 479) or to the secret disclosed by God in the Hermetic literature (I.16; II.46). In the LXX usage the mysteries largely concern divine Wisdom (Wis 2:22; 6:22; Job 15:8 Theodotion), a special bequest to those who fear the Lord (Ps 24 (25):14 Theodotion). In the NT the word refers to the secrets of the kingdom (Matt 13:11) and concerns Jewish-Gentile kinship in God's plan (Rom 11:25; 16:25; Col 1:27; 2:2; Eph 3:3). This mystery is both the secret of the Lord and about the Lord, the Gospel long kept secret but now revealed (Eph 3:9; Rom 16:25), especially in Paul's preaching (1 Cor 2:7; Eph 6:19). First Timothy connects the word with the summary of faith, as outlined in credal statements at 1 Tim 3:16. Revelation and preaching are key concepts there. The doctrinal content of faith is stressed here and summarized at v. 13. See the Note on *conscience* at 1 Tim 1:5.

10. *irreproachable:* See the Note on 1 Tim 3:2.

11. *the women:* These women are probably not the assistants'/deacons' wives. There is no possessive pronoun or article, nor are there parallel requirements for the overseers' wives, who would surely be more prominent. It makes little sense to interrupt the flow of thought with a reference to assistants'/deacons' wives (John Chrysostom, *Hom. I Tim.* 11 (NPNF 1 12:441), *pace* Ambrosiaster, *Commentary on the First Letter to Timothy* [CSEL 81 3:268]). Women were given the title "assistant" before at Rom 16:1 (Phoebe, and compare Luke 8:3; 10:40). Since teaching is not one of their tasks and since they are assistants and not directors, the strictures at 2:12 are not contravened. If these were not assistants/deacons like the men, there might have been a class of women assistants in the Pauline churches. In the final analysis, however, the evidence does not definitively support any conclusion about the status of the women.

12. *married only once, supervising their children:* See 1 Tim 3:2. Possibly telling against the possibility of women assistants/deacons is this requirement, since it refers to having only one wife. See the Note on "supervising children" on 1 Tim 3:4. In addition to how they supervise their household itself, the care they take of their children is a particular indication of their ability. In the obedience relationship of the household, children are to be "under control" (*en hypotagę̄*, 1 Tim 3:4; Titus 2:5) along with wives (1 Tim 2:11) and slaves (Titus 2:9). By analogy, all in the household of the church are to obey proper civil authorities (Titus 3:1).

The implication is that the officials are also to be obeyed in the authority structure represented by the church-household.

13. *confidence in the faith:* In secular Greek the word *parrēsia* referred to the "freedom of speech" enjoyed by free citizens in Athens. Later, as a moral concept, this free speech of morally wise persons expressed itself in praise or blame of friends, enemies, and the public at large for their moral improvement. In the LXX the word acquires a new and unique significance, i.e., freedom, confidence, joyous trust (Job 22:26) enjoyed by persons delivered by God from bondage and led by him in freedom with raised heads (Lev 26:13). Here the confidence rests on faith in Christ. Successful service as assistant expresses the faith they have (v. 9). This service and success result in good standing for them, which matches the letter's concern for reputation (3:7, 10). Freedom of expression toward others is one of the consequences of this good standing. At the same time the assistants' standing before the judgment of God is solid and renders them confident. This, in turn, coincides with the eschatological perspective of the letters. While at v. 9 faith refers to the complex of beliefs, here the aspect of relationship with Christ is noted (see 1 Tim 1:14; 2 Tim 1:9). The personal tone is already established by "standing" and "confidence."

Interpretation

The assistants' qualities echo those of the overseers (3:8-13), except for teaching ability (3:2). Once again the opinion of the wider public is considered, while the promise of good standing and the privilege of confident speech (see 1 Tim 5:20) are offered as motivations for good service (3:13).

The qualifications, with their parallels in lists of virtues from contemporary non-Christian philosophers, outline character traits that are not necessarily specific to the particular positions identified. The catalogues of qualifications appear to serve an exemplary function for the letters' audience. The positions themselves are best considered as distinct from the offices of bishop and deacon as these developed in the church hierarchy over time. While competition for those offices has been looked down on from the start, the service functions described here are open to individuals' ambition. This might well reflect the honor/patronage system in society at large and in the Pauline communities.

For Reference and Further Study

Danet, Anne-Laure. "1 Timothée 2:8-15 et le ministère pastoral féminin," *Hokhma* 62 (1990) 335–52.

Gritz, Sharon Hodgin. *Paul, Women Teachers, and the Mother Goddess at Ephesus: A Study of 1 Timothy 2:9-15 in Light of the Religious and Cultural Milieu of the First Century*. Lanham, MD: University Press of America, 1991.

Heine, Susanne. "Diakoninen-Frauen u. Ämter in den ersten Christlichen Jahrhunderten," *IKZ* 78 (1988) 213–27.

Lorenzen, Thorwald. "Die christliche Hauskirche," *TZ* 43 (1987) 333–52.

Malherbe, Abraham J. "'Gentle As a Nurse': The Cynic Background to 1 Thess II," *NovT* 12 (1970) 203–17.

________. "Hellenistic Moralists and the New Testament," in Wolfgang Haase and Hildegard Temporini, eds., *ANRW*. Principat 26/1. Berlin and New York: Walter de Gruyter, 1992, 267–333.

Marrow, Stanley B. "Parrhesia and the NT," *CBQ* 44 (1982) 431–46.

Scholer, David M. "1 Timothy 2.9-15 and the Place of Women in the Church's Ministry," in Amy-Jill Levine with Marianne Blickenstaff, eds., *A Feminist Companion to the Deutero-Pauline Epistles*. Cleveland: Pilgrim Press, 2003, 98–121.

Sigountos, James G., and Myron Shank. "Public Roles for Women in the Pauline Church: A Reappraisal of the Evidence," *JETS* 26 (1983) 283–95.

Torjesen, Karen Jo. *When Women Were Priests: Women's Leadership in the Early Church and the Scandal of Their Subordination in the Rise of Christianity*. San Francisco: HarperSan Francisco, 1993, 53–87, 117–52.

Turner, Nigel. "Mystery, mysteries," *Christian Words*, 281–85.

van Unnik, Willem C. "The Christian's Freedom of Speech in the NT," *BJRL* 44 (1961/2) 466–88.

Witherington, Ben III. *Women in the Earliest Churches*. SNTSMS 59. Cambridge: Cambridge University Press, 1988, 2–23, 42–61, 117–27, 201.

8. *Credal Summary* (3:14-16)

14. These instructions I write to you in the hope of coming to see you soon. 15. Now if I should delay, they are written for you to know how one must behave in the household of God, which surely is the church of the living God, pillar and foundation of the truth.

16. Yes, demonstrably great is the mystery of piety:
he, who was revealed in flesh,
was vindicated in spirit,
became visible to angels,
was preached among nations,
was believed in on earth,
was taken up in glory.

Notes

14. *These instructions:* The demonstrative pronoun refers to the instructions already given and corresponds with similar summations that punctuate the directives in the rest of the letter (4:6, 11, 15; 6:2). In fact, the promised visit and anticipated delay at 3:14-15 are echoed at 4:13. This makes a unit of the two chapters and places it within the extended station code material.

hope of coming: Often at the close of the body of the Pauline letters, although that is not the case here, is the so-called "apostolic *parousia*" by which Paul announces his intention to visit the addressee. This increases the authority of the letter by signaling that Paul would be on the scene to see how his instructions have been received. It is another aspect of the apostolic presence that the letter itself and the apostle's emissary (in this case Timothy) represent. The intention to visit is reiterated at 4:13, where attention falls on the example of Timothy's progress (4:12, 15) and its salvific effects (4:16).

15. *if I should delay:* The rhetorical nature of the promised visit in the near future ("soon," *en tachei*) is indicated by the retraction of the promise indicated in the "possible" delay. The delay is reinforced at 4:13. This does not anticipate a speedy visit, but one that allows time for Timothy to accomplish his tasks.

how one must behave in the household of God: The stress on behavior here in the codes for men and women and in the qualification lists (with the exception of 2:4 and 3:9) is striking. Orthopraxis takes precedence over orthodoxy as the objective of Timothy's efforts and is the underlying thrust of the credal section in 4:16. Calling this the mystery of "piety" (*eusebeias*), stresses that it is the way of living out one's Christian faith (see 2:2). See the Note on household at 3:4.

church of the living God, pillar and foundation: Used only three times in the PE (1 Tim 3:5, 15; 5:16), the word *ekklēsia* ("church") refers not to the household church communities but to all the believers in Ephesus. The architectural image, pillar and foundation, relates to the church as household. Unlike Eph 2:19-22, the image here is static. While James, Cephas, and John were the reputed pillars of the church in Jerusalem (Gal 2:9, and see *1 Clem.* 5.2), that function is universalized here in typically Pauline fashion. The generic use of "column" is attested at Sir 24:4; 36:24. It, together with foundation (related to *hedraios*, firm or steadfast), offers an image of static solidity that contrasts with the wanderings of the apostate teachers (1 Tim 1:6). Truth, or the Pauline doctrine, is the matter at stake here, and the PE claim to keep to it unswervingly (see 1 Tim 2:4, 7; 4:3; 2 Tim 2:15, 25; Titus 1:1, and contrast 1 Tim 6:5; 2 Tim 2:18; 3:7, 8; 4:4; Titus 1:14). See Plutarch, *Mor.* 1 85F 1,457.

16. *demonstrably great is the mystery of piety:* "Without a doubt," "uncontestably" (*EDNT*) or "demonstrably" (Hanson) is the meaning of *homologoumenōs* in *4 Macc.* 6:31; 7:16; 16:1 (see also Philo, *Worse* 18; *Unchangeable* 71). *Fourth Maccabees* uses the word to introduce the moral drawn from the courageous behavior of the martyrs. The author of the PE, who shares other language with *4 Maccabees*, might have adopted this "academic" term here, and it reflects the author's acquaintance with Jewish apocryphal works as well as a "philosophical" bent. It fits the assuredness of the author in expressing both the content of faith and the way of life in consequence of it. The immediate context offers the bedrock of the church and the virtues of faithful men and women as well as the officials, overseers, and deacons to support the claims of proper behavior in God's household.

The word *eusebeia* ("piety") appears not at all in the letters of undisputed Pauline authorship, but only in the Pastorals (1 Tim 2:2; 3:16; 4:7, 8; 6:3, 5, 6; 2 Tim 3:5; Titus 1:1, and see 1 Tim 5:4; 2 Tim 3:12; Titus 2:12), 2 Peter (1:3, 6; 3:11, and see 2:9) and Acts 3:12 (and see 17:23). In the Septuagint, where the word appears fifty-nine times, it is found largely in *4 Maccabees* (47x). Unlike "faith" (*pistis*), "hope" (*elpis*), and "love" (*agapē*), which are not Greek virtues, piety is a virtue in *4 Maccabees* and here. By creating a parallel with "the mystery of faith" at 3:9 the author might well be referring to doctrine and praxis as two fundamentals of Christian existence.

The christological statement, apparently a hymn fragment, relates to the preceding practical instructions as the kerygmatic message, proclaimed and believed, which calls for appropriate behavior in response. Likewise it establishes the goal calling for a halt to behavior that thwarts the progress of the message and of salvation. The hymn details the mystery of piety. It can be broken up into three couplets, the strophes in each in antithetical parallelism, following the conventions of Hebrew poetry.

The first line alludes to Christ's preexistence, incarnation, and human existence. Romans 1:3-4 has a similar flesh/spirit antithesis. "Flesh" (*sarx*) refers to the humanity of Jesus (e.g., John 1:14; Rom 8:3; Col 1:22; 1 Pet 3:18). The incarnation is referred to at 1 Tim 1:15. "Reveal" (*phaneroō*) is a quasi-technical term here referring to Jesus' human history (John 1:31; Heb 9:26; 1 Pet 1:20; 1 John 1:2; 3:5, 8, and compare 2 Tim 1:10; Titus 1:3). While the death of Christ is the central moment of his human existence, a comparison with the more explicit 1 Pet 3:18 suggests a general meaning here. The contrast in lines 1 and 6 between entrance into and departure from the human sphere also confirms this.

"Vindicated" in spirit is preferred on the basis of LXX, NT, and other parallels (e.g., Rom 3:4; Ps 51:6; *Pss. Sol.* 2:16; 3:5; 4:9; 8:7). "In spirit" suggests a contrast between the natural (in the flesh) and supernatural spheres of existence. The first is characterized by limited humanity, the second by the Holy Spirit as its operative agent. The vindication was at the resurrection, thus implying the death of Christ as the dividing point of Jesus' earthly career.

Line 3 continues the thought in v. 2, where angels are witnesses of the resurrected Jesus (Luke 24:23; Matt 28:2; John 20:12). Although the appearance here may have been thought to be different from the resurrection itself, *ōphthē* could mean "show oneself to" in LXX theophanies and angelophanies (and see Acts 7:26; Luke 22:43; Mark 9:4; 1 Cor 15:6; *EDNT*), a power now exercised by the risen Lord. The manifestation could be parallel to that at Phil 2:9-11; Col 2:15; Eph 1:21; Heb 1:3-4; 1 Pet 3:22; Rev 5:8-14.

The appearance and announcement of the risen Jesus to the heavenly realm finds an antithetical parallel in line 4. The preaching among the nations recalls Paul's self-description as herald (1 Tim 2:7, and see 2 Tim 1:11; compare Luke 24:47; Rom 15:19; 16:25-26; Gal 1:16) and refers to the Jesus (he who) of vv. 1 and 2, incarnate, crucified, and risen.

Line 5 continues (with a synthetic parallelism as between vv. 2 and 3) the idea of v. 4 and completes it. Belief brings eternal life (1 Tim 1:16), and this is accomplished in the world, the universal arena of Jesus' salvific efforts (1 Tim 1:15). The humanity of Jesus thus underlines the historical reality of Christ's saving work (and see 1 Tim 2:5-6). Line 6, by contrast, refers to Jesus in the glorified state of his resurrection/ascension. Just as he is received in faith by believers in the world, so he is taken into the heavenly realm (Phil 2:9-11; Acts 1:2, 9-11).

The song has Jesus end where he started, and the ascension completes the process begun in the incarnation.

The function of the hymn is to provide a model for believers and at the same time to counteract the adversaries who are lost in arguments and speculations (1 Tim 1:6; 4:7; 6:4-5; 2 Tim 2:14; 4:4; Titus 1:10; 3:9). Thus the earthly ministry of Jesus receives attention from the first line (compare Titus 2:11; 3:4-5), as does the quality of his life under the action of the Holy Spirit in the next line (with the Spirit in the dative in an instrumental sense, and see references to the Spirit's action at 1 Tim 4:1; 2 Tim 1:14). Thus the audience sees the human response to the Spirit to which all creatures are called. Timothy above all is to learn appropriate conduct (1 Tim 3:12), which finds a model here, and to model it for others (1 Tim 4:12). Moreover, the "mystery of piety" is not a vague notion but finds embodiment in a historical person and with a practical attitude shown in deed as well as in word (see 2 Tim 2:15; 4:5; Titus 3:8).

Despite the allusion to Jesus' preexistence here (and even more clearly in 2 Tim 1:9-10), the emphasis rests on Jesus' first (earthly) and second (eschatological) appearances, both here and in the letters generally. At the same time the PE contain pre-Pauline christological formulas (compare Acts 2:22, 32-33, 36; 10:38; 13:23, 33) when they speak, for example, of Jesus' human, Davidic lineage (2 Tim 2:8, and compare Rom 1:3-4) and earthly ministry (1 Tim 2:5; 3:16; 6:13; 2 Tim 1:10), his being raised (2 Tim 2:8), and his return (1 Tim 6:14-16; 2 Tim 1:12; 4:1, 8; Titus 2:13).

Interpretation

Paul interrupts the station code prescriptions with an expression of hope to visit soon. The foreseen "apostolic *parousia*," a standard feature in Pauline letters, contributes to the function of the pseudepigraphical letter in the Pauline community after his death. The readers have Paul's instructions to guide them in his absence. Despite the standard caution about possible delays (3:15 and 4:13), the trope furthers the friendly character of the letter and heightens the apostolic authority of the prescriptions. The rhetorical nature of the announcement of a visit can be seen from the Pauline letter form, from the promise itself, which is unexpected in view of Paul's apparently recent departure from Ephesus (1:3), from the fact that Timothy is already the surrogate presence of Paul in his task of wrapping up the work to be done, and from the intimations of delay in returning. The section forms a loose *inclusio*, with the announced visit (3:14) reiterated at 4:13. General exhortation and credal statements (3:15-16, the christological hymn) lead to a description of the activity and teaching of "latter day" false teachers (4:1-5). This negative picture serves as the shadow against which direct advice to Timothy is set (4:6-16).

Paul expresses the hortatory purpose of the letter at 3:15, to convey rules for behavior in the church. Here the PE propose a clear understanding of what the church is: the household of God (for the same image see 1 Pet 2:5; 4:17; Heb 3:6; Eph 2:20-22; and compare 1 Cor 3:16; 2 Cor 6:16). It is not the community that makes the church what it is, but rather the regulations and church order (1 Tim 3:1-13; 5:1-6; Titus 2:1-10). Adherents of the sound teaching dwell in it, while those pursuing heretical views are excluded (2 Tim 2:20-26; Brox, *Pastoralbriefe*, 157–59). The basis for the ethical and doctrinal imperative is that it is the church of God and solid foundation and guardian of the truth (3:15). The image is static and unmoving, but the house includes a variety of inhabitants (2 Tim 2:20-21). The church officials, in an unbroken succession (2 Tim 2:2), exercise authority that is apostolically authenticated (i.e., by Paul) to preserve the church's order and true teaching.

That truth is expressed solemnly in a christological summary (3:16). Whether a quotation from a liturgical hymn or a kerygmatic tradition, the faith declaration employs alternating references to Christ's connections with earth and heaven in his redemptive work. Universal preaching and belief (3:16, strophes 4 and 5) refer to the summary of church conduct noted at 3:15 and expanded at 4:1-16. For the author of the PE the way of life that properly expresses one's faith is as important as the content of faith and the believers' claims to adhere to them and to Christ. All of this constitutes "piety" (*eusebeia*). The structures of one's ordinary life provide the context for and are in continuity with the faith life of the Christian. This is true of both the leaders and the church members generally. Thus the virtues in the list of qualifications for leadership are both secular values and applicable across the community.

For Reference and Further Study

Deichgräber, Reinhard. *Gotteshymnus und Christushymnus in der frühen Christenheit: Untersuchungen zu Form, Sprache und Stil der frühchristlichen Hymnen*. Göttingen: Vandenhoeck & Ruprecht, 1967.

Fowl, Stephen E. *The Story of Christ in the Ethics of Paul: An Analysis of the Function of the Hymnic Material in the Pauline Corpus*. JSNTSup 36. Sheffield: Sheffield Academic Press, 1990, 155–94.

Funk, Robert W. "The Apostolic Parousia: Form and Significance," in William R. Farmer et al., eds., *Christian History and Interpretation. Studies presented to John Knox*. Cambridge: Cambridge University Press, 1967, 249–68.

Gundry, Robert H. "The Form, Meaning and Background of the Hymn Quoted in 1 Timothy 3:16," in W. Ward Gasque and Ralph P. Martin, eds., *Apostolic History and the Gospel: Biblical and Historical Essays Presented to F. F. Bruce on His 60th Birthday*. Grand Rapids: Eerdmans, 1970, 203–22.

Hasler, Victor. "Epiphanie und Christologie in den Pastoralbriefen," *TZ* 33 (1977) 193–209.

Lampe, G.W.H. "The Evidence in the New Testament for Early Creeds, Catechisms and Liturgy," *ExpTim* 71 (1960) 359–63.

MacDonald, Margaret Y. *The Pauline Churches: A Socio-Historical Study of Institutionalization in the Pauline and Deutero-Pauline Writings*. Cambridge: Cambridge University Press, 1988, 167–68, 231–32.

Metzger, Wolfgang. *Der Christushymnus 1 Timotheus 3:16. Fragment einer Homologie der paulinischen Gemeinde*. Arbeiten zur Theologie 62. Stuttgart: Calwer, 1979.

Murphy-O'Connor, Jerome. "Redactional Angels in 1 Tim 3:16," *RB* 91 (1984) 178–87.

Schwarz, Roland. *Bürgerliches Christentum im Neuen Testament?: Eine Studie zur Ethik, Amt und Recht in den Pastoralbriefen*. Klosterneuburg: Österreichisches Katholisches Bibelwerk, 1983.

Schweizer, Eduard. *Church Order and Development in the New Testament*.Trans. Frank Clarke. Studies in Biblical Theology 32. London: SCM, 1961.

Towner, Philip H. *Goal of Our Instruction*, 87–93, 233–37.

Watson, Nigel M. "Some Observations on the Use of *dikaioō* in the Septuagint," *JBL* 79 (1960) 264–65.

White, John L. "Apostolic Letter Tradition," 440.

Williams, David J. *Paul's Metaphors: Their Context and Character*. Peabody, MA: Hendrickson, 1999.

9. *False Teaching; Asceticism; Exhortation to Timothy* (4:1-16)

1. Now the Spirit expressly says that in the latter days some will turn away from the faith while they pay attention to deceitful spirits and demonic teachings; they act 2. in the godlessness of liars, with their own consciences seared; 3. and prohibit marriage or order abstention from certain foods which God created for people who are faithful and know the truth to be received by them with thanksgiving. 4. The reason is that every one of God's creatures is good and nothing is to be rejected when received with thanksgiving, 5. for it is rendered holy through calling on God in a prayerful appeal. 6. If you lay these instructions out for the brothers and sisters, you will be a fine assistant of Christ Jesus, nourished on the words of the faith and of the fine teaching, which you have followed. 7. Only avoid the profane old wives' tales. Thus, train yourself for a pious life. 8. Clearly, "physical training is useful for a few things, while piety is useful for everything, since it carries a promise of life, that is, the present life and the life to come." 9. This saying is trustworthy and deserving of full acceptance.

10. It is for this, you see, that we toil and strain, since we have placed our hope in the living God, who is savior of all people, especially the faithful. 11. Instruct and teach these things. 12. May no one look down on you because of your youth, but become an example for the faithful in word, in conduct, in love, in faith, in purity. 13. Until I arrive, apply yourself to the

public reading, exhortation, and teaching. 14. Do not neglect the gift in you, which was given to you at the pronouncement of a prophetic word along with the laying on of hands by the assembly of elders. 15. Take care of these things, devote yourself to them, so that your progress might be visible to everyone. 16. Attend to yourself and to your teaching; be persistent in them, for by doing this you will save both yourself and those who listen to you.

Notes

1. *the Spirit expressly says:* This is the Holy Spirit (compare 1 Tim 4:14; 2 Tim 1:6) despite the absence of the adjective here (but see the adjective "holy" at 2 Tim 1:14; Titus 3:5). At times "spirit" (*pneuma*) is used in a general way for the supernatural realm (1 Tim 3:16), the human spirit (2 Tim 4:22), or deceiving spirits (1 Tim 4:1). The Holy Spirit, without the adjective, is also referred to at 2 Tim 1:7 (where it is identical with Holy Spirit at 2 Tim 1:14). The revelatory activity of the Holy Spirit here is consistent with the traditional activity of the Holy Spirit (Acts 20:23; 21:11), and the PE speak of the experience of prophetic activity elsewhere (1 Tim 1:18; 4:14, and compare Titus 1:12). The expectation of end-time apostasy, noted also at 1 Tim 1:10; 2 Tim 3:1; 4:3, coincides with the end-time expectation elsewhere (2 Thess 2:3; 2 Pet 3:3; Jude 18; Mark 13:22; Rev 2:7, and compare Dan 11:36). For the expression "expressly" in connection with prophetic utterances see also Justin, *1 Apol.* 1.63.10; 1.35.10. In *Dial.* 1.7 (JMD 21) Justin argues that the prophets of the Christian Bible are more true than those of the pagans since, among other reasons, they are more ancient (see also Origen, *Cels.*).

   in the latter days: The "latter" or last times (2 Tim 3:1), foretold in prophecy, are referred to the church at Ephesus' current experience of apostasy. This eschatological reading of the present was also made by the Thessalonians (1 Thess 5:1; 2 Thess 2:2) and by Paul as he interpreted his "suffering" (*thlipsis*, Rom 8:18-25; Phil 1:17, 21-23) and God's plan (Rom 13:11-14). This strengthens the polemic against the false teachers, since they are seen to be in league with the opponents of God (thus "demonic teachings" here, and see "accuser" at 1 Tim 3:6, 7; 2 Tim 2:26; *Satanas* at 1 Tim 1:20; 5:15, and see also Rev 12:17; 2 Thess 2:3-4; Mark 13:8). The truth of the tradition is also confirmed by the fact that a situation prophesied has come to be.

   The false teaching might well be occasioned by an over-realized eschatology (see 2 Tim 2:18), which confused physical resurrection with the spiritual resurrection at baptism (cf. Rom 6:1-10). The ascetical teachings aim to promote the conditions of the resurrection life. In reaction to this, 1 Timothy 4:8 stresses what is yet to come and worthy of all expectation. Nonetheless, the letters suggest a turning point has been reached in the present age (1 Tim 1:9-10; Titus 1:2-3, and cf. Rom 16:25; 1 Cor 2:6; Eph 3:4-11; Col 1:26) with the Christ event (1 Tim 3:16; 2 Tim 1:10; Titus 1:3). This transformation of the present age results in "the last days" (1 Tim 4:1; 2 Tim 3:1), the time of the church, before the final consummation, and requires new modes of behavior. Thus there is a shift in the commands at v. 6 from the future to the present (cf. 2 Tim 3:1, 5).

The church is between two epiphanies of Jesus—living in a christocentric interim. The grace of God has appeared (Titus 2:11; 3:4) as a saving and helping event. A new mode of existence is now made possible and required. The *parousia* and coming judgment (near at hand: 2 Tim 4:1) will require all to render accountability for their actions in all spheres of their activity. Used with *hysterois* ("latter"), the term *kairois* ("times" or "days") refers to Jesus' *parousia* (1 Tim 6:15), to Jesus' saving death (1 Tim 2:6), and to the apostle's preaching of salvation for eternal life (Titus 1:2-3), all at foreordained times in the divine plan (and see 1 Cor 15:20, 23; Rom 8:23). The latter times here are called troublesome and final at 2 Tim 3:1 (and compare the singular at 2 Tim 4:3) and refer to end-time apostasy. The singular at 2 Tim 4:6 refers to Paul's impending death, again as foreordained by God (*EDNT*). The comparative here could be in place of a superlative (Zerwick, 631), which matches 2 Tim 3:1.

from the faith . . . to deceitful spirits and demonic teachings: The doctrinal side of the word *pistis* ("faith") is suggested in the contrast with "teachings" (*didaskaliais*). The danger of deceptive teachings (an eschatological threat), from which some have been rescued (Titus 3:3), persists (2 Tim 3:13) and provoked the strictures against women (1 Tim 2:14 and see 2 Tim 3:6). The deceiver is the Antichrist in 2 John 7 (see Matt 24:4-5, 11), and the eschatological weight of deception is expressed by Paul (1 Cor 6:9; Gal 6:7).

2. *godlessness of liars, with their own consciences seared:* The aim of the instruction in the letter is to counter godlessness and defective conscience (1 Tim 1:5). Paul's honesty (1 Tim 2:7) contrasts him with the liars. While cautery is an image for the extreme and harsh criticism by Cynics who aim at rooting out advanced moral disease (*Ep. of Diogenes* 29.5), here the image of being "seared" is more akin to that of Lucian in *Downward* 24. There, searing scars are caused by ignorance and vice and must be removed by the philosophic life before Cynics can begin their work to correct others (see also Tacitus, *Annales* VI 6, 1-2).

3. *prohibit marriage:* The restrictions on marriage and food indicate an ascetical movement, perhaps based on the over-realized eschatology in the belief that "the resurrection has already occurred" (2 Tim 2:8). Similar ascetical tendencies surface elsewhere in the NT; e.g., restricting marriage at 1 Cor 7:36-38 (where anti-marriage extremes are rejected at 1 Cor 7:28, 36), and food regulation and over-spiritualized religiosity at Col 2:20-21 (rejected at Col 2:16-19). The PE already established themselves in support of marriage at 1 Tim 2:15 (and see 1 Tim 5:14) and the ignorant teachers of the Law (1 Tim 1:7) might be in view here in connection with the food regulations. In any case, eccentric practices such as these would not suit the letters' agenda of presenting a familiar face to onlookers outside the church. Jesse Sell finds in second-century Gnostic works the literary end point of the gnosticizing thought patterns contested here and elsewhere in the PE. The later works' extreme antisexual and food asceticism echoes the PE's opponents' forbidding of marriage and restricting foods (and see 1 Tim 5:14, 23 and Titus 1:15). The Gnostic restriction of salvation to the most adept finds a refutation at 1 Tim 2:3-4, 6; 4:10; Titus 2:11, where the savior is said to desire the salvation of all people. The mode of salvation by the ransoming death of the historical Jesus (1 Tim 2:5-6; 6:13; 2 Tim 2:11; Titus 2:14) contests salvation by esoteric knowledge. The esoteric teachings of full-blown Gnosti-

cism of the later works seem to have their beginnings in the speculations and vain discussions warned about at 1 Tim 1:4-7; 2 Tim 4:3-4; Titus 3:9. Sell contends that the anti-Jewish orientation of this polemic at 1 Tim 1:6b-7; Titus 1:10, 14; 3:9 represents only one-third of the polemical passages noted here. Moreover, the extreme asceticism and restriction of salvation are not characterized as Jewish. Sell concludes that the Pastorals are concerned with a variety of opponents. The abstinence from marriage might stem from a tactic among women in the community to escape the patriarchal household structure with its expectation of a wife's submission to her husband. The later apocryphal Acts suggest this practice among independent ascetic women (but see 1 Corinthians 7).

God created: The appeal to God's creation and its goodness (v. 4) recalls Genesis 1–2, where food was created and marriage was instituted (see Gen 1:31; Rom 14:14; 1 Cor 10:25-26; Wis 1:14). The appeal to the created order recalls the argument on women's silence and submission (1 Tim 2:13-14) and also the plan of God as an alternative to speculations (1 Tim 1:4). Similar speculations and pretense of wisdom (Col 2:4, 23) were behind the asceticism in Colossae.

know the truth: See the note on 1 Tim 2:4.

thanksgiving: The term "thanksgiving" (*eucharistia*) later takes on the meaning of the Lord's Supper (*Did.* 9.1-5; Ign. *Eph.* 13.1; *Smyrn.* 8:1; *Phld.* 4; Justin, *1 Apol.* 1.65). Here it refers to a table blessing. Perhaps *Didachē* 10 contains the gist of such a prayer, which is subsequently taken over and expanded into a prayer for the Lord's Supper (i.e., "Thou, Lord almighty, didst create all things for thy name's sake, and didst give food and drink to all for their enjoyment, that they might give thanks to thee"). A. T. Hanson prefers to see a direct reference to the Eucharist from a source that the *Didachē* also uses.

4. *good:* The positive evaluation of the created world and of the creator God marks the author's theological optimism, as opposed to the pessimistic dualism of his ascetical opponents. The world around us and we ourselves are good inasmuch as we are creatures God has made. Jesus reaffirmed this goodness by his appearance in human form and the witness of his life and death as a fact of human history and not just a spiritual event. The faith of Christians finds expression in the concrete circumstances of daily life. Thus everyday activities such as eating open onto a spiritual horizon that recognizes their divine origin. The intimate relations of married life participate in this same reality. Marriage, which receives tentative approval by Paul in 1 Corinthians 7, gets wholehearted endorsement here.

5. *calling on God in prayerful appeal:* The phrase refers not to the word of God in creation but to table prayers that use biblical expressions. The author is assertive and confident about the power of prayer (compare the more tentative Rom 8:22 and 26 and the more indirect sanctification process at 1 Cor 7:14). This recalls 1 Tim 2:1, where all are enjoined to pray, give thanks, and make intercession. There people were in mind, here other created reality, but the common belief is that prayer has a sanctifying effect on them all.

6. *these instructions:* While the word could refer to the instruction about the end-time (actually current) promotion of asceticism by false teachers, it seems more likely that it is coordinated with *tauta* ("these things") at 3:14 to refer to the content

of the letter in general. It is this that Timothy is to promulgate in Ephesus in fulfilling the task entrusted to him by Paul (1:3). The second half of the verse explains why Timothy is qualified for the task. He has been reared (see 2 Tim 1:5) on the teaching and has followed it himself (see 2 Tim 3:10).

brothers and sisters: David Horrell describes the shift in the Deutero-Pauline letters (letters whose Pauline authorship is in question) away from kinship language to more hierarchical relationships in God's household (see 1 Tim 3:15; 2 Tim 2:20, and note that running a household is one of the officials' qualifications at 1 Tim 3:4, 5, 12; Titus 1:11, and compare Titus 1:7; 2 Tim 1:16; 4:19). The PE thus employ the language of brother/sister for members of the community in only three places, far less often than Paul does in the undisputed letters (see 1 Tim 4:6; [5:1]; 6:2; 2 Tim 4:21, and not in Titus at all).

assistant: Since Timothy is involved in teaching, he is not an assistant like those above whose qualifications do not include teaching ability (3:8-13). See 2 Tim 4:5, where Timothy's service is linked with his being an evangelist, and compare Paul, who is given the "service" (*diakonia*) of the Gospel at 1 Tim 1:12; also see 2 Tim 4:11 for Mark. The Cynic was considered a *diakonos*, "servant" of Zeus (Epictetus, *Diatr*. 3.22.69) and his *hypēretēs* ("assistant," Epictetus, *Ench*. 3.22.82, 95). Here Timothy's good service comes to the fore in his contesting false asceticism and food prohibitions.

7. *old wives' tales:* The myths are identified as Jewish and are associated with the Law at Titus 1:14 (and see 1 Tim 1:7), but they are unspecified here and at 2 Tim 4:4. The stress on the historicity of Jesus' incarnation and saving death provides the letter's alternative to myths (see 1 Tim 1:15; 2:5-6; 3:16; 6:13; 2 Tim 1:8, 10; 2:8, 11; Titus 3:4-7, and see 2 Pet 1:16). In another explanation these unspecified myths might have been spread by women, such as the idle widow gossips of 1 Tim 5:13 who speak of unmentionable things. They might have been legends of Paul and his women followers as found in the *Acts of Paul and Thecla*, which champion asceticism and celibacy (see 2:15). The myths are most likely not those of the Gnostics that are attested in the second century and later, although there might have been a Jewish proto-Gnostic movement that disturbed the Pauline church at Ephesus.

train yourself for a pious life: Athletic imagery reappears at 2 Tim 2:5 and 4:7-8. The first refers to Timothy and the second to Paul. At 2 Tim 4:7-8 the image characterizes Paul's life of faith and action in his ministry of spreading sound doctrine as a model for everyone. Dedication to the service of the Gospel by Timothy and other faithful persons is the point of the image at 2:5. This echoes 1 Cor 9:24-27 and the Cynics' understanding of the philosopher's life as a contest in the stadium of life against pleasure and passionate desires such as those advanced, for example, by the Epicureans (see Dio Chrysostom, *Alex*. [Or. 32] 20-24, and compare Isocrates, *Nicocles* 11, 14, 35 and *Demonicus* 21. See also Gal 2:2; 5:7; Phil 2:1; 3:12-14). This is a struggle for virtue in the philosophers themselves as well as in people generally. First Timothy 5:7–6:1 uses the athletic image and the explicit application to the idea of putting the Spirit-given virtues into practice and keeping away from desires of the flesh. The PE carry forward the conviction that a life of godliness is not automatic or passive. In fact, the striving implies work, struggle, and even suffering (2 Tim 2:9-12; 3:10-12, and see Col 1:29) in imitation of Paul. Thus Timothy is to engage the community in this effort (4:6, 11, 16; see 2:2 for pious life). Echoing the sentiment expressed here, Philo, *Worse* 72-73, critiquing Sophistic insincerity, notes that piety (*eusebeia*) is of greatest use (*ōphelimōtaton*), and together with other virtues is both healing (*hygieinōtaton*) and salvific (*sōtērion*). These outcomes of a virtuous life are also referred to at 4:16 (and see Isocrates, *De pace* 33).

8. *physical training:* Timothy, who is to train for piety, is contrasted to those who follow false teachings and myths. These are also proponents of asceticism (4:1-3). So the call that Timothy train for piety and the contrast with the limited usefulness of physical exercise is sarcastic, in that it removes any spiritual value from asceticism and reduces it to just another physical exercise. Similarly, Epictetus, *Diatr.* 3.12.1, 3, 16, warns away from strenuous actions that do not lead to "training" (*askēsis*) that has philosophy as its aim (and see Diogenes Laertius, 6.70 where the Cynic Diogenes of Sinope recognizes a two-dimensional *askēsis*, physical and spiritual, that leads to virtuous activity). Plutarch, *Mor.* 793F distinguishes athletic exertions for worthless goals from those in public life whose efforts aim at ends that are worth the effort expended. The advantage of piety in the PE's sense has an eschatological as well as a present dimension. The present dimension is tied to the letters' soteriology, in that piety brings life in Christ Jesus (2 Tim 1:1), who abolished death and brought life and immortality to light (2 Tim 1:10). The exercise image connects with eternal life at 1 Tim 6:12, as does the word *mellō* ("to come") at 1 Tim 6:19 (and compare 1 Tim 1:16; 2 Tim 1:1, 10; Titus 1:1-2; 3:7). Titus 1:1-2 speaks of the promise of eternal life and links it with the recognition of piety. These references carry forward the letters' eschatological focus, and the two aspects of life now and to come are echoes of Luke 18:29-30 and parallels.

9. *The saying is trustworthy:* The faithful saying is that in v. 8. It is pithy and in stereotypical form, like a proverb. It has unusual words for the NT, such as the *hapax* "exercise" (*gymnasia*) and the non-Pauline "physical" (*sōmatikē*). The saying flows from the preceding remarks (*gar*) and is a comment on the command to Timothy at v. 7b. In structure it reveals antithetical parallelism in words and concepts; physical training versus piety, "for a few things" versus "for everything," "usefulness" in both members. The original saying most likely arose in a contrast between widely popular physical exercise and athletic prowess and Greek moral philosophy (Spicq, *Les Épîtres Pastorales*, Excursus VII). This was then taken over by the Christians to show the enduring worth of Christian belief and practice as opposed to the fading crown of athletic victory (see Paul's contrast of the athlete's perishable crown with the Christians' imperishable one at 1 Cor 9:24, and compare 2 Tim 4:7-8). First Timothy uses this saying to expand the call to Timothy to develop his life of piety and suggests even more. In an oblique reference to the apostates' ascetical practices on the basis of their deceptive teaching, he reduces their practice of the faith to asceticism and then goes on to interpret it as a purely physical exercise like any other. As such, despite its claims, asceticism offers only temporary and limited ("for little," *pros oligon*) payoffs.

The practice of asceticism has reached unprecedented heights in our day. With widespread obesity in the United States roundly condemned as a medical and social problem and a contributor to chronic diseases, food is often seen as an enemy and eating as something to be carefully controlled. Gyms proliferate and exercise equipment fills our homes as people strain to offset advancing age. Paradoxically, the practice of Christianity has plummeted to historically low levels in traditionally Christian Europe and the developed West. Nor has the practice of Christianity in formerly atheistic countries rebounded dramatically. As a consequence, a self-centered individualism has begun to take hold, and this leads people away from choosing and acting in favor of the common good. This situation of contemporary Christianity demonstrates the abiding applicability of this message in 1 Timothy and the need for a reassessment of the value of the world's goods and the faithful person's use of them.

10. *for this . . . we toil and strain:* "This" looks back to the content of v. 8. The language of exercise in the saying carries over in the explanation, in the words "toil" (*kopiōmen*) and "strain" (*agonizometha*), with the words describing spiritual and not physical exertion in light of the hope in God.

we have placed our hope in the living God, who is savior of all people: The perfect tense expresses an abiding attitude of hope. Hope at Titus 1:2 and 3:7 is for eternal life and for the appearance of God's glory (Titus 2:13), the time of transition from this age to the age to come. The adjective "living" for God declares God to be the master of life, and the relative clause clarifies God's identity as savior of all. The salvation process begun by God will end in eternal life (Titus 3:4-7). The idea of hope helps maintain the letters' end-time perspective. The belief in universal salvation is reiterated here, perhaps prompted by the reference to the deceptive and demonic teaching of the apostates. The salvation of the faithful stands as a source of hope for the Ephesian community and a threat to the apostates.

11. *instruct and teach these things:* This reiterates the orders referred to at 1 Tim 1:3, and the content of the teaching refers to all the specifics in the letter (see 1 Tim 4:6, 15, and 3:14). This protracted apostolic *parousia* section directly commands Timothy three times to attend to these teachings. While the teachings are general here, a specific focus falls on Timothy as "assistant." Thus his being rooted in the tradition (4:6), his training in piety (4:7), his Christian life and fidelity to duty (4:12-13), and the example of his progress in all these (4:15) are laid out.

12. *look down on you because of your youth:* Timothy can avoid scorn for his youth only by not giving occasion for such scorn. Thus he is to demonstrate personal excellence and be exemplary in his ministry (4:12-16). He is also expected to avoid youthful passions (2 Tim 2:22), unsubstantiated accusations against elders (1 Tim 5:19), prejudice (1 Tim 5:21), and imprudent selection of leaders (1 Tim 5:22). This advice to a young leader parallels that found in Isocrates, *Ad Nicoclem* and *Demonicus*, and in the kingship treatises of Plutarch and Dio Chrysostom. First Corinthians 16:10-11 suggests difficulties and disdain that faced Timothy on his embassy to the Corinthian community. See 1 Tim 1:2 for a reference to Timothy's youth. Although he is Paul's fellow worker (Rom 16:21), Timothy is also his "child" (Phil 2:22). In 1 Timothy he stresses Timothy's youthfulness,

although by the end of the third missionary journey Timothy is no longer a youth. Paul in 2 Timothy suggests the same youthfulness in mentioning his mother and grandmother at 1:5, the threat of youthful passions at 2:22, Timothy's education, his teachers, and his childhood at 3:14-15. In the letters' concern for preserving the authentic Pauline tradition, Timothy represents the next generation. The elders and overseers represent a leadership class that grows out of seniority, and even the assistants are drawn from household masters, another senior adult category. Timothy is cautioned to deal with them carefully (5:1-2). Timothy's youth would not sit well with traditionalists in the authority structure and he risks not being taken seriously. See Fiore, *Personal Example*, 210 n. 68 for parallels in hortatory literature.

an example: As Paul is an example of the saved sinner (1 Tim 1:16), so here Timothy is to be an example of the conscientious leader (and see 2 Tim 1:13). The two figures exhibit qualities that overlap, making Timothy (and Titus) successors to Paul in the fullest sense. Thus Paul and his successors engage in similar tasks (*parakalein*, "exhort"; *parangellein*, "charge"; *didaskein*, "teach"; *kēryssein*, "proclaim"; *mimnēskein*, "remind"; *mnēmoneuein*, "recollect"; *hypomenein*, "endure"; *paschein*, "suffer"; *terein pistin*, "keep faith"), and Timothy is said to have followed both Paul's teaching and his way of life (2 Tim 3:10-11). In this way he counters critics of his youthfulness, for his actions meet the requirements of teaching (4:6) through the grace of Jesus (1:14; 2 Tim 11:13). The list of virtuous qualities fills out the contours of the example. Both official functions and personal qualities are specified. It is in the latter sense that the example is not just for leaders but for the community of the faithful. The treatises on kings and leaders had a parallel aim of making the king or leader the epitome of personal qualities expected of the citizenry. Xenophon, *Cyropaedia* 1.2,8, describing Persian methods of education, finds that the young learn by observing the example of their elders. This was a commonplace in Greco-Roman education. In 1 Timothy the relatively young Timothy is thrust into the position of an elder *vis à vis* his charges as he is called upon to be an example for them. This seems to indicate that Timothy is an ideal rather than a real figure.

in word, in conduct, in love, in faith, in purity: The sound teaching that false teachers abandon (1 Tim 6:3) is to be the hallmark of Timothy's preaching (2 Tim 4:2), as it is of Paul's (2 Tim 1:13, and see Titus 2:8 for the same expectation about Titus, and Titus 1:9 for a reference to overseers appointed by him). Conduct was an essential part of piety (see 1 Tim 2:2). See 2 Tim 1:13 for love and faith as the setting for Paul's exemplary preaching of the sound doctrine. The PE use the formula "in faith" (*en pistei*) differently from earlier Pauline letters. It lacks any association with "in Christ" mysticism and appears in different combinations with other Christian realities. Nonetheless, the PE see "in faith" as the new situation (1 Tim 1:2; Titus 3:5) that characterizes the Christian, and roughly parallel with Paul's earlier "in Christ." While faith often refers to the objective content of faith and the assent to it (as at 1 Tim 4:11), it is also typically, as here, linked with other Christian virtues. It is, in fact, in all the virtue lists of the PE and can therefore be considered not just a random virtue but the indispensable attitude on which the other virtues rest. It is the basis of the intellectual truth of the Christian movement and of the proper way of life. The virtue "purity" (*hagneia*) is expected both of Timothy (1 Tim 5:2, 22) and of the young women in the community (Titus 2:5). Timothy's example extends to the community at large. It is related to being "pure" (*katharos*, see 1 Tim 1:5).

13. *apply yourself to the public reading, exhortation, and teaching:* Attention to one's assigned tasks was common advice to young leaders in Isocrates, Dio Chrysostom, and Plutarch (see 4:12). Reading Scripture aloud (the First Testament in the synagogue, Luke 4:16; Acts 13:15, 27; 15:21, and compare 2 Cor 3:15) had been carried over from Judaic practice into the Ephesian Christian community. The letters of Paul were read publicly to his community addressees in a liturgical setting (1 Thess 5:27; 1 Cor 16:20-24; Phlm 2; Eph 3:4, and see 1 Cor 5:3-5; also Mark 13:14 *parr.*). The letters were also read in other communities (Col 4:16). A collection of Paul's letters may have been known and read in Asia Minor (see 2 Pet 3:15-16 for the collection and 2 Pet 3:1, which alludes to 1 Peter, addressed to Asia Minor among other locales). *Second Clement* 19.1 alludes to "readers" in the church. In the official activities of exhortation and teaching, Timothy (1 Tim 4:11; 5:1; 6:2; 2 Tim 4:2, Titus 1:9; 2:6, 15) follows Paul, who does these (1 Tim 1:3; 2:1, 7; 2 Tim 1:11) and sets the pattern for other community leaders (1 Tim 3:2; 5:17; 2 Tim 2:2). The interest of the letters in the content of faith and right conduct is covered by these activities.

14. *Do not neglect the gift:* The gift of God, like faith, as noted earlier (see 2:2; 4:7), needs practical exercise to come to full expression in the recipient. Second Timothy 1:6-7 recalls the reception of the gift of God and specifies it to be the spirit of strength, love, and moderation.

prophetic word along with the laying on of hands: The setting of the prophetic word here is parallel to that at Acts 13:2, where the prophets' oracle designated Paul and Barnabas for mission, a designation subsequently formalized by the laying on of hands. Here the preposition *dia* ("through") indicates that the prophecy was effective in the transmission of the charism and task to Timothy, although the imposition of hands appears to be an "accompanying" (*meta*) act rather than an effective gesture as it is at 2 Tim 1:6. The task Timothy has is unique and is linked to his completion of Paul's apostolic task (1 Tim 1:3). In Acts his selection as Paul's assistant (Acts 16:2-3) is not confirmed by a commissioning ceremony, although he was circumcised for reasons of missionary access to Jewish congregations. In view of Timothy's being an intermediate example between Paul and the Ephesian community and leaders, his apostolic delegation in the PE through the laying on of hands is described here and at 2 Tim 1:6 as being like an ordination ceremony (compare the designation of presbyters at 1 Tim 5:22, and see 1:18). Thus these words to him would be applicable to any ordained community official. For an OT precedent for the rite of appointment see Num 27:18-23 and Deut 34:9. The LXX fails to distinguish between the different Hebrew words and gestures—that is, "press" hands on the recipient for installation in office and "place" hands for blessing. Our author has both installation and blessing occurring, so the Hebrew distinction does not appear relevant. At Acts 6:6 and 13:3 the laying on of hands does not transmit the Holy Spirit but recognizes the Spirit's presence (contrast Acts 8:17 and 9:17, where the imposition of hands at conversion does release the Holy Spirit). The imposition of hands in 1 Tim 4:14 and 2 Tim 1:6 is a similar ordination to ministry, and at 2 Tim 1:6 it is a solemn gesture both of installation in office and the release of the Spirit charism from one who has it (Paul) to one who does not yet possess it (Timothy). First Timothy 5:22 indicates that the ordination links the one laying on hands to the recipient and makes the first responsible for the growth and activity of the second. The PE is the expression of Paul's care that the ones on whom he imposed hands (Timothy and Titus) follow his example and effectively execute their mission.

assembly of elders: "Assembly of elders" (*presbyteriou*) is unique in the NT as a reference to a body of Christian elders and has thus been "corrected" by one of the later scribes of Codex Sinaiticus to "of an elder" (*presbyterou*). Modern interpreters, also troubled by the unique word, see in the phrase a translation of the rabbinic technical term *semikat zeqenim* for an ordination to the presbyterate. This, however, does not explain the choice of *presbyteriou* rather than *presbyterōn*, the direct translation. The use of this rabbinic idiom is unexpected, and it is also a late ritual in Judaism, not current until the second and third centuries. Moreover, Timothy is not called an "elder" (he is "assistant," *diakonos*, at 1 Tim 4:4, and "evangelist," *euangelistēs*, at 2 Tim 4:5). The word therefore describes the participation of the assembly of elders in the ceremony (and compare 2 Tim 1:6, "my," *mou*, and Acts 8:18, "of the apostles," *apostolōn*).

John Chrysostom, *Hom. 1 Tim.* 13 (LCC 5:386), declares that the reference here is to bishops, since presbyters could not be conceived of as ordaining a bishop. He thus understands Timothy's office to be the same as that of bishops in his own time and speaks from the perspective of a more developed liturgical as well as ecclesiastical tradition. While sharing the same liturgical presupposition about ordination ceremonies, Jerome, on the other hand, in *Epist.* 146.1, finds that Paul in Titus 1:5 equates presbyters with bishops and so they rightfully lay on hands here. Theodore of Mopsuestia in *Commentary on I Timothy* (TEM 2:150) agrees that Paul does not usually allow a presbyter the power to ordain by the imposition of hands. He further explains that the term presbyter in the letter does not refer to the same office as it did in his day. He notes that Paul imposed hands in the company of the apostles, and he calls this gathering the "council of presbyters," a designation of honor. He traces the practice of having several bishops at bishops' ordinations to this.

Paul speaks only of his imposition of hands at 2 Tim 1:6, but this may be due to the personal perspective of 2 Timothy and the effort of Paul there to have Timothy rededicate himself to the Gospel work that shoulders the shame and suffering of Paul's and Jesus' witness.

15. *Take care of these things:* That Paul commands Timothy's persistence here and suggests he might slack off at 1 Tim 4:14 is surprising, given the reliance he places on Timothy in delegating the task to him to begin with, as well as the consistently high praise of Timothy in earlier letters (Phil 2:19-24; 1 Cor 4:17). In the context of a bitter struggle against false teachers these commands and exhortations look beyond Timothy to the community at large. The Pauline delegate is therefore a mirror of the Ephesian church in a moment of crisis and a model of their plucky resistance to apostasy. Titus, who reflects a different

situation in Crete, is not painted with such dark features. See the note on 3:14 for the referent of "these things."

progress: Paul worked for the advancement of the Gospel (Phil 1:12) and of the community in faith (Phil 1:25). His own model is that of one who is making progress toward the Christian Gospel (Phil 3:13-17). It was also an aim of the Greco-Roman moralists that their charges would cultivate moral philosophy by practicing proper habits and self-criticism (see also Sir 51:16). Emulation of an example is particularly useful for this (e.g., Plutarch, *Virt. Prof.* 84E).

The PE have a similar aim and method in mind here. "Progress" fits Timothy's youth and clarifies the kind of example he is expected to set for believers (1 Tim 4:12). He is to be a diligent church minister, and as such he is to develop the way of life that all Christians are expected to pursue. Open manifestation is a recurrent theme in the letters, whether it be applied to Christ, to Paul, to his apostolic delegates, to community leaders, or to Christians in general.

16. *Attend to yourself and to your teaching:* The two aspects of the Christian life of piety, i.e., practice and doctrine, are reiterated.

by doing this you will save both yourself: If taken literally, this is clearly non-Pauline. Moreover, the letters elsewhere refer to salvation by God (2:3) and Christ Jesus (1:15; 2:6). Like childbearing at 2:15, Timothy's exemplary way of life and transmission of sound teaching establish the context in which God and Christ are able to save. A disposition to be saved is needed. Thus Hymenaeus and Alexander are prodded by excommunication to reassess their apostasy (1:19-20). Also, a way of life that encourages maintaining a faith commitment is the letter's aim (1:5). The situation of apostasy has demonstrated that salvation, though accomplished by Christ (2:5-6), accepted by believers (3:16), confirmed by the Spirit (Titus 3:4-7), can be rejected in a loss of fidelity (2 Tim 2:11-13).

Interpretation

In specifying correct belief and consequent conduct the letter contrasts apostate teachers in the "final days" to Timothy. The contrast originates in the teachings of ungodly spirits (4:1). The letter uses medical imagery to describe the obtuse conscience of the faith-rejecting apostates. The meaning of the image of "seared conscience" was elusive from early on. John Chrysostom, *Hom. 1 Tim.* 12 (NPNF 1 13:444), refers this to the false teachers' evil lives; Theodore of Mopsuestia, *Commentary on I Timothy* (TEM 2:141), says it means not having a whole conscience but living the opposite of what they teach; Theodoret of Cyr, *Interpretation of the First Letter to Timothy* (PG 82:811D-812D), sees it as the deadening of their consciences; Ambrosiaster, *Commentary on the First Letter to Timothy* (CSEL 81 3:272-273), explains that falsehood corrupts them by leaving a brand on their consciences like that on skin. Their ascetical abstinence is set against the goodness of God's creation (4:3-5). The incarnational emphasis of the christological summary, the expression of the church's truth (3:15-16), has already laid the groundwork for the letter's rejection of the deceptive ascetical option for those who know the truth (4:3). Proper practice flows from correct belief in the letter's understanding of Christian living.

By contrast, Timothy, faithful follower of the teaching, is to mediate the instructions mentioned at 3:14 to others (4:6). The letter rejects asceticism at 4:3-5. In the early church the Encratites, while doctrinally in agreement with the church, diverged in their practice of abstaining from animal food, drinking water, forbidding marriage, and devoting themselves to ascetical practices. Based on Paul's words in 1 Timothy here, Hippolytus, *Haer*. 8.13 (ANF 5:124), considers them more akin to Cynics than to Christians.

Asceticism is further denigrated in the unfavorable contrast (4:7b-8) between minimally useful physical training, i.e., the ascetical practices, and training in religion, useful both now and in the future. True spiritual exertion leads to a life of piety and eternal reward made available by God (4:10). Timothy's labors are boosted by Paul's assertion of a common effort. The permanence of the faith stance is expressed by the perfect tense ("we have hoped," *elpikamen*), another contrast to the wayward.

The admonition to the young Timothy in imperative commands continues the call for him to be an example in teaching, conduct, and attitude (4:12-16). Both behavior and teaching are at issue in the positive example as they were in the contrasting negative one. The Spirit, who foretold the current conflict (4:1), now appears as a resource (4:14) transmitted through the church officials. In this way Paul clarifies a way in which the church is a foundation of the truth (3:15). The example is rendered dynamic and accessible by Paul's relating it to the reality of visible progress in Timothy's application of Paul's advice (4:16). Timothy's hortatory and teaching efforts will prod his charges into moral advancement. Thus the spiritual training (*gymnasia*, 4:7) will achieve its desired results now and in the future, for the purpose of all this is salvation for Timothy and his hearers (4:16). This associates Timothy's work with God, the savior of all (4:10 and see 1:15). And these efforts of his are to occupy the interim until Paul returns (4:13), a reference to the latter's *parousia* (3:14), which creates the context for the extended direct exhortation to Timothy in anticipation of the promised visit.

Basil, *The Long Rules* Q.43.R (FC 9:273-274), explains that the example is so that there may be no excuse for those under his guidance to think the Lord's commands impossible or readily to be set aside. He wisely assesses the interrelation between a leader and those being led. The most effective leaders require nothing of their subordinates that they themselves would not do. Thus Jesus sets the standard of this leadership by maintaining fidelity to God's plan even to his own death. Here Timothy establishes a lived pattern of the Christian life expected of the members of the community.

For Reference and Further Study

Brox, Norbert. *Pastoralbriefe*, 180–83.

Dewey, Joanna. "1 Timothy," in Carol A. Newsom and Sharon H. Ringe, eds., *The Women's Bible Commentary*. London: SPCK; Louisville: Westminster John Knox, 1992; expanded ed. 1998, 444–49.

Fiore, Benjamin. *Personal Example*, 6, 34, 36, 45–78, 87–92, 115, 210 n. 68.

Hanson, Anthony Tyrrell. *Studies in the Pastoral Epistles*. London: SPCK, 1968, 97–109.

Harvey, Anthony E. "Elders," *JTS* 25 (1974) 318–32.

Hoffman, Lawrence A. "Jewish Ordination on the Eve of Christianity," *Studia Liturgica* 13 (1979) 11–41.

Horrell, David. "From *adelphoi* to *oikos theou:* Social Transformation in Pauline Christianity," *JBL* 120 (2001) 293–311.

Kilmartin, Edward. "Ministry and Ordination in Early Christianity Against a Jewish Background," *Studia Liturgica* 13 (1979) 42–69.

Knight, George W. III. *Faithful Sayings*, 62–79.

Malherbe, Abraham J. "Medical Imagery," 127–36.

________. "The Beasts at Ephesus," in idem, ed., *Paul and the Popular Philosophers*. Minneapolis: Fortress Press, 1989, 79–89.

Meier, John P. "*Presbyteros* in the Pastoral Epistles," *CBQ* 35 (1974) 523–45.

Parratt, J. K. "The Laying on of Hands in the New Testament: A Reexamination in Light of the Hebrew Terminology," *ExpT* 80 (1968–1969) 210–14.

Roberts, C. H. "Elders: A Note," *JTS* 26 (1975) 403–405.

Sell, Jesse. *The knowledge of the truth—two doctrines : The Book of Thomas the Contender (CG II,7) and the false teachers in the Pastoral Epistles*. Frankfurt: Peter Lang, 1982.

Towner, Philip H. "Present Age," 427–48.

10. *Dealing with the Elderly; Care for Widows* (5:1-16)

1. By no means should you attack an older man; rather urge him like a father and younger men like brothers, 2. older women like mothers, younger women like sisters, in total purity. 3. Give honoraria to widows who are truly widows. 4. But if a particular widow has children or grandchildren, let those learn first of all how to show piety to their own household and to make repayment to those who reared them. This, you see, is acceptable to God. 5. Now the woman who is really a widow and left alone has placed her hope in God, and keeps at her supplications and prayers night and day. 6. On the other hand, the woman who lives a life of indulgence is dead. 7. Yes, give these instructions, so that they might be irreproachable. 8. Now if someone does not provide for his own dependents,

and especially those of his household, he has abdicated his faith and is worse than a nonbeliever.

9. Let a widow be registered if she is not less than sixty years old, married only once, 10. attested by good works, if she brought up children, showed hospitality, washed the feet of the saints, helped those in distress, followed every good work. 11. On the other hand, reject younger widows; for when their impulses turn them away from Christ, they want to marry 12. and thus they incur the condemnation that they have nullified their first pledge. 13. Besides, in their idleness they also learn to circulate from house to house, yes and not only idle but gossipy and meddlesome as well, saying things they shouldn't. 14. Therefore it is my decision that the younger widows marry, bear children, be mistresses of their households, give no occasion to an opponent for abuse. 15. I say this because some have already turned away after Satan.

16. If one of the faithful women has widows to care for, let her attend to their needs and don't let the church become burdened, so that it might attend to the needs of the real widows.

Notes

1. *By no means should you attack an older man; rather urge him:* The practice of exhortation among the moral philosophers of the time favored gentle persuasion over harsh rebuke (see *Ep. Socrates* 1.2; 9.3; 13.2; Dio Chrysostom (*Or.* 32) *Alex.* 8; Lucian, *Demonax* 19.48; Philodemus, *On Frank Speech* XVIa.12). The letter returns to the station code sequence and deals now not with officials but with groups in the community according to gender and age. The purpose of Timothy's assiduousness in his task was identified as salvation of himself and his hearers. That provides a transition point to consider the community members. The station code here largely departs from the traditional three pairings (husband-wife, father-children, master-slave), retaining only the gender distinction and the admonition to slaves at 6:1-2.

   The older men are not the officials called elders at 5:17, since the elders are men at Titus 1:6, and this passage speaks of both men and women. Moreover, there as here the qualifications for officials (1 Tim 3:1-13; Titus 1:6-9) are followed by material concerning false teachers (1 Tim 4:1-5; Titus 1:10–2:1) and then a consideration of older and younger men, older and younger women, and slaves (1 Tim 5:1–6:2; Titus 2:2-10).

   like a father: The fictive kinship of the Pauline (and early Christian) communities takes on a programmatic purpose here to motivate gentleness in the leaders. In the letter to the Colossians the argument against the false teachers' severity, abasement, and ascetical practice based on human teachings (2:16-23), and all hostile and aggressive behavior (3:8-9), are contrasted with the new self (3:10) characterized by gentleness and forbearance (3:12-15). This suggests that the polemic against the false teachers in 1 Timothy was depicting the teachers as excessively and purposelessly harsh (they disdain Timothy's youth at 4:12) by contrast to how the Christian leaders are to conduct themselves. Iamblichus,

Vit. Pyth. 40, records among the philosopher's rules for the citizens of Croton that, as sons, they maintain a well-ordered relationship with their elders (see also Plutarch, *Mor.* 120 A; Valerius Maximus, II 1,9; Aulus Gellius, II 15,1), with benevolent comradeship toward others as brothers. More like our passage is Libanius' instruction (Loc. 3, 7) to doctors to treat contemporaries as brothers, to relate to elders as a son and younger persons as a father.

2. *in total purity:* As a model of purity (1 Tim 4:12) Timothy is to be impeccable with respect to young women (and see Titus 2:5). Youthful passions (2 Tim 2:22, and compare Titus 2:12; 3:3) are to be avoided, in contrast with the false teachers who play up to passions of women (2 Tim 3:5).

3. *honoraria:* The verb *timaō* itself means "honor, assess the value," but this section deals with providing support, either from the family or from the church, for widows. *Timē* at 5:17 refers to an honorarium. These influence the meaning of the verb here, as does v. 16 (see also Sir 38:1). It is not clear how the practice of community support for widows evolved. The Jews distributed food to the needy in Jerusalem (pilgrim sojourners, the poor, among whom were widows). This daily dole was carried over into the practice of the Jerusalem church (Acts 6:1-6). Care for widows was an ethical obligation in Judaism and continued as such into Christianity (Jer 7:6; Prov 23:10; Deut 24:19; Mark 12:40; Pol. *Phil.* 6:1).

In Rome all citizens received the corn dole. At public festivals in the East food was distributed to all, but not according to need, for honored persons received larger portions. There were also child allowances in some parts of the empire from Nero's time on. In light of a variety of regular and emergency distributions, there was a tendency to take advantage of the system and shift one's dependents to other providers. The church may have been caught in this, for there seems to have been no needs test in place.

widows: The letter takes up, as the next group in the household of the church, the widows. Widows received charitable support from the Christian community from the earliest days (Acts 6:1; 9:39, 41; Jas 1:27). In the Old Testament widows are protected against oppression (Exod 22:21-22; Deut 10:18; 24:17; 27:19; Jer 7:6; 22:3; Zech 7:10). God himself is their defender (Pss 68:6; 149:9; Exod 22:22; Deut 10:18; Wis 15:25), and the prophets decried their exploitation (Isa 1:23; 10:2; Jer 5:28; Ezek 22:7; Ps 94:6). Thus the PE carry forward this longstanding concern for the widows' well-being (Brox, *Pastoralbriefe*, 185–98). The issue here is to determine which are "real" widows who need church support (5:3-8, 16). A second matter has to do with those to be registered in the list of "widows" as an official status. With Timothy instructed to look into this matter, the situation of discriminating among widows and enrolling some is given a general rather than a local aspect. The activity of widows and their families achieves exemplary status. The formal ecclesiastical status of widows continued into the post-apostolic period (Ign. *Smyrn.* 13, 1; *Pol.* 4,1; *Phld.* 4,3) but has since disappeared.

4. *to show piety:* Religious piety (see 2:2) takes on a very practical face here, as fulfilling familial and religious obligations to parents. Aristotle expresses the obligation in *Eth. Nic.* IX 2, 1165a21-27 (and see Simplicius, *Epict.* I, p. 320, 9-19, Schweighäuser).

acceptable to God: The author appeals to religious grounds (the Decalogue) rather than to social custom to motivate the audience. In Greece a widow could stay in her husband's home, if the couple had children, and be maintained by her new supervisor (*kyrios*, usually her son) or return to her parents' home, taking with her a part of her dowry. The obligation of maintaining her fell legally on the men who took charge of her dowry.

5. *really a widow . . . keeps at her supplications and prayers:* The real widow has no relatives to look after her, but instead depends on God. This reliance on God is expected of all in the community, beginning with Paul and mediated through Timothy (4:10). This is consistent with the attitude of widows in the Old Testament (Deut 10:18, and see Luke 4:25-26). Anna (Luke 2:36-37) is the prototype of these real widows. (For other widows as paradigms of dependence on God see Mark 12:42-43; Luke 7:12; 21:2-3.) The widow meets the common requirement of prayer at 2:1-2 (and see Luke 18:3-5 for a widow at prayer).

6. *who lives a life of indulgence:* The author's preference for contrasts leads him to this sketch of a self-indulgent widow. Instead of living in hope (v. 5, and in the PE hope is for eternal life in God, 1 Tim 4:10; Titus 1:2; 2:13; 3:7), she is as good as dead in her reckless life (the perfect tense shows ongoing effects of a past action in the present). While the life of pleasure is generally looked down on in the letters (1 Tim 6:9; 2 Tim 2:22; 4:3; Titus 2:12; 3:3-4), women are singled out as particularly susceptible to this temptation (2 Tim 3:6, and compare Titus 2:5, and for the Greco-Roman view see Epictetus, *fr.* 15).

7. *irreproachable:* The letters' general concern for the opinion of the church in the wider community (see 3:2), and the particular caution to bring social relations within the community into conformity with accepted societal norms regarding the activity of women (2:11-15; Titus 2:3-5) lead the author to try to rein in excesses among the women.

8. *does not provide for:* The letter reminds men of their duty to look after their dependents and household members, and this places care for the widows within the larger context of social roles and obligations. Within the family its head (*paterfamilias*) ruled, but outside the family patron-client responsibilities were also institutionalized and supported by ritualized behavior, such as the clients' morning salutation of the patron at which they received a gift or food ration (*sportula*). Supervising the household, a qualification for office (3:5, 12), includes caring for its members (Epictetus, *Diatr.* 3.24.3), and the observation here singles this out as a special (*malista*) duty. Not caring for family members would make one worse than an unbeliever because it would mean not only shirking the legally established dowry and household duties but also violating the Decalogue.

   As noted above at 1:9, care for elderly parents is enjoined by the fourth commandment. With the extended average life span today the responsibility of adult children, sandwiched between demands for the support of their elderly parents and the requirements of rearing their own children, has led to an acute problem. Coupled with this is the enormous rise in the cost of medical care, which leaves the elderly with hard choices between paying for medicines and other necessities. The reduced size of the nuclear family and the scattering of family members across the country add to the problem of elder care. Now, as in the first century, the resources of church charities are stretched to the breaking point. Private and public agencies, as well as government assistance, help close the gap. Church members, whether they have elderly parents or other relatives under their care or not, cannot ignore and exempt themselves from working to address this problem. In addition to material care, social and psychological concerns comprise another dimension of elder care. Unlike the social system of the first century, which was based on large households, today's family units are increasingly diminished in size and isolated. Even where material resources abound, the needs of the spirit call out for a response.

has abdicated: Once again one's conduct of life and faith stance are intimately related, such that abandoning Christian duty is tantamount to abandoning the faith itself. The seriousness of denying the faith has a negative impact on salvation (2 Tim 2:12-13). The apostates show the emptiness of their faith claims by their deeds (Titus 1:16, and see 2 Tim 3:13). So these masters who shirk their responsibility are like them and worse than unbelievers, since they have known the faith and have turned away from it (compare 1 Tim 1:19).

9. *Let a widow be registered:* The letter shifts focus from urging care for widows by those responsible for them to describing those who are to be registered on the official list of widows. This is another instance of the author's insertion of traditional material into the letter. (See the "true sayings," the qualification lists, ordination exhortation, household codes.) The abrupt shift without a connective between vv. 8 and 9 indicates the introduction of a new topic. A different set of qualifications emerges here that does not coincide with the list in v. 5 (i.e., left alone, hoping in God, persistent in prayer, not wanton but blameless). Age and marriage history could well exclude women who fit the earlier mentioned criteria. Would they then be disqualified from church support? Moreover, what happens to the young widow who remarries, as ordered at v. 14? Is she therefore excluded from support should her second husband die and leave her stranded in destitution? Other considerations below indicate that in vv. 9-15 the author is discussing widows in a different sense. The treatment of widow as a household category has provided the author with the occasion to deal with an official category that had grown troublesome. The verb "be registered" (*katalegesthō*) can refer to a formal enlistment, as of soldiers (Josephus, *C. Ap.* 1.131), but need mean no more than writing down on a list. In either case an official list is being drawn up.

   sixty years old, married only once: The age limit reflects the average age of the "elderly" in antiquity (see v. 14). Plato, *Leg.* VI 759c-d establishes sixty years as the minimum age for sacral duties (see also Plutarch, *Comp. Lyc. Num.* 26, 1-2; Poll. II 11 and, specifically for women, Demosthenes, *Or.* 43,62. See also *Abot. R. Nat.* 5, 21). At Titus 2:3 older women are given the task of educating younger women and of setting an example of upright behavior. A single marriage indicates their fidelity (see also 3:2) even after the death of the spouse (*Anth. Graec.* VII 324; Propertius, IV 11,33-37.41-42.67-69; Livy, X 23,5.9; Valerius Maximus, II 1,3, and see Josephus, *Ant.* XV 65-66; XVII 352; Pausanias, II 21,7; VII 25,13 as a requirement for priestly service). The age and marriage requirements suggest that this is an "office" with institutional requirements and not a personal charism or condition brought about by circumstance. First Timothy carries forward its anti-ascetic perspective by expecting the qualified widows to have been married and reared children, a qualification similar to that of the overseers, elders, and assistants.

10. *attested by good works:* The clearly forensic tone of the testimony at 2 Tim 1:8; 1 Tim 6:13 (and see 2:6); 1 Tim 5:19 (and compare Titus 1:13), and the implication of public verifiability of declarations by witnesses at 1 Tim 6:12 and 2 Tim 2:2 suggest a solemn and public quality to the attestations of worthiness here and at 3:7 (and compare 4:7). The list that follows describes the qualifications, not the duties, of the widows. They match qualifications for other community officeholders. These good works are specified in the five conditional clauses that follow. The first two deal with domestic activities, the second two with service to those in God's household, the church. The last is another general, open-ended reference to good works. The widows in this category live out their Christian piety. This is an expectation for all in the community (1 Tim 2:10; 6:18; 2 Tim 2:21; 3:17; Titus 2:7, 14; 3:1, 8, 14).

    brought up children, showed hospitality, washed the feet . . . helped those in distress: The author does not specify whose children they are (contrast 2:15, *teknogonias*, "childbearing"). In the admonition for relatives to care for widows at vv. 4 and 8, children and grandchildren are mentioned. There the author also speaks in general terms of the widows as forebears (*progonoi idiōn . . . oikeiōn*). The mention of *idioi* and *oikeioi* is vague. The *idioi* can refer to dependents such as freed slaves or paid day laborers, among whom widow-nannies might be included. If these were not living in the home, perhaps the master felt a lessened responsibility to support them and may even have used manumission of the slaves as a ploy to reduce his obligations, despite laws to the contrary. *Oikeioi* would refer to the master's close relatives (compare *Barn.* 3.3). Thus they may not have been the parents of the children they reared or even have lived in the household. Care for the children in a household was required of the overseer (3:4), assistants (3:12), and elder-overseers (Titus 1:6). Hospitality, an expectation in the Greco-Roman friendship relationship, was a characteristic of the Christian communities (Rom 12:13; 15:24; 16:23; 3 John 5-6; Heb 13:2; 1 Pet 4:9) and a requirement at 1 Tim 3:2 and Titus 1:8. This qualification for enrollment might be one of the widows' official functions, along with service to the community members themselves. For washing the feet see John 13:14-15. It is a sign of Jesus' and his followers' humble service and a mark of a woman's virtue: see Plutarch, *Mor.* 249 D, and *Abot. R. Nat.* 16 (6a). For helping those in distress see Phil 4:13, and compare Rom 12:13 (and note similar expectations of friends in Greco-Roman friendship treatises).

11. *younger widows:* Widowed women under fifty were expected to marry under Augustus' *Lex Papia Poppaea*. Among Greeks, too, remarriage provided a secure option for women. But their marriage would violate the "married once" qualification and disqualify them from inclusion on the list of widows.

12. *nullified their first pledge:* LXX usage (e.g., 1 Macc 11:36; 2 Macc 13:25; Ps 88:35) suggests the verb *ēthetēsan* means a formal renunciation or violation. *Pistin*

means a solemn promise or oath (Xenophon, *Cyropaedia* 7.1.44; Plato, *Leg.* 3.701C; *3 Macc.* 3:10; Josephus, *Ant.* 12.382). The pledge has to do with not marrying again, which would signal their dependence on God, like the "real" widows at v. 5. Paul encouraged not remarrying for eschatological reasons at 1 Cor 7:40, and at 2 Cor 11:2 he reminds the Corinthians that he espoused them to Christ. This echoes ideas about Christ the bridegroom at Mark 2:19; Matt 22:1-14; Matt 25:1-13; Rev 19:7. Here in 1 Timothy the ministry of the widow is related to fidelity to Christ. The pledge indicates a formal association of registered widows.

13. *in their idleness:* Contrary to the dedication to good deeds that qualifies them for the registry of widows, these slip into idleness. When they do act they are "meddlesome" (*periergoi*) and spread inappropriate teaching and behavior from house to house (for criticism of such women see *b. Sotah* 22a and *y. Sotah* 3.19a.37). This pejorative view of women who fail to remain within the framework of household duty was common among moral philosophers of the day (see Musonius, *Or.* 3.43-44; Plutarch, *Mor.* 508 C). Cynics and Epicureans were exceptions to the insistence on female domesticity, but these movements were widely criticized for their excesses and socially ambivalent values. The activity of the idle widows mirrors that of the false teachers at 2 Tim 3:6-7, and their idle talk could well consist of the old wives' tales of 3:7.

14. *it is my decision:* See 1 Tim 2:8.

marry . . . give no occasion . . . for abuse: Like women in general in the community at 1 Tim 2:9-15, the widows are to assume the traditional domestic role of women. Disruption of households continues to be an issue at Ignatius, *Eph.* 16.1. For concern with opponents' abuse see 3:2. The focus of the opponents' criticism is on the domestic role of women, thus similarly to 2:9-15. The young widows' reluctance to marry, the house-to-house activity, speaking unmentionable things, the pledge, and the obvious discredit they are bringing to the Ephesian church suggest two problems with regard to widows in the community. The first has to do with making equitable and manageable arrangements for their support, the second with actions engaged in by registered widows. The registry seems to have grown without adequate scrutiny. The assurance of church support and the Pauline encouragement of celibacy as an eschatological virtue (1 Corinthians 7) might well have combined with emancipatory claims based on the baptismal unification formula (Gal 3:28, and see its reformulation in 1 Cor 12:13; Col 3:11; compare Eph 6:8 and Ign. *Smyrn.* 1.2), the tradition of women's participation in a wide range of Pauline church activities (e.g., Rom 16:1-2, 3-5, 6, 7, 12, 15; 1 Cor 11:5), a tendency toward asceticism (1 Corinthians 7; Col 2:16-18, 20-21; 1 Tim 4:3), and patterns of equality in Epicurean communities as well as the debunking of conventional social models among the Cynics to encourage a large number of women to pursue a life unattached from family responsibilities, male dominance, and household confinement. The letter gives no indication that these women are not actually widows, although later Ign. *Smyrn.* 13.1 refers to "virgins" (*parthenous*) who are "called widows" (*tas legomenas chēras*). Here "widow" is a technical term for an unmarried or even never-married woman who is dedicated to the Lord's service (see also Tertullian, *Virg.* 9).

More in line with the explicit problem of 1 Timothy, however, in his *Pol.* 4.1-3 Ignatius is concerned that Polycarp bring the widows under his control.

Likewise, Pol. *Phil.* 4:3 wants widows to "exercise moderation" (*sōphronousas*), to pray ceaselessly, and to avoid "slander," "negative criticism," and "calumny" (*diabolēs, katalalias, pseudomartyrias*). Here in the PE the house-to-house circulation is not the problem (for older women are urged to teach domestic virtue to young wives at Titus 2:4-5). Rather, what the young widows say on their rounds is. Turning away after Satan is the accusation against some of them (5:15). The fact that the letter finds only some (*tines*) to be guilty of this suggests that this is a paraenetic warning. The widows might be tending toward, but have not yet reached this point; still, they have to beware. At 2 Tim 4:4 the end-time apostasy will have some turning from sound truth and toward myths. At 1 Tim 1:6 the false teachers are already doing this and Timothy (1 Tim 6:20) is urged to turn away from this empty talk and deceptive knowledge. The younger gadabout widows might thus be spreading the false doctrines and questionable myths of the false teachers and are in danger of falling in with Satan and the forces of opposition in the end-time struggle currently underway at Ephesus (see 4:1, and also the dangers to the inexperienced overseer at 3:6, as well as the prohibition against women teachers at 2:12). The widows are not yet directly condemned and expelled from the community as apostates or heretics (contrast 1 Tim 1:20; 6:3-5; 2 Tim 4:14-15; Titus 3:8-11). If the widows here are making house calls in which they are spreading legends (4:7, old wives' tales like those in the *Acts of Paul and Thecla*) and teachings that justify their celibacy and emancipation from domestic roles, then the church will fall under criticism as a socially subversive association in the community at large. So the letter tries to rein in the widows by paring down the list to include only older women, married once.

Are these the same as the "real" widows who receive church support? The insertion of the qualification and exclusion material (3:15) within the consideration of household versus church support (vv. 3-8, 16) suggests that the author did not make a distinction. On the other hand, he does distinguish between widows and "real" (*ontōs*) widows, with support going only to the latter (vv. 3 and 16). This would mean that the officially registered widows are a special ministerial group in the community (perhaps they do household visitation, v. 13, and domestic instruction; compare Titus 2:4-5). The group comprises qualified widows from among all the community's widows. It also means that church support would be available for "real" widows, those with no support from their household affiliations, whether they were among the registered widows or not. An inscription from the next generation reflects the application of the instructions in 1 Timothy:

> To the well-deserving Rigina, her daughter beautifully fashioned this tombstone. Rigina, mother, widow, who remained a widow sixty years and never burdened the church; a *univira* who lived eighty years, five months, twenty-six days.

16. *has widows:* This might well be addressed to the mistresses of households and thus match the admonition to household masters at v. 8, from which it has been severed by the inserted instruction on widow registration. A less likely but intriguing possibility is that it refers to women who have taken widows under their care. Acts 9:36-42 refers to Tabitha/Dorcas who supplied clothing for a circle of widows. Later, *Acts Thom.* 59 and *Acts Pet.* 2, 20-22 refer to widows

taken into others' homes, or to homes for widows. This later practice coincides with evidence of interdependence among widows in Ign. *Pol.* 4.1-3 and Pol. *Phil.* 4.3. The story from Acts confirms at least that some women took on assistance to needy widows as their charitable project. The admonition here might well be aimed at encouraging this practice. The situation, from the viewpoint of traditional household management, might have led to the addition of *pistos* before *pistē* in some manuscripts at this point.

Interpretation

The next section of the body of the letter (5:1–6:2), a continuation of the station code, begins in the mode of a *Haustafel* but moves from a discussion of household categories to a consideration of church ministries with the same titles. Timothy's official status supersedes that due to age among his community's members. Nonetheless, he must deal with his elders with due respect. Thus the familial respect one expects to be shown to the old and young men and women (5:1-2) leads into a protracted discussion of widows, presented in an *inclusio* pattern. *Tima* ("give honoraria") at 5:3 fits the command for gentle and respectful treatment for other household members at 5:1-2. So Timothy is to see that "honor" is given to "real" widows (i.e., those with no other sources of support) at v. 3. This honor includes support from the church (5:16). Timothy must make sure that other widows receive support due them from family members and household patrons (5:4, 8). The expectation rests on the fourth commandment of the Decalogue and on Christian practice (see Jesus' criticism of nonsupport at Mark 7:10-13). In this letter Paul makes withholding such support a demonstration of denial of faith (5:8), a negative option that balances the one approved at 5:4. The letter then clarifies what constitutes a real widow: that is, hope in God and unceasing prayer (5:5). This contrasts with a pleasure-seeking widow, who is spiritually dead (5:6). Timothy has to direct an admonition to be blameless to the widows faced with the choice between patterns of behavior, but this is ultimately for the good standing of the church in general.

The treatment shifts at 5:9 to describe widowhood as a service ministry in the church. What these widows were supposed to do remains unexplained, but the qualifications sketch the good works by which they gave witness to their faith. These include parental duties and service to the community (5:10). A minimum age requirement and a prohibition of remarriage (supported by the widow's pledge) are laid down for those wishing to be enrolled. The minimum age requirement is justified (5:9, 11-13) by a summary of younger widows' frivolity and infidelity, which sets out the contrasting image. Paul follows that with a wish list of proper domestic activities (5:14-16) by which the younger widows can avoid occasions of rebuke and moral dereliction. The church, too, will avoid community disapproval.

This discussion has led Paul away from the actual widow ministers and parallels the remarks at 5:6-7, where the reference to a wayward few led to a call to Timothy to exhort widows to avoid public blame. Just as 5:9-10, 14 expand the implications of 5:5, so 5:11-13 expand those of 5:6. As at 5:8, in an address to male household masters, he concludes at 5:16 with a command that the faithful women take responsibility for widows in their care, either as mistresses of the households referred to at 5:8, or as women who have taken up the care of widows as their special responsibility. He gives the reason for this: so that the church may not be unduly burdened.

For Reference and Further Study

Bangerter, Otto. "Les Veuves des épîtres pastorales, modèle d'un ministère feminin dans l'église ancienne," *FoiVie* 83 (1984) 27–45.

Bassler, Jouette M. "Limits and Differentiation: The Calculus of Widows in 1 Timothy 5.3-16," in Amy-Jill Levine with Marianne Blickenstaff, eds., *A Feminist Companion to the Deutero-Pauline Epistles*. Cleveland: Pilgrim Press, 2003, 122–46.

Duncker, Peter G. "'*Quae vere viduae sunt*' (1 Tim 5.3)," *Angelicum* 35 (1958) 121–38.

Fiore, Benjamin. "Paul, Exemplification, and Imitation," in J. Paul Sampley, ed., *Paul in the Greco-Roman World: A Handbook*. Harrisburg: Trinity Press International, 231–37.

________. *The Function of Personal Example in the Socratic and Pastoral Epistles*. AnBib 105. Rome: Biblical Institute Press, 1986, 117–23.

Lightman, Marjorie, and William Zeisel, "*Univira:* An Example of Continuity and Change in Roman Society," *CH* 46 (1977) 29.

Malherbe, Abraham J. "Hellenistic Moralists and the New Testament," (1992) 267–333.

________. "Gentle as a Nurse," 35–48.

Malina, Bruce J. *The New Testament World: Insights from Cultural Anthropology*. Atlanta: John Knox, 1981, 116.

Synge, Francis C. "Studies in Texts: 1 Tim 5:3-16," *Theology* 108 (1968) 200–201.

Thurston, Bonnie Bowman. "1 Timothy 5.3-16 and Leadership of Women in the Early Church," in Amy-Jill Levine with Marianne Blickenstaff, eds., *A Feminist Companion to the Deutero-Pauline Epistles*. Cleveland: Pilgrim Press, 2003, 159–74.

________. *The Widows: A Women's Ministry in the Early Church*. Minneapolis: Fortress Press, 1989.

Verner, David C. *Household of God*, 161–66, 134–39.

Veyne, Paul. *Private Life*, 89–91.

Winter, Bruce W. "*Providentia* for the Widows of 1 Timothy 5:1-16 (. . . Acts 6:1-5)," *TynBul* 39 (1988) 83–99.

11. *Presbyters; Public Correction* (5:17-25)

17. Consider the elders who have supervised well as deserving of double honor, especially those who work hard in preaching and teaching. 18. The scripture, we know, says, "You shall not muzzle an ox while it is threshing," and "The worker deserves to be paid." 19. Do not accept an accusation against an elder, except with the corroboration of two or three witnesses. 20. Correct those who are at fault publicly, so that the others might have fear. 21. I solemnly testify before God and Christ Jesus and the elect angels, that you follow these procedures without prejudgment, doing nothing out of favoritism. 22. Do not impose hands on anyone hastily, nor become a party to another person's sins. Keep yourself pure. 23. From now on, do not drink only water; rather take a little wine for the good of your stomach and your frequent ailments. 24. For some people, their sins are known to all, preceding them to judgment; but sins follow after others. 25. Likewise, their good works also are known to all, and those of the other sort cannot be hidden.

Notes

17. *elders:* The next group in the prolonged station code is the elders, here an official function as opposed to the domestic meaning at 5:1. The mixture of ecclesiastical and ordinary uses of a title was just seen in the case of the widows. The NT knows elders as members of the lay nobility in the Sanhedrin (Acts 4:5-6), as synagogue elders (Luke 7:3), as Pharisaic scribes who developed the Mosaic Torah (Matt 15:2; Mark 7:3, 5), or as predecessors in the faith (Heb 11:2). None of these correspond to the elders here. On the Christian side, elders in Jerusalem form a sort of Hellenistic *gerousia* as a governing body of elders next to the apostles (Acts 11:30; 15:2, 4, 6, 22-23; 16:4) and secondary to them. Later, James assumes leadership of the church and the elders serve in the manner of an authoritative board for the church at large (Acts 21:18). The elders of the PE, however, are more like those appointed for individual churches by Paul (Acts 14:23; 20:17), and are like shepherds of the community (Acts 20:28 and 1 Pet 5:1-4; *EDNT*). They are akin to synagogue elders in the limited extent of their authority. Synagogue elders (*zeqenim*), however, formed a council but were not pastors. At Qumran the overseer (*mebaqqer*) or supervisor (*paqid*) had pastoral responsibility. The PE seem to have combined these two Jewish offices, for its elders form a council, some of whom have oversight duties (*episkopoi*; see 3:1).

who have supervised well . . . deserving of double honor: The term for supervise, *proistēmi*, is the same as that for the activity of a household supervisor (compare 3:4, 12). This is in keeping both with the image of the church as God's household (3:15) and the fact that household masters and mistresses constitute the pool of candidates for church ministries. Nonetheless, a more technical sense of the word is used here (and compare 1 Thess 5:12 and Rom 12:8). Thus some supervise the church, some do this in an exemplary way, and some exert themselves further in preaching and teaching. The honor may be doubled because of the dual activity, secular and ecclesiastical, of these men. It might suggest a double form of honor, i.e., praise and a stipend (see Ambrosiaster, *Commentary on the First Letter to Timothy* [CSEL 813:284]). The justification of paying workers in v. 18 indicates that the author has an honorarium in mind here. On the other hand, in the honor-based Greco-Roman society praise cannot be ruled out as insignificant, as it might in contemporary societies where worth is calculated in economic terms. Since firm evidence of a local clergy given regular pay on which to live is clear only in the second century, since presbyters as a major clerical office developed after bishops and deacons at the turn of the second century (Ign. *Smyrn.* 8.1; *1 Clem.* 14.5; *2 Clem.* 17.3), and since the church is already hard pressed to provide for its widows (5:16), a double salary might not be what the phrase means. It might well refer to a double portion at the *agapē* meal (a practice known from Tertullian and the Montanist controversy). In Greco-Roman cult celebrations the wealthy were often invited to share the sacrificial meat, a rare item in the diet of the lower classes (1 Cor 8:10; 10:27). Also, at Greco-Roman formal dinners the more honored guests commonly received better food than did the other guests (1 Cor 11:21). While Paul argued against pressing his own claims to apostolic prerogatives, he recognized their validity and defended them at 1 Cor 9:3-12, where he quotes a passage from Scripture that the PE also use to support the call for the "double honor" (1 Cor 9:9). In a letter in which traditional roles of honor (the public sphere, dominance, male) and shame (the private sphere, submission, female) are reestablished, the trappings of honor might well be introduced also, even into the egalitarian context of the *agapē* meal (1 Cor 11:33-34).

work hard in preaching and teaching: The verb "work" (*kopiaō*) is used for ministerial activity at 1 Thess 5:12; 1 Cor 15:10; Gal 4:11; Rom 16:12; Phil 2:16; Col 1:29; 1 Tim 4:10. Obviously not all presbyters preach and teach, but some do. Teaching puts them in the pool of possible overseers (3:2, and Titus 1:9).

18. *The scripture:* The saying about muzzling an ox is from Deut 25:4 and is also quoted at 1 Cor 9:9. The second saying about the worker is found at Matt 10:10 and Luke 10:7. First Timothy quotes the version known to Luke. The Q saying may have circulated with scriptural authority even at the time of the PE, or the author might have known Luke. It is more likely that the designation of "scripture" applies only to Deuteronomy.

19. *Do not accept:* This is the reverse of the consideration of presbyters who deserve honor. This second topic concerns elders who are accused of wrongdoing. The protocol of requiring two or three corroborating witnesses in these cases was in force in Jewish practice at the start of the Christian movement (Matt 26:60), and was laid down in Deut 19:15, which made its way into Christian community rules for handling disputes (Matt 18:16, and see Heb 10:28; 2 Cor 13:1). The discussion of both topics relies on a similar structure: that is, the presentation of the recommended action and then the scriptural warrant for it. Elsewhere the author of 1 Timothy prefers to substantiate the exhortation with authoritative statements, credal and liturgical fragments, as well as lists, explanations,

examples, and other rhetorical devices. This reflects familiarity with the process of establishing one's position taught by rhetoricians (Quintilian, *Inst.* 1.9).

20. *correct those who are at fault:* The correction has improvement in view (Titus 1:13, and compare Titus 1:9). This was the popular moral philosophers' tactic and goal (see Dio Chrysostom (Or. 77/78) *Invid.* 38; Plutarch, *Adul. Amic.*; Philodemus, *On Frank Speech*). Public reproof, a characteristic of frank speech (*parrēsia;* see Diogenes, *Ep.* 20; Philodemus, *On Frank Speech* 31), offered a salutary lesson to all onlookers (see Eph 5:11). While the fault is not specified, one can assume it has to do with false teaching, the overriding concern of the letter (1:3-4). Apostasy is in the background of Timothy's labors, with correction as one aspect, at 2 Tim 4:2-5. Titus too refutes (*elenchein*) opponents in support of sound teaching (Titus 1:9 and 13, and compare 2:15). Also double honor is to be extended in this context (5:17) to elders who manage well, especially those who teach.

21. *without prejudgment:* After outlining procedures to be followed in accusing an elder, the author concludes the point with a call to Timothy to act without prejudice. This also echoes Deuteronomy 19, which supplies the rules for witnesses. Deuteronomy 19:16-21 describes the procedure for determining whether a charge against someone for breaking the Law was brought by an unjust witness. This coincides with the requirement that Timothy act without prejudice or favoritism. The adjudicators in Deuteronomy are God, the priests, and the judges. In 1 Timothy they are God, Christ, and the chosen angels. Angels are involved in heavenly judgment at LXX Ps 81:1 and may stand here, with God and Christ, as reminders of eschatological judgment. Josephus, *Bell.* II 401, has Agrippa give witness before the angels of God.

22. *Do not impose hands . . . hastily:* The warning to Timothy looks back to the process against an elder at fault and forward to the ordination of worthy new elders after due deliberation by the laying on of hands (see 1 Tim 4:14; 2 Tim 1:6). This corresponds to the testing of the assistants at 3:10. Leo the Great, *Letters* 12.2 (NPNF 2 12:13) interprets the laying on of hands as conferring priestly dignity. On the other hand, Tertullian, *Modesty* 18 (ANF 4:94) seems to apply the laying on of hands in 1 Tim 5:22 to a ritual of penance preceding the Eucharist.

23. *do not drink only water:* Perhaps the admonition to keep pure led the author to introduce this advice to Timothy. It is decidedly anti-ascetical. John Chrysostom, *Hom. Tit.* 1 (NPNF 1 13:523), declares that bodily infirmity no less than spiritual infirmity injures the church. If we could practice virtue with the soul alone, we would not need to take care of the body. And why then were we born at all? The Christian pastor, like the faithful, is fully human and has physical as well as spiritual needs for leading a healthy life. One might even argue that the commandment "You shall not kill" requires action to maintain one's health, both of body and soul. First Timothy expects the addressee to look after his physical health while avoiding excesses, whether in abstention or overindulgence. He is also to cultivate a good self-image despite disparities of age and experience between him and those he serves. Moreover, he is to develop good social and management skills. These "human" skills work with spiritual qualities to make for an effective church leader.

As at 4:8, asceticism is severed from its spiritual basis and is treated as misguided medical practice. Nonetheless, asceticism is still one of the hallmarks of false teaching, and the suggestion here is an oblique reminder to potential presbyters to preserve their doctrinal integrity. By contrast, Epictetus, *Diatr.* 3.13,21 connects asceticism, including drinking only water, with the effort to control one's passions. But Plutarch, *Mor.* 652 B, is clear about the benefits of wine (and see Pliny, *Nat.* XXIII 38).

24–25. *judgment . . . cannot be hidden:* Secrecy and manifestation run as undercurrents throughout the PE. The sins of some are known, and they are exposed by name in the PE (1 Tim 1:20; 2 Tim 1:15), where judgment hangs over them (2 Tim 2:17; 4:10, 14) unless they repent (1 Tim 1:20). The secrecy of false teachers who sneak into homes will be exposed, as will their victims (2 Tim 3:6-9). The widows who are enjoying an overindulgent life are as good as dead (1 Tim 5:6), despite appearances to the contrary, and the rich who are immersed in greed are on their way to ruin (1 Tim 6:9), whether they or others know it or not. Doers of good are also known by name (2 Tim 1:5, 16-18; 3:10-11; 4:6-8, 9-13), and Timothy is encouraged to let his progress be evident to all (1 Tim 4:15). Christ Jesus manifested his justice to the world (1 Tim 3:16) and his forgiveness to all believers (1 Tim 1:16). All the community is to be known for its members' good works (1 Tim 2:10; 3:2, 7, 13; 5:10; Titus 2:7; 3:1, 8, 14). Christ will reward those who are good (1 Tim 6:11-16) when he appears for judgment at the end-time (2 Tim 4:1; Titus 3:4-7, 13).

To manifest good in the larger community is part of the PE's strategy for community acceptance. By this strategy all are involved in establishing the credibility of the Christian faith and attracting others to it. This offers a reason for some (such as the women and the household masters with widowed dependents) to accept restrictions and obligations. The assurance that evil will be exposed and judged is a source of encouragement for the beleaguered and a threat to the wayward. Both the attractiveness of positive examples and the threat of public exposure for wrongdoers were tactics employed by popular philosophical moralists of the day (e.g., Philodemus, *On Frank Speech*). Augustine, *Letters* 95 (FC 18:118), acknowledges a dilemma. If you punish a man you may ruin him. If you leave him unpunished you may ruin another. The aim of correction (*nouthesia*) in this letter, in the letters undisputedly by Paul, and in moral exhortation of the first century is the eventual awakening of self-awareness in the offending person and a return to upright action and choices. While this repentance, sometimes coming late and after enormous misdeeds, might occasion questions about God's justice, God's mercy requires it (Ezek 18:21-22). Paul's spiritual autobiography in this letter demonstrates this.

Interpretation

The topic of honor continues in the next section dealing with elders, now in a ministerial sense (contrast 5:1). This section on elders has four subsections: honor for excellent ministry, reproof of faulty elders, verification of charges, policy about ordaining new elders. The letter recommends that some of the elders receive a double honor (5:17-18). *Timē* ("honor" or "respect") comes into play in another way in the rules for publicly censuring elders. These include a reminder to accept an accusation only when supported by scripturally warranted verification (5:19). The latter goes on to recommend public reprimand for those at fault, as an instructional example for everyone (5:20).

The letter then has Paul turn his attention to Timothy himself as the preeminent official. The charge opens with almost forensic solemnity and requires impartiality in bringing forth the condemnation of an elder. It also expects restraint in designating new elders, as well as Timothy's personal integrity (5:21-22). This caps off the consideration of widows and elders and relates to the discussion of community officials' qualifications at 3:1-13. The command to keep himself pure (5:22) receives a curious sequel in Paul's advice on drinking to maintain health (5:23). Asceticism, debunked above, has no spiritual advantage, only damages health, and so should be dropped.

More to the point are the observations on the eventual disclosure of people's sins, good works, and misdeeds (5:24-25). This remark fits the advice not to rush and risk becoming implicated in others' sins (5:22) as also the call for public reproof of the guilty (5:20). In terms of the advice on drinking in the immediately preceding verse, with its recollection of the ascetical false teachers of the final days, this comment suggests that their current success (4:1-3) will be short-lived. The positive side of the remark, that good works are in the open (*prodēla*), continues the letter's insistence on good works and good public reputation among community members and officeholders, an apologetic and perhaps missionary stance.

For Reference and Further Study

Bartlett, David L. *Ministry in the New Testament.* Minneapolis: Fortress Press, 1993, 167–77.

Brox, Norbert. *Pastoralbriefe*, 199–200.

Colson, F. H. "Quintilian I,9 and the *'chreia'* in Ancient Education," *Classical Review* 35 (1921) 42–44, 150–54, 198–208.

Fiore, Benjamin. "The Pastoral Epistles in the Light of Philodemus' 'On Frank Criticism,'" in John T. Fitzgerald, Dirk Obink, and Glenn Holland, eds., *Philodemus and the New Testament World.* Leiden: Brill, 2004, 271–94.

________. *Personal Example*, 97–100.

Fuller, J. William. "Of Elders and Triads in 1 Timothy 5:19-25," *NTS* 29 (1983) 258–63.

Harvey, Anthony E. "Elders," 318–32.

MacArthur, J. S. "On the Significance of *hē graphē* in 1 Timothy v. 1," *ExpTim* 53 (1941) 37.

Malherbe, Abraham J. *Moral Exhortation*, 48–51, 55, 60, 92.
________. *Paul and the Popular Philosophers*, 85–87.
Meier, John P. "*Presbyteros* in the Pastoral Epistles," *CBQ* 35 (1973) 323–45.
Powell, Douglas. "Ordo Presbyterii," *JTS* 26 (1975) 289–328.
Roberts, C. H. "Elders," 403–405.
Schoelgen, Georg. "Die *diplē timē* von 1 Tim 5.17," *ZNW* 80 (1989) 232–39.

12. *Slaves; False Teaching; Contentment* (6:1-8)

1. Those who are under the yoke as slaves should regard their own masters as deserving of total respect, so that the name of God and the Christian teaching not be defamed. 2. Furthermore, those who have believing masters should not look down on them because they are brothers. Rather they should give even more service because those who devote themselves to beneficial activity are believers and beloved. Teach and exhort these things. 3. If someone teaches otherwise and does not adhere to the sound words of our Lord Jesus Christ and the teaching according to piety, 4. that person has become swollen with conceit, while understanding nothing and on the contrary suffers from an unhealthy interest in investigations and disputes over words. From these interests arise envy, discord, abusive speech, malicious suspicions, 5. endless squabbles of people who have been intellectually destroyed and stripped of the truth, people who consider piety to be a profit-making enterprise. 6. Now piety is a major source of profit; piety, that is, with contentment.

7. You see, we have brought nothing into the world;
So that we are unable to carry anything out of it;
8. But if we have food and clothing,
Let us be content with these.

Notes

1. *under the yoke as slaves:* The heavy tone of oppression is captured by Gal 5:1, where the yoke of slavery is the image that describes the Jewish Law's burden as opposed to Christian freedom. Like women, slaves may have been pushing the emancipatory implications of Gal 3:28, although there is no clear indication of such pressure in the letter to Philemon. The fact that the admonition to slaves is not balanced by a matching admonition to masters, typical in household codes (compare Col 3:22–4:1 and Eph 6:5-9), makes it plausible that the slaves were causing a problem for the Christian community. Paul already confronted pressures toward manumission at 1 Cor 7:21. Evidence of slave discontent is noticeable among the writings of Christians in Asia Minor, where Christian

motives are added to the call for slaves' obedience in the household codes (Col 3:22-25; Eph 6:5-8; 1 Pet 2:18-25, and see Ign. *Pol.* 4.3, where he resists the idea that the church should purchase the slaves' freedom). The disruption of the Greco-Roman social and economic order that the pressure for manumission represented, if left to grow, could only bring the church trouble from the larger community (see Cicero, *Leg.* 2.7.19-27 for the Greco-Roman belief that foreign religions corrupted slaves). John Chrysostom, *Hom. 1 Cor.* 19.4 (CMFL 37), referring also to Ephesians and Colossians, concludes that obviously Paul did not intend to abolish slavery as a social institution. Rather he attacks slavery in its worst form, the slavery to evil that pays no respect to any external freedom. The image of slavery to sin (Romans 6 and 7) and to the Law (Galatians 4 and 5) helps Paul advance his views about faith and justification.

On the other hand, the way he addresses Philemon in his letter to him about the Onesimus affair demonstrates that Paul expected the master/slave relationship within the Christian community to reflect the reality that all are made kin through Christ. The insistence that all in the Corinthian community share the *agapē* meal together and with the same food and drink (1 Corinthians 11) brings the ideal of equality into the reality of everyday Christian practice. The egalitarian nature of Christianity defines a goal to be striven for even today. The separation of people in our society, sometimes from prejudice but more often on economic and social grounds, has religious consequences as people end up worshiping together in homogeneous groups. The separation also affects intergroup attitudes, leading to prejudicial views and participation in discriminatory practices under the cloak of community cohesiveness and economic interest.

be defamed: The immorality of the faithful as an occasion for deriding God's name is criticized at Rom 2:24 and later at *2 Clem.* 13.2 (both applying Isa 52:5). First Timothy expands this theological position to include occasioning defamation of the church's teaching. The latter is also a concern at Titus 2:15 (see also Ign. *Trall.* 8.3). The letter has Paul use "blasphemer" (*blasphēmos*) to characterize himself in his preconversion life (1:13) and describe blasphemy as a product of false teaching (1 Tim 6:4, and see 2 Tim 3:2) and corrupted faith (1 Tim 1:20).

2. *because they are brothers:* A second aspect of the slave problem is slaves' chafing at servitude to Christian masters who presumably subscribe to Pauline egalitarianism. The justification for their claim to manumission rests in the slogan "because they (i.e., the masters) are kin in the faith."

they should give even more service: Paul used something akin to this argument in Philemon 11 ("once useless and now useful to you and to me") and 16 ("more than a slave, a brother, beloved to me and more so to you"). Ephesians 4:6-9 and Colossians 3:23–4:1, since they address masters as well, refer to the Lord as the true master whom the slaves serve and to whom the masters are subordinate as well.

those who devote themselves to beneficial activity are believers: The beneficial activity goes from superior to subordinate and not vice versa in the honor-based Greco-Roman world. The word *euergesia* ("beneficial activity") derives from *euergeteō* ("be a benefactor"), which led to the title *euergetēs*, adopted by Hellenistic kings (e.g., Antigonus) and Roman emperors (e.g., Trajan). *Antilambanō* in the middle voice usually means "devote oneself to" (*LSJ*). Thus the clause refers to the household masters and the "good works" that are expected of all in the community (see 5:24) and that the wealthy household leaders are in a good position to do (e.g., 2:9-10; 6:18). The slaves expected their masters' beneficial activity to extend to them. Since the community's officials (elders, overseers, assistants) are all drawn from the ranks of household leaders, the problem is compounded, because recalcitrant slaves would not demonstrate their masters' good household management. Moreover, these unresolved household tensions would not win them a good name in the community at large. Both of these were qualifications for selection. The author thus tries to focus on their beneficence as a demonstration of fulfilling the requirements of their station in a Christian life of faith and love. Slaves, on their part, are expected to do likewise through their willing service. The reputation of the community, its leaders, and its teaching would thus be secure. The author alludes to the slogan ("because they are kin in the faith") by which the slaves were claiming their right to freedom. The phrase is expanded with "beloved" (*agapētoi*; see Philemon 16), derived from the peculiarly Christian attitude among coreligionists. The word is the equivalent of "brothers" (*adelphoi*). At Rom 1:7 Paul expands the Jewish epithet "beloved of God" (see Rom 11:28) to make it an expression for all Christians (see 1 Pet 2:11; 4:12, and compare 1 Cor 4:14 and 2 Cor 11:15). Paul uses the word to refer to the new reality of the Christian's life in the Spirit. Faith and love are both gifts of God to the members of the church (1 Tim 1:14; 2 Tim 1:13) as well as objects of the letter's instruction (1 Tim 1:5). As such, these gifts are focuses of the community members' way of life (1 Tim 2:15; 4:12; 6:11; 2 Tim 2:22; 3:10; Titus 2:2). Use of the adjective here carries with it the presumption that the believing masters should be loved.

these things: The word for "these things" (*tauta*) again refers to all the instructions in the letter and stands at the end of the expanded station code section. As such it forms the transition to the concluding exhortation. This section mentions traditional hortatory material, both from the general Christian tradition and from the particular apostolic instruction given to the addressee. Here the author weaves segments of an ordination exhortation together with commonplace teaching about riches and a polemic against false teachers (see 1:3-7 and 4:1-11 for the two previous critiques of false teachers). While it derives from a variety of sources, the diverse material is not thrown together haphazardly. The arrangement juxtaposes three sets of exhortations and warnings

I	2b	3-10
II	11b-19	11a
III	20a	20b-21a

Within this structure, vv. 6-10 correspond to vv. 17-19, and vv. 11-16 correspond to vv. 20-21.

3. *If someone teaches otherwise:* In the first section of the concluding exhortation and warning the author often uses the indefinite pronoun for the false teachers (compare 1 Tim 1:3, 6, 19; 4:1; 5:15, 24; 6:10, 21, and 2 Tim 2:18). By this device the author creates a bond with the addressees, who are presumed to know those

to whom the author is referring. It also allows any in the audience who tend toward the apostates' position to correct their views without losing face. The same tactic appears in the letter's treatment of those reluctant to shoulder their burden of care for widows (1 Tim 5: 4, 8, 16). Finally, it suggests that the opposition is not numerous, thus putting a good face on a critical situation. The reference to heterodox teaching recalls the basic purpose of Timothy's work, which is to stop such false teaching (1 Tim 1:3), and echoes earlier references to false teachers (1 Tim 1:6-7, 19-20; 4:1-3, and compare 2 Tim 2:14, 16-18, 23; 3:1-9, 13; 4:3-4; Titus 1:10-16; 3:9-11). For sound teaching and moral illness see 1:10. For piety see 2:2. The intellectual dead-end of the false teaching receives emphasis here and throughout the letters (1 Tim 1:7; 6:9, 20; 2 Tim 2:18; 3:7-9, 13; 4:4; Titus 1:14-16; 3:3, 9) as does the intellectual side of the faith (1 Tim 1:10; 2:4, 7; 3:2, 15; 4:3, 6, 13, 16; 5:17; 6:1; 2 Tim 1:11; 2:2, 24-25; 3:10, 16; 4:2; Titus 1:1, 9; 2:1, 3, 6, 10).

the sound words of our Lord Jesus Christ: This does not mean the sayings of the Lord, of which the letters give little evidence, but rather refers to the preaching about the Lord (e.g., 1 Tim 1:11; 2:7).

4. *swollen with conceit:* Possible conceit that might lead to falling into the devil's trap was enough to strike new converts from the list of overseer candidates at 3:6. Here the nature of the trap receives expanded attention.

suffers: The PE characterize the false teachers as ill (here mentally unbalanced) and their teaching as unsound. See 1:10, and also Plutarch, *Mor.* 546F.

From these interests arise: The second half of the polemical statement against the false teachers focuses on the divisiveness the false teaching and its disputations induce. The list of vices in vv. 4 and 5 focuses on divisiveness. This contrasts with the unanimity promoted by the letter, with its protracted station code. More particularly, the pursuit of peace and the avoidance of disputes are attitudes modeled for all by Timothy and Titus (1 Tim 5:19; 6:11; 2 Tim 2:23-24; Titus 3:9). Furthermore, community leaders (1 Tim 3:3, 11; Titus 1:7; 3:2), men (1 Tim 2:8), women (1 Tim 2:11, 12), indeed all (2 Tim 2:14; Titus 1:3) are called to adopt their peaceable lifestyle. Paul himself manifested the hostility and abusive speech of the false teachers but became a model of conversion and of Christ's forbearance for all (1 Tim 1:13). While the example is primarily that all, even the worst sinners, can be saved, the insistence on patient self-control in the letters suggests that Christ's forbearance is part of the pattern for believers as well (see the exhortation to patience at 6:11, and compare 2 Tim 3:10 and Titus 2:2 and the exhortation to forbearance at 2 Tim 3:10; 4:2). The PE make use of the common view among Greco-Roman moralists that pointless rebuke is characteristic of false teachers (see Isocrates, *Ad Nicoclem* 46-47). The hostility and divisiveness here, however, have theological implications in view of their juxtaposition to salvation at 1:13, the remedy by the extreme step of excommunication at 1:20, the association with end-time hostility at Titus 3:2, and the contrast with the condition of those renewed by the Holy Spirit at Titus 3:1-7.

5. *consider piety to be a profit-making enterprise:* See the Note on 2:2. Without truth the false teachers cannot achieve a way of life that accords with true faith. Thus "piety" for them was an impossibility. Another commonplace charge against

false teachers is that they are only interested in making money (Dio Chrysostom (Or. 32) *Alex.* 11-12; Lucian, *Peregr.* 13; *Vit. auct.; Ep. of Socrates* 1.1-2; 1 Thess 2:5). The letter uses this in connection with material about wealth from the Christian (Lukan) tradition to demonstrate the profit to be gained from the Christian faith and way of life. Dionysius of Halicarnassus, *Ant. rom.* V 21, 2, reports that the Tarquinii lost good sense due to power and riches, a problem of those criticized here. Philo, *Embassy* 242, similarly contrasts piety and material gain.

6. *with contentment:* The philosophical ideal of Cynics and Stoics (*Ep. of Diogenes* 28.8; Epictetus, *Gnom.*; Stobaeus, *fr.* 33; *Ecl.* 3; Dio Chrysostom (*Or.* 30) *Charid.* 33) had been adapted to Pauline Christianity in Phil 4:11 (and compare 2 Cor 9:8). It is also contrasted with greed by the Greco-Roman moralists (*Ep. of Diogenes* 46; *Ep. of Socrates* 8), and 1 Timothy does that here. Finding contentment within oneself and not in one's external possessions or situation suits the theology of the letter, which finds salvation by Christ to be the key experience that transforms the believers' consciousness and way of life (1 Tim 1:13-15 and Titus 3:1-7). Isocrates, *Demonax* 21, 46 and *Ad Nicoclem* 29 links the pursuit of wealth to enslavement to pleasure.

7. *we have brought nothing:* This commonplace saying, found in Scripture at Job 1:21 and Eccl 5:14, is completed with an exhortation in v. 8 (and see *Anth. Graec.* X 58; Seneca, *Ep.* 102,23-25, and compare Seneca, *Prov.* 6,6; *Ep.* 20,13; Horace, *Carm.* II 14,21-24; Propertius, III 5,11-14; Ovid, *Trist.* V 14,11-14). The exhortation applies the virtue of contentment (compare Philo, *Rewards* 99-100; Juvenal, *Sat.* 14, 316-321). The first person plural middle verbs suggest that these are two strophes.

   "So that" (*hoti*) has troubled scribes, who have "corrected" the text by adding "truly" (*alēthes*), "clearly" (*dēlon*), or "indubitably" (*haud dubium*, Vlg) before it. It is an unusual *hoti consecutivum*.

8. *content with these:* The source of contentment, food and clothing, does not fit the letter's spiritual viewpoint. The material here rather serves to develop the argument about the danger of seeking wealth that follows in vv. 9-10.

Interpretation

In the concluding section of the body Paul instructs Timothy to maintain the teaching and exhortation outlined in the letter (6:2, "these things," *tauta*). In this, the exhortation section, Paul reaffirms the soundness of the teaching by contrasting it (6:3-5) with the heterodoxy of anyone who fails to adhere to it. Medical images of illness and charges of ignorance and moral depravity bolster the contrast. These reiterate the warnings and criticisms at 1:4-11 and 4:1-3 and ultimately direct the audience's focus to the contrasting positive examples offered earlier in the letter and here in the rest of the chapter. The contrast is reiterated succinctly at the end of the chapter (6:20-21). The positive recommendations to Timothy are interspersed with a consideration of the morality of riches and those who pursue them. The warnings about riches here function like those against the heterodox teaching of false teachers in that both serve to contrast with the acceptable position and Timothy, its adherent and proponent. Timothy is warned away from both in a formal, almost scripted admonition. The topic of riches, expanded here, follows from Paul's final comment about the heterodox teachers who seek to make money from religion (6:5). Paul sees another type of gain from religion (6:6) and posits contentment rather than avarice as a precondition.

For Reference and Further Study

Bartchy, S. Scott. "Slavery (Greco-Roman)," *ABD* 6:65–73.

________. *MALLON CHRĒSAI: First-Century Slavery and the Interpretation of 1 Cor 7:21*. SBLDS 11. Missoula: Scholars Press, 1985.

Harrill, J. Albert. *Slaves in the New Testament: Literary, Social, and Moral Dimensions.* Minneapolis: Fortress Press, 2006.

Perkins, Pheme. *The Love Commands in the New Testament*. New York: Paulist, 1982.

Thurén, Jukka. "Die Struktur der Schlussparänese 1 Tim 6, 3-2," *TZ* 26 (1970) 241–53.

Towner, Philip H. *Goal of Our Instruction*, 175–80.

Turner, Nigel. "Beloved," *Christian Words*, 266–68.

Veyne, Paul. *Private Life*, 107–10, on euergetism.

White, John L. "Apostolic Letter Tradition," 441.

Wischmeyer, Oda. "Das Adjektiv *AGAPĒTOS* in den Paulinischen Briefen: Eine traditionsgeschichtliche Miszelle," *NTS* 32 (1986) 476–80.

13. *On Riches; Final Charge to Timothy; Conclusion* (6:9-21)

9. Those, however, who want to be rich are stumbling into temptation, and a trap, and into many foolish cravings any of which plunge people into destruction and ruin. 10. For the root of all evils is the love of money, and in their striving for it some have strayed from the faith and pierced themselves with many woes.

11. But you, O Man of God, flee these things,
and pursue justice, piety, faith, love, patience, gentleness.
12. Compete in the noble contest of faith;
take hold of eternal life. You were called for it
and pronounced the noble confession in the presence of many witnesses.

13. I instruct you before God, who gives life to everything, and Christ Jesus
who gave testimony before Pontius Pilate to the noble confession, 14. that
you observe the commandment spotless and blameless until the appearance
of our Lord Jesus Christ, 15. which he will display at the proper time.

He who is the blessed and only Sovereign,
King of kings,
And Lord of lords,
16. He who alone has immortality,
Who inhabits unapproachable light,
Whom no human has seen or is able to see.
To him be honor and eternal sovereignty. Amen.

17. Instruct the rich in the present age not to be proud nor to rest their hope
in the uncertainty of riches but rather in God, the one who offers us everything in rich abundance for our enjoyment, 18. and instruct them to do
good, to be rich in good deeds, to be generous, liberal, 19. storing up a
noble treasure for themselves for the time to come, so that they might take
hold of what is really life.

20. O Timothy, safeguard what has been entrusted to you, turning away
from profane, empty chatter and from contradictions of what is errone-
ously called knowledge. 21. Some, in preferring this, have deviated with
regard to the faith.

Grace be with you all.

Notes

9. *temptation . . . trap . . . cravings:* The temptation is the end-time test of the Adversary at Matt 6:13 *parr.*; 26:41 *parr.*; Luke 8:13. At 2 Tim 2:26 the trap can be escaped, but the context (2 Tim 3:1) is eschatological. At 1 Tim 3:7 the trap constitutes a serious danger to be avoided. Passionate cravings, given in to by Epicureans but to be avoided in the other philosophical schools, lead to destruction and ruin (perhaps a hendiadys for total ruin), which is an eschatological condition (Rev 9:11; Matt 7:13; Rom 9:22; Phil 1:28; 3:19-20; and see Philo, *Spec. Leg.* IV 65; Pseudo-Phocylides, *Sent.* 42-47; Stobaeus, III 10,37; Cicero, *Rosc. Amer.* 75; Seneca, *Clem.* I 1,4-2,1; Aulus Gellius, XI 2,2). The opposite of that condition is salvation. The promise of eternal life at the end of a life of Christian virtue stands in contrast to the result of a life of greed and makes the same eschatological point here in the final exhortation of the letter. Thus the stakes are high and the exhortation accords with the eschatological tenor of the letter and the reiteration of belief in salvation. The teaching on riches agrees with that in Luke (e.g., Luke 16:19-34, and see Propertius, III 7, 1-4; Seneca, *Ep.* 87, 28.31). The NT characterizes the poor as people in a wretched condition (Matt 5:3-5; 11:4-5; Luke 6:21; 14:13-21; 21:2-3; Jas 2:3-6; Rev 3:17), as people who were unable to maintain their inherited status or were born into a condition of need, a class that included people who had to work for a daily wage (and cf. Philo, *Spec. Leg.* IV, 195-196). By contrast, the rich are considered to have ready access to God because they have access to human powers (Mark 10:23-24 *parr.*; Matt 27:57).

They are satisfied and proud (Luke 1:63; 6:24-25) and are depicted as greedy (Luke 12:16; 16:14; 19:1-10). Second Timothy 3:1-4 ranks avarice second after selfishness (and compare Jas 1:10-11; 5:1-7; Rev 3:17-18; 6:15; 18:3, 15, 19). In the ancient world wealth was considered a means to another end, such as contentment. To accumulate it for itself was thought to be greedy and evil (Pseudo-Pelagius, *On Wealth* II, PL Supp I, 1381; XX,4; PL Supp I, 1417; Plutarch, *Cupid. divit.* 525 A 17; 526 BC 19, 25).

11. *Man of God:* Here and at 2 Tim 3:17 the title by which Timothy is addressed describes the person equipped for the task of upholding the confession of the Gospel in the face of opposition. Philo, *Giants* 61, finds that the priests and prophets, who are models of the wise and citizens of the kingdom, are men of God. The *Letter of Aristeas* 140 uses the title for true worshipers of God. Shepherd of Hermas, *Mand.* 1.32; 13.20 calls the reborn "your man." Psalm 89:1 LXX identifies the psalmist as Moses, man of God (and for prophetic servants of God in the OT see also 1 Sam 2:27 and Deut 33:1). In Hellenistic Judaism the title seems to refer to a Spirit-filled person (Käsemann).

    flee . . . pursue . . . gentleness: The way of Christian living contrasts with the pursuit of riches, which the author describes in this second warning/exhortation section. While the passage contains elements of an ordination address, they are employed here in a general exhortation intended for the whole community. The virtues listed are not just commonplaces but comprise fundamental features of Christian life that are expanded on elsewhere in the letter. For "justice" (*dikaiosynē*) see 1:9; for "piety" (*eusebeian*) see 2:2; for "faith" and "love" (*pistin* and *agapēn*) see 1:5; and for "patience" and "gentleness" (*hypomonēn* and *praupathian*) see 6:4.

12. *Compete:* The athletic image was used at 4:10 in reaction to the false teachers' asceticism. See v. 19 for the exhortation of the rich to victory in life and compare 2 Tim 1:9; Titus 1:2; 3:7. See also 2 Tim 4:7, which summarizes Paul's apostolic career. This is the example put before Timothy here.

    eternal life: Thus the profit of "piety" (*eusebeia*) is great indeed (and see 4:8 and 6:19). Eternal life is, in the end, a gift from God (v. 13).

    You were called for it: As Paul is an exemplar of salvation for believers (1:16), so is Timothy (4:12); this leads to their and his salvation (4:16). The idea is alluded to in the fact that he is called to eternal life, as are all people, for God wants to save all through Christ (2:4, 6). The later scribal insertion of "and" (*kai*) before the verb "pronounced" (*homologēsas*) tries to clarify the grammar in the predicate by making explicit the link between the two verbs. Both verbs are in the relative clause. The preposition "for" (*eis*) expresses the purpose or goal of the calling. Timothy is a minister in service of eternal life, to advance its acceptance. The confessional statement also has to do with eternal life. It most likely refers to Christ's redemptive deed, to which the author refers in v. 13. That deed is the basis of eternal life and the message to be heralded.

    in the presence of many witnesses: The presence of witnesses (compare 2 Tim 2:22) indicates a formal, liturgical ceremony for the confession. The imperatives, promise of eternal life, start of a lifelong struggle, command to live Christian virtues, and the double formula in v. 13 (God and Christ), which marks a transition to the triple formula (the eschatological outlook), all suggest baptism as the context of the declaration. Ordination is more likely, however, because the reference to Pilate indicates a struggle with a hostile world for which Timothy was appointed (1:3, 18-19). His task includes suffering (see 2 Tim 4:7), and the letter here has Timothy engaged in the effort to preserve the tradition entrusted to him (6:20 and 2 Tim 1:14). Furthermore, the verb "call" (*eklēthēs*) suggests selection for a particular ministry (compare 2 Tim 1:9). Finally, imposition of hands, a part of an ordination ritual, receives mention elsewhere in the letters (4:14; 5:22; 2 Tim 1:6). The author seems to be quoting from an ordination exhortation in this chapter (6:11-12, 15-16) but that exhortation has some baptismal themes as well.

13. *I instruct:* The author expands the traditional material and refers to themes used elsewhere: God as creator at 1:4 and 4:4, Christ's witness before Pilate at 2:6 and 2 Tim 1:8.

the noble confession: The phrase repeats that at v. 12 and links the confession of Christ to that of the ordained person. Jesus' goal has been identified as the redemptive salvation of sinners (1:5; 2:5-6, and compare 3:16; 2 Tim 1:1, 10; 2:10-12; 3:15; Titus 3:17-18). The confession Jesus made was in word, as the trial before Pilate implies, but also in the deed of giving himself up to death and then rising (3:16; 2 Tim 1:8). This is the Gospel message (1 Tim 2:7; 2 Tim 1:10-11; 2:8, and see 3:15 and the confessional statements at Acts 3:13; 4:27; 13:28; Ign. *Magn.* 11.1; *Trall.* 9.1; *Smyrn.* 1.2). Timothy is committed to preach it (2 Tim 4:2, 5) in imitation of Paul (1 Tim 1:11; 2:7; 2 Tim 1:11; 4:17; Titus 1:3). Part of Timothy's and other ordained persons' ongoing task is to suffer with Paul in advancing the Gospel, as Jesus suffered (2 Tim 2:3, and see 2 Tim 3:4). In all, the virtuous life outlined in the list at vv. 11-12 provides some of the ways in which Timothy and other ordained persons will keep the confession pure and blameless. Consistently throughout the PE, one's way of life has to coincide with the confession of faith for there to be true piety.

14–15. These verses may be taken from the ordination address, or at least it may be using language from such an address.

observe the commandment spotless and blameless: This refers to the charge to the newly ordained. Its preservation as pure and blameless parallels the effort to safeguard "what has been entrusted" (*parathēkē*, 6:20). Care to preserve blamelessness has already been seen in the qualification lists (3:2; 5:7).

appearance: The end-time appearance of Christ is part of the letters' eschatological expectation (2 Tim 1:18; 2:12; 4:1, 8; Titus 2:13). The end-time expectation looks to the future, but sees the present as the beginning of the final days (see 4:1). The revelation of Jesus Christ is expected at 1 Cor 1:7 and 2 Thess 1:7, but the word "epiphany" appears only at 2 Thess 2:8. The mercy of God to save all has already appeared (Titus 2:11; 3:4) in Jesus Christ (2 Tim 1:10 and Titus 3:6). The completion of the saving action is foreseen in the future (2 Tim 1:12, 18; 4:8) at the time appointed by God (1 Tim 6:15), when Jesus will again appear (Titus 2:13).

15. *he will display:* The idea is common in the PE, but the word is used only here. Christians live between the first appearance of God's favor (1 Tim 3:16; 2 Tim 1:10; Titus 1:3; 2:11) and the one yet to come (2 Tim 4:1, 8; Titus 2:13). From the first, Christians draw assurance of salvation; from the second, warning and hope. See Heb 9:28 for a similar expectation of the saving appearance of Jesus.

the blessed and only Sovereign: The PE reflect their Hellenistic environment in some of their descriptions of God. For "blessed" (*makarios*) see 1:11. For the title "King of Kings" see Diodorus Siculus, I 55, 7; Aeschylus, *Persians* 21-28; and as a divine title see Horace, *Carm.* III 1, 5-8. "Lord of Lords" is found in Deut 10:17 LXX; Ps 136:3 LXX, and the Targum translations for these verses. The word "sovereign" (*dynastēs*) describes God in later Jewish writings (Sir 46:5; 2 Macc 12:15; 15:3; *3 Macc.* 2:3; *Sibylline Oracles* 3.719; *Letter of Aristeas* 139). In the only other NT appearances, Luke uses the word for earthly rulers (Luke 1:52; Acts 8:27).

16. *immortality:* This word, *athanasia*, appears five times in Wisdom, once in *4 Maccabees*, and nowhere else in the LXX (see Plutarch, *Pericles* 39,2; Vergil, *Aeneid* IV 356-359).

To him be honor . . . eternal sovereignty: The doxology is typical of traditional Judaism, although a gnosticizing tendency can be detected in the stress on God's being unseen. In all, the Hellenistic syncretism of the diaspora synagogue seems to have influenced the author.

17. *the rich in the present age:* To balance the first section's dire description of the destruction of the greedy at vv. 7-10, which stems from the linkage between greedy persons and delusional false teachers who are described at vv. 3-5, the second section of the final exhortation offers the wealthy a program of reform. The latter issues in an outcome like that of the faithful struggle noted in the ordination exhortation, that is, eternal life (see vv. 12 and 19). Warnings to the rich about their attachment to riches are found in Lucian, *Dial. mor.* 1, 3. The admonitions here echo those in the gospels (Matt 6:20; Luke 12:21; 16:9). The contrast between the present age and the age to come is common in Jewish apocalyptic dualism. In the PE the present age (1 Tim 4:8; 2 Tim 4:10; Titus 2:12) is identified with the last times (1 Tim 4:1; 2 Tim 3:1). New threats to the faith are balanced by new possibilities of living the life of faith, for the age of salvation is now.

for our enjoyment: Compare 4:4. In the LXX the word "enjoyment" (*apolausis*) only appears at 3 Macc. 7:16 (and Aquila Ps 118:143). The creator God is viewed positively, as is the enjoyment of created reality (see also *Did.* 10.3; *1 Clem.* 20.10, and contrast Heb 11:25 and *2 Clem.* 10.3-4 for enjoyment of vice).

19. *storing up a noble treasure for themselves:* The rich, too, can live true piety by acting in accord with their faith. The advice parallels Luke's, which is to hope in God and not in riches (Luke 12:22-32; 19:29), to use wealth for doing good (Luke 12:33; 14:12-14; 18:22), and to heap up a treasure for the eternal life to come (Luke 12:16-21; 18:23, and see also Tob 4:8-9). Plutarch, *Mor.* 786 C, notes that once passions diminish with age, a person can be devoted to works that benefit the commonality of people, and Lucian, *Pisc.* 35, advances the philosophers' ideal as one who shares what they have (see Diogenes Laertius, 4.37-38 and 7.123). This advice appears to be "after the fact," following as it does on the doxology (vv. 15-16). On the other hand, the epiphany of Jesus Christ is brought

about by God, who alone is immortal and supreme in power. God, then, is a reliable basis of hope and the only guarantor that a converted life of generous good deeds will be rewarded. Hebrews 13:1-9 contains many of the same exhortations and warnings.

20. *safeguard what has been entrusted:* The letter ends, as it began, with a direct admonition to Timothy to act to safeguard the tradition of faith (1:3). The third section of the final exhortation places before Timothy both the admonition to safeguard and the warning against false teaching. This commercial image refers to money given in trust, which must be surrendered intact at the request of the depositor (*MM*). Philo, *Worse* 65, applies the word to knowledge of sacred things and Pseudo-Isocrates, *Or.* 1, 22 uses it for the advice being entrusted to the listener. Paul entrusted (*paratithemai*) the apostolic instruction to Timothy (1:18), and Timothy is to hand on what he heard from Paul to trusted teachers (2 Tim 2:2, and see also 2 Tim 1:12 and 14). It is a fitting charge in the context of an ordination exhortation.

    from profane, empty chatter and from contradictions: The empty chatter (see Epictetus, *Diatr.* 2.17.8) of false teaching constitutes a danger to the entrusted teachings, since it leads to apostasy. The coincidence that the word *antitheseis* is also the title of one of Marcion's works (Tertullian, *Marc.* 1.19.4; 2.29.1) is not enough to establish an anti-Marcionite polemic here. Such a polemic would demand a late date for the PE, but their undeveloped ecclesiology alone would argue against this. They are anti-Jewish and so agree with Marcion. Like him, they favor Lukan ideas. They show only a confrontation with gnosticizing tendencies, but not with fully developed gnostic systems of the second and third centuries. Moreover, the Marcionites adopted the PE within their canon of scriptures, as indicated by the set of Marcionite prologues to the letters. The word "contradictions" (*antitheseis*) here is consistent with the letter's references to theological debates (1:4; 6:4, and see 2 Tim 2:14, 23, 25; Titus 3:9). It could very easily refer to the rabbinic mode of theological argument, known in Christianity as well (Matt 5:21-48; Mark 11:27-33; 12:13-27, 35-37). Similarly "knowledge" (*gnōsis*) carries on the letter's concern with the faith as truth, as opposed to false and misleading speculations.

21. *preferring:* Declaring allegiance. For the use of this word for women professing reverence for God in the PE community see 1 Tim 2:10.

    Grace be with you all: The letter concludes with a brief farewell. Without greetings from or to other community members, personal references, or elaboration on the final wish, this conclusion stands out as exceptional among the Pauline letters, including the other two PE. Perhaps the author wanted to keep the "official memorandum" tone consistent throughout. Although the letter is addressed to Timothy, the plural pronoun "you" (*hymōn*) here indicates the expectation that a wider audience will read and be directed by the letter's instructions and exhortations. Paul and Timothy have been seen to be examples not just for community leaders, but for the community members in general.

    Descriptions added at the end of manuscripts give information about the letter. The major majuscule codices identify it as the first written to Timothy. A few majuscule codices add "written from Laodicea" (or "Nikopolis"). Still others add the explanation "which is the metropolis of Pakatian Phrygia" (or "Kapatian" or "Parakatian"). Colossians 2:1 and 4:13, 15 suggest that Paul had not been to Laodicea before his imprisonment in Rome, although he had an interest in the Christians there (Col 4:16). The letter could only have been written in Laodicea, therefore, if it were composed after the Roman imprisonment we know from Acts, and from which Paul would have had to have been released to enable him to carry on with further mission activity.

Interpretation

The observations turn from the false teachers to people who seek riches generally and the woeful results of this preoccupation (6:9-10). Inserted into the comments on the pursuit of riches (6:7-10, 17-19) is advice to Timothy (6:11-16). This is based in part on a hortatory address from an ordination ritual. Before getting to that, however, Paul describes the philosophical virtue of contentment (6:7-8). The contrasting group, who crave riches, are characterized as prompted by ignorant and dangerous passions. The distressing loss of faith that befalls some money seekers sets up the contrasting advice to Timothy ("but you," *sy de*) to flee that, pursue virtue, and struggle to maintain the faith and his public commitment to it. Casting the matter in life and death terms, Paul underlines its urgency (6:11-12).

Greed itself is not addressed in the advice to Timothy, and only the unspecified "these things" (*tauta*) provide a link to the discussion on riches, which precedes. The advice to Timothy thus reveals the author's real target, i.e., the false teacher of 6:3-5. The discussion on riches amplifies the lesson about the teachers-for-profit by relating commonplace opinions on the hazards of riches.

The admonition to Timothy is reiterated more solemnly by invoking God and Jesus Christ (6:13). In referring to Jesus' witness before Pilate, the author cites the primary model for the public confession Timothy is said to have made at his own ordination and that Paul here reminds Timothy to adhere to (6:12). The connection between Timothy's and Jesus' witnesses is furthered by mentioning, in parallel with Pilate witnessing, Jesus' confession and the "many witnesses" of Timothy's confession. The characteristic concern for blamelessness in preserving the ordination charge (6:14) is set in eschatological perspective. While terminology of the last days in the letter indicates the nearness of the epiphany of Christ (see 4:1), the church order regulations suggest a long-term waiting period. Consistent with the credal affirmations at 2:5-6 and 3:16, Jesus is described as the visible Lord whom the unseen God will reveal (6:16).

As can be concluded from the qualifications for leadership roles in the community (3:1-13), which presume the ability to run a household well (and see 6:1), the rich are an important segment of the community and deserve attention suited to their station. Thus Paul returns to those who are currently rich and suggests that Timothy tell them to cultivate humility and to hope in God. Real riches consist in salvation for eternal life ("real life," *tēs ontōs zoēs*) and not secular ("in the present age," *en tǭ nyn aiōni*) wealth. A symbolic treasury can be built up now, he says, through good works (mentioned twice: "do good works," *agathoergein*, and "be rich in good works," *ploutein en ergois kalois*) and paradoxically through generous sharing of one's wealth. Thus, unlike the false teacher or the ordinary rich person, the member of the PE community is to engage in works of charity toward others and so get a grasp of "real life" (*tēs ontōs zoēs*, and compare Luke 12:16-21; Jas 1:9-11). This recalls the advice to those who have obligations toward widows (ch. 5) and also provides motivation for household heads to seek to be church elders and assistants (ch. 3).

The contrast between Timothy and the false teachers that occasioned the treatment on riches receives a brief reiteration. Here the defensive effort of Timothy on behalf of the treasury of teaching stands against the influence of the empty and ignorant propositions of the faithless apostates (6:20-21). The letter ends abruptly, which is uncharacteristic for both the PE and the other Pauline letters.

For Reference and Further Study

Barclay, William. "Paul's Certainties: Our Security in God: 2 Timothy 1:12," *ExpTim* 69 (1958) 324–27.

Bartchy, S. Scott. "Slavery (Greco-Roman)," *ABD* 6:65–73.

Berger, Klaus. "Jesus als Pharisäer und frühe Christen als Pharisäer," *NovT* 30 (1988) 231–62.

Borse, Udo. *1. und 2. Timotheusbrief*, 71–72.

Cipriani, Settimio. "La dottrina del 'depositum' nelle lettere pastorali," in *Studiorum Paulinorum Congressus Internationalis Catholicus 1961 : simul Secundus Congressus Internationalis Catholicus de Re Biblica : completo undevicesimo saeculo post S. Pauli in urbem adventum*. 2 vols. AnBib 17-18. Rome: Pontifical Biblical Institute, 1963, 2:130–42.

Fiore, Benjamin. "Passion in Paul and Plutarch," in David L. Balch, Everett Ferguson, and Wayne A. Meeks, eds., *Greeks, Romans, And Christians: Essays in Honor of Abraham J. Malherbe*. Minneapolis: Fortress Press, 1990, 135–43.

Käsemann, Ernst. "Das Formular einer neutestamentlichen Ordinationsparänese," in idem, *Exegetische Versuche und Besinnungen*. Göttingen: Vandenhoeck & Ruprecht, 1964, 1:101–108.

Lampe, G.W.H. "The Evidence in the New Testament for Early Creeds, Catechisms and Liturgy," *ExpTim* 71 (1960) 359–63.

Malina, Bruce J. "Wealth and Poverty in the New Testament and Its World," *Int* 41 (1987) 354–67.

Schlarb, Egbert. "Miszelle zu 1 Tim 6:20," *ZNW* 77 (1986) 276–81.

Spicq, Ceslas. "Saint Paul et la loi des dépots," *RB* 40 (1931) 481–502.
Stambaugh, John E., and David L. Balch. *The New Testament in Its Social Environment*. Library of Early Christianity 2. Philadelphia: Westminster, 1986.
Towner, Philip H. "Present Age," pp. 427-448.
Zeilinger, Franz. "Die Bewertung der irdischen Güter im Lukanischen Doppelwerk und in den Pastoralbriefen," *BL* 58 (1985) 75–80.

2 Timothy

2 TIMOTHY

INTRODUCTION

With its assertion of the faithful completion of Paul's ministry, its warning about troubles ahead, and its exhortation to maintain the tradition faithfully, this letter resembles the farewell discourse and final testament of Paul to the Miletan elders at Acts 20:17-38.

The letter presents Paul as awaiting his second trial in Rome (1:17). Although "rescued from the lion's mouth" at his first defense, he now foresees his "rescue" to be his being taken into God's heavenly kingdom (4:17-18). Therefore he speaks of his life's work as coming to an end with the expectation of a crown of victory for his faithful ministry (4:6-8). The faithless abandonment of Paul by members of his churches, some of whom are named (1:15, 4:10 [including Titus?], 14-16), provides a contrast to his faithfulness. Timothy's unstinting adherence to the persecuted Paul in the past (3:10-11) and Onesiphorus' unashamed succor to Paul in his Roman imprisonment expand the contrast and establish a positive example of community faithfulness.

After a brief opening greeting (1:1-2), the thanksgiving section follows (1:3-5). This is a common feature in classical epistolary correspondence but is absent from the other two PE. The thanksgiving establishes the long tradition of faith to which Paul and Timothy are heirs.

The exhortations that follow provide the main content of the letter, and, as in 1 Timothy, they alternate with statements of the true doctrine and warnings about destructive false teaching. An additional feature of 2 Timothy is the references to Paul's sufferings and prospective death. So Timothy is reminded of the spiritual charism from Paul's imposition of hands that empowers him to stand unashamed with the imprisoned Paul and to assume the hardship of Gospel preaching (1:6-8).

The acknowledgement of God's eternal saving plan, manifested through Jesus and apart from any human works (1:9-10), establishes the normative sound teaching for which Paul suffered as he preached, and that Timothy is to guard with the Holy Spirit. This spiritual help had supported Paul and will likewise aid Timothy, unlike the defection of the cowardly deserters (1:11-18). Timothy as the model preacher is reminded of the Pauline tradition he received as he takes up the challenge to entrust it to successive teachers, all the while working with tireless focus and drawing his sustenance from that work (2:1-7).

The Gospel of Jesus' death and resurrection receives mention, as does Paul's suffering and imprisonment because of it. Just like Jesus, who died and rose, Paul and all those who, remaining faithful, die with him, will rise to glory (2:8-13). False teachers engage in useless and harmful disputes and are to be avoided. Timothy's correction of them might lead them to repent and regain their senses (2:14-26).

The false teachers are set in an end-time context, which gives the doctrinal disturbances they bring to church households an air of ultimate consequence. Timothy has to avoid these vice-filled pseudo-believers, who are ignorant and bring down those whom they are unable to lead to true piety (3:1-9). By contrast to them Timothy is the faithful and consistent follower of the work and sufferings of Paul. His childhood teachers and the Scriptures have set him on the path to salvation and have given him the tools for refuting false teachers and accomplishing good works of righteousness. Since those who live piously in Jesus Christ can expect to suffer, Timothy too is urged to put up with hardships as he fulfills his evangelistic ministry, heedless of personal preferences (3:10–4:5). Mention of Paul's heavenly crown, the end-time reward for keeping the faith in the struggles of his life and work, puts the task of Timothy and his successors in the end-time context that counterbalances the end-time apostasy mentioned earlier (4:6-8).

Notices of the movements of his associates, warnings to Timothy, a statement of Paul's reliance on God for ultimate rescue, and personal information and greetings conclude the letter (4:9-22).

Outline

1:1-2	Greeting	
1:3-5	Thanksgiving	
1:6–4:18	Exhortation to Timothy	
	1:6-8	Timothy's calling
	1:9-17	Paul's suffering and imprisonment
	2:1-7	Timothy's task
	2:8-13	Suffering and perseverance
	2:14–3:9	Warnings about false teaching
	3:10-13	Paul's suffering
	3:14–4:1-5	Timothy's task
	4:6-18	Paul's abandonment and imminent death
4:19-22	Closing greetings	

TRANSLATION, NOTES, INTERPRETATION

1. *Greeting; Timothy's Faith; Salvation* (1:1-10)

1. Paul, apostle of Christ Jesus through the will of God, with a view to the promise of life which is in Christ Jesus, 2. to Timothy, beloved child, favor, mercy, peace from God the Father and Christ Jesus our Lord.

3. I thank God, whose worship I carry on from my ancestors with a clean conscience, while I keep an unfailing remembrance concerning you in my prayers, night and day. 4. Your tears I remember, as I long to see you in order to be filled with joy. 5. I hold on to the memory of your sincere faith. It first found a home in your grandmother Lois and in your mother Eunice, and I am convinced that it abides in you as well.

6. For this reason I remind you to fan into flame the gift of God, which is in you through the laying on of my hands. 7. As you know, God did not give us a spirit of cowardice, but of strength, love, and moderation. 8. Therefore do not be at all ashamed of the witness of our Lord or of me his prisoner. On the contrary, share in the suffering on behalf of the gospel, resting on strength from God,

9. who saved us
and called us with a holy calling,
not according to our works, but according to his own plan and favor,
granted to us in Christ Jesus before all time,
10. but revealed now
through the appearance of our Savior, Christ Jesus, who both brought death to an end and brought life and immortality to light through the gospel.

Notes

1. *Paul, apostle of Christ Jesus through the will of God:* Awaiting trial, Paul writes to Timothy. The prospect of death looms (4:6-8) before the suffering prisoner (2:9). The letter has the tone of a final testament, as Paul asserts his faithfulness to God and to his apostolic task. He sums up his career, warns Timothy of impending opposition, and takes his leave (compare Acts 20:17-38). See the Note on "apostle" at 1 Tim 1:1. God's plan for the salvation of all, a theme throughout 1 Timothy (2:4; 4:10; 6:17-19, and compare *oikonomia*, "God's order," 1:4) and

Titus (1:2; 3:4), is addressed here as well (see *epangelian zoēs*, "promise of life," 1:1). In the plan of God, Paul is designated to be the herald of the Gospel, which promises life (see 1 Tim 1:11-12; 2:7; 3:16e; Titus 1:2, and in this letter 1:11; 2:3, 8; 4:17).

the promise of life which is in Christ Jesus: The promise of eternal life in the age to come is an expression of the PE's eschatological hope (see 1 Tim 4:8). Jesus Christ is mediator of salvation by his historical appearance, culminating in his redemptive death (see also 1:9; 2:10-13; 3:15, and also 1 Tim 1:15; 2:5; Titus 2:11, 13-14; 3:6). See 1 Timothy 1 for the form of the name. The phrase at 3:15 suggests that Jesus is the object of personal faith, and 2:10-13 as well as 3:12 imply a lived association with Jesus. First Timothy (1:14 in light of Titus 3:6) suggests that Jesus mediates divine virtues (and see 2 Tim 1:9, 13; 2:11). A relationship on the basis of these shared qualities can be assumed, but the idea is not developed.

2. *Timothy, beloved child:* See the Note on 1 Tim 1:2. Paul uses this Jewish form of address at Rom 11:28 (see LXX Ps 59:5) and applies it to all Christians at Rom 1:7 in connection with their being called (like the Jews at 11:28). It is also a Hellenistic friendship word, and so the uses in the Pauline letters often cluster at the beginnings and ends of the letters. When the word is applied to community members, as here, it is likely to carry not friendship but familial (father-child) overtones (1 Cor 4:14, 17; Philemon 1, 16). The term then indicates election by God and an ongoing relationship with Paul, which comprise the new reality of the spiritual life made possible by God. For the form of the introduction and the remainder of its expressions see 1 Tim 1:1-2.

   favor, mercy, peace: See 1 Tim 1:2 (favor, mercy, peace); 1:12 (I give thanks); 1:14 (favor of God has been abundant); and Titus 1:4 (favor, peace); 2:11 (favor of God appeared); 3:7 (justified by his favor); 2 Tim 1:9 (favor given to us); 2:1 (favor that was in Christ Jesus).

3. *I thank God:* The formula of thanks introduces the thanksgiving section (see 1 Tim 1:12). In its more customary position following the greeting, the thanksgiving alludes to two themes to be developed in the letter: Paul's faithfulness and Timothy's carrying on the tradition of faith. A personal and friendly chord is struck with Paul's expression of longing and recollection of Timothy's tears (v. 4).

   worship I carry on from my ancestors: The LXX uses the word "worship" (*latreuein*) largely for Israel's cultic worship of God. This is more restricted in meaning than "worship" (*douleuein*). The NT continues this usage, especially for false worship (Rom 1:25). Paul specifies spiritual worship (Rom 1:9) in distinction from that of the Jews (Phil 3:3) and the worship is carried out in his service of the Gospel (Rom 1:9). Luke at Acts 24:14 closely parallels the link expressed here between Paul's worship and that of his ancestors in faith. Both passages quote Paul on trial speaking in his own defense. Although the trial in 2 Timothy is to be conducted by Romans, Paul's apologetic centers on his fidelity to God and the Gospel mission. The "defense" actually aims to encourage the Christian audience of the letter to emulate Paul's fidelity to tradition and missionary zeal. Mention of ancestors underlines a continuity with Jewish tradition, which is implied at 1 Tim 1:8 even though Jewish teachers are criticized for excesses

(1 Tim 1:7; Titus 1:14). In a sense, however, the absence of a specification of these ancestors as Jewish, the proximity of this claim to the reminiscence of Timothy's faith ancestors at v. 5 (and see 2:2, *par' emou dia pollōn martyrōn*, "from me through many witnesses"), and the requirement that Timothy appoint teachers for others (2:2) suggest the presence and continuity of a Christian tradition of faith.

with a clean conscience: See 1 Tim 1:5. First Timothy makes the clean conscience the object of the exhortation to everyone (1:5, and see 3:9) and to Timothy as a model (1:19). That letter also paints the false teachers as exemplars of bad conscience (1:19; 4:2, and compare Titus 1:15). Here the focus is on Paul's example.

an unfailing remembrance . . . in my prayers: Constant remembrance strikes a familiar tone for the letter, as does Paul's ceaseless prayer on Timothy's behalf. Prayer for others is highly valued in the PE (see 1 Tim 2:1-2 and 5:5, "day and night"). Paul claims constant remembrance of the Romans (Rom 1:9) and also that his prayer to see them is ceaseless (Rom 1:10, and see Phil 1:4 and also 1 Thess 3:10).

4. *Your tears I remember, as I long to see you:* The tearful memory is juxtaposed to the joyful anticipation of a reunion. This suggests that a significant span of time intervened since their last parting. Paul gives no indication of a tearful parting at 1 Tim 1:3. The context must be a separation at another time, perhaps tears in view of Paul's being taken to Rome for trial (1:17). The tears echo those of the Ephesian elders at Acts 20:37. Timothy seems to have been there (Acts 20:4-6), but he also seems to have left with Paul to continue on to Jerusalem and may have gone with Paul to the Temple (Acts 21:1, 18-19). There Timothy's trail fades away. The desire for a reunion is a common feature in friendly letters, finding fuller expression in a section of its own near the salutation (4:9-18, and see 1 Tim 3:14).

5. *I hold on to the memory of your sincere faith: Hypomnēsin* is the third word for "memory/remember" in three verses. They indicate the author's tendency to vary the terminology and heap up synonyms (more usually in lists, e.g., 1 Tim 6:9, 18). In addition to the connotations of friendship and affection, the words also fit the idea of tradition, which the author seeks to preserve. Contrast 1 Tim 4:2, and compare 1 Tim 1:5.

in your grandmother Lois and in your mother Eunice: The name Lois means either "from Lystra" (*EDNT*) or "pleasant, desirable" (*BAGD*). At Acts 16:1 Eunice has a Greek (unbelieving) husband and an uncircumcised son (Timothy). Her unlawful marriage to a Gentile conflicts with her description as a believing Jewish woman. Thus the sincere faith here more likely refers to her Christian faith. The name is Hellenistic rather than traditionally Jewish, and means "easy victory," a name of mythological figures in Hesiod, *Theogony* 246, Theocritus, 246, Pseudo-Apollod., 1.2.7, CIG IV. 8. 139. The reference to Timothy's mother and grandmother but no male forebears might indicate that the latter were not Christian. The mention of the women attests to the importance of women in the spread of early Christianity.

I am convinced that it abides in you as well: The reiteration of the assurance of Timothy's faith noted at the start of the verse appears redundant. It can be seen, however, as a way of establishing individual faith in a line of transmission (see 3:16). Family faith traditions are now a possibility, for no longer is everyone a new convert (1 Tim 3:6), and elders are coaching younger persons in the Christian life (Titus 2:4). Furthermore, while Timothy, the fellow worker with Paul, enjoyed Paul's full confidence, Timothy the model for the Christian community and its leaders is depicted with flaws and hesitations likely among ordinary members of the community. Finally, the stated assurance of the possession of a quality by another is an indirect admonition to be sure the quality is indeed firmly in hand in the one praised.

6. *I remind you to fan into flame:* This is yet another reference to remembering. Here the paraenetic intent is clear. Exhortation aims at transmitting traditional, well known, agreed on instructions and teaching and calling the addressees' attention to them. The verb introduces the body of the letter, which comprises exhortations to Timothy, apostolic reminiscence by Paul, and warnings about apostasy. In the Bible the word "fan into flame" (*anazōpyrō*) appears only here and at 1 Macc 13:7. The rekindling indicates that the gift abides in the person but is revived when called on as a resource for the recipient's ministry (v. 8, and see 1 Tim 4:14). Seneca, *Ep.* 94,28-29 uses the same image for the seeds of everything upright fanned to flame through admonition and leading to moral maturity (and see Iamblichus, *Vit. Pyth.* 70; Marcus Aurelius, VII 2).

through the laying on of my hands: While 1 Tim 4:14 could mean that the gift of God came on the occasion of a prophetic word and the imposition of hands, the preposition *dia* ("through") with the verb "to be" here recognizes the imposition of hands as the means by which the gift has come to reside in Timothy. This formalizes and institutionalizes the indiscriminate and free bestowal of God's gifts on all in the Pauline churches (1 Cor 12:4-11; Gal 2:2). In the Pauline communities the gifts seem to have come at the reception of the Gospel in faith (see 1 Thess 1:6, and see also Acts 10:44-46).

At 1 Tim 4:14 the presbyteral assembly imposed hands. Here only Paul does. Since Paul's relationship to Timothy is in focus in this letter, only Paul receives mention. First Timothy treats church order and various officials, and so the whole presbyteral assembly comes into focus. After 70 and before the Bar Kochba revolt in 132 C.E. and Hadrian's prohibition of ordination of rabbis, each rabbi would ordain his own followers with the laying on of hands. After 130 C.E. rabbis were simply proclaimed. Matthew 18:20 seems to reflect a situation in which qualified men receive a commission as teachers of a fixed deposit of doctrine. The commission is based on a rite similar to that of the rabbis after 70 C.E., with a parallel concern for maintaining the tradition. While 1 Pet 1:10 reveals a charismatic prophetic ministry, 4:12–5:1 describes a presbyteral church with Peter as presbyter (5:1) and a college of elders (5:5). No ritual laying on of hands appears. There was none for elders in Judaism, either. The meaning of the laying on of hands at Acts 6:1-6 and 13:1-3 is not clear. Parallel to Acts 13:1-3, the appointment of elders at Acts 14:23 includes a commendation to God, which may be the rite and meaning of the laying on of hands. In 1 Tim 4:14 and 2 Tim 2:6 the practice is already established. Prophets make the selection (compare Acts 13:2), a solemn exhortation is delivered (1 Tim 6:11-16), the teachings are handed on before witnesses (2 Tim 2:2), the one selected and appointed pronounces a confession (1 Tim 6:12), and elders impose hands. The last rite is linked to the bestowal of a specific gift of God (2 Tim 1:6-8). The gift is a power for the office, not a bestowal of the office itself. The task is to maintain the deposit of tradition. While the ordination of elders has become ritualized and is mirrored in Timothy's ordination, Timothy is not an elder himself, but like Paul functions apart from the local ecclesiastical structure. He, like Paul, can appoint and impose hands on new elders (1 Tim 5:22), and so can Titus (Titus 1:5). The apostle and his two delegates share some of the duties of the elders and overseers (e.g., they teach and defend the true doctrine against false teachers), but they are not permanently associated with the local churches at Ephesus and Crete (2 Tim 2:9; Titus 3:12).

7. *God did not give us:* The plural pronoun "us" associates the readers with the addressee. Even though all are not officially designated for the evangelist's task, all believers will suffer (3:12) and so will have to call on God's gifts.

   but of strength, love, and moderation: See 1 Tim 1:5. The virtue of love is present in the individual through the indwelling Spirit (see 1:14). It comprises activity among people, the "good works" side of piety. Once again the virtue of "moderation" (*sōphronismos*) is made possible by the indwelling Spirit. Similarly at Titus 2:12 the grace of God in Christ has trained the believer to live in moderation (and compare Titus 2:2, 4, 5, 6). While the virtue is highly esteemed in Greco-Roman society, it is a fundamental aspect of the new life in Christ (see 1 Tim 2:9, 15; 3:2; Titus 1:7-8, and see Rom 12:3). The perverse and disruptive behavior of the false teachers leads the author of the PE to highlight this quality.

8. *do not be at all ashamed of the witness of our Lord:* Paul at 1 Cor 1:18–2:10 declares the paradox of the cross as an expression of divine wisdom and power and the basis of true boasting in the face of the human calculation of shame and folly. The Greco-Roman society of honor/shame would encourage avoiding situations that could compromise one's honor. Paul rises above the shame of imprisonment by looking at the advance of the Gospel (Phil 1:20) and the example of Jesus (Phil 2:1-11). Jesus exchanged his honorable status of sovereign for the shameful condition of a slave and went further to accept the ultimate shame of crucifixion. Second Timothy here recalls the same situation and offers a parallel restoration of honor in the life to come, where Jesus Christ is already in glory. The witness is the historical Jesus Christ's saving mediation wherein he gave himself as a ransom for all (1 Tim 2:5-6) and in the process gave testimony before Pontius Pilate (1 Tim 6:13). This is the kernel of the Gospel proclamation (1 Tim 6:13), which Timothy made at his ordination and about which he now is warned not to be ashamed. A convicted revolutionary associated with outlandish claims to save all people by his execution hardly constitutes an honorable religious leader and creed of belief. Lucian, *Peregr.* 13, and Tacitus, *Annales* XV.44, indicate the ridicule to which Christian belief was exposed. The title "Our Lord" (*ho kyrios hēmōn*) counters the dishonorable aura surrounding Jesus' death (see 1 Tim 1:2).

   or of me his prisoner: As at Phil 1:20, so too at Phlm 9 being a prisoner causes Paul no shame, nor does it interfere with his *parrēsia* ("frank speech," Phlm 8).

Here, too, Timothy and other Pauline community members have no reason to be ashamed, for Paul is a prisoner of the Lord Jesus Christ and not of the Roman emperor.

suffering on behalf of the gospel, resting on strength from God: The suffering Timothy is to shoulder with Paul ultimately benefits the Gospel (see 1:12). Paul is entrusted with the task of spreading the Gospel (1 Tim 1:1, 11-12; 2:7; 2 Tim 1:1, 11; 2:8; Titus 1:1-3), and Timothy receives other exhortations to engage in the struggle for the Gospel (1 Tim 1:18; 4:10; 2 Tim 2:3). "Suffering" associates the Christian sufferers with the suffering of Christ and the life won for them by it (see 2:11-12). If all Christians are to suffer (3:12), then Paul's suffering contributes to making him the model Christian, as does Timothy's and, at the head of the chain of models, Jesus'. Being able to suffer stems from God's power, not from the believer's own endurance. Since all have the same gift, they can likewise bear the suffering.

9. Verses 9 and 10 comprise a series of antithetical phrases, most of them participial. In all, they provide a capsule summary of the Christian Gospel message. The aorist participles emphasize the once-for-all character of the redemptive act of Jesus Christ.

who saved us and called us: See 1 Tim 1:1, 15. The salvation of all people is a basic and reiterated teaching in the PE, perhaps because the false teachers taught otherwise (see 1 Tim 2:4). Similar to 1 Tim 6:12, the calling is the divine summons to salvation and the Christian existence implied by it. See "church" (*ekklēsia*, 1 Tim 3:5, 15; 5:16), a usage that prevails in the Pauline literature.

not according to our works: Although the letters urge the audience to excel in good works, these are not the source of redemption (see also Titus 3:5) but one of its effects. Thus evil works betray faithlessness (Titus 1:16) and good works express the life of piety (1 Tim 2:10, and see 1 Tim 5:10, 25; 6:18; Titus 2:7, 14; 3:8, 14). The first antithesis in these verses speaks of the salvation to which people were called, but notes that it was God's plan at work and not anything people did. This faith/works dichotomy may not have been the main issue in the PE as it was in Galatians. Law is debated at 1 Tim 1:7, but the focus there is on general morality, and food restrictions (1 Tim 4:3) are motivated by asceticism. The "works" in the PE, then, might refer to a Greco-Roman question of the value of human striving. Ps-Heraclitus 4.3 expresses the philosophers' striving against tendencies toward vice (pleasures, cowardice, flattery, fear, drunkenness, grief, anger) to achieve the status of a sage.

according to his own plan and favor: See 2 Tim 1:1. God's plan is for all to be saved; it excludes no one. See 2 Tim 1:2 for "favor."

in Christ Jesus: Christ Jesus is called the mediator of divine favor at 1 Tim 2:5. First Timothy implies Jesus' preexistence (1 Tim 1:15) and consequently his mediation. Similarly, this verse describes the gift of divine favor in Christ in eternity.

10. *revealed now:* The second half of the antithesis asserts that this eternal favor became known in the historical saving appearance of Christ (1 Tim 1:15 and Titus 3:4). The emphasis rests on the saving death of Jesus but includes Jesus'

incarnation and historical existence. *Nyn* ("now") stretches from then into the time of the letter.

brought death to an end and brought life and immortality to light: The Pauline idea is that Christ conquered death (1 Cor 15:26, 54, and see Heb 2:14) and brought in an eschatological new creation (*EDNT*). Second Timothy refers explicitly to the death of Jesus Christ as lifebringing at 2:11. For the spiritual meaning of death see also 1 Tim 5:6. The second member of the antithesis speaks of new and eternal life as a consequence of Jesus' death (see 1 Tim 6:12). The letter uses immortality, a Hellenistic Jewish concept that appears in Wis 2:23; 6:19; and *4 Macc.* 9:22; 17:12, and nowhere else in the LXX. The late concept of immortality does not appear in the earlier OT. Illumination carries forward the PE's stress on bringing all into the open (see 1 Tim 5:24) as well as on appearance (e.g., *epiphaneia*, "appearance," as Jesus' historical life at 2 Tim 1:10; 3:16, and his second coming at 1 Tim 6:14; 2 Tim 4:1, 8; Titus 2:13).

through the gospel: Timothy and, through him, the audience are urged to suffer for the Gospel (2 Tim 1:8). If the three antitheses are traditional material, then the phrase "through the gospel" appears to have been tacked on by the author to relate the antithetical Gospel summary to the exhortation to Gospel preaching in the immediate contexts.

The antitheses lay out the essential features of belief in salvation through Jesus' redemptive death and resurrection (see also 1 Tim 2:6; 3:16). At the time of the letter, however, it is the Gospel preaching and its effects that bring salvation and life. Salvation is a reality achieved in the present (see the aorist *sōsantos*, "who saved," 1:9, and illumination "now" by the savior's appearance, 1:10). But it has a future prospect as well (physical death to pass into immortality, 1:9, in the future resurrection, 2:18). Both aspects are expressed at 2:13-14.

Interpretation

The second letter to Timothy, while related thematically to the other two PE, differs from them in content and genre. Highly autobiographical, the letter presents an introspective Paul taking stock of his apostolic career and offering advice and encouragement to the younger Timothy in the first years of his ministry as evangelist.

John Chrysostom, *Hom. 2 Tim I* (NPNF 1 13:475), explains the encouragement Paul offers Timothy. His apostleship is given by God to prepare him for eternal life, where there is no danger, grief, or mourning. Thus Paul refers to the promise of life in Jesus Christ. Following God in faith neither makes one immune from life's troubles nor necessarily implicates one in them. Rather, the faithful are directed toward the promise of life, not seen in life's circumstances, for then it would not be the object of hope.

With little church order material, the letter resembles a farewell discourse or last will and testament. In this letter Paul describes the saving action of God in his life and the subsequent conduct of his ministry in such a way as to make him a model not just for Timothy but for the church's faithful as well. As such, the letter might well be considered the introduction to the PE corpus.

The ordinary greeting form finds elaboration of the sender's title, "apostle." The apostolic ministry proceeds from God's will and plan and centers on the promise of life gained by Jesus Christ and made accessible through association with him. Paul sees himself as sent by Christ Jesus, which gives a Christian specificity to his work. The friendly tone is established by Paul's calling Timothy his "beloved child." Paul was a key figure in Timothy's coming to the fullness of faith (1:13) and to the experience of the Spirit's gifts (1:6). So Paul can consider himself a spiritual father (see Phlm 10). Christ Jesus and God the Father, mentioned separately in v. 1, are the common source of "grace, mercy, and peace" (NAB) in v. 2. A distinction is, nonetheless, maintained between God, who is Father, and Jesus, who is Lord. Moreover, the title "Christ" usually precedes Jesus' name here and throughout the PE.

The thanksgiving section focuses on the tradition of faith in God for Paul (v. 3) and Timothy (v. 5). Unceasing prayerful remembrance and the longing to reunite advance the letter's friendly tone, as do the mention of Timothy's tears and the contrasting expectation of a joy-filled reunion (vv. 3-4). References to the reality of faith, which frame the personal recollection and expectation, open this personal letter to the wider audience of the faithful and suggest a context of maturity in the Christian faith as opposed to one of recent conversion. Paul establishes a momentum of belief: from his own ancestors, to himself, to Timothy's grandmother and mother, and finally to Timothy himself. This momentum receives affirmation for Timothy in Paul's expression of confidence about it (*pepeismai*, v. 5). The "sincerity" of Timothy's faith (*anypokritou*, v. 5) echoes Paul's worship of God with a "clear conscience" (NAB) (*katharą*, *syneidēsei*, v. 3).

The recollection of Timothy's early introduction to the faith and of the tradition of belief going back to his grandmother fits the letter's conception of the church as the household of God (1 Tim 3:15). The family continues to be the social and religious context in which faith is richly nurtured. Those who profess a neutral stance toward imposing value commitments when bringing up their children seem disingenuous and, at the very least, reluctant to engage seriously in religious thought and action. Their professions of neutrality as far as values are concerned is belied by the fact that they readily accede to the mores and presuppositions of their social and political contexts and do not leave these bracketed until the time when their children are able to choose for themselves.

Paul refers to the continuity of faith in God from his Jewish ancestors to his Christian faith. This realization might well serve as the basis for interfaith dialogue and understanding between these two sometimes historically antagonistic faith communities. Perhaps the appreciation of the oneness of God for all peoples could also show a way of rapprochement among other religious communities as well.

From the thanksgiving and its stress on faith flows a hortatory reminder to Timothy to rekindle the gift of God with its virtue and power, which Paul mediated to him (v. 6). John Chrysostom, *Hom. 2 Tim. I* (NPNF 1 13:477), observes that the gift of God requires zeal, as fire requires fuel, to stir it up. Just as sloth and carelessness can extinguish it, so do watchfulness and diligence keep it alive. The exhortation here forms an *inclusio* around the christological statement. Paul's opening call for Timothy to recover his initial charism finds expansion in his description of the spiritual resource (v. 7). He uses a typical negative/positive structure to emphasize the reliability of the spiritual gift in the struggles of the Christian ministry. Thus cowardice is ruled out in favor of power, love, and self-control. On this basis he can ask Timothy to exclude shame over association with the witness of Christ and with the prisoner Paul (v. 8). The link with the imprisoned Paul indicates that it is the Christ of the Passion and death that is the point of reference. On the positive side, Paul calls for suffering along with Paul and Christ through reliance on the gift of power.

The credal summary recalls God's eternal design and favor to save and call the faithful (*hēmas*, "us," v. 9). People's deeds do not tilt God's designs one way or the other. Paul notes that the favor of God, while mediated through Christ Jesus eternally, has recently been made manifest (v. 10) in Jesus' appearance in his saving work, which encompasses his death destroying death and life bestowing resurrection. In view of these positive effects, the Passion and death of Jesus are nothing to be ashamed of (v. 8). For the faithful at the time of the letters it is the Gospel preaching and teaching that make this a reality (*dia tou euangeliou*, v. 10).

For Reference and Further Study

Brox, Norbert. *Die Pastoralbriefe: übersezt und erklärt*. Regensburg: Pustet, 1969, 224–25, 242.

Dewey, Joanna. "2 Timothy," in Carol A. Newsom and Sharon H. Ringe, eds., *The Women's Bible Commentary*. London: SPCK; Louisville: Westminster John Knox, 1992; expanded ed. 1998, 450–51.

Ferguson, Everett. "Laying on of Hands: Its Significance in Ordination," *JTS* n.s. 26 (1975) 1–12.

Fiore, Benjamin. *The Function of Personal Example in the Socratic and Pastoral Epistles*. AnBib 105. Rome: Biblical Institute Press, 1986, 41 n. 60.

Hahn, Ferdinand. *Worship of the Early Church*. Trans. David E. Green. Edited, with an introduction, by John Reumann. Philadelphia: Fortress Press, 1973.

Klein, William W. "Paul's Use of *kalein:* A Proposal," *JETS* 27 (1984) 53–64.

Koester, Helmut. "The Purpose of the Polemic of a Pauline Fragment," *NTS* 8 (1961/62) 317–32.
Malherbe, Abraham J. *Paul and the Popular Philosophers*. Minneapolis: Fortress Press, 1989, 51, 74, 153.
________. "The Beasts at Ephesus," in idem, *Paul and the Popular Philosophers*. Minneapolis: Fortress Press, 1989, 79–89.
Meeks, Wayne A. *The Moral World of the First Christians*. Library of Early Christianity 6. Philadelphia: Westminster, 1986, 40–64.
Parratt, J. K. "The Laying on of Hands in the New Testament: A Reexamination in Light of the Hebrew Terminology," *ExpTim* 80 (1968–69) 210–14.
Read, David H. C. "Eunice and Lois' Homemade Religion," *ExpTim* 97 (1985) 307–308.
Stendahl, Krister. "The Called and the Chosen: An Essay on Election," in Anton Fridrichsen and Krister Stendahl, eds., *The Root of the Vine: Essays in Biblical Theology*. New York: Philosophical Library, 1952, 63–80.
Towner, Philip H. *The Goal of Our Instruction: The Structure of Theology and Ethics in the Pastoral Epistles*. JSNTSup 34. Sheffield: Sheffield Academic Press, 1989, 161–63.

2. *Paul as Exemplar; Support in Prison* (1:11-18)

11. It was for this that I was appointed herald, apostle, and teacher, 12. and because of this I suffer even these hardships; but I am not ashamed, for I know the one in whom I have believed and I am convinced that he is able to guard what has been entrusted to me until that day. 13. Look to the model of sound teachings, which you have heard from me in faith and love, which are in Christ Jesus. 14. Guard the noble trust through the Holy Spirit who dwells in us.

15. You are aware of this. Everyone in Asia, including Phygelus and Hermogenes, abandoned me. 16. The Lord grant mercy to the household of Onesiphorus, because he frequently refreshed me and was not ashamed of my imprisonment. 17. On the contrary, upon arriving at Rome, straight off he searched for and found me. 18. The Lord grant that he find mercy from the Lord on that day. All the services he rendered at Ephesus, you yourself know full well.

Notes

11. *I was appointed herald . . . teacher:* See 1 Tim 1:12 and also 2:7, of which this verse is an abridged version (compare also 1 Tim 1:11; Titus 1:3). Cognates of the word "herald" (*kēryx*) express Paul's preaching to the Jews and Gentiles (1 Tim 3:16; 2 Tim 4:17), which carries over from Paul's description of his mission work at

Rom 10:14-18; 1 Cor 1:23; Gal 2:2. It is the Gospel of Jesus' death and resurrection that he preached (1 Cor 1:23), and Timothy is to take up the task as well (2 Tim 2:8; 4:2). See the Note on "teacher" at 1 Tim 2:7. Overseers (1 Tim 3:2; Titus 1:9) and some presbyters (1 Tim 5:17) teach in the PE. Timothy, as slave of the Lord, is also to teach (2 Tim 2:24, and see Titus 2:7 and 1 Tim 4:11). The latter references and Titus 1:9 are in contexts of false teaching and opposition. Older women are to teach younger women domestic responsibility (Titus 2:3). The freedom to teach publicly, however, is denied to women at 1 Tim 2:12. The author is bent on restricting teaching to those with approval in view of (1) the conflicts caused by false teachers (see 1 Tim 1:7; 4:1; 6:3-4; 2 Tim 2:19; Titus 3:9), (2) the doctrinal confusion and moral misbehavior that resulted from community members' spreading unauthorized beliefs (1 Tim 5:13; 2 Tim 3:6-7; 4:3-4), and (3) the disrepute the church found in the community at large because of this (see 1 Tim 3:2). Thus a line is established that extends from Paul, to Timothy and Titus, to the authorized overseers and elders, older women, and finally to the teachers of future generations (2 Tim 2:2).

12. *I suffer even these hardships:* Enduring hardships, particularly in manual labor, was a prized example for the Greco-Roman popular philosophers of the way to progress in wisdom and happiness (Musonius Rufus, *fr.* 11; *Ep. of Diogenes* 27). Some Stoics even saw hardship as part of life's divine purpose and a means to exercise oneself in virtue and obtain happiness. In a less self-confident vein, Paul refers to his weakness and suffering from opponents and adverse conditions in his ministry at 2 Cor 11:23-30. At 2 Cor 12:7-10 he goes on to describe sufferings in his own body. All demonstrate the sufficiency of Christ's power to enable him to endure, and so he is willing to go on suffering for the sake of Christ. The expressions of personal knowledge of Christ in faith and confidence in his power to safeguard the entrusted Gospel message here echo Paul in 2 Corinthians.

able to guard what has been entrusted: The word "guard" (see Philo, *Heir* 102-106; Philo, *Abraham* 258-259; Josephus, *Bell.* III 369-372) is used with *parathēkēn* ("deposit," "what has been entrusted") almost as a technical term (see also 1 Tim 6:20; 2 Tim 1:14). This may be an ironic allusion to Paul's imprisonment. The earlier letters of Paul are concerned with accepting and passing on the Christian tradition under the term *paradosis* and its cognates (1 Cor 11:2, 23; 15:3; 2 Thess 2:15; 3:6). In the context of apostasy and conflict the PE look to guarding the tradition intact (so 1 Tim 1:18; 6:20; 2 Tim 1:12, 14; 2:2). The tradition is the Gospel entrusted to Paul (1 Tim 1:11; 2:7; 2 Tim 1:10) and outlined in the antitheses (vv. 9-10) and in the other credal and liturgical fragments that dot the letters. Thus it did not originate with Paul but is passed on through him (2 Tim 1:13; 2:2).

until that day: The PE look ahead consistently to the day of the Lord and the *parousia* (1 Tim 6:14; 2 Tim 4:8; Titus 2:13), while they see the present as the beginning of the final days (1 Tim 4:1).

13. *the model of sound teachings:* The Gospel message is given in pattern or outline form (Strabo, 2.5.18; Sextus Empiricus, *Pyrrhyo inscriptio*) in these letters to guide fundamental Christian preaching and faith. The "pattern" refers to the words,

but it also includes behavior ("heard in faith and love"). The Gospel was proclaimed in the testimony of Jesus, which included suffering and death, of Paul, which also includes unashamed suffering and looks forward to death, and of Onesiphorus, who defies shame in serving Paul and thus establishes his Gospel witness in Rome and in Ephesus.

in faith and love: See 1 Tim 1:14; 2:15; 4:12; 6:11; 2 Tim 2:22. Whereas faith describes the relation of the Christian to God, love describes the relation to other people.

14. *Guard the noble trust:* See v. 12.

the Holy Spirit who dwells in us: The indwelling Holy Spirit corresponds to the gift of God (v. 6), i.e., the Spirit of strength (v. 7), which is the strength of God (v. 8). Thus it is not just human fortitude. Moreover, love and moderation are also divinely prompted attitudes.

15. *You are aware of this. Everyone . . . abandoned me:* The mention of other members of the Ephesian church gives the exhortation's root in an actual context of personal fidelity and betrayal. The word "abandoned" (*apestraphēsan*), used for apostasy at 2 Tim 4:4; Titus 1:14, refers to abandonment by two persons known to Timothy. Since the Gospel is the message of redemptive suffering and death (1:10, and see 1 Tim 2:5-6; 3:16), and since it implicates the Christians in suffering (3:12) and death (2:11), abandoning the suffering Paul in shame at his imprisonment is an abandonment of the Gospel itself, a practical apostasy. In this way the letter broadens the readers' understanding of apostasy from an intellectual denial to a denial of suffering in one's lifestyle (see *eusebeia*, "piety," 1 Tim 2:2). Those who abandoned Paul, however, are not condemned. The letter simply records the fact of their lack of support and then goes on to praise and bless the ones who stood by Paul. The two responses to Paul in need establish examples that need no elaboration.

16. *frequently refreshed me and was not ashamed of my imprisonment:* Lucian, *Peregr.* 11-13, mentions matter-of-factly that Christians were known to rush to the aid of imprisoned brothers and sisters. Paul, imprisoned as he writes the letter to Philemon, asks the addressee to refresh him by giving him the services of Philemon's slave Onesimus (Phlm 13-14, 20).

17. *arriving at Rome:* Another visit to his mission field after the Roman imprisonment described in Acts is needed to fit 1 Timothy (and Titus) into what is known of Pauline chronology. Second Timothy, if written before 1 Timothy, could have been written during the first imprisonment, except that Trophimus at 4:20 accompanied Paul to Jerusalem (Acts 21:29) and was not left sick at Miletus. Another visit to Miletus has to be postulated, with a second imprisonment during which 2 Timothy would have been written. The abandonment by all in Asia could have been as a result of Paul's first trial, or it could have been after the initial arraignment.

18. *The Lord . . . from the Lord:* The first "Lord" refers to God the Father, the Lord of Lords (1 Tim 6:15). The second is Jesus Christ, "our Lord" (1 Tim 1:1; 1 Tim 1:2), who is also mediator between God and humanity (1 Tim 2:5) and the conduit of grace and mercy (1 Tim 1:13-16).

at Ephesus: Onesiphorus' name is known and connected with Ephesus only in this letter.

Interpretation

The holy calling (v. 9) takes on specificity in Paul's elaboration of his ministry as apostle, preacher, and teacher (v. 11). This in turn sets up his autobiographical reference to his own unashamed and confident reliance on God's power to preserve the integrity of faith. This echoes his exhortation to Timothy not to be ashamed and to suffer along with him for the Gospel (v. 8). He returns to his opening exhortation in which he urges Timothy to safeguard the integrity of faith, the model of which he heard from Paul. As earlier (v. 7), Paul calls Timothy's attention to the spiritual power within him to carry out the task (v. 14), and this encouragement is substantiated by his own experience of God's protective power in his unashamed suffering (v. 12). The audience, who are assured of the same spiritual resources (*hēmin*, "to us," v. 12) are thereby encouraged with Timothy to accept the exemplary teaching (*hypotypōsin*, "model," v. 13) and thus to hold fast to the integrity of faith, to endure suffering for the Gospel, and not to see anything shameful in the sound words of the Christian tradition.

To clarify his call to join the struggle to defend the tradition unashamedly, Paul gives Timothy and the readers of the letter negative and positive examples. Deserters are mentioned first, some are named, and they are then dismissed with no further discussion. Onesiphorus, on the other hand, incarnates unashamed and even eager support for the imprisoned Paul (v. 17). He went to Rome and sought Paul out to extend long-term support, unlike those in Rome who abandoned him. His actions are consistent with his longstanding service to the church at Ephesus (v. 18). The experience and testimony of persons imprisoned for matters of conscience and human rights, as well as that of whole societies oppressed under authoritarian regimes, declare the importance of solidarity between them and those who know of their affliction and support them. The fact that others know and care, even if they cannot effect changes in fact, serves to bolster the spirit and endurance of the afflicted. The work of groups such as Amnesty International in writing letters to those imprisoned for conscience' sake demonstrates the importance of these expressions of solidarity with those unjustly deprived of freedom.

For Reference and Further Study

Fitzgerald, John T. *Cracks in the Earthen Vessel: An Examination of the Catalogues of Hardships in the Corinthian Correspondence*. SBLDS 99. Atlanta: Scholars Press, 1988.

Hodgson, Robert. "Paul the Apostle and First-Century Tribulation Lists," *ZNW* 74 (1983) 59–80.

Lee, E. Kenneth. "Words Denoting 'Pattern' in the N.T.," *NTS* 8 (1961–62) 166–73.

Malherbe, Abraham J. *Moral Exhortation: A Greco-Roman Sourcebook*. Library of Early Christianity 4. Philadelphia: Westminster, 1986, 141–43.

________. "Antisthenes and Odysseus and Paul at War," in idem, *Paul and the Popular Philosophers*. Minneapolis: Fortress Press, 1989, 91–119.

Plank, Kurt A. *Paul and the Irony of Affliction*. Atlanta: Scholars Press, 1987.

Spicq, Ceslas. "L'Imitation de Jésus Christ durant les derniers jours de l'apôtre Paul," in Albert Descamps and André de Halleux, eds., *Mélanges bibliques en homage au Béda Rigaux*. Gembloux: Duculot, 1970, 313–22.

Stambaugh, John E., and David l. Balch, "Asia Minor: Ephesus and Other Cities," in *The New Testament in Its Social Environment*. Library of Early Christianity 2. Philadelphia: Westminster, 1986, 149–54.

Towner, Philip H. *The Goal of Our Instruction*, 124–26.

Wolbert, Werner. "Vorbild und paränetische Autorität: zum Problem der 'Nachahmung' des Paulus," *MTZ* 32 (1981) 249–70.

3. *Designated Teachers; Credal Summary* (2:1-13)

1. And so, as for you, my child, be strong in the grace that is in Christ Jesus 2. and, what you heard from me through many witnesses, entrust this to faithful persons, who will be competent to teach others as well. 3. Share in the suffering like a good soldier of Christ Jesus.

4. In order to accommodate the one who enlisted him, no one serving in the army wants to be entangled in the affairs of everyday life. 5. And should someone compete as an athlete, the competitor will not be crowned except by competing according to the rules. 6. The hard-working farmer ought to be first to receive a share of the crops. 7. Take note of what I am saying, for the Lord will give you insight into everything. 8. Remember Jesus Christ, risen from the dead, from the seed of David, according to my gospel. 9. Because of this gospel I am suffering hardship to the point of being imprisoned like a criminal. The word of God, however, has not been imprisoned. 10. Therefore, I endure everything on behalf of the ones who were chosen, so that these also may obtain salvation, which is in Christ Jesus, along with eternal glory. 11. This saying is credible,

For if we died with him, we will also live with him;
12. if we endure, we will also reign with him;
if we will deny (him), that one will also deny us;
13. if we are unfaithful, that one remains faithful,
for he is unable to deny himself.

Notes

1. *my child, be strong:* See "child" at 1:1 and 1 Tim 1:2. The command restates 1:6 and incorporates the insight of 1:7 about the strength that comes from God. Here, though, it is linked with grace bestowed through (1:9) association with

Christ Jesus (see 1:1). As in 1 Timothy, apostasy and false teaching are serious threats, and so images of strength and battle are employed.

Paul gives substance to his call to Timothy to "be strong" with his own spirit unbowed despite his imprisonment. As John Chrysostom, *Hom. 2 Tim.* 4 (NPNF 1 13:487-488), points out, a general gives his captain great encouragement when the latter sees him wounded and then recovered. So here Paul has been exposed to great sufferings but has not been made weak by them. Furthermore, there is more here than a master/servant relationship, since Paul is asking his "son" to imitate him, his "father."

2. *what you heard . . . entrust this to faithful persons . . . competent to teach:* For the Gospel teaching see 1:13 and also *parathēkē*, "entrusted tradition," at 1 Tim 6:20 and 2 Tim 1:12. A public ceremony, probably of ordination, is the context referred to here (see 1:6). Timothy serves as an example for others ordained to teach the Gospel. The phrase curiously suggests intermediary witnesses to the Pauline tradition between Paul and Timothy. This carries forward the tradition-of-faith idea from the first chapter but obscures the direct relationship between Paul and Timothy as coworkers in the mission. Timothy is to entrust the *parathēkē*, "deposit," to reliable bearers of the tradition. In this way others share his task to "guard what is entrusted" (1 Tim 6:20). Fidelity is a prime qualification in a time of doctrinal conflict. As a quality ascribed to Christ, fidelity carries great weight, and is expected of his followers (2:13, and see 1 Tim 1:12; 3:11; 4:3, 10; Titus 1:6). In the PE, "faithful" (*pistos*) is used to refer to community members (see 1 Tim 4:10, 12; 5:16; 6.2). On the basis of 1 Timothy 2:12 and the qualification for elder and bishop one can assume that these persons, official teachers, will be men. The restriction, however, appears linked with the community's efforts to establish its reputation as posing no threat to prevailing social norms. The persistence of teaching in the domestic sphere by women (Titus 2:3-4) indicates a willingness to maintain the earlier Pauline practice of women teachers (e.g., Acts 18:26) where that is socially acceptable. Accommodating social custom is a strategy in service of the goal of gaining a sure foothold for the Gospel in the world it means to save. By teaching, they continue the work of Paul (1:11) and Timothy (1 Tim 4:11; 6:2) in a line of tradition that looks to the future (*kai heterous*, "others as well").

3. *Share in the suffering:* See 1:8, and compare 1:12. The suffering of Jesus included abusive captivity, false accusations at his trial, execution as a traitor (Mark 14:43–15:41 *parr.*; John 18:1–19:36). He was remembered in the Greco-Roman world with ridicule as a crucified Sophist (Tacitus, *Annales* 15.44.3; Lucian, *Peregr.* 11-13; Pliny, *Ep.* 96). Paul's sufferings include his missionary hardships (1 Cor 4:11-13; 2 Cor 6:3-10; 11:21b-33), opponents' abuse (2 Cor 11:1-15), and imprisonments with the prospect of execution (Phil 1:22-26; Acts 20:23). He proudly asserts that he suffers all this unashamedly (1:12), implying that others would find shame in this. The PE are clearly concerned with the community's reputation in belief and practice (see 1 Tim 3:2). The suffering called for on the part of Timothy and the Ephesian audience of the letter is to endure the shame of their association with Christ, Paul, and the Christian community, which occasions suspicion, derision, and even condemnation in the community at large. Onesiphorus is the model of this unashamed association with the dishonorable Paul and the Ephesian church (1:17-18).

There is also the suffering involved with carrying on the struggle with false teachers (here, and also 1 Tim 1:18; 6:4). The community is not under a physical threat, for it has a good number of wealthy (1 Tim 6:17) as well as well-to-do members who are in leadership positions (see 1 Tim 3:4). The community's slave members can expect good treatment from non-Christian masters (1 Tim 6:1). The community also expects favorable treatment from rulers and people of influence (1 Tim 2:2).

4. *entangled in the affairs of everyday life:* The word "affairs" (*pragmateiai*) appears only here in the NT. This letter contrasts getting taken up in the affairs of ordinary life with undiluted attention to Christ Jesus (see also Philo, *Spec. Leg.* 2.65). Epictetus, *Diatr.* 3.24.34-36, uses the image of a soldier closely attentive to his general's signals. Luke's version of the parable of the sower (Luke 8:14) has a similar warning against entanglement in the thorns of life's cares, riches, and pleasures (and compare Demas' abandonment of Paul at 2 Tim 4:10). False teachers give their attention to deceitful spirits (1 Tim 4:1), and wayward widows abandon their pledge to Christ (1 Tim 5:12). Timothy is expected to be free of the ordinary household responsibilities that elders, overseers, and assistants have. As a model for them, however, he proposes the ideal of single-minded service of Christ Jesus. Service of the Gospel is also given a military image in 1 Tim 1:18; Phil 2:25; Phlm 2.

5. *compete as an athlete:* See 1 Tim 4:7. While the military image describes undivided readiness to follow Jesus Christ's orders despite other concerns of life, the athletic image stresses the proper (*nomimōs*) exercise of one's duty. This contrasts with the people who teach falsely and those who behave improperly. Compare the concern with qualifications, testing, and rules of behavior (1 Tim 3:15; Titus 2:14; and contrast 1 Tim 4:3). The crown of victory, promised to the successful athletic competitor, is claimed by Paul at 4:8. Epictetus, *Diatr.* 3.10.7-8, applies the athletic image to the study of philosophy.

6. *The hard-working farmer:* The farmer, the third image, echoes 1 Tim 6:18 and suggests a recompense to Timothy and community officials for their labors. First Corinthians 9:7 offers a close parallel. The context at 1 Cor 9:7 contains a soldier image as well, and the saying from Deut 25:4 at v. 9 is also quoted at 1 Tim 5:18, which specifies a double honor for certain elders. In 1 Corinthians, however, Paul forgoes his rights to salaried support in his ministry.

7. *the Lord will give you insight:* In the LXX the word "insight" (*synesis*) appears particularly in Wisdom literature (Ps 110:10 LXX; Prov 2:1; Sir 5:10; 34:11) and refers to God-given insight into God's activity and will. Here the God-given insight is into everything. The PE frequently focus on the intellectual side of faith (see *epignōsis alētheias*, "knowledge of the truth," 1 Tim 2:4; 2 Tim 3:7; Titus 1:1), and contrast the failed attempts of the false teachers to reach true knowledge (1 Tim 1:7; 4:3; 6:5, 20; 2 Tim 2:18; 3:7-8; 4:4; Titus 1:16). Timothy's coming to insight parallels the converted Paul's being taken out of ignorance (see 1 Tim 1:13).

8. *Remember:* The call to remember, another paraenetic reminder (see 1:6), proceeds from a credal summary to an exhortation.

risen from the dead, from the seed of David, according to my gospel: Jesus' Davidic origins noted here recall Rom 1:3-4. This verb form should be regarded as perfect tense, middle voice, and takes the intransitive meaning of *egeirein* as "stand up," "awaken," and "rise" (at the end-time). Elsewhere in the NT the verb is used as a synonym for *anestē* ("he rose"). Thus the formulation with the active form of the verb, "God raised Jesus" (Rom 10:6; Acts 2:32) and the passive form "Jesus was raised" (Rom 6:9) are secondary in tradition-historical terms. See the early resurrection preaching (Luke 24:34; Rom 4:25; 6:4; Mark 16:6 *parr.*; Matt 27:64; John 2:22) and also the passive participles at 2 Cor 5:15; Rom 6:9; 7:4; 8:34; John 21:14, and the Passion predictions. Although a passive nuance cannot be excluded, the middle sense predominates. The verb declares the end of the condition of death and, more than that, what follows death, a new life. The PE use the word only here and never use *anistanai* ("rise"). The noun *anastasis* ("resurrection," 2 Tim 2:18) refers to the resurrection of all at the end-time. Jesus' resurrection is referred to in the PE by its effects (1 Tim 3:16c; 2 Tim 1:10). The resurrection of Jesus Christ is alluded to at 1 Tim 3:16c and 17; 2 Tim 1:10b; 2:11b, as part of the Gospel. With expressions such as "from the seed of David" the letters reiterate the fact and significance of the incarnation and human life of Jesus. See 1 Tim 1:15; 2:5; 3:16; 6:13; 2 Tim 1:10; Titus 3:4. Here the early credal formula of Rom 1:3-4 is reversed. The reference to the Gospel here, which is implicit in the word (*synkakopathēson*, "share in the suffering," v. 11, and see 1:8, 11-12; 2:9), gives priority to the resurrection. The Davidic lineage looks ahead to 2:12 (*symbasileusomen*, "we will rule together with") and to 4:1, 18 (*basileian*, "kingdom"). See 1:11, 12 for reference to Paul's Gospel.

9. *I am suffering hardship . . . like a criminal:* See 2:3 for "suffering." The letter uses a word for "criminal" that was common in legal and popular speech and was so used in the LXX (Prov 21:15; Sir 11:33) and Josephus, *Ant.* 1.270. Only Luke (23:32, 33, 39) and 2 Timothy use it in the NT. In Luke's gospel the crucifixion of Jesus with two criminals associated him unjustly with their guilt. Paul protests his innocence (*hōs*, "like," with the meaning "as if") and his unjust imprisonment thus creates a likeness with the suffering Jesus (compare 1:8). The *hypotypōsin* ("model," 1:13) of the Gospel is, again, not just the words but the career of Paul in its resemblance to Jesus' career.

   has not been imprisoned: At Phil 1:14, 18, Paul makes a similar comment about his imprisonment. The declarative statement serves as a challenge by which Paul exhorts Timothy and the wider audience. The suffering he wants them to bear (see 2:3) pales before the criminal conviction and imprisonment he, like Jesus, is undergoing.

10. *I endure . . . on behalf of the . . . chosen:* By endurance under pressure on behalf of the chosen ones, Paul exemplifies a quality of steadfastness in the best interests of the community. This is a characteristic of Jesus (2:13). Timothy receives admonitions to persist in his duties and in his fidelity to the Gospel (3:14; 4:2; 1 Tim 4:15). Women (1 Tim 2:15) and widows (1 Tim 5:5) receive a commendation for persistence in prayer and the practice of faith. This contrasts with the waywardness of the apostates and false teachers (1 Tim 1:6; 6:10; 2 Tim 2:18; 4:4; Titus 1:11, 14; 3:11). See Titus 1:1, where the word "chosen" designates the

Christians. The same word is used in connection with the end-time gathering of the chosen ones (*1 Enoch* 62:2; Zech 2:10 LXX; *1 Enoch* 5:7; 1 Thess 4:13-18) and, in general, in eschatological contexts (Mark 13:20, 22, 27 *parr.*). Romans 8:33 uses it of God's faithful. There, end-time acquittal of the chosen ones against all charges and their final rescue from all persecution and distress echo the context here. Moreover, eschatological salvation links this passage to the usages noted above.

obtain salvation, which is in Christ Jesus, along with eternal glory: Paul's endurance of suffering is in service of the Gospel (1:8), which mediates salvation to the contemporary audience (1:10-12). See 1 Tim 1:15 for Christ's role in salvation, and see 1 Tim 3:16 for a reference to "the glory of Christ Jesus." See 1 Tim 1:11 for glory as linked with God in the Gospel. Here the glory of the heavenly realm, into which Christ was taken, is promised to the faithful as well (1 Pet 1:6-12; 4:13; 5:1, 4, 10; Rom 8:17) after they have suffered. The crown of righteousness that Paul awaits at 4:8 is called the crown of glory at 1 Pet 5:4.

11. *This saying is credible:* The saying does not precede the corroborating affirmation. The material before the affirmation is personal and not gnomic. The most likely candidate for a saying in the text before the affirmation is at v. 8, too distant from v. 11. Furthermore, there is no other indication to guide the audience to identify it as the credible saying. The lines from vv. 11-13 have a hymnic or credal character. There are four simple conditional sentences: the first two apodoses (second halves of the sentences) begin with *kai* ("and"); the second two apodoses start with a form of *ekeinos* ("that one"); a temporal progression from past to present to future in the first three protases (the "if" clauses) returns to the present in the fourth; all the four protases have first plural subjects; the first plural subjects in the first two apodoses (the main clauses) become third singulars with the emphatic *ekeinos* ("that one") in the second two; the last strophe explains the fourth condition by repeating the verb in the third strophe; and by emphasizing its unacceptability, the conjunction *gar* ("for") was probably a connective between the fragment and the verses that preceded it in the lost original. The *syn-* ("with-") compounds, which refer to verbs in those verses, serve to link the fragment with the personal observation in vv. 8-10.

if we died . . . we will also live: This is not an exhortation to embrace martyrdom in view of a future reward. In the preceding verses Paul refers to his suffering and imprisonment. Martyrdom was not a common expectation in the church at this time. The order of ideas in the "if" clauses is rendered illogical by martyrdom. Moreover, a martyr would die "for" rather than "with" Christ. Romans 6:8 and its context provide an almost exact parallel. Although Christ is named in Rom 6:8, he is not mentioned here presumably because he was referred to in the last verses prior to this quotation. The context indicates here and in Romans that the exhortation is not to martyrdom, but to death to sin by all Christians in their being crucified with Christ in the baptism ritual (Rom 6:11; see also Gal 2:20; Col 2:12; Mark 14:31; 2 Cor 7:3). For "life" see Rom 6:11 and Gal 2:20. "Life" at Rom 6:5-11, although it is expressed in the future, refers to the new life lived in the present by Christians. The new life, of course, encompasses eternal life (see Rom 6:22, and also 2 Tim 1:10; 6:12).

12. *if we endure . . . we will also reign:* See Matt 10:22 and Mark 13:13 for endurance under hatred and affliction in the final days. The examples of Christ (Heb 12:2-3; 1 Pet 2:20-21) and Paul (2 Tim 2:10) inspire Christians' endurance. The eschatological perspective is never far away in this letter (2:10) and in the parallel NT passages (Matt 10:22; 24:13; Mark 13:13; Heb 10:36). The present tense emphasizes ongoing endurance in the face of persistent trials and difficulties (see 2:3). The rule is shared by all the faithful with Jesus Christ. First Corinthians 4:8 helps readers understand that the reign is eschatological, with endurance as the lot of Christians in the present. That passage also helps show that the reign is shared by all and at the same time with Christ (see Luke 22:28-30, where those who endure receive a place in the kingdom; compare Matt 25:34-36, and see also Matt 25:46 and Rev 22:5 for the kingdom as eternal).

    if we will deny . . . that one will also deny: Matthew 10:33 (and Luke 12:9), possibly the source of this idea, clarifies that this is a denial of Christ before people. The context shows it to be the opposite of confessing Christ (see 1 Tim 6:12, and compare Titus 1:16). Denying a person implies refusal to admit one's prior relationship with that person (see Matt 26:69-75 *parr.*). In the PE the unfaithful manifest their denial by their actions (1 Tim 5:8; 2 Tim 3:5; Titus 1:16). Mark 8:34-38 and Luke 9:23-26 speak of shame that provokes one to deny Christ rather than denying self and bearing the cross that is required of Christians. Shame and endurance are a preoccupation in this letter and this passage.

    Christ's future denial in response to our final stance of rejection will take place at the end-time judgment before the Father (Matt 10:33, and see Luke 12:9). This eschatological warning adds punch to the exhortation here.

13. *if we are unfaithful, that one remains faithful:* The word "unfaithful" (*apisteō*), appears only six times in the NT (in Luke, Paul, and 1 Peter, with two more uses in the long ending of Mark). Only at Rom 3:3 and here does it mean "be unfaithful." In both cases the contrast is not with belief but with divine faithfulness (of God in Romans, and of Christ here). Since the apodoses express a relationship with the subject of the protases ("if" clauses), so here Christ remains faithful "to us." That his attitude contrasts with ours is demonstrated by the omission of *kai* ("also") from the preceding parallel clauses. Christ's faithfulness is positive, as indicated by the verb "remain" (*menei*), which indicates an abiding relationship and not a new attitude. Thus Christ is not faithful here in order to "punish" our waywardness. God's faithfulness is to save people on the final day, as promised (1 Cor 1:9; 10:13; 2 Cor 1:18-20; 1 Thess 5:22-24; 2 Thess 3:3, and compare Heb 10:23; 1 Pet 4:19). See 2:2.

    he is unable to deny himself: See Heb 6:17-18. The apodosis (main clause) and elaboration in response to the protasis ("if" clause) of our faithfulness underline Jesus Christ's fidelity to his promises to forgive and save all. The declaration encourages Christians who might tend to unfaithfulness that forgiveness is an offer that will not be revoked (see 1 Tim 1:15-16).

    The first statement suggests an origin in Paul's own words as expressed in Romans 6 and used in a baptismal context. The second statement seems linked structurally and in content with the first. The third appears to have its origins in a saying of Jesus recorded in Matt 10:33. While the latter statement and the next one vary somewhat in form from the first two, the basic structure remains the same. The application to the context of the warning against denial and faithlessness is not as close as that of the first two statements. The explanatory v. 13b was also part of the original. It is unlikely to be an addition by the letter's author for various reasons: The addition is insignificant to the context. The length corresponds to the length of the other verses. The addition supplies the rationale for Christ's faithfulness, which the fourth protasis, unlike the first three, does not include in itself. The likelihood is that the author did not write any of this, but used a fragment of a (baptismal?) hymn that originated in the Pauline church, perhaps at Rome. The credal statement in v. 8, again from Romans (1:3-4), might possibly preserve another excerpt from the hymn, but it and the rest of the verses down to v. 11 are so tied up with personal references as to make finding other fragments there unlikely.

Interpretation

Directed emphatically (*sy de*, "but as for you") toward Paul's protégé Timothy, the next section in the exhortation and instruction reiterates and applies the observation about spiritual power from the thanksgiving (v. 1), the concern for preserving the tradition (v. 2), and the call to share in suffering (v. 3). Three images illustrate aspects of Timothy's labors (vv. 4-7), positive and negative examples illustrate and confirm the exhortation, and the section concludes with a return to direct instruction to Timothy.

This section of the exhortation has four parts. In the first (vv. 1-7) the pronoun "you" (*sy*) and the coordinating conjunction "therefore" (*oun*) turn attention emphatically to Timothy in light of the opening exhortation and its examples, especially those just mentioned at 1:15-18. Association with Christ Jesus gives continuous access to divine favor. Thus the command to "be strong" (*endynamou*) has assurance of its realization in the gift of the spirit of "power" (*dynamis*) noted at 1:7. This connection carries forward the spiritual gift of his ordination (1 Tim 4:14; 6:12) and also has relevance to the Christian community generally, who enjoy the gift of the Spirit by virtue of their baptism.

The effort to preserve the tradition of faith that Paul urges finds a practical strategy in the designation and instruction of capable teachers. A line of tradition is established from the witness of Paul to the "many witnesses" to Timothy and then to his trusted "faithful people" and the "others" whom the last-mentioned will teach. This echoes the tradition of faith suggested at 1:3-5, i.e., the ancestors, Paul, grandmother Lois, mother Eunice, and finally Timothy. The contact between Paul and Timothy at his conversion seems to be more reduced here than what Acts 16:1-5 implies.

The letter completes the call to be strong (vv. 1-2) with three comparisons (vv. 3-7). The first, to a soldier, carries on from 1:8 the theme of unashamed and vigorous suffering for the Gospel shared with Paul (*synkakopathēson*, "suffering along with," and see 2:3) as well as of guarding (1:14) what has been entrusted (*phylaxon*, "safeguard"). The soldier image (v. 4) expresses a distinction between church work and common business affairs, from which Timothy is expected to separate himself totally as he dedicates himself exclusively to satisfying Christ Jesus, his recruiter (1:3-4). Timothy, the exemplary community leader, apparently is less self-supporting than the tentmaking Paul (Acts 18:3). Ambrosiaster, *Commentary on the Second Letter to Timothy* (CSEL 81 3:302-303), from a later vantage point notes that business affairs often evoke greed in the participants and thus should be avoided by faithful servants of the church. Leo the Great goes even further when he recommends severing all obligatory ties to others, lest these call the church soldier away from God's encampment (*Letters* 4 [FC 34:24]). The trend toward asceticism in these later applications of the ideas in this verse is clear, and it helps explain the subsequent adoption of the discipline of clerical celibacy, not envisioned in the letters themselves. As it is, the call for disentanglement from worldly affairs is more practical than the theological motivation for remaining unmarried offered by Paul in 1 Corinthians 7: that is, to give undivided attention to preparation for Jesus' imminent return (1 Cor 7:29-31).

The second comparison, to an athlete (v. 5), includes an end-time suggestion in the crown, which echoes the immortal life referred to at 1:10 and the final day at 1:12. Here the focus is not on the athlete's exertion but on competing according to the rules (*nomimōs*), which throws emphasis on orthopraxy rather than orthodoxy and recalls the praise of Onesiphorus' household (1:16-18) as opposed to the Asian deserters (1:15).

The use of athletic images here and at Phil 3:13-14; 1 Cor 9:24-27 mirrors the interest of Greek and Roman society in physical culture and athleticism. The revival of the Olympic Games in our time brings this reality clearly to our attention. Then, as now, athletes subjected themselves to an ascetical regimen of diet and exercise in order to prepare themselves to compete well and to win the prize of the victor (drinking bowls, crowns, wreaths, free dining privileges, commemorative statues) and the adulation accorded by the crowd. The PE, following Paul's lead, capitalize on this interest and make appropriate applications to the spiritual life.

The third comparison is to a farmer (v. 6). Here hard work displaces the suffering connected with evangelical work, and the image promotes prompt payment for church workers as their just share. Rural references like this one are rare in the epistolary literature of the NT (see 1 Cor 9:7-11; Rom 11:17-24), with its urban focus.

The call to reflect and the promise of divine enlightenment (v. 7) conclude the image section on a positive note, and one that lays emphasis on knowledge. Thus the emotional and volitional aspects of the Christian life (1:7) receive an intellectual balance that picks up the teacher (1:11) and the normative words (1:13) mentioned earlier.

In the second part of this exhortation section (vv. 8-13) the Gospel of the dead and risen Christ and Paul's suffering in connection with it provide an example to imitate (vv. 8-9), as well as the motivation for it: salvation and future glory (vv. 10-13). The Pauline Gospel summary includes Jesus' messiahship (Christ), Davidic lineage, death, and resurrection. Paul's mention of his sufferings recalls earlier references to them (1:8, 12, 16) and backs up his call to Timothy to share in the suffering (2:3). The Gospel of Jesus' death and resurrection, repeated from 1:10, is elaborated in the "credible saying" below (2:11-13).

The Incarnation of Jesus lends reality to his sufferings and completeness to his resurrection. Paul in his suffering is following the pattern of the sufferings of the human Jesus, and the audience of the letters is to follow this example as well. The resurrection of Jesus affected his entire being, body and soul. This establishes the outline of the promised resurrection of the faithful as well. This will not be an event involving the human spirit alone, but will include the body, albeit in a transformed condition (1 Cor 15:36-54; 2 Cor 5:1-5). This gives the physical side of human life and activity an eternal dimension. Human existence bears a divine imprint and manifests the Spirit. Believers recognize this privilege and challenge in their very nature. Similarly, as the human destiny is not restricted to the mind or the soul but involves the physical human reality as well, human words and deeds are set against the horizon of eternity.

The inability to chain God's word (v. 9) coordinates with Paul's assurance of God's guardianship over the Gospel words entrusted to Paul (1:12) and serves as a comment on Timothy's task to entrust the Gospel to other teachers (2:2).

The power of the word to shape humans' hopes and sustain their spirits despite efforts to suppress these has been demonstrated throughout history. The Spirit of God calls forth and sustains the expressions of truth. In the first centuries of Christianity, Paul's Gospel was announced despite his imprisonment (Phil 1:12-14), and the Christian message filtered throughout the Roman empire even in the face of concerted attempts to silence it, especially in the third century. More recently the word of justice and human rights, encouraged by papal teachings, took root in movements for freedom that could not be silenced by government repression and led, for example, to the collapse of communism in Poland and then throughout the Soviet bloc. Efforts to stifle human expressions of religious belief and longing for basic human rights and freedoms in other countries, which have included such tactics as suppressing religious assemblies, public demonstrations, and even internet exchanges, have had only partial success and that most likely for the short term.

The audience of the Gospel for which Paul toils and suffers (1:8) is the elect, which suggests a restricted number of faithful. The end-time focus introduced by "eternal glory" (*doxēs aiōniou*) helps explain the less-than-universal reception of the Gospel as a consequence of end-time apostasy and deception (3:1-9, and see 1:9). As a hortatory device, the suggestion that few may remain faithful serves as a warning for a church in a time of conflict and opposition. The defensive stance of the beleaguered church's insiders finds further expression at 2:19.

The Gospel's aim is twofold: salvation in Christ Jesus and eternal glory. The eschatological perspective of the latter is continuous with present salvation in the church, where the faithful enjoy the security of divinely sanctioned true belief and virtuous action.

The "credible saying" (vv. 11-13) reiterates the themes of the section and universalizes their application with the use of "we." Death with Christ echoes the suffering of Paul (vv. 8-9) and Timothy (v. 3) and Jesus' death (v. 8); life with Christ echoes Jesus' being raised (v. 8) and the promise of eternal glory (v. 10, and see 1:10). Perseverance (v. 12) relates to "bearing with everything" (v. 10) and being strong (v. 1) and hard-working (v. 6). Reigning expresses Christ's Davidic lineage (v. 8) and eternal glory (v. 10). Fidelity (vv. 12-13) is the hallmark of Paul as exemplary Christian (2:12-13). It is presumed of Timothy (1:5, 8, and see 2:4) and is expected of Timothy's designees (2:2). The apparent exclusivity of God's election receives correction here, where only human infidelity occasions alienation from an ever-faithful savior (see 2:25-26 for hope of eventual repentance).

For Reference and Further Study

Allen, John A. "The 'In Christ' Formula in the Pastoral Epistles," *NTS* 10 (1963–64) 115–21.

Borse, Udo. *1. und 2. Timotheusbrief, Titusbrief*. Stuttgarter Kleiner Kommentar, Neues Testament 13. Stuttgart: Katholisches Bibelwerk, 1985, 83–84.

Broneer, Oscar T. "The Apostle Paul and the Isthmian Games," *BA* 25 (1962) 2–31.

________. "The Isthmian Victory Crown, " *AJA* 66 (1962) 259–63.

Elliott, John H. *The Elect and the Holy: An Exegetical Examination of 1 Peter 2:4-10 and the Phrase basileion hierateuma*. NovTSup 12. Leiden: Brill, 1966.

Jeremias, Joachim. *Theology of the New Testament*. London: SCM, 1973, 13 n.1.

Knight, George W. III. *The Faithful Sayings in the Pastoral Letters*. Grand Rapids: Baker, 1979, 112–37.

Pfitzner, Victor C. *Paul and the Agōn Motif*. NovTSup 16. Leiden: Brill, 1967.

Ridderbos. Herman N. *The Coming of the Kingdom*, trans. H. de Jongste; ed. Raymond O. Zorn. Philadelphia: Presbyterian and Reformed Press, 1962.

Riesenfeld, Harald. "The Meaning of the Verb *arneisthai*," in Seminarium neotestamenticum upsaliense, eds., *In honorem Antonii Fridrichsen: sexagenarii*. Coniectanea Neotestamentica 11. Lund: Gleerup; Copenhagen: Munksgaard, 1947, 207–19.

Schürmann, Heinz. "Haben die paulinischen Wertungen und Weisungen Modellcharakter? Beobachtungen und Anmerkungen zur Frage nach ihrer formalen Eigenart und inhaltlichen Verbindlichkeit," *Greg* 56 (1975) 237–51.

Viviano, Benedict T. *The Kingdom of God in History*. Good News Studies 27. Wilmington: Michael Glazier, 1988.

Wolbert, Werner. "Vorbild und paränetischer Autorität; zum Problem der 'Nachahmung' des Paulus," *MTZ* 32 (1981) 249–70.

4. *False Teachers; God's Household* (2:14-23)

14. Remind them of these things, as you emphatically declare before God that they not dispute about words, which is good for nothing and leads to the ruin of those who listen. 15. Be eager to show yourself to God as proven, a worker with no need to be ashamed, straightforward in teaching the word of truth. 16. Avoid the profane, empty chatter, for they will go on to even more impiety 17. and their teaching will spread like gangrene. These include Hymenaeus and Philetus, 18. who deviated with regard to the truth, declaring that the resurrection has already taken place, and they are overturning some people's faith. 19. Nevertheless, the solid foundation of God stands, with this inscription: "The Lord knows those who are his" and "Let everyone who calls on the name of the Lord keep away from wrongdoing." 20. Now, in a grand household there are vessels not only of gold and silver but also of wood and clay. The former serve honorable uses, the latter lowly ones. 21. Accordingly, if someone should purge oneself of these unseemly things, that one will be a vessel for honor, made holy, useful to the master, readied for every good deed. 22. But flee the passionate desires of youth and pursue uprightness, faith, love, peace with those who call on the Lord with a clean heart. 23. Yes, avoid foolish and stupid controversies, since you know that they give rise to quarrels.

Notes

14. *Remind . . . declare before God:* This is another paraenetic reminder (see 1:6). The forensic background of the word "declare" (*diamartyromenos*) matches the trial-and-imprisonment setting of 2 Timothy (see 1 Tim 5:10). God observes the sworn declaration, which adds to its solemnity (see 1 Tim 6:12, and for a direct courtroom image see 1 Tim 5:21; 2 Tim 4:1).

dispute about words . . . to the ruin: This disputatious characteristic of the false teaching is repudiated repeatedly in the PE (see 1 Tim 6:4). Varro satirizes the philosophical debate between Stoics and Epicureans as a *logomachia*. Plutarch, *Virt. prof.* 80B-F, notes that contentiousness is useless for useful correction (and see Stobaeus, II 2,18.22). See 1 Tim 1:13; Titus 1:11.

15. *Be eager:* Compare Onesiphorus at 1:17. The letters, while organizing a socially unremarkable community, seem to expect a high level of commitment to an energetic ministry in support of church doctrine at a time of doctrinal crisis.

    proven . . . with no need to be ashamed, straightforward in teaching the word of truth: See 1 Tim 3:10; 5:20-22. Paul (1 Tim 1:12) was judged faithful, and his follower Timothy is to prove himself, too. Scrutiny on the basis of unashamed dedication to correct preaching fits the view at 1 Tim 5:25 that good deeds are inevitably manifest to all (and see the Note on 2:3). The PE propose an uncomplicated doctrine and a preaching that follows clear lines, as opposed to the nuances and alternative proposals debated by the opponents. The doctrinal content of faith is emphasized, but this is not surprising in this context, where disputes about words are the contrasting alternative (see also 1 Tim 2:4).

16. *profane, empty chatter:* This is the opposite of "piety" (*eusebeia*). See 1 Tim 2:2. Since piety comprises sound teaching and an appropriate way of life, the false teachers cannot avoid impiety. Since it involves deeds, their progress into impiety will be obvious to all, as explained at 1 Tim 5:24, and contrast 1 Tim 4:15. The catchphrase "empty chatter" (*bebēlous kenophōnias*, see 1 Tim 6:20) derisively characterizes the opponents' doctrine. While the PE caution Timothy and Titus and, through them, the community to avoid controversies with opponents, they are not above caricaturing the opponents' teaching (see also 1 Tim 4:7). This was standard in doctrinal polemic of the day.

    they will go on: See the note on 1 Tim 4:15.

17. *like gangrene:* For medical imagery as applied to false teaching see 1 Tim 1:10.

    Hymenaeus and Philetus: Hymenaeus was named at 1 Tim 1:20; Philetus is named only here. Nothing further is known about them. Singling out named individuals gives concreteness to the warning and puts into practice the public rebuke of the wayward prescribed at 1 Tim 5:20, there in the case of elders. The threat of such dishonor before the community would be a strong deterrent against taking up the false teachers' views.

18. *deviated with regard to the truth:* See the note on 2:10. The tradition of faith, as the truth (see v. 15 and 1 Tim 2:4, and the Introduction), is the reference point. While Timothy is to cut a straight path (v. 15) with his teaching, the false teachers wander about.

    resurrection has already taken place: This is one of the few clear descriptions of the false teachers' doctrinal error. Interpretation of the resurrection as a spiritual event in the life of the believer is known from 1 Cor 15:12. The PE's reiteration of the belief in the end-time appearance of Christ Jesus to judge the wicked and reward the faithful (2:11-13, and see also 1 Tim 6:14; 2 Tim 1:18; 4:1,8, 14, 18; Titus 3:7), the contrast between the present (Titus 2:12; 1 Tim 6:17) and future ages (2 Tim 1:12), and the balance maintained between present (2 Tim 1:9-11; Titus 2:11; 3:5) and future salvation (1 Tim 4:8, 16; Titus 2:13) all provide the traditional, Pauline focus on both the "already" and the "not yet" (see 2 Thess 2:2-12; 1 Thess 5:1-11; Col 3:1-17; Rom 6:5-14; Phil 3:8-16). Belief in an anticipated resurrection might have led to the false teachers' exhortations to ascetical practices to express the spiritual transformation of the believer (1 Tim 4:3-10, which reminds the audience of both the present and future life, and compare Col 2:16-23). The PE also make a strong point of the universality of salvation (see 1 Tim 2:4), which might be a response to a limiting of salvation by the false teachers to a spiritual elite who exempt themselves from obedience to the law (1 Tim 1:8-11, and compare 1 Cor 6:12) and who have pretensions to special knowledge (1 Tim 6:20-21; 2 Tim 3:7, and compare 1 Cor 3:18-20). John Chrysostom, *Hom. 2 Tim.* 5 (NPNF 13 1:493), observes that if the resurrection were already past, then so too is the retribution. The unjust, however, still flourish, while the good suffer persecutions and afflictions. Thus to him it would be better to say there is no resurrection than that it is already past.

overturning some people's faith: Plato (*Leg.* 709a; *Rep.* 471b) uses the verb "overturn" (*anatrepousin*) to describe the ruin or overthrow of a city or a household, and Aristophanes (*Wasps* 671) applies it to the overthrow of a city. The conflict image suggested in the verb fits the defensive tone of the letters (e.g., *phylassein,* "guard," 1 Tim 5:21; 6:20; 2 Tim 1:12, 14; 4:15) and carries over into the next verse with the "solid foundation" (*stereos themelios*). Moreover, in an earthquake-prone region like western Turkey total ruin would be a familiar occurrence. By using the indefinite pronoun "of some people," (*tinōn*) the author can suggest that the apostasy is still a small problem. It also leaves open the door for reconciliation by keeping the faithless ones anonymous.

19. *solid foundation of God stands, with this inscription:* In Isa 28:16 the foundation stone of Israel is laid by God in Zion as a sure basis for the faithful. Paul speaks of Jesus Christ as the foundation he laid for the Corinthian community (1 Cor 3:31; Rom 15:20, and compare Heb 6:1). The letter to the Ephesians notes that the foundation of the Ephesian community is the apostles and prophets, with Jesus as the cornerstone (Eph 2:20). The image here accords well with the PE's view of the church as household of God (2:20, and 1 Tim 3:15). While 1 Tim 6:19 relates the foundation image to the works done in Christian piety, here the foundation is the true teaching of the faith (2:15) in contrast to the faith-destroying teachings of the false teachers (2:14, 16-18).

The impression of a seal identified an owner or author or, when unbroken, signified that the contents of a container or chamber were undisturbed. The image is stretched here, since a stone foundation could not receive the seal's impression. Moreover, the "impression" is not a mark but a quotation, hence an inscription. The notion of the seal carries over, however, since the inscription declares God's ownership as well as the uprightness of the members of God's household.

"The Lord knows those who are his": While the declaration is not found verbatim in Scripture, Num 16:5 is similar. There, in the context of the rebellion of Korah and his Levitical followers against Moses, the appeal is made to God to make known who belongs to him. The optimistic, universal belief of 1 Tim 3:16 receives a sobering second look here. Exclusion from the household of God's own is the implied threat.

"Let everyone who calls on the name of the Lord keep away from wrongdoing": Again this does not exactly quote a scriptural verse. Isaiah 26 speaks of God's judgment on the wicked who do not learn justice from God's forbearance, and of

the faithful calling on God's name (26:13) in contrast to these (compare Sir 35:5).

20. *in a grand household:* The household image moves from foundation to utensils.
serve honorable uses: See Rom 9:21, where the image of household vessels applies to God's use of people to express faith or resist it (see also Isa 29:16, 45:9; Wis 15:7). Here the image differentiates the church ministers who promote the authentic Gospel from the false teachers. Once again the honor/shame distinction enters in, with honor associated with the Gospel message and its purveyors (see 1:8). Thus at 2:15 Timothy is to be a worker with nothing to be ashamed of. There is a pun here on Timothy's name, for he does give "honor" (*timē*) to "God" (*theos*).

21. *purge:* As the image develops, the possibility of a change of heart in the false teachers is mentioned as a hope and an invitation (compare 1 Tim 1:20 and Titus 1:13). The verb "purge" (*ekkatharizō*) is used in 1 Cor 5:7 in a similar context of a threat to the community's integrity, moral in this case. The image is that of the pre-Passover cleaning out of all leaven as a symbol of impurity. In 2 Timothy the author's expansion on the image leads to an inconsistency, for he implies that the purgation will change vessels from lowly uses into ones for honorable service. But the material of the vessels, precious metal or commonplace matter, determines the use. The developed image mentions only a change of use, but not the change of material.
Vettius Valens, 242, using the word in a moral sense, has "cleanse of all evil and every blemish." A clean conscience is the hallmark of Paul (1:3) and the qualified assistant (1 Tim 3:9). It is also the aim of the letters' exhortation for the whole community (1 Tim 1:5). Timothy is expected to have a clean heart (2 Tim 2:22). This is possible because Jesus cleansed the whole community and rendered it capable of and eager for doing good (Titus 2:14).
holy, useful to the master, readied for every good deed: First Thessalonians 4:7 contrasts "holiness" (*hagiasmos*) with "uncleanness" (*akatharsia*). In the LXX the word suggests consecration of persons (Exod 13:2) and things (e.g., Sabbath at Gen 2:3; prophets at Jer 1:5) to God, which is the meaning here. At 2:14 the false teachers' disputes over words were declared useless. On the other hand, Paul notes that Mark is useful for service at 4:11. God is the master of the household, the church (see 1 Tim 3:15). Good deeds are complementary to sound teaching in the faithful life of piety (see 1 Tim 2:2). Good deeds are characteristic of the Christian (1 Tim 2:10; 5:10, 25; 6:18; 2 Tim 3:17; Titus 3:1, 8, 14) and Timothy is to be a model in doing these (1 Tim 6:18; Titus 2:7). Similarly, the false teachers cannot achieve good deeds (Titus 1:16). The good works, however, do not acquire salvation (2 Tim 1:9; Titus 3:5), and in the end it is Jesus Christ who does the cleansing and renders the believers eager for good deeds (Titus 2:14). Titus 2:14 thus balances this verse by identifying the ultimate source of cleansing in connection with the believers' efforts to become clean and prepared for good deeds.

22. *passionate desires of youth:* See 1 Tim 6:9 for a similar excess among the rich, but contrast the desire for a good occupation among applicants for community

office at 1 Tim 3:1. A life under the sway of unbridled passions contrasts with the sober life of piety that the PE promote (see Titus 2:12). The false teachers and their followers give themselves to passion (2 Tim 3:6; 4:3) as the believing community also did prior to the action of God's saving grace (Titus 3:3). See 1 Tim 4:12 for further comments on youthfulness.

pursue . . . peace: See 1 Tim 6:11 and 1 Tim 1:5, 9. While the vice catalogues characteristically use plural nouns, suggesting the wanton confusion of the apostate and heretical way of life, the virtue catalogs use singular nouns (1 Tim 1:5; 4:12; 6:11; 2 Tim 3:10). The same holds true for descriptions of the heretical teachings, again using plurals (1 Tim 1:4; 4:1, 7; 6:4, 20; 2 Tim 2:16, 23; 4:4; Titus 1:14; 3:9) as opposed to the sound teaching, faith, and truth, which are singular (1 Tim 1:10; 4:1, 6, 13; 5:17; 6:1, 3, 20; 2 Tim 1:12, 14; 3:10, 16; 4:3; Titus 1:9; 2:1, 7, 10). In this way the unity and stability of the faithful tradition receives emphasis. Peace here is not the eschatological peace brought in at the *parousia* (1 Thess 5:23; Rom 8:6) but the peace that is a bond between Jews and Gentiles (Eph 4:3). Thus Timothy and his appointees are to pursue peace with those who believe in God.

call on the Lord with a clean heart: The Lord here is Christ Jesus (Phil 2:11, and see 1 Tim 1:2), and Christians were known as those who call on the name of the Lord (Acts 9:14, 21; Rom 1:12-13). Purity is mentioned at 2:21 (and see Joel 3:5).

23. *avoid foolish and stupid controversies . . . they give rise to quarrels:* One of the principal defensive tactics of the PE is to counsel the addressees to avoid misleading, false teaching and unproductive controversies as well as to keep at arm's length persons prone to wayward behavior (1 Tim 4:7; Titus 3:9-10, and compare 1 Tim 5:11, 22; 6:11; 2 Tim 2:16; 3:5). Direct rebuke of wrongdoers (1 Tim 5:20; 2 Tim 4:20; Titus 1:9; 2:15) will make the offense clear to all, as a deterrent to others and a remedy for the wrongdoers (1 Tim 1:20; Titus 1:13). The PE often focus on the intellectual aspect of faith (see "knowledge of the truth," 1 Tim 2:4) and this supplies the perspective for their criticism of the false teaching (see also 2 Tim 2:16). Controversies and quarrels receive comment at 1 Tim 6:4.

Interpretation

The second unit of this exhortation section urges Timothy to an eager demonstration to God of his worthiness and his adherence to the truth, as a worker who has done nothing of which he is ashamed (vv. 15-17a). It also warns him away from empty talk that leads to impiety and harm. Adherence to the truth contrasts with the useless disputes in the previous unit. In fulfilling his charge Timothy would be setting an example for his selected teachers (2:2). The discussion of shame is shifted here from a preoccupation with association with criminals (Paul and Jesus) to a consideration of its true cause; that is, useless and ruinous teaching. Moreover, God, not human society, is noted as the one who determines shamefulness. The distinction between the religious and the secular continues as the letter warns Timothy away from "profane, idle chatter" (NAB) that leads people away from God.

The debate is religious in nature, not one pitting the secular against the religious. The letter, however, condemns its opponents as proposing ideas that are tantamount to godlessness. Reiterating what was said at v. 14, the letter applies the graphic image of gangrene to the opponents' teaching (contrast 1:13, *hygiainontōn logōn*, "sound teachings").

The third unit of the exhortation provides the examples of named, negative proponents of unsound, irreverent apostasy and untrue and destructive teaching to reinforce the warning (vv. 17b-18). The apostasy consists in an over-realized eschatology, which contrasts with Pauline belief in a resurrection life of eternal glory with Christ in the future (1:1, 12, 18; 2:10, 11, 12). This deviation from the truth (v. 18) contrasts with Timothy's longstanding adherence to it (1:5), and the destruction of people's faith (v. 18) puts at risk the Gospel promise of salvation of the elect (v. 10).

Finally, images and scriptural warrants confirm the teaching (vv. 19-20) and offer hope of conversion (v. 21). The strong defense of the church of the PE finds expression in the image of the solid foundation (compare 1 Tim 3:15). It is decidedly on God's side according to the inscription (*sphragis*, literally "seal") that asserts God's acceptance and demands a blameless life. The assurance for the letter's audience from this scripturally based inscription receives further confirmation in the image of household vessels (vv. 20-21). The idea of the church as household of God (see 1 Tim 3:15; Titus 1:7) gives rise to the image.

A second image makes use of household vessels to refer to community members and their functions (see Pseudo-Aelius Aristides, *Rhet.* II 138). The image is stretched under the pressure of the idea behind it. Although presumably the gold and silver vessels are for honorable purposes and the wooden and clay ones for shameful use (v. 20), the letter promises an upward change in usefulness for those who cleanse themselves from "these things" (v. 21). The change in usefulness as a result of cleansing does not account for a change in material, the initial premise of the image. "These things" refers to the empty, ruinous, and untrue teachings (vv. 16-18). An open-ended, conciliatory note is thereby struck as the letter offers the possibility of repentance and reintegration of the wayward into the household of God. The image characterizes the false teachers as shameful and their teaching as vile refuse. By contrast, Timothy, his colleagues, and their teaching are all of them beneficial and honorable.

The fourth unit of the exhortation section returns to Timothy and urges him to flee youthful passions, join the Christian pursuit of virtues, and embrace a peaceable paraenetic style, again with the hope of rescue of the wayward (vv. 23-26). The directives addressed to Timothy (vv. 22-26) close this hortatory section by returning to where it began. The specific instructions here flow from the images in the immediately preceding part and from the exhortation in the entire section. Thus Timothy (v. 22) is urged to turn from "youthful desires" (*neoterikas epithymias*) and to pursue virtue in the company of those "with purity of heart" (NAB) (*ek katharas kardias*, and compare *ekkatharei heauton*, "cleanses himself," [NAB 2:21]). The "youthful passions" refer to uncontrolled, vehement, and aggressive dealing with opposition (see Plotinus, IV 4,21,96; Cicero, *Cael.* 42-43; Tacitus, *Historiae* I 15, 3; Aulus Gellius, X 3, 4-5). This is indicated in the contrasting virtues of "love" (*agapē*) and "peace" (*eirēnē*). The implication of immaturity falls on the opponents, who press on with their vain argumentation. More directly, the exhortation reiterates (v. 23) the charge from the first and second units to avoid speculation and quarrels (see vv. 14, 16) which, presumably, constitute the refuse in the shameful vessels.

In a society such as that in the United States, where the individual's rights and prerogatives are paramount, the social consequences of individual choice receive short shrift. This is particularly troubling when the inviolate conscience of the individual is in error. Decisions taken in the boardroom on compensation and perquisites for a company head have been shown to create a culture of ethical obtuseness with a negative impact on the business climate and the financial status of workers and investors. Individual choices in the bedroom likewise have been catalogued to contribute to a social climate of abusive and exploitative relationships, a deadening of the respect for life, and a breakdown of the family. Contemporary society is at a disadvantage when compared with the society of the Pastoral Epistles, since it lacks the corrective and cohesive force of the family honor code and the sense of obligation and duty toward one's class and society as a whole.

For Reference and Further Study

Baughen, Michael. *Chained to the Gospel* (*24 Studies on 2 Timothy*). Glasgow: Marshall Pickering, 1986.

Malherbe, Abraham J. "Medical Imagery in the Pastoral Epistles," in W. Eugene March, ed., *Texts and Testaments: Critical Essays on the Bible and Early Church Fathers.* San Antonio: Trinity University Press, 1980, 19–35.

________. *Paul and the Popular Philosophers*, 125–26 and n. 12.

Schlarb, Egbert. "Miszelle zu 1 Tim 6:20," *ZNW* 77 (1986) 276–81.

Towner, Philip H. "Gnosis and Realized Eschatology in Ephesus (of the late Pastoral Epistles) and the Corinthian Enthusiasm," *JSNT* 31 (1987) 95–124.

5. *Strategy for Correction* (2:24-26)

24. A slave of the Lord, you see, must not fight, but rather must be gentle toward everyone, skillful in teaching, patient, 25. correcting opponents courteously. It may well be that God will give them repentance leading to the knowledge of the truth. 26. And they will come to their senses and escape from the devil's trap, after being captured by him for his will.

Notes

24. *A slave of the Lord . . . must not fight:* The designation "slave" is suitable to the household image for the church. Titus 1:1 applies the image to Paul and follows Pauline usage (Rom 1:1; Phil 1:1; Gal 1:10). Submissiveness is encouraged in slave members of the church (1 Tim 6:1; Titus 2:9). At 1 Tim 4:6 Timothy is called an "assistant" (*diakonos*, and compare *diakonia*, "ministry," 2 Tim 4:5, 11, and 1 Tim 1:12). This is the image preferred by the PE and its suits the air of respectability promoted in the letters. "Slave" here underlines 2 Timothy's effort to show that criteria for shame and honor in the Christian community differ from those in the secular world (see 2:3). The gentleness required here is a qualification for overseers at 1 Tim 3:2-3 and Titus 1:7-9 (contrast the false teachers at 1 Tim 6:4). Timothy is thus a model for other community officials; compare the peacefulness urged on the community at 1 Tim 2:2, 11, 12; 2 Tim 2:22. The noble fight (1 Tim 1:18) does not employ the same weapons used by the opponents. Debates and controversies give place to correction and rebuke on the basis of a sure grasp of truth (v. 25).

25. *correcting . . . to the knowledge of the truth:* Correction by the grace of God in Christ led to the community's rebirth (Titus 2:12), and the excommunication at 1 Tim 1:20 aims at correction of blasphemous activity. So, too, courteous correction might well render the wayward person open to God's influence and bring repentance and recognition of the truth. John Chrysostom, *On the Priesthood* 2.4 (COP 58), refers to this verse when he stresses that admonition accomplished without rancor has a better chance to lead to the improvement of the admonished (see also Philodemus, *On Frank Criticism*, 12.7, 38.4-5). Repentance and recognition of the truth in the PE is God's desire for all people and is the equivalent of salvation (see 1 Tim 2:4). The PE are consistent with Pauline usage that salvation comes from God and is not acquired by human effort (see 1 Tim 4:16, and compare 1 Tim 1:4). "Knowledge of the truth" is discussed at 3:7, and see also 1 Tim 2:4; Titus 1:1.

26. *devil's trap . . . captured by him for his will:* The expression appears in the PE in its secular sense to describe old women calumniators (Titus 2:3), end-time wanton people (2 Tim 3:2), and the type of people women deacons should not be (1 Tim 3:11). But in the LXX the word translates "Satan" or "adversary" (12 times) and "accuser" (Zech 3:1-3; Ps 108:5 LXX). Here the "devil" (*diabolos*) is the archenemy of God, for God wishes repentance and rescue from the devil's trap. This is consistent with the eschatological interpretation of the current apostasy and

conflict, with false teachers noted in the letters (see 3:1 and 1 Tim 4:1). At 1 Tim 3:7 the devil's snare is set to capture overseers whose inexperience in the faith provokes community contempt. The word appears in eschatological contexts at Luke 21:35 and Rom 11:9, and the contrast here with repentance and the will of the devil suggests a similar end-time urgency. Since it is the devil's snare, "his" (*autou*) refers to the devil as the one who captures. "That one's" (*ekeinou*) is best taken to refer to the devil also. The flow of thought is easiest, with the use of the demonstrative pronoun explained for stylistic variety's sake and also as pointing back to the noun in the first half of the verse. The idea of the devil's will behind the capture contrasts nicely with the action of God to bring repentance and knowledge of the truth in v. 25. This is a reference to God's will to save everyone. The end-time conflict is in view here (see 3:1-5).

Interpretation

The household image returns in the next verses (24-25a), which describe the behavior of a slave of the Lord and spell out the implications of v. 22. Gentleness, tolerance, capable teaching, and humbly setting opponents straight constitute the desired aims. The ultimate objective, repentance and coming to know the truth (vv. 25b-26), expands the idea in v. 21 and sets the community conflict against the cosmic struggle between God and the devil, who has ensnared the opponents to advance demonic aims. This characterization gives the struggle clear outlines that disfavor the opponents' stance. Getting out of the devil's trap is occasioned by a "change of mind" (*metanoia*), which leads to knowledge of the truth. The emphasis on knowledge of the truth (v. 25, *alētheias*), sensibleness (v. 26, *ananēpsōsin*), and teaching (vv. 24-25, *didaktikon, paideuonta*) captures the focus begun at v. 14 ("stop disputing about words. This serves no useful purpose"). Knowledge and action are both at issue in the letter, with knowledge a critical issue in this section.

For Reference and Further Study

Harris, J. Rendel. "The Influence of Philo upon the New Testament," *ExpTim* 37 (1926) 565–66.

McEleney, Neil J. "Orthodoxy and Heresy in the New Testament," *CTSA Proceedings* 25 (1970) 54–77.

________. "The Vice Lists of the Pastoral Epistles," *CBQ* 36 (1974) 203–19.

Turner, Nigel. "Devil," in idem, ed., *Christian Words*. Edinburgh: T&T Clark, 1980, 109–10.

6. *Vices of False Teachers; Paul's Virtues; Timothy's Teaching* (3:1-17)

1. Now understand this, that in the final days difficult times will come; 2. for people will be selfish, avaricious, arrogant, haughty, blasphemous, disobedient to their parents, ungrateful, unholy, 3. unloving, implacable, slanderers, dissolute, wild, not loving the good, 4. traitors, reckless, conceited, lovers of pleasure rather than lovers of God, and 5. bearing the outward form of piety, but denying its power. Avoid these people. 6. The reason is that among these are people who slip into households and captivate silly women loaded with sins, led on by passionate desires of all kinds. 7. They keep on learning but are never able to come to the knowledge of the truth. 8. In the way in which Jannes and Jambres opposed Moses, so even these oppose the truth. They are people depraved in mind, unqualified when it comes to the faith. 9. However, they will make no further progress, for their folly will be plain to all, as the folly of that pair also was. 10. You, on the other hand, followed my teaching, way of life, purpose, faith, patience, love, steadfastness, 11. my persecutions, sufferings. What sufferings happened to me in Antioch, in Iconium, in Lystra! What persecutions I endured! But from them all the Lord rescued me. 12. Yes, all those who wish to live piously in Christ Jesus will also be persecuted. 13. But wicked people and frauds will go from bad to worse, deceivers who are deceived themselves. 14. As for you, on the other hand, keep to what you have learned and become convinced of, since you know those from whom you learned it, 15. and are aware that from childhood you have known the sacred scriptures, which are able to give you wisdom for salvation through faith in Christ Jesus. 16. Every scripture passage is divinely inspired and useful for teaching, for correction, for improvement, for instruction in righteousness, 17. so that God's servant might be capable and equipped for every good work.

Notes

1. *in the final days difficult times will come:* The final days are once again identified with the present (1 Tim 4:1, and compare 2 Tim 3:13; 4:3. See also Joel 3:1 and Acts 2:17). So Timothy is to avoid people characterized by the list (v. 5). The urgency of the situation for the church is expressed by the adjective "difficult" (*chalepoi*). The letter does not appeal to eschatological arguments to deal with the eschatological crisis, but insists on sound teaching, guarding the deposit, and transmitting it faithfully to the next generation. The letter's equation of the contemporary false teaching and evil deeds with the end-time tells against its being authentically Paul's. Paul consistently looked forward to the final days (1 Cor 7:29-31; Rom 13:11-14; 1 Thess 4:15-18).

2–4. *people will be selfish:* The plurals of the vices and their wide-ranging character suggest the moral disorder of the opponents (see 2:22). The list, with parallels in Rom 1:29-31, Wis 14:25-29, and Philo, *Flight* 15, reflects a characterization of idolaters in Judeo-Hellenism. This contrasts with the list of virtues that describes

Timothy and those who acknowledge Jesus as Lord (2:22-24). While the list is a general indictment, many of the vices reflect criticisms and instructions elsewhere in the letters. Thus the list outlines the qualities the leaders and the community are consistently warned away from, while the PE encourage their opposing virtues.

For parallels to *philautoi* ("selfish"), *alazones* ("arrogant"), *hyperēphanoi* ("haughty"), and *tetyphōmenoi* ("conceited") see *typhōtheis* ("puffed up," 1 Tim 3:6), *tetyphōtai* ("swollen with conceit," 1 Tim 6:4), *hybristēs* ("insolent," 1 Tim 1:13), *hypsēlophronein* ("proud," 1 Tim 6:17), and *authadē* ("self-willed," Titus 1:7).

For *philargyroi* ("avaricious") see *aischrokerdeis* ("greedy for dishonest money," 1 Tim 3:8), *porismon* ("piety as profit-making," Tim 6:5), *philargyria* ("love of money," Tim 6:10), *ploutou* ("rich," Tim 6:17), *aischrou kerdou* ("shameful gain," Titus 1:11).

For *blasphēmoi* ("blasphemous") see *blasphēmon* ("blasphemer," 1 Tim 1:13), *blasphēmein* ("blaspheme," 1 Tim 1:20; Titus 3:2), *blasphēmiai* ("abusive speech," 1 Tim 6:4).

For *apeitheis goneusin* ("disobedient to their parents") see *patrolōais* and *metrolōais* ("killers of their fathers and mothers," 1 Tim 1:9).

For *acharistoi* ("ungrateful") see *eucharistias* ("thanksgivings," 1 Tim 2:1; 4:3, 4), and *charin* ("I thank," 2 Tim 1:3).

For *anosioi* ("unholy") see *asebesi* ("impiety"), *anosiois*, *asebeia* ("profane," 2 Tim 2:16; Titus 2:12), and *hosion* ("devout," Titus 1:8).

For *astorgoi* ("unloving") see *agape* ("love," 1 Tim 1:5, 14; 2:15; 6:11; 2 Tim 1:7, 13; 2:22; 3:10; Titus 2:2), *agapētoi* ("beloved," 1 Tim 6:2; 2 Tim 1:2), *dakryōn* ("tears," 2 Tim 1:4), and *philoteknous* ("loving their children," Titus 2:4).

For *aspondoi* ("implacable") see *dioktēs* ("persecutor," 1 Tim 1:13), *makrothymian* ("forbearance," 1 Tim 1:16; 2 Tim 4:2), *philoxenon* ("hospitable," 1 Tim 3:2; Titus 1:8), *eris* ("discord," 1 Tim 6:4; Titus 3:9), *logomachein* ("dispute about words," 2 Tim 2:14), *machas* ("quarrels," 2 Tim 2:23; Titus 3:9), *machesthai* ("fight," 2 Tim 2:24), *misountes* ("detesting," Titus 3:3), *hyponiai* ("suspicions," 1 Tim 6:4), *hypomonēn*, ("patience," 1 Tim 6:11; 2 Tim 3:10; Titus 2:2).

For *diaboloi* ("slanderers") see *diabolous* ("slanderers," 1 Tim 3:11; Titus 2:3).

For *akrateis* ("dissolute") see *anypotaktois* ("disobedient," 1 Tim 1:9; Titus 1:6, 10), *pornois* ("sexually immoral," 1 Tim 1:10), *sōphrosynē* ("moderation," 1 Tim 2:9, 15), *sōphrona* ("self-controlled," 1 Tim 3:2; Titus 1:8; 2:2, 5), *spatalōsa* ("lives a life of indulgence," 1 Tim 5:6), *autarkeias* ("contentment," 1 Tim 6:6), *sōphronismou* ("moderation," 2 Tim 1:7), *enkratē* ("self-controlled," Titus 1:8), *sōphronizōsin* ("give good sense," Titus 2:4, 6), and *sōphronos* ("self-control," Titus 2:12).

For *anēmeroi* ("wild") see *ēmeron* ("tranquil,") and *hēsychian* ("quiet," 1 Tim 2:2, 11, 12), *orgēs* ("anger," 1 Tim 2:8), *dialogismou* ("disagreement," 1 Tim 2:8), *plēktēn* ("violent," 1 Tim 3:3; Titus 1:7), *epieikē* ("kind," 1 Tim 3:3), *amachon* ("peaceable," 1 Tim 3:3), *nēphalion* ("clear-headed," 1 Tim 3:2, 11; Titus 2:2), *praupathia* ("gentleness," 1 Tim 6:11), *prautēti* ("courteously," 2 Tim 2:25; Titus 3:2), and *orgilon* ("irascible," Titus 1:7).

For *aphilagathoi* ("not loving the good") see *agathos syneidēseos* ("good conscience," 1 Tim 1:5, 19), *philagathon* ("loving what is good," Titus 1:8).

For *prodotai* ("traitors") see *pseustais, epiorkois* ("liars, perjurers," 1 Tim 1:10), *piston* ("trustworthy," 1 Tim 1:12; 3:11; 2 Tim 2:2), *apistou* ("nonbeliever," 1 Tim 5:8, 12), and *apistoumen* ("we are unfaithful," 2 Tim 1:13).

For *propeteis* ("reckless") see *proklisin* ("favoritism," 1 Tim 5:21), and *tacheōs* ("hastily," 1 Tim 5:22).

For *philēdonoi* ("lovers of pleasure") see epithymias ("cravings," 1 Tim 6:9; 2 Tim 3:6; 4:3; Titus 2:12; 3:3).

For *dynamin* ("power") see *pneuma* ("spirit of strength," 2 Tim 1:7).

5. *bearing the outward form of piety:* The contrast between appearance and reality here resembles Titus 1:16, where claims are belied by deeds. The wayward people here also act contrary to their claims, since piety involves action as well as confession. The power of piety was described at 1:7; i.e., the spirit of strength, love, and moderation. This was the power on which Timothy was to rely as he stood up against the ordinary honor/shame code in proclaiming the Gospel of the crucified Jesus as handed on by the often beleaguered and imprisoned Paul. The wayward must include those who, unlike Onesiphorus (1:16-18), abandoned Paul (1:15; 4:10, 16) and even opposed him (4:14).

   avoid: The strategy of avoiding is mentioned and explained at 2:23.

6. *slip into households:* The ecclesiastical organization of the church is still decentralized, which allows teachers to influence households directly. The situation seems similar to that in 2 and 3 John. That women are the prime targets identified here is not surprising. The statement reflects the prejudice that women are more susceptible to deception (1 Tim 2:14) and that they are easy prey to the influences of new cults (see 1 Tim 2:9, 12). Gentile women associated with the synagogue were incited by Jewish opponents of Paul to get him expelled from Antioch in Pisidia (Acts 14:50). On the other hand, Lydia invited him to her home, where he baptized the household (Acts 16:15, and see also the activity of Pauline women at Acts 17:4, 12, 34). The overseers, whose special charge concerns teaching and oversight, appear to constitute the part of the community structure that is to deal with the diffusion of unacceptable teaching (1 Tim 3:1). The false teachers of the end-time are loosely described in terms of their vices and wanton excess. In other places the opposing teachers have a Jewish cast (1 Tim 1:7; Titus 1:10; 3:9), or are excessively ascetical (1 Tim 4:3), or proclaim a knowledge-based Christianity (1 Tim 6:20), or tend toward mythologies (1 Tim 1:4; 4:7; 2 Tim 4:4; Titus 1:14). The PE seem to have incorporated strains from all sorts of opponents (for example, traditional Judaizing Christians, over-spiritualized ascetics, proto-Gnostics) to sketch a picture of the false teaching that threatens the community.

   passionate desires: Unbridled passions are a principal target of the PE's criticism (see 2:22). The problem here is different from the asceticism denounced in other false teaching (1 Tim 4:3).

7. *They keep on learning:* The interest of the letters in the intellectual side of faith provides a good basis for their criticism of the false teachers. They have only a pretense of knowledge (1 Tim 6:20), but their deeds belie their claims to theological knowledge (Titus 1:16, and see 1 Tim 1:7). Whereas Timothy can pass on the tradition to designated teachers (2:2), these cannot lead the women to

know the truth (see 1 Tim 2:4). Their position is further belittled in that their audience, silly, sinful, passion-led women, is unqualified. The opprobrium that the PE wish to save the community from, they drop onto the false teachers (1 Tim 2:11).

8. *Jannes and Jambres:* In rabbinic texts (e.g., *T. Pseudo-Jonathan* on Exodus 1:15; 7:11), these are two magicians of Pharaoh, sometimes identified as sons of Balaam (*T. Jer.* I Ex 1:15, Num 22:22; in pagan literature they are mentioned in Apuleius, *Apol.* 90,5; Pliny, *Nat.* XXX 11). They used their art against Moses and Aaron and are even credited with instigating the apostasy of the golden calf (*Tanch. ki toseh* 15 on Exodus 32). The variant Mambres in some manuscripts indicates confusion in the sources. Their stories might have been contained in a text known to the author of 2 Timothy but subsequently lost. However, Origen, *Cels.* 4.51 and his comments on Matt 27:9, and Pope Gelasius, *Decretum de libris recipiendis et non recipiendis* 303, both mention apocryphal books of Jannes and Jambres. The apocryphal pair are good representative figures for the apostates and heretics. Their resistance to Moses fits the criticism of the false teachers at 1 Tim 1:7 as those who have no knowledge of the Law and promote lawbreaking.

   depraved in mind, unqualified: The phrase "depraved in mind" is repeated from 1 Tim 6:5, as is their distance from the truth (and see Titus 1:5). As unqualified with respect to the faith, these teachers are the opposite of Timothy (2:15), who is to demonstrate himself approved by an orthodox presentation of the truth, an important aspect of faith in the PE.

9. *no further progress, for their folly will be plain to all, as the folly of that pair also was:* See 1 Tim 4:15. The fact that they are making advances in their unorthodox teaching indicates the seriousness of their threat to the community. See 1 Tim 5:24-25, where all know the quality of the works being done. The appeal to the example of the apocryphal figures indicates the widespread acquaintance of the community with them. The letters use personal examples widely in their exhortation. These include Jesus, Paul, Timothy, and Titus, named supporters such as Onesiphorus, named opponents such as Alexander, Hymenaeus, and Philetus, and these apocryphal characters. Association of the end-time heretics with these Egyptian magicians places the false teaching outside the tradition of faith from Moses (and see 1 Tim 1:7) through Paul.

10. *You, on the other hand, followed my teaching, way of life, purpose, faith, patience, love, steadfastness:* The address to Timothy is made emphatic by the use and position of the personal pronoun "you." The focus shifts by contrast from the foolish, vice-filled opponents and their models in Jewish legend to the present reality of Timothy's attention to Pauline tradition and Paul's example of steadfastness under persecution for the Gospel. The objects of the verb "you followed" (*parēkolouthēsas*) indicate that Timothy has not only been faithful to Paul's teaching but has also taken Paul as a model for his own way of life. See 1 Tim 4:6. Of prime concern in the context of doctrinal conflict, teaching is mentioned first in contrast to the foolish ignorance of end-time teachers at 3:7. For correspondences between Paul and Timothy/Titus as teachers see 1 Tim 2:7; 4:6, 13; 6:2; 2 Tim 1:11; 3:10; 4:2; Titus 2:1, 7. The "way of life" (*agōgē*) is given specificity in

the remainder of the list (note the singular forms as opposed to the plural vices at 3:2-4, and see 2:22), and the list fills out the example of Paul. "Purpose" (*prothesis*) in the NT primarily refers to God's eternal purpose for his chosen ones (Rom 8:28; 9:11; Eph 1:11). Ephesians 3:11 clarifies this as God's plan for Paul to preach to the Gentiles. Second Timothy 1:9-10 reiterates the eternal purpose as the saving call effected through Christ Jesus' death and resurrection and the Gospel message about this. God's will to save all people (1 Tim 2:4) has become the aim of Paul's work and that of those who labor with him (1 Tim 4:10, 16; 2 Tim 1:11; 2:2-3). The two virtues of faith and love, often mentioned together, express the Christian life as directed toward God and other humans (see 1 Tim 1:14). The coordination between Paul and Timothy is seen by noting 1 Tim 2:7; 2 Tim 1:12, 13; 3:10; 4:7; Titus 1:1; and 1 Tim 1:14; 4:6, 12; 6:11, 12; 2 Tim 1:7; 2:22; 3:14. Paul enjoyed the "patience" (*makrothymia*) of Christ Jesus (see 1 Tim 1:16), has incorporated that into his own dealings with others (2 Tim 3:10), and expects the same of Timothy (2 Tim 4:2). The patience is in evidence in his expectation of the conversion of Hymenaeus and Alexander (1 Tim 1:20) and of those described as unworthy vessels (2 Tim 2:21). "Steadfastness" (*hypomonē*) is prized in the letters, where the community faces abandonment of the tradition by false teachers and wayward believers (see 2:10). Timothy is expected to have this quality (1 Tim 6:11; 2 Tim 2:12).

11. *my persecutions, sufferings . . . in Antioch, in Iconium, in Lystra:* See 2 Tim 2:12. In that context (1:8; 2:3) Timothy is exhorted to bear a share of suffering for the Gospel (see also 2:9-10; 3:11; 4:5; 1 Tim 6:11). These three cities heard Paul on his first missionary journey, and opponents in the synagogues and in the cities at large attacked Paul and Barnabas, forcing them to leave (Acts 13:14–14:20). Timothy was not part of Paul's mission at that time. He was, however, from Lystra (Acts 16:1) and may have been converted on that first visit by Paul to the city. The record of endurance of persecution and suffering adds credibility to Paul's call to bear suffering in chapters 1 and 2. The pronouns *hoia* and *hoious* ("what!") here introduce an exclamation (BAGD 304).

    the Lord rescued me: The recollection of rescue by the Lord is important in view of the call to suffer along with Paul (see 3:11). The ultimate, otherworldly nature of the Lord's rescue receives clarification at 4:18. The Lord there is Christ Jesus, end-time judge and king (4:1), so Christ is the rescuer here as well.

12. *those who wish to live piously in Christ Jesus will also be persecuted:* See 1 Tim 2:2 for more on piety, and Ps 34:20. At issue here and throughout the PE is both faith based on true teaching and action expressive of that faith. The salvation in Christ Jesus the believers receive (2:10) is a future hope (1 Tim 2:15; 4:16; 2 Tim 4:18) and a present reality (1 Tim 2:4; 2 Tim 1:9; Titus 3:5). It brings the indwelling Spirit (2 Tim 1:14), faith and love (2 Tim 1:13), and the grace of God, which appeared in the incarnation of Christ Jesus (Titus 2:11). The latter enables one to live devoutly (Titus 2:12). Consequently, those who live in Christ Jesus live in a relation with him that enables them to live a transformed life (1 Tim 1:12). In referring to the inevitability of persecution the PE offer their audience no illusions. Despite the measures they set in place to gain approval, the memory of Jesus' and Paul's suffering (1:10-11, and Acts 20:19), as well as that of the

Christian community members in Jerusalem (Acts 8:1-3, 1 Thess 2:14-16) and in the diaspora (1 Pet 4:12-19), serves to characterize one consequence of Christian belief. The resistance to true teaching currently experienced at Ephesus is another aspect of the persecution. The prediction of suffering fits well with the PE's eschatological perspective (see 2:3).

13. *frauds will go from bad to worse, deceivers who are deceived:* Literally "sorcerers," the word "frauds" (*goētes*) echoes the comparison to Jannes and Jambres (3:8). The predicted decline from bad to worse expresses what is found at 3:9 in positive form and reiterates 2:16 (see 1 Tim 4:15). In the dualistic conception of Jewish literature the opposition of deception to truth (*T. Jud.* 20.1) is a sign of the end-time (*1 Enoch* 56:5; *T. Levi* 10.2; 16.1). The spirits of deception (*T. Reu.* 2.1; 3.2; *T. Sim.* 6.6) work as instruments of Beliar and of Satan, the prince of deception (*T. Sim.* 2.7; *T. Jud.* 19.4), who tries to lure people from the right path. Second Thessalonians 2:10-12 depicts the end-time as a struggle of deception against truth. See also 1 John 1:8; 2:26; 3:7-8; 4:6. The end-time snare set by greed leads some to stray from the faith at 1 Tim 6:10, and, more generally, end-time deceitful spirits are at work to lead some away from the faith by lies and false teaching at 1 Tim 4:1-2. These apostate teachers receive the same condemnation here. The deceived are not beyond hope, as some in the community attest at Titus 3:3. In this context, however, there is less interest in offering reconciliation than in drawing clear lines between the inauthentic and authentic teachers in the Pauline tradition.

14. *As for you, on the other hand, keep:* The contrast between Timothy and the wicked frauds and deceivers is emphatic (see 3:10). See 2:10 for the promised reward for endurance.

    what you have learned and become convinced of, since you know those from whom you learned it: The verbs emphasize the intellectual side of faith. The learning acquired and held on to from childhood on contrasts with the failure of the weak-minded opponents to teach and the failure of their followers to grasp the truth (3:7-8). The firm grasp of his faith contrasts with the opponents' unreliability in matters of faith (3:8). The teaching has come from known and reliable sources: Paul and many witnesses, (2:2; 3:10), Lois and Eunice (1:5). The verification of the source of the teaching tradition is a key concern. Once Paul is established as the originator, his apostolic authority guarantees the reliability of the tradition. It is a genealogical argument for the tradition behind the PE. The PE do not argue it (1 Tim 1:4; Titus 3:9), but claim it as foreknown.

15. *from childhood you have known the sacred scriptures, which are able to give you wisdom for salvation:* Jewish children began their scriptural instruction at age five or six (*ʾAbot* 5.21, and see Prov 4:3-5 and Dan 13:3). The Jewish practice would have been carried out by Timothy's Jewish mother. The fact that she was married to a Greek and did not have Timothy circumcised (Acts 16:1-3) suggests that she was not a fully observant Jew. This, together with the observation that Timothy is a model figure, supports the view that this reference to childhood rearing in the faith (see 1:3-5) is not biographical but paradigmatic. So the education in Scripture mentioned here suggests a practice to be carried over from Judaism into the early church. For "sacred scriptures" (*hiera grammata*) as a way of referring to the Hebrew Bible see Philo (*Abraham* 61; *Prelim. Studies* 34.90; *Decalogue* 8, 37;

Moses 2 (179) 21), 1 Macc 12:9, and Josephus, *Ant. proem.* 3; 3.7.6; 5.1.17; *Life* 75; *Bell.* 5.5.7). Contrast Paul (Rom 1:2), who uses *hagiais* ("holy"). The usage here is thus a Hellenistic Jewish one (and see *1 Clem.* 45.2; 53.1). The PE maintain the Christian view that the Hebrew Scriptures, when read from a christological perspective, provide saving wisdom. They offer the Christian an interpretation of the career and saving work of Jesus (Matt 26:56; Luke 24:44-47; John 5:46; Rom 1:2-4).

16. *Every scripture passage is divinely inspired:* While the singular "scripture" (*graphē*) can refer to Scripture as a whole (1 Pet 2:6; 2 Pet 1:20; Gal 3:8, 22, where it is personified), it often refers to particular passages (Gal 4:30; Rom 4:3; Luke 4:21). There is no NT usage of the word for a book of the Bible, which is common in Jewish and later Christian writings. Here the phrase means every Scripture passage. "All scripture," another possible translation, seems to state what would be obvious to all. "Every scripture passage" admittedly could be seen as an exaggeration. Nonetheless, it fits a polemic situation where the interpretation and application of some passages might have come into question. For example, those passages that are taken to refer to God's plan for universal salvation or to the resurrection and judgment at the final days would be disputed by the false teachers. The word "inspired" (*theopneustos*) is used only here in the Bible. God's Spirit filled the prophets Balaam (Num 24:2-4) and Hosea (Hosea 9:7) and gave Moses the words of the Decalogue (Exod 34:27). Similarly, Philo calls all writers of the First Testament prophets (*Heir* 259-266; *QE* 1.49; *Moses* 2.188; 2.246-292; *Decalogue* 175, and compare Josephus, *C. Ap.* 2.39-40; *4 Ezra* 14:22). The translation of the LXX was divinely guided (*Ep. Aris.* 301-302). Paul suggests a similar notion when he personifies Scripture (Gal 3:8, 22) and thereby indicates that Scripture expresses God's will and can be identified with God speaking. Paul in Rom 15:4 comes close to this idea when he says: "what was written in former days was written for our instruction."

useful for teaching, for correction, for improvement, for instruction in righteousness: One would expect greater application of this conviction about Scripture's usefulness in the PE. They cite Scripture, and not always clearly, only at 1 Tim 1:18; 5:19; 2 Tim 1:19, and allude to Scripture only a bit more often (see, for example, 1 Tim 4:3; 6:7, 19; 2 Tim 4:15, 18). The importance of teaching is noted at 1 Tim 2:7 and 3:10; 4:2. The task of correction for Timothy and Titus finds expression at 4:2 and 1 Tim 5:20; Titus 1:13; 2:15. The officials appointed by them are also to practice it (Titus 1:9). The reproof aims at conversion (Titus 1:13, where, as here, it is linked with teaching, and compare 3:10). This contrasts with the destructive results of the false teaching (2 Tim 2:14). As a common hortatory technique the condemnation of shortcomings is actually constructive criticism aimed at the improvement of the object (Isocrates, *Ad Demonicum* 45; *Ad Nicoclem* 42, 49). This technique contrasts with mutual and pointless rebuke (Isocrates, *Ad Nicoclem* 46-47; Dio Chrysostom (*Or.* 32) *Alex.* 8). The noun "instruction" (*paideian*) and the corresponding verb form "teach" (*paideuein*) focus on forming proper habits of behavior. See also 1 Tim 1:20; 2 Tim 2:25; and Titus 2:12. For righteousness see 1 Tim 1:9.

17. *God's servant . . . equipped for every good work:* See 1 Tim 6:11. Timothy's adherence to the tradition of faith that he learned and that is expressed in the Scriptures

sets the pattern for the successors he is to designate (2:2). They will also be expected to teach (2:2, and compare Titus 1:9. See also 1 Tim 4:12, *typos* ["model"], and compare Titus 2:7). See 1:9 for another reference to work.

Interpretation

An eschatological urgency overhangs the final unit of the exhortation section (3:1–4:8). The unit has four divisions: the end-time situation, Paul's experiences, the charge to Timothy, and a resumptive conclusion. In this unit the letter relates the current situation of conflict and apostasy to the upheavals expected in the final days. It thereby sets the disturbing circumstances in a framework that helps the audience explain them through traditional faith expectations. The letter also adds urgency to its call for preserving the tradition by casting this as the final and definitive struggle. The characters in the struggle serve as models of attitudes and actions to avoid and to choose.

First, the people of vice in the final days (vv. 1-5), likened to Moses' opponents (v. 8), are depicted in the act of secretly ensnaring helpless women but ultimately being found out (vv. 6-9). In this initial explanation of the difficult days (*gar*, "for," vv. 2-5) a vice list describes the people who will cause the end-time disturbances, i.e., the interpersonal, not the physical upheavals. Their hollow show of religion denies its power (v. 5). This description is particularly pertinent to Timothy and, through him, to the letter's audience. From the start the prisoner Paul has been urging unashamed suffering in adherence to and advancement of the Gospel of the dead and risen Christ in reliance on the God-given power of the Spirit. The command to "avoid them" (*apotrepou*, v. 5) advances the future timetable to the present.

It has long been noted, and is one of the repeated themes of the PE, that not performing the works that characterize godliness ultimately produces negative results and could lead to doctrine and belief being belittled (John Chrysostom, *Hom. 2 Tim.* 8 [NPNF 1 13:505]). From Gandhi's disaffection with Christianity over the inconsistency he saw between theory and practice to G. K. Chesterton's wry comment to the effect that the trouble with Christianity is that it has never been tried, those within and without the Christian community look to the community of the faithful for belief and conduct that matches the high ideals of doctrine and morality. While "cafeteria Catholics" might blend in easily with their secular neighbors, compromise on essentials ultimately leads to the discrediting of the body of doctrine as a whole and of those who uphold and teach it.

The second explanation (*gar*, "for," vv. 6-9), in the present tense, seems to focus on the contemporary struggle and thereby fully collapses the future into the present. The targets of these secretive teachers are women, sinful, passionate, and always missing the mark of truth despite their efforts to learn (vv. 6-7). The damage done to faith and knowledge of the truth by these teachers recalls the warnings at 2:14-18, 25, and the blame ascribed to passion echoes the admonition to Timothy at 2:22 and the criticism of the false teachers as being "without self-control" (*akrateis*, 3:3) and "reckless" (*propeteis*, 3:4). The correlation between theology and morality is again maintained, for passion-provoked sin impedes advancement in knowledge.

Jannes and Jambres, opponents of Moses in some Jewish writings, further illustrate the point. They opposed the truth by their opposition to Moses. Moses stands for Paul, the Gospel's divinely designated proponent (1:1, 11-13; 2:2, 8-9), who suffers opposition and imprisonment from various quarters (1:8, 12; 2:3, 9-10) including named pairs of community members (1:15; 2:17). The association of Paul with Moses and his plight provides impetus for his exhortation and a justification for the criticism of the opponents. The uncomplimentary description of them as mentally corrupt and untrustworthy in faith matters (v. 18) spells out the grounds of criticism. The threat of public disclosure of their ignorance hangs over them (v. 9), while the prediction of a halt to their progress is some encouragement to those holding the Pauline tradition. Nonetheless, the progress made to date constitutes a real danger to the PE community.

The mention of Jannes and Jambres shows that the evildoing is not new. If even Moses found opposition, it is no wonder that similar troubles afflict the church in the time of the PE (John Chrysostom, *Hom. 2 Tim.* 7 [NPNF 1 13:500]). The awareness of significant difficulties faced by the church in the past puts current distressing situations into perspective. As the faith community continued to prosper over time despite setbacks, so too will one who trusts in God have confidence that the church of God will continue on under God's nurturing care.

Second, a survey of Paul's own evangelical activity and suffering establishes the positive model (vv. 10-13) in contrast to the ignorant and harmful teachers just described. Unlike Jannes and Jambres, Timothy, as the addressee who represents all in the community, receives praise for following Paul and as such establishes the model of desired relation to the Pauline tradition. Paul's doctrine, way of life, virtues, and sufferings are all included in his example. While his teachings have first place, in keeping with the doctrinal focus noted above (1:11-13; 2:2, 7, 11, 15-17, 24-25; 3:7-8), conduct of life receives more extended comment. In connection with the attention to conduct of life the letter recalls specific qualities mentioned earlier, such as faith (1:3, 4, 12, 13; 2:2, 13, 22, and contrast 2:18; 3:8; see 4:14), love (1:7, 13; 2:22, and contrast 3:2), self-control (contrast 3:6), longsuffering (1:8, 12, 16; 2:3, 9-10, 24, and see 4:2), and endurance (2:12, and contrast 1:15). The virtues of endurance and longsuffering are amplified by mention of persecution and suffering, which give this catalogue its dominant tone, a tone that pervades the letter's recollection of Paul's ministry (1:8, 12, 15-16; 2:3, 9, 11) and the witness of Jesus (1:8, 10; 2:8, 11). The letter emphasizes the suffering of Jesus' witness to counterbalance the opponents' overemphasis on resurrection life.

The letter goes on to declare the inevitability of suffering for all who live religiously in Christ Jesus (3:12), a prediction that coincides with the repeated challenge to Timothy to suffer along with Paul for the sake of the Gospel (1:8; 2:3), as well as with the suffering at the heart of the Gospel itself (2:11). The recollection of Paul's deliverance by the Lord (3:11) repeats the description of the refreshing support from Onesiphorus (1:16) and coordinates with his expressions of confidence of divine assistance and salvation (1:8, 12, 14; 2:11, and see 4:8). The autobiographical declaration adds an encouraging personal testimony to the otherwise dire prediction of suffering. Despite the dramatic emphasis given to the idea of suffering, the ensuing advice does not envision difficulties for Timothy.

Third, in order for him to become a versatile "man of God" Timothy is told to stand pat on the ground of the instruction received from childhood, with particular attention to Scripture for its value in instruction, exhortation, and constructive reproof (vv. 14-17). Once again he is told to endure the suffering connected with the fulfillment of his ministry as evangelist (see 4:5). The commendation of Timothy for following the various facets of Paul's example, implicit at 3:10, becomes more direct at 3:14-15, where Timothy is told to remain faithful. This reiterates the assurance expressed at 1:5 and serves as a hortatory tool, for it adds the presumption of compliance based on prior experience. Thus the letter urges him to "rekindle the earlier flame" (*anazōpyrein*, 1:6).

The elaboration of the Pauline example (vv. 10-13) and this section are closely related because they both ultimately place the focus on Timothy with the same introductory formula ("you, on the other hand," 3:10, 14). The tradition of faith is the focus first (*mene en hois emathes kai epistōthes*, "keep to what you have learned and become convinced of"), and it is authenticated by its transmitters (*eidōs para tinōn emathes*, "since you know those from whom you learned it"). These can be traced back to Paul through the "many witnesses" mentioned at 2:2. Attention to the intellectual side of faith (*emathes*, "you learned") continues the doctrinal emphasis found throughout the letter (1:11-13; 2:2, 7, 11, 15-17, 24-25; 3:7-8), with the related concern over authentic (1:1, 11-13; 2:2, 15, 24) and inauthentic teachers (2:16-18, 25-26; 3:5-9).

The letter also urges Timothy's fidelity on the basis (*hoti* as "because" not "that") of his knowledge of Scripture from childhood. The Sacred Scriptures are most probably the First Testament, and Timothy's grandmother, Lois, and mother, Eunice, might well have been the initial source of Timothy's acquaintance with them (1:5). The importance attributed to the Sacred Scriptures complements Paul's tracing the tradition of his faith back to his ancestors (1:3) and it expresses an awareness of Christianity's roots in Judaism. Despite that continuity, the wisdom provided by the Scriptures offers salvation only through faith in Christ Jesus. The letter offers an instance in a typological understanding of King David (2:8), a moral reading of the apocryphal Jannes and Jambres (3:8), perhaps a Wisdom reinterpretation of the creation accounts (1:9), a Christianized eschatology (2:10-12; 3:1; 4:1, 8, 17-18), and a direct appropriation of scriptural phrases (2:19), images (the vessels at 2:20), and personages (the devil at 2:26; Moses at 3:8).

The letter thus presents a demonstration of the multiple uses of Scripture outlined at 3:16-17. The Scriptures serve the *anthrōpos theou* ("man of God" or "God's servant") as a tool for his own good work, which encompasses all aspects of his didactic and hortatory activity. They are indispensable for the competence of these church workers.

For Reference and Further Study

Barrett, C. K. "Pauline Controversies in the Early Church," *NTS* 20 (1974) 229–45.

Brox, Norbert. *Pastoralbriefe*, 253, 260–61.

Cook, D. E. "Scripture and Inspiration: 2 Timothy 3:14-17," *Faith and Mission* (Wake Forest) 1 (1984) 56–61.

de Boer, Willis P. *The Imitation of Paul: An Exegetical Study*. Amsterdam/Kampen: Kok, 1962, 200–201.

De Virgilio, Giuseppe. "Ispirazione ed efficacia della scrittura in 2 Tim 3, 14-17," *RivB* 38 (1990) 485–94.

Fiore, Benjamin. *Personal Example*, 201 n. 27; 160 n. 217; 205–208.

Glasson, T. F. *Moses in the Fourth Gospel*. London: SCM, 1963, 96–97.

Grabbe, Lester L. "The Jannes-Jambres Tradition in Targum Pseudo-Jonathan and Its Date," *JBL* 98 (1979) 393–401.

Meier, John P. "The Inspiration of Scripture: But What Counts as Scripture? [2 Tim 1:1-14; 3:14-17]," *Midstream* 38 (1999) 71–78.

Reck, Reinhold. "2 Tim 3, 16 in der altkirklichen Literatur; eine urkundsgeschichtliche Untersuchung zum Locus Classicus der Inspirationslehre," *Wissenschaft und Weisheit* (München-Gladbach) 53 (1990) 81–105.

Schenke, Hans-Martin. "Das Weiterwerken des Paulus und die Pflege seines Erbes durch die Paulus-Schule," *NTS* 21 (1974–75) 505–18.

Schweizer, Eduard. "Gottesgerechtigkeit und Lasterkataloge bei Paulus (inkl. Kol u. Eph.)," in Johannes Friedrich, Wolfgang Pöhlmann, and Peter Stuhlmacher, eds., *Rechtfertigung. Festschrift for Ernst Käsemann zum 70. Geburtstag*. Tübingen: J.C.B. Mohr; Göttingen: Vandenhoeck & Ruprecht, 1976, 461–77.

Strack, Hermann L., and Paul Billerbeck, *Kommentar zum Neuen Testament aus Talmud und Midrasch*. 6 vols. 6th ed. Munich: Beck, 1974–1975, 3:664–66.

Whitaker, G. H. "2 Timothy III.10," *Expositor* 8 ser. 18 (1919) 342–44.

________. "Note on 2 Timothy III.10," *Expositor* 9 ser. 1 (1924) 456–57.

7. *Charge to Timothy; Paul's End Foreseen* (4:1-8)

> 1. I emphatically declare before God and Christ Jesus, who is going to judge the living and the dead, and by his appearing and his kingdom; 2. preach the word, stand ready both when convenient and inconvenient, correct, rebuke, exhort, with complete patience and every kind of instruction. 3. I say this because a time will come when they will not put up with sound teaching but, following their own passions, will heap up teachers for themselves to tickle their ears. 4. What's more, they will turn their ears away from the truth and will turn them toward myths. 5. As for you, on the other hand, be self-possessed in all circumstances, bear up under evil, perform the work of an evangelist, fulfill your ministry. 6. I, as you know, am already being offered up and the time of my passing on has arrived. 7. I have competed in the noble contest; I have run the race; I have kept the faith. 8. For the rest, the crown of righteousness is reserved for me, and the Lord, the just judge, will award it to me on that day, and not just to me but also to all who have yearned for his appearance.

Notes

1. *I emphatically declare:* Timothy, who was to give a solemn declaration to the Ephesians (2:14), receives one himself. In both instances the solemnity of the charge suits the critical situation, which the succeeding verses outline.

   judge the living and the dead: The future judgment was part of the Christians' end-time expectation (2 Cor 5:10; Rom 14:9-12; 2 Thess 1:5-9; Matt 25:31-46; Mark 13:26-27; 1 Pet 4:5; 2 Pet 3:7; Jude 6; Acts 10:42; 24:25; Heb 6:2; Rev 20:4; *2 Clem.* 16.3; 17.6; 18.2; Pol. *Phil.* 7.1; *Mart. Pol.* 11.2; Ign. *Smyrn.* 6.1; *Barn.* 19.10; 21.6). This expectation carried with it the threat of damnation and divine vengeance (Matt 12:40 *parr.*; Rom 2:3; 3:8; 13:2; Jude 4; Rev 17:1; 18:20). The belief in a future resurrection is affirmed here, as opposed to the belief of the opponents (2:18). "The living and the dead" echoes the belief in the *parousia*'s imminence, which Paul described at 1 Thess 4:15-17.

   by his appearing and his kingdom: The appearance of Jesus is identified as his *parousia*, when Christ Jesus will judge (see also 1 Tim 6:14; 2 Tim 4:1; Titus 2:13). At 2 Tim 1:10 the epiphany was the incarnation. The term is one aspect of the "already/not yet" eschatology of the PE. God is king of the ages (1 Tim 1:17; 6:15), to whom honor is due. The kingdom spoken of here is the heavenly kingdom (4:18). There is no advance appearance of the kingdom in the preaching and deeds of Jesus as in the Synoptic Gospels (e.g., Mark 1:15 *parr.*; 4:26). Jesus is messianic king as descendant of David (2 Tim 2:8). In Paul's view he will return at the end-time to rule, exercise judgment, subject all opponents, and then hand over the kingdom to God the Father (1 Cor 15:24-28).

2. *preach the word, stand ready both when convenient and inconvenient:* See 1 Tim 2:7 and 2 Tim 1:11 for preaching, and 1 Tim 4:12 for the word. Writers on moral philosophy in the first century such as Plutarch (*Adul. amic.* 65E-75E), Dio Chrysostom ([*Or.* 38] *Nicom.* 4-5), and, later, Dio Cassius (*Rom. Hist.* 65.12.1)

note the importance of using *parrēsia* ("frank speech") at the right time (*en kairǭ*) and not unseasonably (*akairos*) in order to achieve the desired healing effect (notice the medical images throughout the PE and at 2 Tim 4:2-3, and see Plutarch, *Rect. rat. aud.* 43 E-44 A; *Adul. amic.* 69 A-74 E). This was in contrast with the harsh Cynics' habit of heaping censure on their audience, heedless of the circumstances and condition of the audience (Lucian, *Iupp. trag.* 43; Epictetus, *Diatr.* 3.22.50). The readiness to preach with urgency here deliberately departs (the phrase without a conjunction connecting the nouns appears flippant) from the caution employed by contemporary moralists. It also lays Timothy open to the charge he is to place at the door of the false teachers who are contentious, disputatious, and abusive. The passage, unlike Titus 1:13, does not explicitly look to a healing effect from Timothy's actions, although at least some may be open to accept correction, as suggested by 2b. Rather, Timothy's actions are presented as necessary to stop the progress of false teaching (3:9). The mode of teaching also contrasts with that of the false teachers. The latter sneak into homes and corrupt gullible women (2 Tim 3:6; Titus 1:11), while Timothy and Titus are directed to minister in public (1 Tim 4:12-15; 5:19-21, 24-25; 2 Tim 2:2; Titus 2:7-8) in keeping with their role as examples for the community. The passage also sees this as a critical end-time conflict (3:1 and 4:3), and as such it is beyond the determination of Timothy or Paul, but rests in the prophesied plan of God. The confrontational preaching thus has to be pursued for the good of the wider audience.

correct, rebuke, exhort, with complete patience and every kind of instruction: See 3:16 for correction. While there are none of Mark's exorcistic overtones here (Mark 1:25; 3:12; 9:25), 2 Timothy does echo the rebukes by Peter and Jesus on the level of narrative, wherein characters call each other to task for unacceptable views (8:32, 33). Luke 17:3b comes closer, where Jesus calls for rebuke of a sinful brother with a view toward repentance and forgiveness (see the repentant thief at Luke 23:40). Repentance and forgiveness are not expressed as a result here, although they are implied by "patience and instruction" (*makrothymia kai didachē*). The action of exhorting is less confrontational than in the previous two (compare 1 Tim 5:1). At 1 Tim 1:3 the word describes Paul's urging of Timothy and of the community (1 Tim 2:1) and is the action expected of Timothy and Titus directed toward community members (1 Tim 6:2; Titus 2:6, 15). Their appointees are expected to exhort in the same way (Titus 1:9, and see 1 Tim 1:3). Patience, the quality of God, exercised by Jesus (see 1 Tim 1:16) and a characteristic of Paul's example followed by Timothy (2 Tim 3:10), is expected to be put into action by Timothy in his preaching work. Since Timothy is a model for successor leaders, the qualities he has taken over from Paul can be expected to be exercised by those who follow him. The persistence and moral optimism (at 1 Tim 1:16 Paul's conversion through Christ's forbearance is a prototype for all future believers) offer a bright prospect as a counterbalance to the urgency and difficulty of the current situation of opposition. See 3:10 for teaching. The hortatory teaching here contrasts with the ineffective efforts of the false teachers (3:6-7). They are deficient in knowledge and deviant in behavior. As a result they fail to live Christian piety. Paul's example and Timothy's actions based on it include both knowledge and behavior.

3. *a time will come:* As at 3:1, the prediction comes directly from Paul and is not attributed to the Spirit (contrast 1 Tim 4:1). Paul also foresees the time of his own death (4:6) and the simultaneous rescue from evil to be saved for the heavenly kingdom (4:18). Paul similarly refers to the possibility of death in prison at Phil 1:21-26. The actual situation of conflict and opposition identifies the present time as the end-time and also enhances the authority of Paul, who predicted accurately. The PE's references to God's and Christ Jesus' revelation of the Gospel reality at the appropriate time (1 Tim 2:6; Titus 1:3) and to the expectation of the final epiphany (1 Tim 6:15) enhance the knowledge expressed here of the schedule by which God's plan will unfold (and see 2 Tim 1:12, 18).

   not put up with sound teaching . . . following their own passions, will heap up teachers for themselves to tickle their ears: See 1 Tim 1:10 for opposition to sound teaching. Stubborn resistance to sound teaching explains the apparently incautious call to use correction and rebuke even if the time is inopportune (v. 8). There is no place now for subtlety and delay. Desires are mentioned at 2:22. Unbridled desires have a strong element of irrationality in them (see 1 Tim 6:9 and 2 Tim 3:6; Titus 2:12; 3:3). This clearly sets them in opposition to the PE with their emphasis on faith as the knowledge of the truth (1 Tim 2:4) and the attendant virtues of self-possession (*nēphalios*, "self-possessed," 1 Tim 3:2, 11; Titus 2:2; *nēphein*, "be self-possessed," 2 Tim 4:5), and moderation (*sōphronein*, "be moderate," Titus 2:6; *sōphronizein*, "make moderate," Titus 2:4; *sōphronismos*, "moderation," 2 Tim 1:7; *sōphronōs*, "moderately," Titus 2:12; *sōphrosynē*, "moderation," 1 Tim 2:9, 15; *sōphrōn*, "moderate," 1 Tim 3:2; Titus 2:2, 5). The plurality of teachers typifies the doctrinal and moral disarray of the opposition teachers (see 2:22). By contrast, there is one true stream of tradition from Christ (1:8), through Paul (1:8; 3:10) and Timothy (1:5; 2:2; 3:10), to the approved teachers (2:2). Dio Chrysostom, (*Or.* 33) *1 Tars.* 15-16, criticizes some people who cannot endure demanding preaching and so seek out flattering preachers who will not disturb their dainty ears. Quintilian, *Inst.* XI 3, 60, censures those whose ears are tickled by pleasures that determine the lives they lead (and see Seneca, *Ep.* 108.6). Philo, *Agriculture* 136, singles out for criticism the ear-appealing but equivocating Sophists. Lucian, *Cal.* 21, imagines lies tickling the ear like feathers.

4. *they will turn . . . away from the truth and will turn . . . toward myths:* The deviation from the truth predicted here is already characteristic of the apostates and false teachers (2:18). It contrasts with the steadfastness that Timothy must maintain (3:14, and see 2:10) and that the faithful in the community must demonstrate (1 Tim 2:15; 5:5). See 3:7 and 1 Tim 2:4 for truth. See 1 Tim 1:4 and Titus 1:14 for myths. The historical appearance of Jesus Christ and his redemptive deed (1:10; 2:8, 11, and see 1 Tim 6:13; Titus 2:11) and the expected reappearance of Jesus as end-time judge (1 Tim 6:14; 2 Tim 4:1, 8; Titus 2:13) are unlike these foolish and untrue myths. The realistic expectation of Jesus' end-time appearance is enhanced by the fact of the false teachers and their followers, which provides the initial fulfillment of end-time prophecies and expectations.

5. *As for you, on the other hand, be self-possessed, bear up . . . perform the work of an evangelist, fulfill your ministry:* Once again the pronoun "you" is expressed and the shift of focus is emphatic (see 3:10, 14). See 1 Tim 3:2, 11 for the virtue of being self-possessed. Bearing up under hardship is a value in the PE (see 2:3).

The saving actions of Jesus Christ brought the light of life and immortality, and people have access to these by hearing and accepting the Gospel (see 1:10). Timothy was encouraged earlier to persist in work for the Gospel despite suffering (1:8), and that charge is reiterated here. Luke gives the ministerial title at Acts 21:8 to Philip in Caesarea. He, as "one of the seven," earlier spread the Gospel after being driven from Jerusalem (Acts 8:4-40). The title is listed at Eph 4:11 between "apostles and prophets" and "pastors and teachers." All these are forms of ministerial service. The title and the work it indicates differ from those of apostle and prophet. Here in 2 Timothy it appears to include proclamation of the Gospel, correction of error, exhortation, and leading a life in keeping with the truth. Neither Timothy nor Titus bears the titles of the community offices they are to establish and to which they appoint community members. They are apostolic delegates sent ad hoc, as was their role in the other Pauline letters and in Acts. Nonetheless, they are models of leadership and belief for the churches they serve. See 1 Tim 1:13; 4:6 for further reference to ministry.

6. *I . . . am already being offered up and the time of my passing on:* The position and use of the pronoun announces another definite shift in focus. In Greek and Roman practice, liquid (wine for the Olympian gods and water for the chthonic deities) was poured onto the ground in sacrifice. Initially this was done at cult sites and on special occasions, but later it became a common practice at meals. The Hebrews also adopted the practice in their temple sacrifices with the sprinkling of blood on altar and earth at the Day of Atonement and on Passover. They did the same with water at the Feast of Tabernacles and used water and wine on other feasts. Philo interpreted the sprinkling spiritually as a symbol of a person's readiness to serve God fully (*Spec. Leg.* 1.205), or of the consecration by the high priest of his reason to God, savior and benefactor (*Alleg. Interp.* 2.56). Similarly, this passage, echoing Phil 2:17, has Paul describe the actual offering of his life with the liturgical and cultic symbol of libation sacrifice. There are no reliable accounts of the date or place of Paul's death.

7. *the noble contest . . . the race; I have kept:* See 1 Tim 4:7 and 6:12, where athletic competition is used as an image. Paul, in the farewell to the Ephesian elders (Acts 20:24), looks forward to finishing the race, which was his ministry (see Demophilus, *Sim.* 22 for the image applied to the workman whose crown in the race at old age is wisdom). Philippians 3:12-16 suggests a similar striving, and 4:1 refers to the community as Paul's crown (and see 1 Thess 2:9). The crown is the symbol of the completed task, which is to transmit the Gospel to them. First Corinthians 9:24-27 more explicitly uses the image of running (and boxing) to win the crown to describe singleminded service of the Gospel.

   At 1 Tim 6:14 Paul urges Timothy to keep to the charge he accepted at his ordination. Here Paul claims to have kept the faith himself. Paul is Timothy's model (3:10), and this includes being a model of faith. Paul's keeping the faith to his approaching end includes having successfully pursued his mission task (the race). Timothy, therefore, is expected to do no less as he follows this example (*kēryxon*, "preach," 4:2). The same holds true for the leaders and community members for whom Timothy is a model. The purpose of this declaration is ultimately hortatory and it is directed at all who wish to live piously (3:12 and 4:8).

8. *the crown of righteousness reserved for me:* Wreaths were used to crown the victors in the panhellenic athletic competitions (olive at the Olympic Games at Olympia in honor of Zeus, wild celery at the Nemean Games at Nemea in the plains of Argolis in honor of Zeus and in the Isthmian Games at Corinth in honor of Poseidon, laurel at the Pythian Games at Delphi in honor of Apollo). Paul has demonstrated his righteousness through his fidelity in executing his mission and living the Christian life (3:10-11, and see 1 Tim 1:9). Paul's certainty rests on his confidence in the fixed plan or will of God, which has often received mention in the PE (1 Tim 1:4; 2:4; 2 Tim 1:9).

   the just judge . . . on that day . . . to all who have yearned for his appearance: See "judgment" (*krisis*) at 1 Tim 5:24. The day Paul looks to is that of the *parousia* of Christ Jesus mentioned at 4:1. The adjective "all" (*pasi*) is omitted in several manuscripts. Its appropriateness can be defended by the consistent theme of universal salvation in the PE (e.g., 1 Tim 2:4). The verb "loved" (*ēgapēkosi*) here implies a high evaluation of or esteem for a person or thing, or receiving something/someone with favor. As such it does not express affectivity to a significant degree. Used of an impersonal object, it suggests striving after or longing for. This leaves the believer more engaged than with a purely intellectual grasp of the idea of the *parousia*. The PE community thus is expected to have a positive thrust toward the end-time.

Interpretation

The themes of the whole eschatological exhortation are reiterated in 4:1-8. The end-time conflicts preceding the final and victorious intervention of the Messiah are described in terms of heresy and apostasy. The letters do not presage the inauguration of the end-time paradise. Their "hang tough" exhortation points to a prolonged, this-worldly, but ultimately successful outcome to the doctrinal and moral struggle. It has been a challenge for believers throughout history to take seriously God's promise of protection and vindication for those who remain faithful in the face of conflict and opposition. Knowing that believers will face hostility prepares them to bear up when it comes. This is the rhetorical and religious strategy at work here in the PE.

Further admonition directed toward Timothy solemnly instructs him to persist in all facets of moral exhortation (4:1-2 and 4, which repeat 3:14-17). The prospect of eschatological appearance and judgment by Jesus Christ gives solemnity to the charge to Timothy and urgent necessity to his work of exhortation and correction. The hope of conversion raised earlier (2:25-26) stands behind the charge. The judgment carries with it a threat of alienation from God implicit earlier (no crown, 2:5; denied by Christ, 2:12; increasingly godless, 2:16; not acknowledged by the Lord, 2:19; entrapped by the devil's snare, 2:26). The judgment will fall on the unrepentant people of vice and error in the final days (3:1-9).

Next, rejection by licentious, self-concerned apostates is foreseen (4:3-4). The false teaching noted at 3:1-9 will result in some people abandoning the truth and sound doctrine. They will prefer the unhealthy teaching described at 3:16-18. Already portrayed as under the thrall of passions (3:6), they will follow these passions (4:3) and will select teachers like themselves (3:2-5), who will lead them from the truth (4:4, and see 3:7-8 and also 2:17-18) to myths.

Fourth and last, the image of Paul as faithful to the end and looking forward to his reward provides motivation to Timothy to persevere in his work despite suffering. The same lesson extends to all who remain faithful (4:6-8). Paul, faithful to the end as described at 3:10-12, was a model of suffering for all believers. Here the deliverance he acknowledged at 3:11 is promised to all the faithful. The image of the athlete from 2:5 finds its application in Paul's career. Competing according to the rules (*nomimōs*, 2:5) in order to qualify for the crown thus means competing well by keeping the faith (4:7). Keeping the faith is the burden of the credal summary (2:11-13) and a constant theme in the letter.

By using the athletic image of competing for a crown of victory the PE tap into athleticism and body culture, major preoccupations of their Greek audience. Applying this metaphor, the letters evoke the ascetic rigor required of successful athletes. People in the contemporary world share this interest in sports and athletics with their classical-period ancestors. Now, as then, analogies to the demands of athletic pursuits can illustrate the implications of the life of faith.

The references to *stephanos* ("crown"), *ekeinę tę hēmerą* ("on that day"), *kritēs* ("judge"), and *epiphaneian* ("appearance") all reinforce the eschatological tenor of the passage, which is juxtaposed with Paul's own death. In Philippians 1, Paul also looked at the possibility of death but expressed optimism that he would live (Phil 1:21-24). The 2 Timothy passage has a sacrificial character (*spendomai*, "I am being offered up," 4:6, and see Phil 2:17 for the same image) and involves a total transformation of human existence (*kairos tēs analyseōs*, "time of dissolution," 4:6). At the same time, the perfect tenses of the verbs (*tetelēka*, "have finished," *teterēka*, "have kept," *ēgapēkosi*, "have yearned for" 2:7) express the permanent accomplishment of life's task, which looks to the promised reward of this righteousness (and see 2:11-12, where death with Christ leads to life and glory with him). The final day, in view of the opening of this eschatological exhortation (3:1, and see 4:3), seems to be collapsed into the present. So Paul's reward is close at hand. The allusion to his immediate circumstance of imprisonment recapitulates 3:10-11 and also takes the reader back to the first chapter of the letter.

For Reference and Further Study

Cassidy, Richard J. *Paul in Chains: Roman Imprisonment and the Letters of St. Paul.* New York: Crossroad, 2001.

Hanson, Paul D. *The Dawn of Apocalyptic: The Historical and Sociological Roots of Jewish Apocalyptic Eschatology*. Philadelphia: Fortress Press, 1979, 123–28, 184–85.

Kolenkow, Anitra B. "The Literary Genre 'Testament,'" in Robert A. Kraft and George Nickelsburg, eds., *Early Judaism and Its Modern Interpreters*. Philadelphia: Fortress Press, 1986, 259–67.

Malherbe, Abraham J. "Self-Definition Among the Epicureans and Cynics," in Ben F. Meyer and E. P. Sanders, eds., *Jewish and Christian Self-Definition. Vol. 3: Self-Definition in the Greco-Roman World*. Philadelphia: Fortress Press, 1983, 46–59.

________. "'In Season and out of Season': 2 Timothy 4:2," *JBL* 103 (1984) 235–43.

________. "Medical Imagery in the Pastoral Epistles," in W. Eugene March, ed., *Texts and Testaments*, 19–35.

________. *Paul and the Popular Philosophers*, 137–45.

Pfister, F. "Zur Wendung *Apokeitai moi ho tēs dikaiosynēs stephanos*," *ZNW* 15 (1914) 94–96.

Rowland, Christopher. *The Open Heaven: A Study of Apocalyptic in Judaism and Early Christianity*. New York: Crossroad, 1982, 42–48.

Sellew, Philip. "Martyrdom of Paul," *ABD* 5:204.

Sint, Josef A. "Parusie-erwartung und Parusie-verzögerung im paulinischen Briefkorpus," *ZKT* 86 (1964) 47–79.

Spicq, Ceslas. "Le verbe *agapaō* et ses dérivés dans le grec classique," *RB* 60 (1953) 372–97.

Turner, Nigel. "Judgment," in idem, ed., *Christian Words*, 237–38.

8. *Final Requests; Support and Abandonment; Closing Greetings* (4:9-22)

9. Make every effort to come to me quickly. 10. Demas, you see, in his longing for the present world has forsaken me and gone to Thessalonica; Crescens went to Galatia, Titus to Dalmatia. 11. Luke alone is with me. Come and bring Mark with you, for he is useful for his assistance. 12. I sent Tychicus away to Ephesus. 13. When you come bring the cloak that I left with Carpus at Troas, and also the scrolls, especially the parchments. 14. Alexander the coppersmith manifested much harm toward me. The Lord will repay him in keeping with his deeds. 15. You, too, have to beware of him, for he has been extremely opposed to our teachings.

16. At my first defense no one stood by me. On the contrary, everyone abandoned me. I hope it will not count against them. 17. Still, the Lord stood by me and strengthened me, so that through me the preaching might be completed and all peoples might hear it. And I was rescued from the lion's mouth. 18. The Lord will rescue me from every wicked action and will save me for his heavenly kingdom; and to him be glory for ages of ages. Amen.

19. Greet Prisca and Aquila and the household of Onesiphorus. 20. Erastus remained at Corinth, and I left Trophimus at Miletus, for he was ill. 21. Make

every effort to come before winter. Euboulus greets you, as do Pudens, Linus, Claudia, and all our kin in the faith. 22. The Lord be with your spirit. Grace be with you.

Notes

9. *Make every effort to come to me quickly:* The apostolic *parousia* (see 1 Tim 3:14) is reversed, for Paul summons Timothy. The quick departure of Timothy is not connected to the situation of false teaching, which he was sent to handle (1 Tim 1:3). This and the various other instructions and comments could well be the author's way of creating a likely epistolary closing.

10. *Demas . . . longing for the present world has . . . gone to Thessalonica; Crescens went to Galatia, Titus to Dalmatia:* Demas is mentioned favorably along with Luke, the doctor, at Col 4:10, and with Mark, Aristarchus, and Luke at Philemon 24. It is a contraction of the name Demetrius. The contrast with longing for the epiphany of Christ Jesus (4:8) is clear. The charge to the rich in the present age (1 Tim 6:17) addresses the focus of the PE. They encourage good works (1 Tim 6:18) now, in view of judgment and reward to come (1 Tim 6:19), nothing less than life itself. Belief in the *parousia*, resurrection, and judgment (4:8) serves as a hortatory motive for upright living in the present. Demas stands with the false teachers as a cautionary example of someone with a misguided outlook, which results in infidelity to and abandonment of Paul and the Pauline tradition. First Thessalonians 3:2, 6 records Paul's sending Timothy to Thessalonica to ascertain the degree of stability in the Christian community there and his return to Paul with a reassuring report. Paul's mission there is reported in Acts 17, and he refers to it in Phil 4:16. Aristarchus and Secundus are from Thessalonica (Acts 20:4, and see 27:2). The name Crescens appears only here. A region of central, modern-day Turkey, Galatia was visited by Paul on his second missionary journey (Acts 16:6). The Roman province also included places evangelized by Paul on his first mission (Acts 13:13-24) and revisited by him later. Antioch in Pisidia, Iconium, and Lystra were mentioned at 2 Tim 4:11 as sites of persecution, with which Timothy is familiar. Paul wrote an epistle to the churches of Galatia. Strong manuscript evidence supports the reading *Gallian*. This place name could designate Galatia, since both Galatia and Gallia refer to areas where Celtic people live, according to Epiphanius, *Pan.* 5. It might, on the other hand, refer to the Roman province of Gaul, another place, like Galatia, of Celtic settlement. This would be the only such NT reference. While it is unlikely that Christians were active in Transalpine Gaul at this time, their presence in Cisalpine Gaul (on the Italian side of the Alps in northern Italy) is not impossible. The reference to Gaul in this context, however, is unlikely, given equally weighty manuscript support for Galatia and the other geographical notices of places in Asia Minor, Greece, and the Balkan Peninsula. Titus, the addressee of one of the PE, is not mentioned in the Acts of the Apostles. Paul calls him a coworker (2 Cor 8:23), and he proved to be an effective intermediary with the troubled Corinthian community (2 Cor 12:18), where he effected a reconciliation with Paul (2 Cor 7:6, 13). From Gal 2:2-3 we learn that he accompanied Paul

and Barnabas to the "council" of Jerusalem and that he demonstrated the Pauline principle of Gentile freedom from the Law by remaining uncircumcised. His close association with Paul makes it unlikely that his departure for Dalmatia was an abandonment like Demas' departure. This also suggests that the reference to Crescens' unexplained departure is also nothing more than an item of information. Dalmatia lies on the Adriatic coast of modern-day Croatia. Paul claims to have preached in Illyricum (Rom 15:19), the Roman province on the Adriatic coast northwest of Greece and including today's Albania, Serbia, and Croatia.

11. *Luke . . . Mark . . . useful for his assistance:* "Luke" referred to here might be the author of the third gospel and the Acts of the Apostles. He is mentioned at Philemon 24 and Col 4:14, where he is identified as a doctor, along with Demas. The conclusion of the letter to the Colossians also makes mention of Mark (4:10) and Tychicus (4:7). In that letter, as here, they are both Paul's emissaries. Philemon 24 also mentions Mark. Some attribute the PE to Luke's hand. The name may be used here because it is known to be connected with the church in Asia Minor. By contrast with Demas, with whom he is paired in Colossians, he exemplifies steadfast fidelity, for he is unashamed to remain with the beleaguered Paul. John Mark, whose mother Mary seems to have hosted a house church community in Jerusalem (Acts 12:12), accompanied Paul and Barnabas, his cousin (Col 4:10), back to Antioch after their relief mission. He continued to accompany them on their first mission journey (Acts 13:5) at least as far as Perga, where he left them and returned to Jerusalem (Acts 13:13). For Paul this "desertion" disqualified John Mark from collaboration on the second journey (Acts 15:37-39). Paul, who lost Barnabas in the conflict about Mark, chose Silas as his companion (Acts 15:40) and later added Timothy (16:3) to replace John Mark as his assistant. Philemon 24 has Mark back among Paul's coworkers, attending to the imprisoned Paul. Colossians 4:10 repeats this, while 1 Pet 5:13 calls Mark (perhaps the same individual) Peter's son. Mark's importance in the Asia Minor church after Acts is attested by 1 Peter, Colossians, and 2 Timothy, which express his closeness to Paul (2 Timothy and Colossians) and to Peter (1 Peter). Second Timothy thus expresses awareness of two persons associated with the Synoptic Gospel tradition as authors. At the same time the names tie the letter to the Pauline mission tradition. At 1 Tim 1:12 Paul describes his being given a ministry of service by Christ Jesus and at 2 Tim 4:5 he recalls Timothy's ministerial duty. Here Mark is included in the service ministry. The prominent, named figures thus enhance the dignity of church service.

12. *Tychicus . . . to Ephesus:* Tychicus is mentioned with fellow Asians Timothy and Trophimus at Acts 20:4, as part of Paul's entourage. He serves as a messenger in Col 4:7 and Eph 6:21, where he is sent to Ephesus. He serves a similar function here and at Titus 3:12. Like Mark, his is a name remembered and respected in the Asia Minor church for his connection with Paul, and thus is an important link to the Pauline tradition. First Timothy 1:3 and 2 Tim 1:18 refer to Ephesus.

13. *the cloak . . . with Carpus at Troas, and also the scrolls, especially the parchments:* The Latin word for "cloak," *paenula*, has been transliterated and altered from

phainolas or *phainolēs* (Epictetus, *Diatr.* 4.8.34) to this Greek form (MM). Ambrosiaster, *Commentary on the Second Letter to Timothy* (CSEL 81 3:317) identifies the cloak as the distinctive garment of a Roman citizen, and thus a garment needed by Paul to identify him on his further journeys. In any case, the request for the cloak seems to run counter to Paul's prediction of his imminent death (4:6-8). The references to visits, requests, news about various individuals, and exchanges of greetings provide the letter with the occasional tone typical of the undisputed letters of Paul. Epictetus, *Diatr.* IV 8,34-35 describes the would-be philosopher as showily cloakless and argumentative rather than self-reflective. Carpus is mentioned only here in the NT. A Christian community existed in Troas. Timothy and his companions waited for Paul there for five days and all then stayed on for a week more (Acts 20:6). During this time Paul broke bread with them and delivered a long sermon (Acts 20:7-12). Paul passed through Troas with Timothy on his second missionary journey on his way to Greece (Acts 16:8-11), and visited the place a second time, meeting up with Timothy and other companions (Acts 20:6). He passed through yet again on his third mission journey (2 Cor 2:12). All of these visits were well in advance of the imprisonment in Rome recorded in Acts. "Scrolls" is probably a reference to papyrus scrolls. Theodoret, 3.695, says this refers to parchment scrolls and that the Jews used this designation, following Roman custom, to refer to their sacred scriptures. Martial, *Ep.* 14.7 and 184, suggests that they are parchment codices (and see 14.186, 188, 190, 192). The Christians adopted the codex for the Scriptures, eventually replacing scrolls as the preferred book form. The content of these books is otherwise unspecified. It is not likely that a gospel is meant, especially Mark or Luke, since those names appear earlier with no reference to the gospels. The parchments in particular more likely refer to the First Testament writings, in keeping with the mention of sacred scriptures at 3:15. John Chrysostom, *Hom 2 Tim.* 10 (NPNF 1 13:514) speculates on Paul's need for books since he was about to go to God. He hypothesizes that Paul intended to deposit them in the hands of the faithful in place of his own teaching. This hypothesis coincides with this commentary's view of the three letters as pseudonymous, in that these three "books" stand as part of the deposit that the addressees and their successors are to maintain and hand on.

14. *Alexander the coppersmith manifested much harm . . . The Lord will repay him in keeping with his deeds:* Perhaps this is the same Alexander who was mentioned at 1 Tim 1:20 as being cut off by Paul in response to his hostility. There, however, some hope of conversion is held out. The Alexander at Acts 19:33, an apparent opponent who supported the Jewish position, may have suggested the name to the author of the PE. Alexander worked his evil in Ephesus, and Paul warns against his continuing to do so. Whether and how this affected Paul's imprisonment and trial in Rome is not clear. The allusion resembles that made by Paul to community opponents in Philippi who mean to cause him distress during his imprisonment, whether in Rome or in Ephesus (Phil 1:15-17). Christ Jesus as Lord and end-time judge has received prior mention in the chapter (4:1, 8, and see Ps 62:13 and Rom 2:6). This threat against the hardened opponent looks ahead to v. 16b with its prospect of pardon for Paul's associates, who were shaken and proved unreliable at Paul's imprisonment. The judgment of Paul

(4:8) produces the opposite result to that of Alexander, just as Paul's life path (3:10-11) differs from Alexander's (4:14-15). Alexander's opposition to the teaching demonstrates itself in evil action, as Paul's good teaching found expression in his good conduct (3:10-11). These misdeeds contrast directly with Timothy's good deeds as a minister of God (see 3:17).

15. *beware of him, for he has been extremely opposed to our teachings:* Timothy's task of guarding the teaching entrusted for safekeeping (1 Tim 6:20) extends to individuals in opposition to it (compare Titus 1:11). Alexander ranks with those opponents of the truth who were compared to Jannes and Jambres (3:8). See 4:2 for a reference to the teaching, the preaching of which is Timothy's task. The preaching here is that of Paul, Timothy, and all those designated by Timothy to teach.

16. *At my first defense:* Paul's defense speeches in Caesarea, before his trial in Rome, are created by Luke in Acts 22:1; 24:10; 25:8, 16; 26:1, 2, 24. The "abandonment" echoes 1:5. This could refer to the first Roman trial, to which the end of Acts looks forward. It might also mean the preliminary defensive statements in the trial process that forms the context of the letter.

    it will not count: The forgiveness of the deserters differs from the threat of punishment to the leaders (4:15; 3:5, 9). The hope for repentance and conversion was mentioned at 2:25 and at 1 Tim 1:16.

17. *strengthened:* See 1:7-8; compare 2:1 and 1 Tim 1:12, and contrast 3:5. This expresses a basic Pauline conviction that his ultimate strength is God's support (Phil 4:13 and 2 Cor 12:9). Recommitment to this conviction is part of the overall strategy to shore up the community in a time of conflict. It complements the station code regulations and the structural development in community ministries.

    the preaching: Paul's preaching task originates in God and Christ Jesus (1 Tim 1:11-12; 2 Tim 1:11). The object of his preaching is all people (1 Tim 2:7; 2 Tim 2:10) and he declares satisfaction with the success of his efforts (2 Tim 4:7, and compare Rom 15:19-20). Some defenders of the letters' authenticity hypothesize the completion of Paul's Spanish mission plans, which verifies his claim here. Otherwise the statement can be taken simply as an echo of the satisfaction expressed in Rom 10:18; 11:25-31, and 15:19-20.

    from the lion's mouth: The image of the lion's mouth has the same meaning as at 1 Macc 2:60, which refers to Daniel's rescue from the jaws of lions (see Dan 6:23 and 14:31-42, and compare 1 Kgs 17:37 LXX). At Ps 22:22 (21:21 LXX) the image is part of the description of the sufferings of the just person. The psalm was read as an allusion to the death of Jesus by the early church (Matt 27:35, 39-40, 43, 46, *parr.*, and John 19:24). And so Paul here refers to his rescue by God from death in order for him to complete his task of preaching. The PE refer to his "first defense" (4:16), which might be the trial at Rome at the end of his imprisonment there (Phil 4:16, 19). Nero, before whom the trial was to be conducted (Acts 25:10-12), was called *leōn* ("lion") by Josephus at *Ant.* 18.228 (*TDNT* 4:253 n. 20). In an expanded sense, rescue from the lion's mouth (death) has eschatological overtones. The suffering of the Christian is an end-time reality (see 3:12) and the snare of the devil is set and ready to capture those who wander from the truth (2:26, and see 1 Tim 3:7; 6:9). Life and death are treated as realities of the end-time (1:1, 10, and see 1 Tim 1:16; 4:8; 6:12, 19; Titus 1:2; 3:7) as well as in the present ("life in the present and future" [NAB] 1 Tim 4:8; "she is dead while she lives" [NAB] 1 Tim 5:6). Thus the devouring lion of 1 Pet 5:8 and the apocalyptic beast of Rev 13:2 (see Dan 7:4) are not far from the point of the image. Paul's rescue from death was a historical reprieve from the death penalty, which had eschatological consequences as a result of the prolongation of his preaching work. Paul's rescue from death was also figurative since his conversion saved him for everlasting life (1 Tim 1:16) and made him a model of conversion for all.

18. *The Lord will rescue me . . . will save me for his heavenly kingdom:* Both the historical and the eschatological aspects of rescue (4:17) are expressed in this verse. Confidence of rescue from evildoing here and now serves to encourage Timothy and all community members who will suffer (1:8; 2:3; 3:12; 4:5). The ultimate rescue, which is salvation for eternal life, is an undercurrent throughout the letters (1 Tim 1:15; 2:4; 4:10, 16; 2 Tim 1:10; Titus 2:11; 3:6-7). The tribulations of the apostle are a recurrent theme in his letters (Rom 8:35, 1 Cor 4:10-13a; 2 Cor 4:8-9; 6:4b-5, 8-10; 11:23-29; Phil 4:12). There, as here, Paul illustrates steadfastness in the face of adversity and a reliance on the saving power of God. The kingdom is mentioned as part of the solemn exhortation at the start of the chapter, at 4:1.

    for ages of ages: The plural of *aiōn* ("age") indicates eternity. The singular, on the other hand, can mean eternity or a prolonged but not unending extension of time. The formula here is used by Paul and Revelation (but see also Heb 1:8; 1 Pet 4:11; 5:11).

19. *Greet Prisca and Aquila and the household of Onesiphorus:* The final salutation includes greetings to individuals, a common feature in the Pauline letters (contrast 1 Tim 6:21). The much-traveled Prisca and Aquila (from Pontus to Rome to Corinth, where Paul met them and worked for them, Acts 18:2-3; to Ephesus with Paul, where he left them, Acts 18:18-19 and 1 Cor 16:19; and back to Rome, Rom 16:3-5) were coworkers with Paul and hosted a household church community at Ephesus and Rome (Rom 6:3). They typify the mobile commercial class (in this case practitioners of tentmaking) whose mobility helped the spread of Christianity and whose relative wealth enabled them to accommodate church communities in their household establishments. They "risked their necks" (NAB) for Paul. Prisca, mentioned first, might have had a higher social standing than her husband Aquila. The mention of their names here, then, is an echo of earlier days in the Pauline churches when Prisca shared the privilege of hosting a church community and helped introduce Apollos to Christian teaching (Acts 18:26). The station codes of Timothy and Titus would rule out such activity on Prisca's part. An alternate name for Prisca, favored by Luke in Acts 18, is Priscilla. For Onesiphorus see 1:16. A fourth-fifth century minuscule, under the influence of the Acts of Paul and Thecla, adds the names of Onesiphorus' wife (Lectra) and two sons (Simaias and Zeno).

    Erastus . . .Trophimus at Miletus: An Erastus is mentioned at Acts 19:22 as a companion of Timothy who went ahead to Macedonia while Paul stayed on at

Athens. He is not on the list of persons who are mentioned with Paul in Macedonia at Acts 20:4. Erastus seems to have stayed in Corinth rather than continue on with Timothy to Macedonia. At Rom 16:20 Erastus sends greetings to the Romans. The letter was written from Corinth during Paul's three-month stay on his way from Ephesus to Macedonia (Acts 20:2-3). As city treasurer, Erastus, as a *quaestor*, would have been at the lower end of the *cursus honorum* (the line of offices in a public career). An inscription on a pavement in Corinth identifies an Erastus as an *aedile*, which, if it is the Erastus of the Pauline church there, indicates that he had risen higher after the letter to the Romans. Persons of such stature were rare in the early Pauline communities, thus meriting an honorific mention. Second Timothy locates him correctly and remembers him as a person of position and influence, perhaps not unlike others, in the increasingly respectable church of the PE. Trophimus, a Gentile, is mentioned along with Timothy at Acts 20:4 as "from Asia," and at Acts 21:29 as "the Ephesian," whose presence with Paul in Jerusalem led to the charge that Paul had desecrated the Temple by bringing Gentiles into it. Paul met the Ephesian elders at Miletus (Acts 20:17-38) for a farewell before going to Jerusalem. His remarks in Acts 20 parallel 2 Timothy as a farewell testament.

21. *before winter:* Travel, particularly by ship, was not attempted in winter. While one could go overland for most of the way from Ephesus to Apollonia or Dyrrachium at the Adriatic end of the Egnatian Way across northern Greece, a sea crossing to Brindisium was required to link up with the Appian Way. More usually, travel from Ephesus to Rome would involve a sea voyage to Corinth, a short portage over the isthmus from Cenchreae to Lechaeum, and then on again by sea through the Saronic gulf across the Adriatic Sea to Brindisium to join the Appian Way and go on to Rome.

Euboulus . . . Pudens, Linus, Claudia: These four are mentioned only here in the NT. Linus, according to Irenaeus, *Haer.* 3.3.3, later became bishop of Rome, having received his office from "the apostles," but there is no historical verification of this claim. Claudia is another Latin name. She and Prisca are the only women named. Contrast Romans 16, where many women are named and their contributions noted. The PE restrict the role of women largely to the household, following social norms common at this time. Lois and Eunice, mentioned at the start of the letter (1:5), fit the latter standard. The list of those sending greetings along with Paul conflicts with his claim of abandonment at 4:10. The lone apostle and beleaguered defender of the Gospel thus appears to be a model for those who follow Jesus Christ (see 1:8, 11-15).

22. *The Lord be with your spirit. Grace be with you:* The first blessing corresponds with that at Gal 6:18; Phil 4:23; and Phlm 25. The concluding benediction follows the Pauline pattern (and see 1 Tim 6:21), although it may have arisen in the Christian worship setting (see Rev 22:1; Heb 13:25; and *1 Clem.* 65.2. "Farewell, in peace" (*errōso en eirēnē*), the more usual Greek salutation, concludes the letter in one uncial codex. Some uncial codices add "amen" to the end of v. 22.

Principal manuscripts identify the letter as the Second to Timothy. Some add "written from Rome" (or Laodicea in one variant). Most go on to say the letter was written from Rome when Paul was there for the second time under Nero, emperor of Rome, to Timothy, appointed first bishop of the church of the Ephesians.

Interpretation

The letter's closing (v. 22) is preceded by lengthy final requests and reports. The friendly requests to Timothy to join Paul (vv. 9 and 21) include reminders about what to bring (v. 13), comings, goings and remainings of mission team members and associates (vv. 10-12, 20), reports of betrayal and warnings (vv. 10, 14-16), expressions of confidence in God (vv. 17-18), and greetings back and forth (vv. 19, 21). The impression of the immediacy of Paul's death is dissipated by his request for Timothy to join him with supplies and also with Mark, who is helpful to him in the ministry (vv. 9, 11, 13, 21). The expected rescue by the Lord, while it looks to heaven (v. 18), is nonetheless associated with the recollection of previous rescues and continued ministry (v. 17). On the other hand, the completion of the proclamation task signals the end of his life's work, the fulfillment of his role in the eschatological plan of God to teach all the Gentiles, and relates to his declaration at 4:7. The reference to the power of the Lord, which enabled this completion, corresponds to the statements at 1:7, 12, 14 and serves to encourage Timothy to act on the exhortation in the letter.

The fault of the deserter Demas is that he "loved the present world" (v. 10), an attitude quite opposite to loving the future appearance of Christ (4:8), which merits the crown of righteousness. This also reflects the future end-time perspective throughout the letter (contrast the opponents' view that the resurrection has already taken place, 2:18, with the insistence on its futurity at 1:10-12; 2:10-12; 4:8, 18). Crescens and Titus also left Paul, but this might just be a travel notice about fellow missionaries and does not necessarily imply that they also abandoned Paul for less than worthy motives.

Alexander merits singular condemnation and negative judgment for resisting Paul's preaching (4:14), a breach of faith according to the Pauline tradition, which this letter repeatedly extols (e.g., 1:3; 2:2, 15-18; 3:14; 4:3-4). He is a typical demonstration (*enedeixato*) of the opposition in the letter. Moreover, while Paul expresses hope that his associates' desertion of him will not be counted against them, the emphasis throughout the letter on the offense involved in failing to remain by Paul, coupled with the suggestion in the prayer that judgment is to be expected, works to underline the importance of remaining faithful. Despite the earlier abandonment, Paul is surrounded by friends as he sends greetings to others in the community with Timothy, probably at Ephesus.

For Reference and Further Study

Brox, Norbert. *Pastoralbriefe*, 274–77.
Cadbury, Henry J. "Erastus of Corinth," *JBL* 50 (1931) 42–58.
Hawthorne, J. G. "Cenchreae, Port of Corinth," *Arch* 18 (1965) 191–200.

Hemer, Colin J. *The Letters to the Seven Churches of Asia in Their Local Setting*. Grand Rapids: Eerdmans, 2001.

Hodgson, Robert. "Paul the Apostle and First-century Tribulation Lists," *ZNW* 74 (1983) 59–80.

McCown, C. C. "Codex and Roll in the NT," *HTR* 34 (1941) 219–50.

Meeks, Wayne A. *The First Urban Christians: The Social World of the Apostle Paul*. New Haven and London: Yale University Press, 1983, 16, 18, 26–27, 41–47, 57–59, 61, 77, 95, 133.

Michaelis, Wilhelm, art. *leōn*, *TDNT* 4:251–53.

Theissen, Gerd. *The Social Setting of Pauline Christianity: Essays on Corinth*. Trans. and ed. by John H. Schütz. Philadelphia: Fortress Press, 1982, 75–83.

________. "Soziale Schichtung in der korinthischen Gemeinde," *ZNW* 65 (1974) 232–72.

Trummer, Peter. "'Mantel und Schriften': Zur Interpretation einer persönlichen Notiz in den Pastoralbriefen," *BZ* 18 (1974) 193–207.

White, John L. "Saint Paul and the Apostolic Letter Tradition," *CBQ* 45 (1983) 438.

Yamauchi, Edwin M. *New Testament Cities in Western Asia Minor: Light from Archaeology on Cities of Paul and the Seven Churches of Revelation*. Grand Rapids: Baker, 1980.

Titus

TITUS

INTRODUCTION

The letter is to a coworker not known from the Acts of the Apostles, but one who receives mention as helping resolve the rift between Paul and the Corinthians at 2 Cor 2:7; 7:6, 13; 8:6, 16-17, 23 and as standing with Paul against the circumcision party at Gal 2:1, 3. Neither Acts nor Paul's other letters mentions the locale of Titus' work, Crete, during Paul's active ministry. The letter presumes that Titus can exercise his authority among all the church communities on the island. Like Timothy in Ephesus, Titus on Crete is more than an emissary of Paul to deal with a specific issue in a particular church.

The greeting is the most expansive of the three Pastoral Epistles and refers to God as savior, to the truth of faith, and to the revelation at the proper time (the incarnation), all themes from the other two PE (1:1-4).

The letter loses no time in detailing church regulations on the qualifications for the office of elder/presbyter = overseer/bishop. Emphasis on virtue, household managing abilities, and blamelessness echo 1 Timothy 3. So, too, does the reference to sound doctrine and refutation of opponents (1:5-9). The presence of apostate teachers is particularly troubling. They are identified as Jewish Christians and the upsetting results of their teaching provoke harsh criticism. Titus must admonish them to get them back to the true teaching (1:10-16).

Household rules for older men and women, younger women and men, and slaves specify behavior that will avoid discrediting the community and its beliefs (2:1-10). The statement of the truth of faith, i.e., universal salvation, behavior consistent with godliness, and expectations of the *parousia* support the call to live as people cleansed by Jesus and eager to do good (2:11-15).

Another call to a life that is upright before secular authority and virtuous toward all finds its basis in a recollection of the faithful people's moral transformation and a restatement of their traditional faith. The faithful have undergone a baptismal transformation and renewal in the Holy Spirit poured out by God through Jesus Christ. Their justification resulted from divine mercy, not from human works, a Pauline tenet (3:1-8a).

The letter concludes with a reminder to Titus to stress good works, to avoid useless quarrels, and to deal sternly with unrepentant heretics (3:8b-11). It ends with particular requests and general greetings (3:12-15).

Outline

1:1-4	Greeting	
1:5-16	Church regulations	
1:5-9		Qualifications: presbyters/bishops
1:10-16		Titus' task to confront false teachers
2:1-8	Domestic regulations	
2:1-2		older men
2:3-5		older women/younger women
2:6-8		younger men
2:9-10		slaves
2:11–3:11	Final exhortation	
2:11–3:7		Transformed life and upright behavior
3:8-11		Titus' task to deal with heretics
3:12-15	Concluding greetings	

TRANSLATION, NOTES, INTERPRETATION

1. *Greeting; Choosing Elders on Crete* (1:1-9)

1. Paul, slave of God and apostle of Jesus Christ for the faith of God's chosen ones and the knowledge of the truth which looks to piety 2. on the basis of hope for eternal life, which God, free of all deceit, promised from time immemorial. 3. Yes, he manifested his word at the proper time in the preaching with which I have been entrusted in accordance with the command of our savior God. 4. To Titus, true child with respect to our common faith, favor and peace from God the Father and Christ Jesus our savior.

5. For this purpose I left you on Crete, to make the additional corrections which are left and to appoint elders in the various urban centers, as I directed you to do. 6. If a man is irreproachable, the husband of one wife, with faithful children, who are not liable to a charge of debauchery nor disobedient. 7. This is because an overseer as a steward of God must be irreproachable, not self-willed, irascible, addicted to wine, violent, or greedy. 8. On the contrary, he must be hospitable, loving what is good, reserved, just, devout, self-controlled, 9. holding fast to the trustworthy message in accord with his teaching, in order for him to be capable both to exhort with sound teaching and to correct those who oppose him.

Notes

1. For the form of the letter opening see 1 Tim 1:1.

slave of God and apostle of Jesus Christ: See the Note on 2 Tim 2:24. Paul refers to himself as slave of Jesus Christ at Rom 1:1; Phil 1:1; Gal 1:10, and so designates Epaphras at Col 4:12 (compare 1 Pet 2:16; 2 Pet 1:1; Jude 1; James 1:1). Acts 16:17 might have been the source for the title "slave of God" (*doulos theou*) here. Submissiveness will be a key idea in the station code of this letter, and Paul here sets the tone (see *epitagē*, "command," at v. 3). God is declared master of Paul and, by implication, of all Christians. This sets the stage for egalitarian mutuality within the social and economic stratification of the day (compare Col 4:1; Eph 6:9; Rom 6:18, 22). See the Note on "apostle" at 1 Tim 1:1, and see 1 Tim 1:1, 12; 2:7; 2 Tim 1:1, 11 for "Jesus Christ."

for the faith of God's chosen ones and the knowledge of the truth which looks to piety: The apostolic witness (v. 3) has the faith of Paul's listeners as its aim (1 Tim 1:2). As at 2 Tim 2:10, the context provides an eschatological setting in *zoēs aiōniou* ("eternal life") at v. 2. The election strikes a note of particularity at 2:14, but the other two PE affirm God's design for universal salvation (see 1 Tim 2:4). See the Note on 1 Tim 2:4 for "knowledge of the truth" (*epignōsin alētheias*). See 1 Tim 2:2 for a discussion of piety. The preposition "in accord with" (*kata*) indicates piety as a result of recognizing the truth. Actually, a grasp of the truth is one component, along with upright action, of piety. See 2:12.

2. *hope for eternal life:* See the Notes on Tim 4:8, 10. While 1 Timothy specifies that hope is in God (4:10; 5:5; 6:17), Titus clarifies the object of hope as eternal life (2:13; 3:7). The diverse emphases do not signal a difference in meaning.

   God, free of all deceit, promised from time immemorial: The designation "free of all deceit" identifies God as the source of the truth, which the chosen are to recognize (v. 1). It contrasts with the deceit of the opposing teachers (1 Tim 4:1; 2 Tim 3:13), which caught some of the audience of the letter as well (3:3). The eternal plan of God, which began to unfold in the events of Christ Jesus' life and death, is a consistent theme in the PE (see 2 Tim 1:1). It looks to completion at the *parousia*, which ushers in eternal life. The incarnation and earthly work of Jesus Christ (1 Tim 1:5) constituted a key turn (v. 3) and gave importance to "now" as the beginning of the final age (see 1 Tim 4:1).

3. *he manifested his word at the proper time:* Compare 1 Tim 3:16b; 2 Tim 1:10. "Word" (*logon*) refers to the Gospel (see 1:9, 2:5 and 2 Tim 4:2, and compare 1 Tim 2:6b-7). The Gospel message is the means of entering into relationship with the saving action of God and Jesus Christ. It is God's word entrusted to Paul for dissemination (see 1 Tim 1:11; 2:7; 2 Tim 1:11). Romans 16:26 speaks of the manifestation of the mystery of the Gospel. The unfolding of the preordained plan of God proceeds at its own pace (see 1 Tim 2:6; 6:15), with the coming of Christ in the flesh (1 Tim 3:16), the appearance of his grace (Titus 2:11, 2 Tim 1:10), and the manifestation of his word in Paul's preaching (1 Tim 1:11).

   in the preaching . . . entrusted in accordance with the command of our savior God: See 2 Tim 4:17 for Paul's preaching task, and compare 1 Tim 2:7; 3:16e; 2 Tim 1:11; 4:2. See 1 Tim 1:11 for Paul's being entrusted with the Gospel. Paul's obedience to the command of God to be an apostle (see 1 Tim 1:1, and compare 1 Tim 2:2) contrasts with the former disobedience, with which all are associated (Titus 3:3), and it sets a pattern of obedience God will expect of children (1:6), wives (2:5), slaves (2:9), and all in the community to those in governing positions (3:1). The title "savior" (*sōtēr*) is ascribed to God at 2:10; 3:4, but at 3:6 Jesus Christ is given the title, as he is in the next verse. See also 1 Tim 1:11; 2:4.

4. *to Titus, true child with respect to our common faith, favor and peace:* From Gal 2:1 and 3 we learn that Titus was a Greek Christian who accompanied Paul to the Jerusalem "council." Like Timothy, he represented Paul to the fractious Corinthians and seems to have effected a resolution of the crisis (2 Cor 7:6-7, 13-15). He is not mentioned in Acts. Titus and his trip to Dalmatia are noted among others in the salutation of 2 Timothy (2 Tim 4:10). His job is to remain on Crete

after Paul leaves and establish elders/bishops for the church communities among the island's cities. See 1 Tim 1:2. The word "child" (*teknon*) suggests that Paul was instrumental in his conversion (compare Phlm 10 and 1 Cor 4:14-15). The genuine relationship in faith is stressed in the face of opponents, deceivers, and false teachers (1:10). With the phrase "with respect to our common faith" (*kata koinēn pistin*) the common front is established against the problem of false teaching and opposition. The formula "favor and peace" (*charis kai eirēnē*) repeats Rom 1:7b, replacing the title "Lord" for Jesus by "Savior" (and compare 1 Tim 1:2; 2 Tim 1:2).

5. *For this purpose:* The body of the letter starts with a reminder of Titus' mission. Like 1 Timothy, Titus presents the anomaly of a letter with instructions to a close associate who would have received them orally, and not very long before. The "official memorandum" might be the letter-type represented here (see 1 Tim 1:3), although this letter, more than 1 Timothy, has the appearance of a personal letter with station code material incorporated into it.

   I left you on Crete to make the additional corrections: No record of Paul's visit to Crete exists except for this reference. Acts 27:8, 12, 13, 21 mention that the ship taking Paul to Rome for trial entered the harbor at Fair Havens, near Lasea, to escape adverse winds. While Paul suggested that they stay there, the ship's officials decided to sail on with the hope of wintering at Phoenix. Instead, the ship and its occupants were driven by a storm away from the island and westward toward Malta. No missionary work was done at this time on Crete, nor is there any indication that Titus might have been with Paul on the ship and was then left behind at Fair Havens. There is no indication of an opportunity to visit Crete at the end of Acts, where Paul is awaiting trial under house arrest in Rome. The letter to Titus traces the founding of the church on Crete to Paul and Titus, but there is no evidence to substantiate this claim. While there is some opposition on doctrinal grounds (1:10-15), the situation does not appear to be as critical as that in Ephesus, where the opponents had made disturbing progress (2 Tim 2:17-18; 3:9).

   appoint elders in the various urban centers: The solution on Crete is a structural change in church organization with the introduction of elders/overseers. In Ephesus elders and overseers already exist but need some reform (1 Tim 5:19-22). Even more important in that letter, however, is a confrontation with the false teachers (1 Tim 1:3). While the author of the Pastorals seems to prefer the "overseer" title in 1 Timothy for the person in a supervisory and teaching role, he might have been drawn to use "elder" here by the reference to Paul's establishing elders in Derbe (Acts 14:23). The elders blend with overseers, who are selected from their number. See 1 Tim 5:17-22 for elders in Ephesus.

   I directed: For other words of command and obedience see v. 3.

6. *If a man is irreproachable, the husband of one wife, with faithful children:* The list of qualifications closely resembles that for overseers at 1 Tim 3:2-4. The author is apparently using a church order source. See the Notes on 1 Tim 3:2 for the expectation of being irreproachable and for a discussion of the marriage regulation. The restriction of elder and overseer functions to males complements the relegation of women largely to the domestic sphere (see 1 Tim 2:9-15). A well

regulated household demonstrates the potential leaders' abilities to direct the church community, the household of God (1:7, and see 1 Tim 3:4-5, 15). As Paul's own "child" (*teknon*), Titus is genuine in the faith and has followed Paul's instructions. He is expected to be a model of good behavior, sound teaching, and blamelessness (2:7-8). The children here are, like Timothy, probably young adults, given the failing of debauchery from which they are warned. Moreover, Paul has a particular concern that Titus exhort the younger women and men to moderation at 2:4-6.

7. *overseer as a steward of God:* See the Note on "overseer" (*episkopos*) at 1 Tim 3:2. The structure to be put in place on Crete is simpler than that in Ephesus. Here there are elders and overseers. The use of the singular for overseer in a continuous discussion of the man's qualifications to be an elder (v. 6) indicates that the office is the same, but has two names. At Ephesus there are elders, overseers, assistants, and widows. The relationship between elders and overseers is not clear. Elders, appointed in all the urban centers, seem to incorporate the more general office. Since household management experience is expected, he might have to look after the affairs of church communities. The overseer seems to have more specific functions, such as teaching (not all elders teach, as suggested by 1 Tim 5:17b), confronting opponents, and, as the title suggests, supervision. The office is cast here in the image of "steward" (*oikonomos*). The steward oversaw the labor of the household and its products. The steward also managed the outside assets of the household. For that reason, trustworthiness and honesty were essential qualifications (*EDNT*). The singular does not indicate a monarchical bishop. Rather, it results from the use of the word at the head of a qualification list (compare 1 Tim 3:2 and the widow's qualification list at 1 Tim 5:9). Assistants at 1 Timothy 3 might be plural because their qualifications are listed by the author *ad hoc*, but with some looser reference to a list. Nonetheless, the description is of an office that is not common in other churches yet, such as the one on Crete.

   must be irreproachable . . . not greedy: See v. 6 and 1 Tim 3:2. For parallels to this list elsewhere in the PE see 2 Tim 3:2. The self-possessed and irenic qualities of the officials here (and compare 2:12; 3:2) are consistent expectations throughout the letters. See 1 Tim 6:4. The Cretan church officials and members are expected to present themselves as clearly distinct from the false teachers in their rivalries and quarrels (Titus 3:3, 9). Plutarch, *Mor.* 454B-C represents Hellenistic philosophical opinion in its denunciation of anger. Overcoming anger was one of the most important signs of the wise person. Polybius, VI 46,1-5.8-9, notes that Cretans set no limits on greed. Drunkenness and greed are typical faults ascribed to opposition teachers in polemic literature of the day.

8. *hospitable, loving what is good:* Hospitality is recommended by Paul at Rom 12:13 (and see Heb 13:2 and 1 Pet 4:9). Paul appeals to the Romans' hospitality for Phoebe (Rom 16:1-2, and compare 2 Cor 7:13; Phil 2:23, 29; 1 Cor 16:11) and himself (Rom 15:24, and compare Philemon 22). Hospitality was critical in the establishment and spread of the church (see Acts 16:15). First Timothy 5:10 approves enrolling widows who practice hospitality. The task may have been part of the widows' official duties. See also 1 Tim 3:2, where it is a qualification of overseers.

The virtue "loving what is good" (*philagathos*) contrasts the end-time (= present) false teachers who are "not lovers of the good" (*aphilagathoi*, 2 Tim 3:3).

9. *holding fast to the trustworthy message:* Holding fast means maintaining the true teaching both in content and as applied to life practice. This will enable positive exhortation and criticism of errors. Paul expects Titus at 2:7-8 to be a model of both. Good works include teaching integrity, dignity, and soundness, which leave no opening for criticism. The character of the teachers and their actions are essential to their effectiveness as teachers in Greco-Roman education. The teachers were expected to teach by their own example. More than the transmission of knowledge, the Christian way of life is at stake in the exhortation and teaching ("knowledge of the truth which leads to piety," 1:1). Thus, by comparison, Timothy is expected at 2 Tim 3:14 to remain faithful to "what he learned and believed" (NAB), which includes Paul's teaching and life practices (2 Tim 3:10). This will suit him for his work of exhortation and correction (2 Tim 4:2).

   exhort with sound teaching and correct those who oppose him: See 2 Tim 4:2 for exhort, and 1 Tim 1:10 for "sound" as a medical image. See 1:13 and 2 Tim 4:2 and the Notes on the strategy behind correction.

Interpretation

Like 1 Timothy, the letter to Titus is concerned with church order matters. The addressee has been left by Paul on the island of Crete with the task of rectifying matters and establishing elders in the island's Christian communities (v. 5)

The friendly greeting follows the standard form, with the name of the sender expanded by christological and theological affirmations (vv. 1-3). These are repeated in abbreviated forms after the name of the recipient (v. 4). Paul's status is twofold: a slave of God and an apostle of Jesus Christ. Both establish his prominent position securely, since they derive from God and the apostolic function is a privileged one in the church. He reiterates his special task and position at 1:3, where he specifies it in terms of the *kērygma* ("Gospel message") he proclaims under God's command. Faith and the recognition of the truth about religion are correlative and promise eternal life. While his kerygmatic message is the hope for eternal life, this end has been God's promise before all ages. The plan was revealed by God in the savior Jesus. The message entrusted to Paul thus includes Jesus Christ as part of that message (v. 24). Truth and lack of deception are highlighted as qualities of God and of the *kērygma* (vv. 1-2). Titus is associated with Paul as his child (= spiritual convert) and partner in faith (v. 4).

John Chrysostom, *Hom. Titus* 1 (NPNF 1 13:520) declares that Paul was entrusted with his apostleship for God's elect as an effect of the goodness of God and not by virtue of any of his own accomplishments. The gift of God makes possible the work of his servants and the faith of those among whom they work. God's ministers do not assume their role by their own will, but rather recognize a divine calling within themselves. The image of the slave underlines Paul's humble position and the title "apostle" highlights the divine initiative that led to his ministry. The designation of the community members as the "elect" continues the recognition of God's call both to be part of the community and to minister to it.

Divine grace is directed toward the acknowledgment of the truth that accords with piety. Faith is a mystery of God's gift and the human response to it. It is undeserved, and it cannot be presumed that any measures taken by people can dispose them to receive the gift of faith and to strengthen it once it is offered and accepted. As this letter indicates, Titus and designated officials are to remove and counteract people whose teaching and actions are obstacles to belief.

The sonship of Titus rests on his acceptance of Paul's preaching. Hence, unlike natural generation, it is not irreversible (Theodoret of Cyr, *Interpretation of the Letter to Titus* [PG 82:859AB-860AB]). By referring to Titus' sonship in a common faith Paul has introduced complexity into the image of the traditional Roman father-son relationship. From the perspective of faith the two are on a par.

Augustine, *Civ.*, explains that God's promise was his Word, who coexisted with God from all eternity and who is eternal life. The promise was predestined and determined from eternity. Paul's preaching manifested it and refers to Jesus' cross (1 Cor 1:18 and 1 Tim 2:6-7). The eternity of God's promise looks backward and forward in time, for God is outside time as its beginning and end. This gives the readers of the letters assurance of the blessings spoken of in Titus as available to them as well.

With no thanksgiving, the letter goes directly to the body, which is largely hortatory. The reminder of his charge (v. 5) serves to introduce the content of the letter and to characterize it as an *aide memoire*.

The qualifications, largely personal virtues of the elder/overseer and the vices to be avoided by him, are outlined (vv. 6-9) with special attention paid to blamelessness (vv. 6, 7). The latter is a key to the elder/overseer's "frank speech" (*parrēsia*, v. 9).

Both Jerome (*Letters* 69.8 [NPNF 1 6:147]) and Augustine (*Tractates on John* 41.10.1 [FC 88:145]) note that, taken at face value, the requirement of blamelessness imposes an impossible expectation of sinlessness. Thus it is more likely that it expresses the expectation that the candidate not be subject to the accusation of a publicly known crime, but rather that he distinguish himself from the crowd of those he is to shepherd. The loss of credibility for the hierarchy in the contemporary church in North America over their ineffectual handling of priests and religious who abused young people is a striking demonstration of the wisdom of this requirement. While church members rightly expect more of their leadership, even those who are not members of the church have found that this issue displays an unacceptable gap between hierarchical pronouncements on moral issues and the lived morality among church authorities. This undermines the position of the church as it tries to apply Catholic teaching to public policy and ordinary life.

Titus is reminded of his task ("as I directed you") to complete the work of establishing elders in the Cretan cities not dealt with during Paul's visit. The new institution seems to be a component of a plan to deal with community disorder, particularly conflicts over teaching, (v. 5, "make additional corrections" [*epidiorthōsę̄*], and see v. 9, "to correct those who oppose" [*tous antilegontas elenchein*]) . The letter establishes the Pauline precedent for the institution both in theory (the letter's content) and in practice (Titus completes what Paul started). The list of qualifications and personal qualities uses the term "overseer" (*episkopos*, v. 7). Unlike the rural focus of Jesus' ministry, Paul's activity was centered in cities. The PE continue this urban emphasis. As a mission strategy, concentration on urban centers, and particularly regional hubs and provincial capitals, made the best use of the mission's thin resources. From the cities, centers of commerce and the location of principal religious, social, educational, and political activities, the Christian message might well be expected to spread among the inhabitants of outlying areas as they came to the cities for other purposes. The density of Christian settlement in the Lycus Valley in the Roman province of Asia is an indication of the success of this strategy. The eventual use of the word "pagan" (*paganus* or "country dweller" in Latin) for one who follows the traditional Roman religion demonstrates the conversion lag between cities and rural areas.

The one office is thus the elder/bishop. The elder/bishop, manager (steward) of God's household, the church community, demonstrates his aptitude for church leadership by his performance in his own household.

Constitutions of the Holy Apostles 6.3.17 applies the regulation about having only one wife to the bishops, presbyters, and deacons of the day and clarifies that the single marriage obligation applies whether the cleric's wife is alive or dead. "It is not lawful for them, if they are unmarried when they are ordained, to be married afterwards; or if they are married at that time, to marry a second time, but to be content with the wife they had when they came to ordination." John Chrysostom, *Hom. Titus* 2 (NPNF 1 13:524) finds Paul here stressing the holy and honorable character of marriage, such that it does not prevent a man from "ascending the holy throne." Jerome, *Commentary on Titus* (PL 26:598C) finds that the bishop must teach monogamy and "best of all, continence, by example." He goes on to note that some monogamous men are less continent than others who have been married twice and widowed. The discipline of the *Constitutions of the Holy Apostles* is still maintained for presbyters and deacons in the Orthodox and Byzantine Catholic churches today, but bishops are not permitted to marry at all. In the Roman Catholic church, where celibacy is in force for bishops, priests, and "transitional" deacons, permanent deacons may marry, but are expected to remain unmarried if their wives die. An argument has been made that even the married deacons are expected to remain continent within their marriages, which explains some of the qualifications, such as having the wife's full understanding and consent before the married person is ordained a deacon. The model of continence, which the PE and their patristic interpreters see in the presbyter, deacon, and bishop, is a countercultural sign for today, when unrestrained and unreflective sexual activity is taken to be normative.

Keeping faithful to his wife and rearing his children in the faith, integrity, and obedience are considered signs of stability of character behind the overseer's faith stance as well as of his effectiveness in transmitting Christian faith and practice.

The picture of children who embrace their parents' life of faith is idealized. Parents are often dismayed at the ineffectiveness of the teaching and example they give their children. The problem is not new. Jerome, *Commentary on Titus* (PL 26:599BC) is sympathetic to parents whose children are raised well but then stray. He cites Isaac's son Esau, whom he calls "profligate and worldly, when he sold his birthright for a single meal," and Samuel, who communicated with God in prayers but "had sons who declined into greed." The faith option, in the end, is highly personal and rests on the individual's reception of and response to the call of God. Nonetheless, the Pastoral Epistles' ideal family rests within a community of faith that prompts and supports the individuals' faith options.

Adherence to the word of faith (v. 9) makes this explicit. The elder/overseer's reputation for virtue and business dealings (v. 8) as well as his personal temperament are to be such as to enable his task of teaching and correcting.

As for the expectation of a nonviolent temperament, both John Chrysostom, *Hom. Titus* 2 (NPNF 1 13:525), and Jerome, *Commentary on Titus* (PL 26:601D), give evidence of a society more accepting of physical abuse than our own when they refer to raising the hand for striking as ruled out for Christian officials. In contemporary interpersonal relations manipulative, abusive, and harassing speech and actions constitute unacceptable violence, whether between officials and subordinates or between persons of equal status. The community officials here establish the norm of behavior for the community at large. Adherence to the traditional doctrinal content and its transmission are key functions to be fulfilled, and even exhortation is informed by sound teaching (v. 9). Jerome, *Letters* 53.3 (NPNF 16:97) insists on intellectual formation by noting that here the letter requires the bishop to seek knowledge of the Scriptures. "In fact, what of education in a clergyman prevents him from doing good to any one but himself? Even if the virtue of his life may build up Christ's church, he does it an injury as great by failing to resist those who are trying to pull it down." The need for a well-educated priesthood and episcopacy is acute today, when church teaching is being increasingly scrutinized and contested by proponents of competing movements and ideologies. Likewise within Catholic parishes, an increasing number of parishioners have a university-level education. This reality also makes it imperative that church officials present convincing arguments as they explain the official church teaching to increasingly independent-minded and even skeptical congregations.The longstanding intellectual tradition of the Catholic Church and the philosophical and reasoned underpinnings for its doctrine and practice provide a faith experience that is more enduring and, in the long run, more satisfying than an emotional religious experience that is short on content. The Pastoral Epistles manifest this intellectual tradition at the origins of the church itself.

For Reference and Further Study

Bartlet, Vernon. "Titus the Friend of Luke, and other Related Questions," *The Expositor* 77 (1917) 367–75.

Borse, Udo. *1. und 2. Timotheusbrief, Titusbrief.* Stuttgarter Kleiner Kommentar, Neues Testament 13. Stuttgart: Katholisches Bibelwerk, 1985, 111–12, 114.

Brox, Norbert. *Die Pastoralbriefe: übersezt und erklärt.* Regensburg: Pustet, 1969, 279, 284–85.

Fiore, Benjamin. *The Function of Personal Example in the Socratic and Pastoral Epistles.* AnBib 105. Rome: Biblical Institute Press, 1986, 33–37.

Harrill, J. Albert. *Slaves in the New Testament: Literary, Social, and Moral Dimensions.* Minneapolis: Fortress Press, 2006.

Karris, Robert A. "The Background and Significance of the Polemic of the Pastoral Epistles," *JBL* 92 (1973) 549–64.

Weiser, Alfons. *Die Knechtsgleichnisse des synoptischen Evangelien.* SANT, 29. Munich: Kösel, 1971.

White, John L. "Saint Paul and the Apostolic Letter Tradition," *CBQ* 45 (1983) 439.

2. *False Teachers* (1:10-16)

> 10. For there are many who are disobedient, idle talkers, and deceivers, especially those from the circumcision faction. 11. It is necessary to gag these, every one of them who are turning entire households upside down, teaching what they should not for the sake of shameful gain. 12. Someone,

a Cretan himself, one of their prophets, said, "Cretans are inveterate liars, wicked brutes, lazy gluttons." 13. This testimony is true, and for this reason correct them rigorously, so that they might become sound in the faith, 14. without giving attention to Jewish myths and commandments of people who reject the truth. 15. Everything is clean for those who are clean, but for the defiled and faithless nothing is clean. Rather, both their minds and their consciences are defiled. 16. They profess to know God, but deny God by their works, since they are detestable and disobedient and unfit for any good deed.

Notes

10. *many who are disobedient, idle talkers, and deceivers:* Association with unruly young people (2:6) compounds the attack by the author who prizes obedience (1:3, and see 1 Tim 1:1). God's message (1:3, and see 1 Tim 4:12)) contrasts with the opposition teachers' idle talk. For deceivers see 2 Tim 3:13, and contrast "God, free of all deceit" (*apseudēs theos*) at 1:2. All three vices conflict directly with things said of God. The letter thus thrusts the polemic onto a higher plane where the opponents are set over against God.

    those from the circumcision faction: Titus remained uncircumcised at the "council of Jerusalem" (Gal 2:3) in opposition to the circumcision faction. The truth of Paul's Gospel (Gal 2:5) was the principle being safeguarded there. Here Titus faces similar opponents, although the issue of circumcision receives no explicit mention. Compare 3:9 and 1 Tim 1:7. Josephus, *Bell.* II 103, and Philo, *Embassy* 282, both give evidence of a Jewish settlement on Crete.

11. *It is necessary to gag these:* The need to silence the opponents is clear since they are "many" (*polloi*, v. 10) and are overturning households. The measure of correcting followed by shunning (3:10) the heretic seems to belie the urgency of the situation, as do the uncomplicated administrative solution of appointing elders/overseers and the optimistic outlook for the opponents' becoming sound again. The countermeasures in 1 and 2 Timothy are more elaborate and the conflict picture is more critical. The end-time cast (see 1 Tim 4:1) to the conflict in 1 and 2 Timothy is absent from Titus.

    for the sake of shameful gain: See 1:7, and compare 1 Tim 3:8; 6:5 for comments about greed. The accusation of greedy motives among false teachers is a Greco-Roman commonplace and seems to have been hurled at Paul, as indicated by his apologetic remarks at 1 Thess 2:5, 8 and 2 Cor 11:7-9, and see his cautious handling of the "collection" at 2 Cor 8:19-21, as well as his boast of preaching without charge at 1 Cor 9:15-19.

12. *Someone . . . one of their prophets:* Clement of Alexandria in *Stromata* 1.14 (MPG 8.757c) identifies the author of the quotation as Epimenides, but he does not give the title of the work. Jerome cites the text as *De oraculis*. The paradox behind the statement "All Cretans are liars" was contrived by Eubulides and is quoted by Callimachus 1,4-9 (and compare Polybius, VI 47,5-6, Diodorus Siculus, XXXI 45,1; *Anth. Graec.* VII 275; Ovid, *Ars* I 295-300), and Hesychius, *k.* 4086 explains

the verb *krētizein* ("to act like a Cretan") as referring to the Cretans' lying character (see Suidas, *k.* 2407).

inveterate liars, wicked brutes, lazy gluttons: Again contrast the true God acclaimed at 1:2. This brutishness of thought and action threatens to undermine true piety and religion. The immoderation (and see 3:3) that characterizes the opponents separates them from the self-controlled faithful (see 1:7, and also 2:2-7, 12; 3:2). Immoderation is similarly criticized in Greco-Roman literature (Juvenal, *Sat.* 4,104-110; Suidas, *s.* 1271; Donatus, *Phormio* V 8,95).

Like the use of Scripture quotations (see 2 Tim 3:16), the testimony of ancient authority here serves to establish the case being argued. The truth of the quotation is accepted without regard to its inherent paradox. The allusion to the unnamed Cretan as a "prophet" expresses the effort of early Christians to find anticipations of their beliefs in both Greco-Roman and Jewish traditions. In the patristic period Vergil, Plato, Socrates, and the Sybils, among others, were all seen to be forerunners of Christian belief and were used, therefore, as missionary tools. Similarly, figures from the Hebrew Scriptures were considered to be types of Christian realities. The latter is already in evidence, for example, in Paul's association of Jesus with Adam at Rom 5:12-21 and 1 Cor 15:20-23, 45-49.

13. *correct them rigorously:* Correction with a view to conversion echoes a similar aim in the other two PE (see 2 Tim 3:16) and in classical moral instruction. At 1 Tim 5:20 the objects of correction are wayward elders. The crisis within the church leadership at Ephesus might account for the more urgent tone of 1 and 2 Timothy. Here in Crete, Titus is appointing officials to deal with heretical views that are not promulgated by officials.

14. *attention to Jewish myths and commandments:* See 1:10, and compare 1 Tim 1:4, 7, where the Decalogue is in view. The myths are not identified beyond their being "Jewish." The author of the PE reveals awareness of Jewish Haggadic and apocryphal works (e.g., Eve's deception at 1 Tim 2:14; Jannes and Jambres at 2 Tim 3:8) and might know of other legendary books (the *Acts of Paul and Thecla,* 1 Tim 2:12). The commandments seem to deal with purity (v. 15).

    people who reject the truth: Deviation characterizes the opponents, while persistence identifies the faithful (see 2 Tim 4:4). "The truth" is a shorthand way of referring to the Christian faith that is favored in the PE (1:1 and see 1 Tim 2:4).

15. *Everything is clean to those who are clean:* Titus varies Rom 14:14 on clean and unclean foods, which is one of the human commandments at issue (see Matt 15:9, quoting Isa 29:13 LXX). As at 1 Tim 4:3-5, the foods are all clean and are received as such by those who know the truth. The defiled, on the other hand, are unable to recognize this since both their minds and their consciences are tainted. Whereas Paul's concern is for the sensitive consciences of those who adhere to food laws, the author of Titus dismisses the proponents of food regulations as themselves defiled in mind and conscience. The issue is no longer subject to compromise in view of community harmony. The Jewish Christian position is no longer viable in the Gentile-dominated church. Dietary regulations, especially those requiring abstinence, might also be connected with erroneous teaching about the resurrection (see 1 Tim 4:1-3 and 2 Tim 2:18).

A clean conscience is expected of the applicants for assistant (1 Tim 3:9), and the vessels for lowly tasks can cleanse themselves for honorable service (2 Tim 2:21). Here a parallel transformation emerges as the result of direct correction (1:13). For the same approbation of a clean conscience see Philo, *Spec. Leg.* III 209.

the . . . faithless . . . their minds and their consciences are defiled: Their opposition has placed them outside the community of the faithful. See 2 Tim 3:8 for a similar vice. Mind and conscience express the two sides of Christian life in the PE: the intellectual and the practical, the first dealing with matters of truth, the second with good deeds (see 2:14 and 3:3). Knowledge claims must be verified by action (see 1:9). Knowledge of God involves not just the acceptance of doctrine; it also looks to a life of virtuous action (1:1). That an evil outlook can turn all to evil, and a good one to good, is a commonplace sentiment (see Seneca, *Ep.* 98,2-3; Ovid, *Trist.* II 253-258, 263-266, 295-302; Seneca, *Ben.* V 12,6-7). Dionysius of Halicarnassus, *Thuc.* 8, praises Thucydides' objectivity and observes that by following his example one will not falsify or belie one's own conscience.

16. *they are detestable and disobedient:* In the LXX the word group refers to things abominable to God, such as idols (see Mark 13:14), the eating of certain animals, incest, or pagan ways of life. In Wisdom literature it came to denote the antithesis between the human and the divine will (Sir 15:3; Prov 29:27; Sir 1:25, 13:20). In general it referred to Israel's duty to keep separate from everything pagan. At Luke 16:15 Jesus declared that what is highest in human esteem is detestable to God. Here the term refers to the human will as expressed in the commandments, which the circumcisionists try to advance (1:14). These are opposed to God's will and are abominable to God. The word thus hurls the charge of uncleanness back upon those who are experts in purity legislation. See "disobedient" at 1:10 and 3:3.

Interpretation

The conflict over teaching and the need for frank criticism (*elenchein*, v. 9) emerges in the ensuing list of unruly traits of individuals (vv. 10-12) to be dealt with (vv. 13-16). Vice, apostasy (especially toward Jewish traditions), ignorance, and wrongdoing afflict them.

Two divergent examples of leaders to follow and avoid emerge as the vices opposed to the virtues required of the elder/overseer characterize the opponents (e.g., *anypotaktoi*, "disobedient," versus *mē anypotaktoi*, "not disobedient," v. 6; *mataiologoi kai phrēnapatai*, "idle talkers and deceivers," versus "holding fast to the trustworthy message," *antechomenon . . . didachēn pistou logou*, v. 9; teachers for profit versus those who are "not greedy," *mē aischrokerdē*, v. 7). Furthermore, the false teachers overturn households with their teaching while the elders/bishops manage households that are models of faith and uprightness (v. 6). The quotation from Epimenides serves the same exemplary function, as it describes Cretans as *kaka theria* ("wicked brutes," v. 12) versus *mē authadē, mē orgilon, mē plēktēn* ("not arrogant," "not irritable," "not aggressive," v. 7) and *gasteres argai* ("lazy gluttons," v. 12) versus *mē paroinon* ("not a wine drinker," v. 7) and *enkratē* ("self-controlled," v. 8). Their godliness is suggested, for they are *pseustai* ("liars"), while God is *apseudēs* ("free of all deceit," v. 2). So the false teachers and their Cretan audience share similar characteristics. Direct and sharp reproof of the Cretans (vv. 13-14) is intended to be therapeutic for their faith (compare 1:9), keeping them from abandoning the truth by accepting the false teachers' doctrine and regulations. John Chrysostom, *Hom. Titus* 3 (LCC 1:334), explains that Epimenides, a Cretan himself, called his countrymen liars in claiming to have the tomb of Jupiter, who never dies: "The Cretans always lie; for they, O King, have built your tomb, and you are not yet dead."

Titus' charge to set things right, in addition to appointing worthy elders/ overseers, includes criticizing the false teachers just described. The elders/ overseers are to continue this criticism of dissident thinkers (v. 9), especially those inclined toward Jewish myths and religious regulations of people who turned from the truth. The rival claims to the truth referred to in this letter (1:2-3, 9, 11, 12, 14-16; 2:1, 2, 3, 7, 8, 10; 3:3, 9-11) and at least some of the thought opposed to the letter's orthodoxy are linked with Judaism (1:10, 14). The clearest proof of doctrinal unorthodoxy is found in practice (*theon homologousin eidenai, tois de ergois arnountai*, "they claim to know God, but by their deeds they deny him," [NAB] v. 16). Dietary restrictions constitute one clear demonstration of faithlessness (v. 15), with the declaration of impurity hurled at the teachers themselves.

In the pluralistic environment of contemporary religious practice in North America such a connection of doctrinal error with immoral activity is simplistic and often erroneous. In fact, adherents of greatly diverse and even historically antagonistic religious bodies have found common purpose and understanding in shared action on projects to benefit the community at large.

For Reference and Further Study

Bauer, Walter. *Orthodoxy and Heresy in Earliest Christianity*. Ed. Robert Kraft and Gerhard Krodel. Philadelphia: Fortress Press, 1979, 86.

Borse, Udo. *1. und 2. Timotheusbrief*, 117.

Colson, F. H. "Quintilian I, 9 and the *'chreia'* in Ancient Education," *Classical Review* 35 (1921) 150.

Fiore, Benjamin. *Personal Example*, 97–98, 119. n. 73; 157–58 nn. 191–203.

Malherbe, Abraham J. "Exhortation in 1 Thessalonians," in idem, *Paul and the Popular Philosophers*. Minneapolis: Fortress Press, 1989, 49–66.

Pelikan, Jaroslav. "The Light of the Gentiles," in *Jesus Through the Centuries: His Place in the History of Culture*. New Haven and London: Yale University Press, 1999, 34–45.

Rahner, Hugo. *Griechische Mythen in Christlicher Deutung*. Zürich: Rhein-Verlag, 1945.

Zimmer, Christoph. "Die Lügner-Antinomie in Titus 1,12," *LB* 59 (1987) 77–99.

3. *Sound Teaching; Rules for the Household; Salvation in Christ* (2:1-15)

1. As for you, however, declare what befits sound teaching, 2. that it is proper for older men to be sober, dignified, self-controlled, sound with respect to faith, love, steadfastness. 3. Likewise for older women to behave as is appropriate for religious people, not to be slanderers, enslaved to heavy wine drinking, teachers of what is good, 4. in order for them to give younger women the good sense to be loving of their husbands and of their children, 5. to be modest, pure, good homemakers, obeying their husbands, lest the word of God be defamed. 6. Similarly, encourage younger men to be self-controlled 7. in every respect, as you show yourself to be a model of good deeds, exhibiting integrity in teaching, dignity, 8. sound preaching beyond reproach, so that someone on the opposing side might be put to shame for having nothing bad to say about us. 9. Encourage slaves to obey their own masters in everything, to give satisfaction, not being obstinate, 10. nor pilfering, but rather showing complete good faith, so that they might adorn the teaching of our savior God in every respect. 11. The salvific favor of God, you see, has appeared to all people, 12. instructing us to lead a life of self-control, righteousness, and piety in the present age by rejecting impiety and worldly passions, 13. in expectation of the blessed hope and appearance of the glory of the great God and of our savior Jesus Christ, 14. who gave himself up for us, that he might deliver us from all lawlessness and cleanse for himself a precious people, eager for good deeds. 15. Declare these things and exhort and correct with complete insistence. Let no one look down on you.

Notes

1. *As for you . . . sound teaching:* The first section of the body of the letter dealt with Titus' mandate and included the first station code material, i.e., the qualifications for elders/overseers. It also described the opposition teachers and directed Titus' energy to deal with them directly, but with optimism. Now attention turns to Titus more directly, with the personal pronoun expressed and in a position of prominence (compare 2 Tim 2:1; 3:10, 14; 4:5). Another segment of traditional station code material appears here in the household rules. It is a two-part instruction with the directives in 2:2-10 followed by teaching on the

believers' ability to fulfill them (vv. 11-14). The categories depart from the conventional order of husband/wife, parent/children, master/slave (masters are actually omitted completely here). The apologetic purpose for including the material is evident (2:5, 8, 10). The author wishes to avoid criticism of the community by outsiders, and so the conventional social expectations of the larger society are promoted (see 1 Tim 2:2). For sound teaching see 1:9 and 1 Tim 1:10.

2–3. *older men . . . older women . . . slanderers, enslaved to drinking, teachers of good:* Older men here are not the community officials, but a household class (compare 1 Tim 5:1). The virtues of sobriety (see 1:7), soundness (see 1:9), faith and love (see 1 Tim 1:14), and steadfastness (see 2 Tim 4:4) are commonly advanced throughout the letters. The charge to older women to maintain appropriate conduct resembles that to women at 1 Tim 2:9-10. Religious claims and proper conduct ought to coincide (and see 1:9). Theodore of Mopsuestia, *Commentary on Titus*, explains that these women are elders in age only and not, as some claimed at his time, officeholders analogous to male presbyters. See the Notes on "devil" (*diabolos*) at 1 Tim 3:11 and 2 Tim 3:3. At 2 Timothy 3:3, 8, the qualifications for overseers and assistants include sobriety. This accords with the repeated rejection of *epithymia* ("unbridled passion," 2:12, and see 2 Tim 4:3). Excessive drinking among women is a common Greco-Roman concern in itself and for its deleterious effects on virtue and practice (Dionysius of Halicarnassus, *Ant. Rom.* II 25,6; Plautus, *Curc.* I/1, 75-81; Valerius Maximus, VI 3,9). They teach, but apparently teach other women and at home, which is the woman's sphere. Thus they do not contravene the prohibition against women teaching at 1 Tim 2:12.

4. *younger women . . . loving of their husbands and of their children:* The attention to younger women, which flows from the teaching responsibility of older women, breaks the ordinary household role pattern of superior/subordinate. Love for husbands (for such love as a common social value see Plutarch, *Mor.* 141F-142B; Pseudo-Plutarch, *Vit. Hom.* B 185) and children, obedience to husbands, and good homemaking are among the domestic virtues the letter promotes among the women members of the church (see 1 Tim 2:9-15 and 5:4-16).

5. *to be modest:* The virtue of self-control, commonly encouraged among both men and women, has diverse expression according to gender status and sphere of activity. Thus young women are to be "modest" (*sōphronas;* for this virtue, in conjunction with others in the list here, see Philo, *Rewards* 139) and "pure" (*hagnas*), as befits their shameful status, which is lived out "in subjection" (*hypotassomenas*) to their husbands and within the confines of the home, the private sphere proper to women (see 1 Tim 2:9-15 and Philo, *Spec. Leg.* III 169; Columella, XII Pr 2-5; Plutarch, *Mor.* 139C, 142C-D, where he adds that the women will be silent at home). The tendency of women to go from house to house is noted at *Gen. Rab.* 18 (12b) and 45 (28c), and at *Gen. Rab.* 8 (6d) husbands are urged to restrict women from the public thoroughfares lest they stumble.

lest the word of God be defamed: The message of God is that preached by Paul (see 1:3) and his associates (for Titus see 2:7-8). See 1 Tim 6:1 for protecting the name of God.

6–7. *encourage younger men to be self-controlled . . . show yourself to be a model:* In their status of honor the young men cultivate their self-control in the public sphere. Titus, a model for them, manifests dignity and teaches. The latter is a public, male function (1 Tim 2:12). He does this with integrity and soundness that is above reproach, which would be dishonorable and shameful. Men also expect the submissiveness of their wives.

8. *the opposing side might be put to shame:* The reason for the exhortation to young men and women is the same here and at v. 5 in that it aims to preserve the church's reputation in the larger society. It is different, however, in that the reason given for Titus and the young men's upright activity includes the shaming of the opponent, a technique of gaining greater honor for the victor in the struggle (compare Matt 22:15-22; Mark 12:13-34; Luke 7:36-50; 2 Corinthians 10–12). This reflects the male concern for the status of honor.

9. *Encourage slaves to obey:* See 1 Tim 6:1, but, unlike the latter, the exhortation here does not distinguish between masters who are believers and those who are not.

9–10. *to give satisfaction, not being obstinate, nor pilfering:* The lack of cooperation and dishonesty of slaves in antiquity, satirized by Plautus and Menander, was a commonplace opinion at the time (see also Plato, *Leg.* 6.776b-8a; Seneca, *Tranq.* 85.8; Phlm 11).

showing complete good faith, so that they might adorn the teaching of our savior God: Once again actions support or demonstrate the authenticity of the teaching (1:9). Public manifestation functions to demonstrate the unfolding of God's plan (1:3), the virtues and good deeds of the Christian life (2:7), and also the error of the opponents (1:9, and see 2 Tim 1:10; 1 Tim 5:20, 24). In addition to not giving cause for a bad public opinion, the slaves, and probably others in the community, can also make Christian teaching attractive, a missionary function. See 1 Tim 2:3 for the title "savior" applied to God. Christ Jesus, savior (v. 13) and redeemer (v. 14), clearly functions as the agent of God's plan of salvation (1:2; 3:6). Both thus bear the title "savior."

11. *The salvific favor:* Second Timothy 1:9-10 explains that the favor of God was bestowed in Christ Jesus and became manifest through Christ Jesus' human life and saving work (compare Luke 2:40; 4:22 and John 1:17; Acts 20:24; Rom 5:15; 1 Cor 1:4). This passage is not as clear, but the hymn at 3:4-7 presents the same soteriological teaching. The favor of God effects the conversion (v. 12, *paideuousai*, "teaching"; v. 14, *lytrosetai*, "purify") from vice to virtue and makes Christians capable (v. 14, *katharisei*, "cleanse") of performing good deeds. The ideas in Titus expand Paul's declaration at 2 Cor 9:5 and move it in a more general soteriological direction. God's historical manifestation is noted at 2 Macc 3:30 and *3 Macc.* 6:9.

you see: The author provides the basis for confidence that the household members will be able to live virtuously, i.e., their training in piety by Jesus Christ.

has appeared to all people: Universal salvation holds a prominent place in the doctrine of the PE (see 1 Tim 2:4). This Gentile Christian and Pauline principle stands opposed to the views of the circumcisionists (1:10), at least as they worked out the practical details of salvation (with restriction of salvation to those who follow specific regulations, as in Gal 3:2-5).

12. *instructing us . . . to lead a life of self-control, righteousness and piety in the present age:* The doctrinal aspect of Christianity, characteristically emphasized in 1 and 2 Timothy, retains its centrality in Titus as well (see 2 Tim 3:7, 10). See the Note on righteousness at 1 Tim 1:9. Contrary to those here caught up with "worldly passions" (*kosmikas epithymias*), to Demas (2 Tim 4:10), enamored of the present age, and to the rich in the present (1 Tim 6:17) who place shortsighted hope in riches, Titus, consistent with the other PE (see 1 Tim 4:8), looks to the present in anticipation of the end-time (*prosdechomenoi tēn . . . elpida*, "in expectation of the . . . hope," v. 13, and *eusebeian ep'elpidi zoēs aiōniou*, "piety based on hope of eternal life," 1:1-2). See Phil 3:20-21 and Col 3:1-4. Diogenes Laertius, VI 5, refers to piety and righteousness as prerequisites for immortality.

    by rejecting impiety and worldly passions: Some choice is involved in reaction to the appearance of divine favor. The wayward make a wrong choice by rejecting truth (1 Tim 5:8), apostate teachers reject the power that belief brings (2 Tim 3:5), people of unclean conscience deny their faith claims by their deeds (Titus 1:16), and they endanger their salvation by provoking Jesus' ultimate denial of them (2 Tim 2:12). Here the denial goes in the other direction. The virtue opposite to "impiety" (*asebeia*), expressed in the adverb "piously" (*eusebōs*), characterizes the Christian way of life (see 1:1; 1 Tim 2:4). The sober PE consistently look down on unbridled passion (see 2 Tim 2:22; 4:3). The juxtaposition of the words "unbridled passions" (*epithymias*) and "with self-control" (*sōphronōs*) expresses the opposing alternatives in the PE.

13. *in expectation of the blessed hope and appearance of the glory of the great God:* End-time expectation here, like the expressions at Phil 3:20; 1 Cor 1:7; 1 Thess 1:10, carries forward the theme found in the other PE (see 1 Tim 4:1; 6:14; 2 Tim 4:1). The hope at 1:2 is for eternal life. See references to the end-time appearance of Jesus at 1 Tim 6:15; 2 Tim 4:1, 8. At 2 Tim 1:10 and Titus 3:4 the epiphany of Christ took place in his historical life and saving work. That was the first phase of a process to be completed at the second epiphany. Both appearances constitute saving help for humanity. The theophany tradition of the Hebrew Scriptures helps Luke describe the nativity of Jesus (2:9), and Paul uses it, but transfers it to Christ (2 Cor 4:3-6). The end-time expectation recorded at Mark 8:38; 13:26; Matt 16:27; 24:30; Luke 21:27 depicts Jesus coming in (his Father's) glory. Revelation 21:23 speaks of the glory of God in the heavenly Jerusalem. Titus hews more closely to the LXX tradition in speaking of the glory of the great God appearing at the end-time. Jesus' end-time appearance thus coincides with the manifestation of the glory of God. To take the passage's reference to the "great God" as designating only Jesus is more difficult. The application of the title "great God" appears nowhere else in the NT. Moreover, Jesus is named alongside God the Father in other parts of the PE, e.g., the letters' address formulas; 1 Tim 1:15-17; 2:5-6; 5:21; 6:14-16; 2 Tim 4:1; Titus 3:4-7. It is equally difficult to see in this verse a reference to a two-person appearance, that of Jesus Christ our savior and of the great God. In scriptural usage the glory of God will appear,

but not God himself. Moreover, does glory belong both to God and to Jesus Christ?

14. *who gave himself up for us:* The credal formula resembles that at Gal 1:4; 2:20; Eph 5:2, 25. The formula also recalls the credal summary at 1 Tim 2:6 (and compare Matt 20:28; Mark 10:45). The formula in Mark incorporates the word for redemption, which is mentioned in the purpose clause here. The formula thus goes back to the christology of the early Christian tradition. As an alternative expression at Rom 8:32 (compare Rom 4:25), Paul says that God handed Jesus over for us all. Titus, following the Synoptic and one Pauline tradition, emphasizes the initiative of Jesus Christ in his redemptive death as the mediator who came to save (see 1 Tim 1:15; 2:5-6). The first person plural pronoun primarily refers to the believers who have accepted salvation (3:3-7; 1 Tim 1:12-16), but ultimately it includes all people, whom God wants to be saved (see 2:11).

that he might deliver us from all lawlessness and cleanse for himself a precious people: See 1 Tim 2:6, which uses the idea of "redemption" (*antilytron*). The verse recalls Ps 130:8 LXX (and compare 1 Pet 1:18). First Peter uses the word in connection with payment of a ransom (not gold or silver but Jesus Christ's blood, and see Heb 9:12). Titus, like the psalm, speaks more generally of deliverance, as do the disciples on the way to Emmaus (Luke 24:21, and see 1:68; 2:38). First Timothy 1:8-11 introduces the dispute with false teachers over the application of the Law. The righteous, who live a life of true piety, will not engage in vice but will follow God's commands (1:3, and contrast *apeitheis*, "disobedient" 1:16). Their actions will be in accord with sound teaching (1:8-9; 2:7). In fact, good deeds are the hallmark of the faithful Christian here (and see 2:7; 3:8, 14; 1 Tim 6:18; 5:10). Compare the disobedience and defiled supporters of human law whose works prove their faithlessness (1:16). See "clean" (*kathara*) and the Note on 1:15. The deliverance and cleansing, associated with the death of Jesus, are linked with baptism in Eph 5:25-26. The meaning "precious" is based on the use of the word in the LXX for the Hebrew *segullah* (see Ps 134:4; Eccl 2:8), which means not just "one's own" but also "heaped up." The word seems to carry the connotation of a rich, prized possession. First Peter 2:9 uses *peripoiēsin* to indicate simple possession. The LXX uses the phrase found in Titus at Exod 19:5; 23:22; Deut 7:6; 14:2; 26:18. As a qualification for being considered God's people they must keep God's commandments (see Exod 19:5; Deut 7:6; 14:2; 26:18, and also Ezek 37:23). This accounts for the final phrase of the verse, *zēlotēn kalōn ergōn*, "eager for good deeds" (a similar ideal can be found in Plutarch, *Ti. C. Gracch.* 41, 4, presented as the Romans' incarnation of the virtue of the Gracchi), and see "deliver us from all lawlessness" above.

Paul at Rom 15:10 cites Deut 32:42 LXX, which distinguishes Gentile peoples from God's people. The word "people" (*laos*), which came to designate Israel in the LXX, was transferred to the church at Acts 15:14. Peter declares that God has acquired a people from among the Gentiles. Paul also refers to the church as *laos* at 2 Cor 6:16 (citing Ezek 37:27) and Rom 9:25 (citing Hos 2:25).

15. *Declare these things . . . insistence:* The content of "these things" (*tauta*) includes both the community rules and the core apostolic "preaching" (*kērygma*) of Jesus' redemptive death and its effects. The author repeats the command "declare"

(*lalei*) from 2:1 at the start of the section and adds two more commands, "exhort" (*parakalei*) and "correct" (*elenche*). Thus he demarcates the conclusion of the section and diversifies Titus' teaching activity to include exhortation and correction. A similar formula at 1 Tim 6:2 concludes the household code section that started at 1 Tim 5:1. Also compare 2 Tim 4:2, which gives the general charge to Timothy. Obedience to God's command is a hallmark of Paul in the PE (1:3 and 1 Tim 1:1, and compare Rom 16:26). In the Pauline epistles (Phlm 8; 1 Cor 7:6; 2 Cor 8:8) Paul refers to apostolic commands with the word "insistence" (*epitagē*). Titus, like the other PE, urges the addressee to be directive and even confrontational (*elenchein*, "correct," 1 Tim 5:20; *epitiman*, "rebuke," 2 Tim 4:2; Titus 1:9, 13; 2:15; *epistomizein*, "gag," Titus 1:11; *paideuein*, "discipline," 1 Tim 1:20; 2 Tim 2:25; Titus 2:12; *parangellein*, "instruct," 1 Tim 1:3; 4:11; 5:7; 6:13, 17). The teaching and correction here have the added emphasis of an apostolic command, through Paul's apostolic emissary.

Interpretation

By way of contrast to opponents, Titus is to offer sound teaching. Personal qualities, in contrast to those of the false teachers and the caricatured Cretans, are outlined in the Household Code of chapter 2, which includes Titus in the exhortation (vv. 7-8). Self-possession, feminine domesticity, good works, and obedience receive stress in view of the good reputation of the community and its teaching (vv. 5, 8, 10). The exhortation and instruction receive confirmation from the theological and christological summary, which stresses conversion from vice to a life of piety and good works (vv. 11-14). The section ends with a reiteration of Titus' task of exhortation and admonition (v. 15) and of the need to rise above contempt (v. 15).

The sound teaching takes shape in this section in terms of instructions in virtue and virtuous behavior directed to the several members of the household (vv. 2-10). In addition to commonplace virtues, specifically Christian ones such as "faith" (*pistis*) and "love" (*agapē*) are to be urged on older men (at 1:2 and here "steadfastness" [*hypomonē*] seems to have replaced "hope" [*elpis*] in the usual trilogy of Christian virtues). Soundness of faith (v. 2) continues to be a concern (see 1:9, 13). Older women, in addition to watching their general behavior, avoiding gossip, and practicing temperance (and compare 1:7), are to be good teachers (compare 1:9). But the audience of their teaching is limited to young women and only within the realm of approved domesticity.

Origen, *Homilies on Leviticus* 7.4 (FC 83:123), refers to Titus when he declares that servants of the Lord must be sober, practice fasting, and be vigilant at all times for, he goes on to say, "sobriety is the mother of virtues, drunkenness the mother of vices." Ascetical practice for the ordinary faithful in the Catholic Church has resisted the extreme of total abstinence from alcoholic beverages. The PE, while critical of excessive drinking, even recommend the moderate enjoyment of alcohol, if only for its medicinal advantages (1 Tim 5:23). It seems that drunkenness, which the letters condemn, falls into the category of uncontrollable behavior, akin to harmful desires (1 Tim 6:9), youthful passions (2 Tim 2:22), feminine desires (2 Tim 3:6), desires of the wayward (2 Tim 4:3), worldly desires as opposed to temperance (Titus 2:12), and enslaving desires and pleasures (Titus 3:3). Willful obsessive behavior and the deliberate surrender of oneself to addictions are what the letters want their addressees and, through them, the readership to avoid.

The younger women (vv. 4-5) are to be taught by the older women to be reasonable as regards loving their husbands and children as well as in exhibiting virtue and right action, particularly obedience to their husbands. In the sensitive area of young wives' behavior, regard for their husbands is spelled out twice, and respect for the entire word of God is seen to be at risk through their attitudes and practices.

Though less urgent a problem, young men, too, must be urged to be reasonable. Titus, a young man himself, must offer them an example of good behavior with respect to teaching impeccability, dignity, and sound speech above criticism. Once again, while sound and impeccable teaching are noted here twice (*logos*, "sound preaching," and, "teaching," *didaskalia*), it is attitude and action that fill out the instruction and the example. As with younger women, an eye on opponents' criticism of the church (v. 8, *peri hēmōn*, "about us") provides the rationale for the instruction.

Slaves also bear their share of responsibility. How they behave in obedience to their masters redounds to the evaluation of the church's teaching. Faith here (v. 10) refers not to belief alone but includes overall fidelity in their station. The duties of masters toward their slaves receive no mention here or in 1 Tim 6:1-2. This contrasts with the household codes in Eph 6:5-9; Col 3:22–4:1, and Philemon, although 1 Pet 2:18-25 echoes the PE. Similarly, the rules for women here enforce the young and older wives' submission, but husbands' responsibilities toward their wives are not addressed. Compare 1 Tim 5:3-16, where the women's domestic roles are stressed but no corresponding male duties find mention. It appears that the aim of finding respectability in the larger society was to be achieved through the sacrifice of a fuller life for women and slaves.

Just as believing slaves affect the attitude of unbelieving masters toward Christian belief, so too all the other household classes are presumably interacting not just with unbelievers who are observing them from other households, but within their own households as well. Domestic virtue and stability of character are telling indicators of the value of Christian teachings to nonbelieving spouses, parents, offspring, and siblings. The young are singled out, Titus among them, to demonstrate that the new way of belief does not disrupt traditional values and longstanding social conventions.

The second part of this section offers support for the exhortation in Christian belief. Speaking at v. 11 of Jesus as the appearance of the universally applicable saving grace of God, the letter refers to the instruction derived from him. That instruction is a moral lesson to avoid worldly passion and lead pious lives (v. 12) . The spiritual ability to do this derives from Jesus' death, which resulted in redemption from waywardness and a fresh ability to strive for good works (vv. 13-14). Good works, the object of the instruction by revealed grace, i.e., Jesus, are the practical outcome of Jesus' redeeming death and the demonstration of the action of grace.

Titus 2:12-13 declares that the Christian life is lived in expectation of the hoped-for appearance of the glory of God and the savior Jesus Christ. This does not leave Christians open to the criticism that they are waiting for relief and restoration only at the end-time and through the intervention of God at the *parousia*. Rather, Titus 2:14 (and see the other admonitions to do good works at 1 Tim 2:10; 3:1; 5:10; 5:25; 6:18; 2 Tim 1:19; 2:21; 3:17; 4:5; Titus 1:16; 2:7; 3:1, 5, 8) expects the Christian community members, renewed in baptism, not just to do what is good but to be eager to act.

While Jewish dietary regulations are superseded (1:15), religious law and lawlessness are still viable categories (2:14). The Christian community is elect and special (v. 14; compare "us" at 2:8 and "our savior," "our God" at 2:10, 13), although with a universal message (2:11 "to all people"). The threefold temporal dimension of Christian belief looks to the past (2:11, 14: the revelation in Jesus of the prior saving plan of God in the death of Jesus), the present (2:12: instruction in the life of piety in this age), and the future (2:13: the expectation of another appearance of Jesus Christ; compare 1:13).

The section concludes with a brief reiteration of the basic charge to teach, exhort, and criticize (2:15). The additional command to Titus not to let anyone look down on him echoes the concern over giving occasion for criticism expressed to him at 2:8 and to community members at 2:5 and 10 (and compare "blameless" at 1:6, 7).

For Reference and Further Study

Balch, David L., and Carolyn Osiek. *Families in the New Testament World: Households and House Churches*. Louisville: Westminster John Knox, 1997, 120–23, 184–85, 219–20.

Bartchy, S. Scott. "Slavery (Greco-Roman)." *ABD* 6:75–73.

Borse, Udo. *1. und 2. Timotheusbrief*, 120–21.

Dewey, Joanna. "Titus," in Carol A. Newsom and Sharon H. Ringe, eds., *The Women's Bible Commentary*. Expanded ed. Louisville: Westminster John Knox, 1998, 452.

Donelson, Lewis R. "The Structure of the Ethical Argument in the Pastorals," *BTB* 18 (1988) 108–13.

Fiore, Benjamin. "The Hortatory Function of Paul's Boasting," *Proceedings of the EGL and MWBS* 5 (1985) 39–46.

Gayer, Roland. *Die Stellung des Sklaven in den paulinischen Gemeinden und bei Paulus*. Bern and Frankfurt: Peter Lang, 1976.

Hannah, Jack. "The Ignatian Long Recension and the Household Rules in the Pastoral Epistles," *Proceedings of the EGL and MWBS* 4 (1984) 153–65.

Mott, Stephen Charles. "Greek Ethics and Christian Conversion: The Philonic Background of Titus II 10-14 and II 3-7," *NovT* 20 (1978) 22–48.

Padgett, Alan. "The Pauline Rationale for Submission; Biblical Feminism and the *hina* Clauses of Titus 2:1-10," *EvQ* 59 (1987) 39–52.

Schrage, Wolfgang. "Zur Ethik der neutestamentlichen Haustafeln," *NTS* 22 (1974) 1–22.

Towner, Philip H. *The Goal of Our Instruction: The Structure of Theology and Ethics in the Pastoral Epistles*. JSNTSup 34. Sheffield: Sheffield Academic Press, 1989, 196.

Turner, Nigel. "Deliverance; redeemer; people of God," in idem, ed., *Christian Words*. Edinburgh: T&T Clark, 1980, 105–107, 322–24.

Walker, William O. Jr. "The 'Theology of Woman's Place' and the 'Paulinist' Tradition," *Semeia* 28 (1983) 101–12.

Weiser, Alfons. "Titus 2 als Gemeindeparänese," in Rudolf Schnackenburg, ed., *Neues Testament und Ethik*. Freiburg: Herder, 1989, 397–414.

4. *Community Profile: Virtuous, Made Righteous, Engaged in Good Works* (3:1-11)

1. Remind them to submit to officials and authorities, to be obedient, to be ready for every good activity, 2. to slander no one, to be peaceable, gentle, exhibiting total consideration toward all people. 3. For once we, we too, were foolish, disobedient, deceived, enslaved to unbridled desires and pleasures of all sorts, spending our lives in wickedness and envy, hateful, detesting one another.

4. Yes, when the generosity and benevolent kindness
  of our savior God appeared,
5. not in consequence of works in righteousness
  we ourselves did,
 but rather on the basis of his mercy,
  He saved us through the washing of rebirth
 and of renewal by the Holy Spirit,
  6. which he poured out on us richly
 through Jesus Christ, our savior.
  7. This was so that, as a result of being rendered righteous by His favor, we might become heirs in accordance with hope of eternal life.

8. The saying is trustworthy, and with regard to these matters it is my decision that you maintain strongly that those who have come to believe in God

take care to engage in good works. These are praiseworthy and beneficial for people. 9. Yes, avoid stupid controversies, genealogies, quarrels, disputes over the law, for they are useless and futile. 10. Dismiss a factious person after one and then another warning, 11. with awareness that a person like this is perverted and goes on sinning under self-condemnation.

Notes

1. *Remind them to submit to officials and authorities, to be obedient:* The third part of the letter's body is a paraenetic instruction. Reminder of generally accepted teaching here resembles the paraenesis in 2 Timothy (see 1:6; 2:8, 14). Obedience emerges as a prime concern in this letter where household rules are conveyed (see 2:5, 9 and 1 Tim 2:11; 3:4, and compare 1 Tim 2:1-2). Compare the attitude toward civic authority at Rom 13:1-7 and 1 Pet 2:13-17. See also Sir 4:27. The exhortation to civil obedience is standard fare in this paraenesis. The exhortation shares the aim of the domestic rules to help the church avoid suspicion and criticism for disrupting the social order. An indirect missionary motive might be at work here as well. The community's obedience would set the faithful apart from the opponents, characterized as disobedient at 1:16.

   to be ready for every good activity: See 2:14, "lawlessness" (*anomias*) and "precious" (*periousion*), and also 1:1, "piety" (*eusebeian*). Compare 2 Tim 2:21. At Luke 1:17 the angel Gabriel describes the work of John the Baptizer, the Messianic precursor, as preparing the people for the Lord's coming. Ephesians 2:20 describes the faithful as created for good works prepared by God in advance to be done by them. Romans 9:23 uses the image of vessels and describes them as prepared by God. That image is used at 2 Tim 2:20-21 and declares readiness for every good work. The preparation is thus not merely a human effort, just as the works are not mere works of kindness with a human focus only.

2. *to slander no one, to be peaceable, gentle, exhibiting total consideration toward all people:* Refraining from slander distinguishes the faithful from the end-time (= present) apostates and opponents (1 Tim 1:20; 6:4; 2 Tim 3:2). Paul himself was led from being a slanderer and sinner to one saved and serving the Gospel (1 Tim 1:3). The virtuous qualities echo those expected of a bishop at 1:7-8. At Rom 12:9-21; 13:8-10, and 1 Pet 2:17, Christian regard for "all people" accompanies the instructions about their obedience to civil authorities. The inclusiveness of the exhortation here reflects the PE's teaching about God's plan for universal salvation (see 2:11, 14, and compare "slander no one" *blasphēma mēden*). The good name that cordiality would gain for Christians would counter the accusation that they "hate the human race," a charge that arose from their withdrawal from public religious rituals. In service of the same end is the command for prayers for the well-being of the community. At the same time the congenial face of the believing community could serve to attract people to it.

   The letter offers two reasons for cultivating the life of virtue. First there is a contrast between what we once were and what conversion made us. Second, we ought to live the life into which we have been reborn. The latter point is developed in Eph 2:3-10; 4:17-24; 5:1-2. The instruction in Ephesians seems to express a pattern, perhaps a baptismal instruction, of which Titus has also made use.

3. *For once we, we too, were foolish . . . spending our lives in wickedness:* Some detect a parallelism in the first four terms of the list. Thus foolishness (see 1 Tim 6:9 and also 2 Tim 3:9; Paul's ignorance was converted to belief, 1 Tim 1:13) led to their being deceived (see 1 Tim 4:1; 2 Tim 3:13), while their disobedience (of God's law, see 1:16 and compare 2:14) resulted in their enslavement (compare 2:3 and Rom 1:29; 6:17-18) to passions and desires. The Greeks spoke of enslavement to passionate desires (Plato, *Phaedr.* 238e and *Ep.* 8, 354e). The negative view of irrational passion is found in Plutarch, *Virt. mor.* 10 (2.449D). The last four terms in the list describe a life characterized by hostility that is the opposite of the gentleness urged at v. 2. Cordiality to all stands over against envy and hatred. For commonplace expressions of the need to resist unbridled passions see Isocrates, *Or.* 2, 29; Pseudo-Isocrates, *Or.* 1, 21; Plato, *Phaedr* 238d-239a; Aristotle, *Eth. Nic.* X I, 1172a27-33; Plutarch, *Pelopidas* 3, 1-2; Diogenes Laertius, VI 66; Cicero, *Amic.* 82; *Verr.* II 1, 58; Seneca, *Ep.* 39, 5-6; Sallust, *Bell. Cat.* 52, 21-23; Quintilian, *Inst.* XII 2,20-21.

4. *Yes, when the generosity:* The letter makes use of a trustworthy saying (v. 8) for the bulk of the reason for carrying out the ethical instruction in vv. 1 and 2. The saying begins at v. 4. Verse 3 is tied closely to vv. 1 and 2 and with discussions of virtue and vice throughout the PE, as the preceding discussion has shown. It is also a separate sentence, and the previous trustworthy sayings all had just one sentence. It serves as an introduction to the saying in vv. 4-7, with "once" (*pote*) looking ahead to "when" (*hote*). The saying goes off in a theological direction, whereas a close sequel to v. 3 would more likely describe current virtues. The uncial codex Sinaiticus separates vv. 4-7 from the preceding verses.

The saying also continues through v. 7. The one sentence constitutes a continuous thought. To remove v. 7, as some commentators do, cuts the saying off from the declaration of its trustworthiness. Verses 4-5a are also appropriate to the baptismal setting and its theological interpretation. "Yes" (*de*) is a connective added by the author that links the saying to the preceding verse. This verse (and compare Rom 2:4; 11:22; Eph 2:7) ties God's "generosity" (*chrēstotēs*) to God's saving action toward humans.

and benevolent kindness of our savior God appeared: The word "benevolent kindness" (*philanthropia*) is used only here of God and appears again only at Acts 28:2 in the NT. This uniqueness constitutes another argument for considering the verse as part of the original saying. The word appears with "generosity" (*chrēstotēs*) at Diodorus Siculus, 34 and 35 *fr.*; Esth 8:12; Plutarch, *Aristides* 27.7; Themistius, *Or.* 1, 8a-c; Philo, *Spec. Leg.* 2.141; Josephus, *Ant.* 10.164; *Diogn.* 9.2, to describe a single attribute of rulers. For the same quality attributed to God see Plutarch, *Mor.* 780F-781A; Artemidorus, IV 22. The saying uses a secular concept to describe the divine king. The salvific benevolence is God's response to the envy and hate of humans (v. 3). The appearance that brings salvation finds expression at 1:3 and also 2:11. Christ Jesus is the embodied presence of God's favor. Both at 2:11 and here, the divine favor brings salvation. The universality of that salvific favor at 2:11, a common theme in the PE and thus a presupposed understanding behind the word here, contrasts with the envy and hatred that separate humans from each other (v. 3). The appearance of God's favor, as clarified at 2 Tim 1:9-10, refers to the first coming of Jesus, his historical life and saving death (John 1:14, 16-17; Eph 2:7). The word also refers to the appearance of personal saving grace in the life of believers, washed and renewed by the Holy Spirit (2 Tim 1:10 mentions the individual's salvation through the Gospel preaching, and see Titus 1:2-3). So salvation, which was in God's eternal plan as his characteristic saving kindness, became historically manifest in the life of Christ Jesus and individually in the believer through the Gospel and the believer's response to it.

5. *not in consequence of works in righteousness we ourselves did:* See 2 Tim 1:9. The divine initiative, safeguarded here, stands at the heart of Pauline teaching about works and righteousness (Rom 3:27-28; 4:2-6; 9:12; Gal 2:16; Eph 2:8-9), although the phrase "works in righteousness" (*ergōn . . . en dikaiosynę̄*) is not Pauline. The works were considered as done in accordance with God's law (see 1 Tim 1:9 and Titus 2:14), although the expression "works in righteousness" rather than "works of the law" (more common to Paul) expands the reference to include good deeds of Gentiles, thus including Titus and the Cretans. The saying does not pass judgment on whether the deeds were righteous or not, but denies the presumptive assertion that they were and that they therefore constitute a claim to salvation. The use of the pronoun "we" (*hēmeis*) adds emphasis to the subject, since it is already known from the verb ending.

on the basis of his mercy he saved us: The possessive pronoun is in the emphatic position (BDF 284.3) and strongly contrasts with the emphatic "we" (*hēmeis*) in the preceding strophe. See 1 Tim 1:1 and compare 2 Tim 1:2, 16, 18. Mercy is a divine quality and gift, exercised by Christ Jesus toward Paul (1 Tim 1:13). God is the agent throughout. God's saving benevolence appeared (v. 4), God saved (v. 5) and poured out (v. 6) the Holy Spirit, and God's favor justified and made the believers heirs (v. 7). See Eph 2:3-5, where that letter describes a similar progression of humans from subjection to sinful impulses to new life in Christ through the merciful action of God. The baptismal context relates that letter and this saying (and see Rom 6:3-14). The aorist indicates that salvation was accomplished for us in a specific past action.

through the washing: The verb "you have been washed" (*apelousasthe*) at 1 Cor 6:11 describes the process of cleansing from immorality and being "justified" (*edikaiothēte*) in the name of Jesus Christ and in the Spirit of God. Acts 22:16 identifies the process of "washing" from sins (*apolousai*) with "baptism" (*baptisai*, and compare Eph 5:26 and Heb 10:22).

The action of the Holy Spirit in connection with baptism is commonplace (Eph 4:30; Acts 2:15-17; 10:47; Mark 1:8; John 3:5), although the relationship between the Spirit and the ritual has been a subject of controversy since the Reformation. Nonetheless, the Spirit's action in connection with the washing here suggests that the washing is baptismal. The same is the case with the mention of the three divine persons, God (v. 4), Holy Spirit (v. 5), Christ Jesus (v. 6), for baptism was done in their name (Matt 28:19). The saying refers to the initial, inner change in the believer that baptism symbolizes. The saying conveys fundamental beliefs in a terse formula suitable for a liturgical acclamation. God's pouring out the Holy Spirit is spoken of as already done in the past (aorist verbs, and see Joel 3:1-2 and Acts 2:17-18). However, only exaggerated literalism would demand a present tense to assert the connection of the outpouring with the ritual washing. The washing is the means of God's saving action, and it brings rebirth and renewal, of which the Holy Spirit is the agent. Jesus Christ mediated the outpouring of the Spirit, and all of this leads to the justification of the believer. The saving washing is thus a reference to baptism and the saying fits a baptismal setting and lays the ground for the sacramental understanding of the baptismal ritual. The meaning of the ritual process comes to expression in the phrase "the washing of rebirth and of renewal by the Holy Spirit" (*loutron palingenesias kai anakainōseōs pneumatos hagiou*).

rebirth and of renewal by the Holy Spirit: Only at Matt 19:28 does the word "rebirth" (*palingenesia*) appear again in the NT. This is another indication that the verse belongs to the saying. There the gospel refers to Jesus Christ's second coming and the new age he ushers in. Here the word describes the effects of the salvific cleansing that is a consequence of Jesus Christ's first coming, although it looks to eternal life in the age to come. The word relates to similar NT expressions of the idea of rebirth such as "to be born again" (1 Pet 1:3, *anagennēsas*, 23, *anagegennēmenoi*; John 3:3, 7, *gennēthenai anothen*); "to be born from God" (John 1:13; 1 John 5:1, *ek tou theou gennēthenai*). Paul at 2 Cor 5:17 speaks of the Christian believer as a "new creation."

Matthew 19:28 reflects the Stoic use of the term, where it refers to a periodic restoration of the world after its consumption by fire (Philo, *Eternity* 89; Marcus Aurelius, *Ant.* 11.1). The rebirth of souls (more like the use in Titus) is paralleled in Plutarch, *De esu.* 2.4 (2.998C) and Lucian, *Musc. laud.* 7. Cicero, *Att.* 6.6, finds his return from banishment to be a "rebirth" (*palingenesia*), signaling widespread use of the word. It is not used in the LXX. A word from the Greco-Roman context thus applies to the Christian reality of an inner transformation. Romans 12:2 marks the only other NT use of the word "renewal" (*anakainōsis*). There Paul encourages an inner transformation, away from the present age and toward doing what pleases God. That usage, like the verbal use at 2 Cor 4:16 and Col 3:10, speaks of gradual inner renewal (and compare Heb 6:6). Romans 12:12 and Col 3:9-10 detail both a moral and a noetic renewal. The passage in Titus contrasts the life of renewal with the foolish and immoral life that preceded it (v. 3). The noun is parallel with "rebirth" (*palingenesias*) as descriptive of the purpose of the washing (*BDF* 166). The absence of a second preposition recommends this interpretation. The renewal, like the rebirth, characterizes the initial transformation, although progressive continuation is also implied.

A subjective genitive indicates that the Holy Spirit effects both the renewal and the rebirth. The Spirit's indwelling (2 Tim 1:14, and see Acts 2:33) enables the faithful to live pure lives as the new creation.

6. *which he poured out on us through Jesus Christ, our savior:* "Pour out" (*ekcheō*) is not a Pauline word and its use in Acts by Luke is influenced by Joel. The antecedent of the relative pronoun is the Holy Spirit rather than the washing. The

genitive is by attraction to the case of the antecedent. While it makes sense to think of God pouring out the bath, the figure of pouring is common for the Holy Spirit (see Acts 2:17, 18, 33, and Joel 2:28) and the adverb "richly" (*plousiōs*) is more appropriate to the Holy Spirit. The pouring is a specific, completed action in the past (aorist tense). The pouring here, despite the Pentecost reminiscences (Acts 2:33), has a personal direction. The occasion of the pouring is the same as that of the saving act of God and is connected with the washing. All of these cause a change in "us." Jesus' involvement in the transmission of the Spirit echoes Acts 2:33. See 2 Tim 1:10. As a result, Jesus Christ is our savior, in a personal relationship of union.

7. *being rendered righteous by his favor:* The saying hews closely to the Pauline explanation of justification as a divine favor that has results both present (*esōsen*, "he saved," an action completed in the past) and future (*klēronomoi . . . zoēs aiōniou*, "heirs of eternal life"). In addition to having immoral and disobedient deeds (v. 3) forgiven, and the sinner declared righteous, the believer is also transformed within by the Holy Spirit (the two effects are mentioned by Paul at 1 Cor 6:11). The pronoun "his" (*ekeinou*) refers to God, although Jesus Christ is involved in the saving work as well (v. 6). See 2 Tim 1:9, and compare Rom 3:24.

   we might become heirs in accordance with hope of eternal life: The purpose stems from God's saving act (*esōsen*, "he saved"), which effected the righteousness of the believers. The idea of the heir is rooted in the promise of the possession of land that originated with the patriarchs, especially Abraham (Deut 6:10; Gen 15:7). The promise of a permanent possession was expanded in an eschatological direction. During the exile, the hope arose of regaining possession of Israel forever (Isa 60:21). This ended with a transfer of the inheritance to the end of days, when it would be bestowed (Dan 12:13 LXX), but only on the righteous (Ps 37:9, 11, and *1 Enoch* 39:8; 71:16). The inheritance thus came to be conceived in spiritualized terms (Deut 10:9; Lam 3:24; Ps 16:5; *1 Enoch* 40:9). Paul uses the image of an inheritance for the promise that Jesus Christ mediates to the faithful (Gal 3:29; 4:7; Rom 8:17). Hebrews 6:12, 17 speaks of inheriting what is promised, in connection with the hope the believers have before them (and see 9:15, eternal inheritance; 1:14, salvation as the inheritance). Titus clearly stands in this tradition when it speaks of those justified as heirs in connection with the hope of eternal life. See 1:2 for a reference to such hope, and see also 2:13, where the hope is explicitly tied to the end-time appearance of Jesus Christ. While the attention here is on the appearance of God's kindness in the historical existence of Jesus Christ and at the Holy Spirit's coming to the individual believer, the ultimate outlook is toward eternal life and the second appearance of Christ Jesus.

8. *The saying is trustworthy:* The saying is found in vv. 4-7, which the author includes in order to provide motivation for the paraenesis at vv. 1 and 2.

   with regard to these matters it is my decision: The demonstrative pronoun "these matters" (*toutōn*) includes the saying as well as the paraenesis and recollection of disobedience and immorality (vv. 1-3), all of which together constitute the paraenetic unit. See the Note on "it is my decision" (*boulomai*) at 1 Tim 2:8.

those who have come to believe take care to engage in good works: Throughout the letters faith has found a complement in action, as it does here (see 1:16; 2:14; 1 Tim 1:14; 5:10; 6:17-18). In the life of Christian piety, good deeds express the reaction to faith (1 Tim 2:4). Unlike the faithful sayings in the PE at 1 Tim 1:15 and 4:9, which recommend full acceptance, this one ends with a call to action, in keeping with the paraenetic setting. The paraenesis began with a call to obedience and good works in the practice of virtue and avoidance of vice. That is repeated here.

beneficial for people: The benefit to other people contrasts directly with pre-conversion envy and hatred (v. 3) and it parallels the divine, benevolent kindness in the saying (v. 4). The universality suggested here reiterates v. 2, which in turn recalls the universal salvation offered by God.

9. *Yes, avoid stupid controversies, genealogies, quarrels, disputes over the law:* The final exhortation, directed to Titus, concerns his manner of dealing with argumentative opponents. The letter lays down as policy here the avoidance of conflict, which has been urged throughout the PE (see 2 Tim 3:5, and compare Rom 16:17; 1 Cor 5:9, 11; 2 Thess 3:6, 14; Matt 18:17). Exasperation with protracted (and "useless," *anōpheleis*) debates and, perhaps, disdain of the truthful position in favor of alternative ("futile," *mataioi*) viewpoints combine to recommend avoiding and finally dismissing dissenters. See 2 Tim 2:23 (*zētēseis . . . machas*, "controversies . . . quarrels," and compare 1 Tim 1:4, *ekzētēseis*, "speculations"). See 1 Tim 1:4 and the Note there; in that passage these disputes were contrasted with the "divine order" (*oikonomia*), which the PE profess to know and uphold (2 Tim 1:9, *prothesis*, "design"; 1 Tim 2:4, *thelei*, "he wishes," and compare Titus 2:11, *epephanē hē charis*, "the favor appeared" and 3:4, *hē chrēstotēs kai hē philanthropia epephanē*, "the generosity and benevolent kindness appeared"). The genealogies, if they be of lines of teachers and their tradition, pale before the primary line of "tradition" (*parathēkē*, 1 Tim 6:20; 2 Tim 1:12, 14) in the PE from God through Christ Jesus to Paul and his emissaries Timothy and Titus and to those they designate as officers and teachers (2 Tim 2:2). See 1 Tim 6:4 (*zētēseis . . . logomachias . . . eris*, "investigations . . . disputes over words . . . discord"). The circumcisionist position and religious regulations have already been critiqued at 1:13-16, particularly regarding purity (see 1 Tim 1:7-11 and 4:1-5). The controversies seem to be over theories that are proven from the Law or Scriptures.

10. *Dismiss a factious person after one and then another warning:* Factionalism reflects the divisiveness and hatred of the former state of the believers (v. 3, and compare 1 Tim 6:4-5; also see Paul's opposition to factionalism at Gal 5:20; Rom 16:17-18; 1 Cor 11:18-19). The two warnings (*mian kai deuteran nouthesian*, "one and then another warning") are a variation on the accusation substantiated by two or three witnesses (1 Tim 5:20); the rule is based on Deut 17:6-7 and 19:15. The result of the process of proven and persistent misconduct is expulsion (Deut 17:7; Matt 18:17; 1 Tim 1:20). The neutral term that designated a school, doctrine, or religious party (Sadducees in Acts 5:17; Pharisees in Acts 15:5; Nazarenes in Acts 24:5, and Josephus *Bell.* 2.118; *Ant.* 7. 347, as well as secular authors Diodorus Siculus, 2.29.6; Diogenes Laertius, 1.18-19; Epictetus, *Diatr.* 2.19.20) later became derogatory for dissensions and divisions (already at 1 Cor 11:18-19).

Galatians 5:20 includes the noun "division" (*hairesis*) among the list of vices with "dissensions" (*dichostasiai*), " rivalry" (*eris*), "plots" (*eritheiai*), "envy" (*phthonos*), all of which threaten church unity. The later church maintains this understanding of *haireseis* as heretical groups or sects (Ign. *Eph.* 6.2; *Trall.* 6.1; Justin, *Apology* 1.26.33 and also 2 Pet 2:1). It is this sense that Titus conveys here. This type of warning, although sharp and unpalatable, includes a desire to help, with the hope of correction as its outcome (see Dio Chrysostom, *Or.* 32.27; Plutarch, *Adul. amic.* 70DE; *Inim. util.* 89B; Philodemus, *On Frank Speech fr.* 77, 84, 86,91 N), and so is unlike fault finding, abuse, or reviling. Paul uses it at 1 Cor 4:14 (and see his recommendation to the Ephesian elders at Acts 20:31) and urges his audience to engage in it (1 Thess 5:14; 2 Thess 3:15; Rom 15:14).

11. *a person like this is perverted and goes on sinning:* See 2 Tim 2:10. Wandering away from the truth is a characteristic of the false teachers. The public correction of sinning elders (1 Tim 5:20) looks to strengthening the community's resolve. While people in the communities at Ephesus and on Crete are charged with sin (1 Tim 1:9; 5:22, 24; 2 Tim 3:6), their forgiveness and salvation is God's desire (1 Tim 2:4) and Jesus Christ's work (1 Tim 1:15), of which Paul stands as a prime example (1 Tim 1:13, 16). Thus the apparently indifferent dismissal of the sinner here is more rhetorical than actual, as the "warning" (*nouthesia*) also indicates.

under self-condemnation: Christ Jesus is the end-time judge (2 Tim 4:1, 8). Nonetheless, Timothy (1 Tim 5:20) exercises judgment, as do Paul and, here, Titus. With the double warning, however, one could say the evildoers have brought judgment on themselves (compare John 3:18). The idea of judgment in the PE is often connected with Jesus Christ's *parousia* (1 Tim 5:24b; 6: 9; 2 Tim 2:12; 4:8).

Interpretation

A second paraenetic section flows from the summary exhortation to Titus in 2:15. The brief list of injunctions and virtues (3:1-2) leads to a statement recollecting the transformation experienced by the Christian community from a wayward life enslaved to evil passions and hostility (v. 3). The exhortation concludes with a renewed call to useful good works (v. 8), avoidance of useless controversy (v. 9), and suggestions for helpful admonition of a recalcitrant heretic (vv. 10-11). The letters' call to community members to perform good works can be understood as a way to demonstrate the profundity of their understanding of and commitment to the faith. In keeping with the preoccupation in the PE with the community's reputation before persons outside, good works might well serve as an evangelistic tool. The letter makes it clear later on (3:5) that works do not constitute a claim on God for salvation. Works thus flow out of the heart of the saved person; they do not lead to salvation.

Here at 3:1 commonplace, public virtues are at issue. Obedience to public officials, echoing the slaves' obedience to their masters (2:9), suggests that the readiness for good works is to be exercised in the larger community.

This is verified in the next verse (2) where the virtues of gentleness and humility are expected to be shown to all people. The community members are to show all humility to everyone (3:3, *endeiknymenous*, "showing"), just as the slaves are to show complete good faith (2:10, *endeiknymenous*). The hoped-for result of the slaves'exemplary conduct is to make the Christian teaching appear all the more decorous (*hina tēn didaskalian . . . kosmōsin*). The exemplary virtues of the community might be expected to achieve a similar effect, i.e., the opposite of the denigrating criticism (2:5, 8). In fact, it aims at more, i.e., at establishing a persuasive demonstration of Jesus' saving work. The conjunction "for" (3:3, *gar*) introduces the explanation of the call to demonstrate humility to all. A contrast is drawn between the believers' former life of ignorance, faithlessness, deception, passion, and alienation and the merciful outpouring of renewal and justifying grace by which Jesus saved them and gave them hope of eternal life (vv. 4-7). The description here spells out the instruction given in the appearance and saving death of Jesus Christ (2:11-14). Ultimately the effect of the deliverance and cleansing in Jesus is the creation of a people uniquely possessed by God and eager for good (2:14). The reiteration of the opening appeal to the believers to excel in good works ends by calling them good and useful for people (v. 8). Their usefulness is their demonstration of the saving work of Jesus and the Holy Spirit (3:5, 6), which is intended for all people (2:11). The demonstrative examples are designed to draw nonbelievers to the transforming faith.

Constitutions of the Holy Apostles 4.13 (ANF 7:436) relates the admonition about submitting to rulers and authorities to Paul's advice in Rom 13:1, 4, 7 and to 1 Pet 2:13. Tertullian, *On Idolatry* 15 (NPNF 1 5:382), adds the proviso that this obedience excludes idolatry, and Jerome, *Commentary on Titus* (PL 26:626 CD), explains that if the emperor or leader orders something evil, then "it is more important to follow God than men" (Acts 5:29). Even before the Roman government under Constantine embraced the Christian church, Christians recognized the legitimacy of civic authority and even fit it into their view of God's rule over creation. This view is an expansion of the Israelites' self-identity as God's people, ruled by kings as God's regents, which in turn reflects the widespread understanding in the Eastern Mediterranean of the religious aspect of kingship. The Pastorals have a less complex political-religious ideology; they see government officials as legitimate rulers whose government can preserve or disturb Christians' peace and tranquillity (1 Tim 2:2). The pacification of the Roman empire proved beneficial not just for commerce, education, and social interaction, but also for the spread of Christianity along with other religious movements of the day. In subsequent ages the interlacing of political and religious authority has led to an increase in the number of Christians, an expansion of the church's influence in shaping public morality and social organization, and the enrichment of the public good through institutions of charity and public service as well as the products of artistic creativity. On the other hand, the entanglement of church and government has sometimes also resulted in the denial of basic human rights and free expression of conscience, the curtailing of scientific research, and the taking of opponents' lives. In the contemporary Western world of secular governments the church competes with other religious and social movements both for adherents and for a voice in influencing public policy. It also sees itself as an essential component of the public common good. As it argues for recognition and support for its contributions to that common good, it advances the legitimate aims of secular government, always reserving the right to criticize and even resist what it sees as immoral and harmful to its own legitimate place and also to the public good.

After the positive exhortation (vv. 1-8), the letter cautions (vv. 9-11) against foolish and useless investigations and legal quarrels. If well-intentioned correction has no effect in the divisive individual, relations with the contentious person must be severed. The concern here is that neither Titus nor any other member of the community become implicated in that person's sinful activity. In this case Paul reminds Titus that such a person's perverse persistence in sin brings its own condemnation. Clearly such an eventuality would be the opposite of the righteousness and eternal life that the saving work and teaching of Jesus has accomplished and that the model lives of the saved faithful should prepare for and demonstrate.

For Reference and Further Study

Barth, Markus. *Ephesians*. 2 vols. AB 34, 34A. Garden City, NY: Doubleday, 1974.

Boismard, Marie-Émile. "Une liturgie baptismale dans la Prima Petri," *RB* 63 (1956) 182–84.

Borse, Udo. *1. und 2. Timotheusbrief*, 126.

Malherbe, Abraham J. *Paul and the Thessalonians: The Philosophic Tradition of Pastoral Care*. Philadelphia: Fortress Press, 1987, 90–94.

Marshall, I. Howard. "Faith and Works in the Pastoral Epistles," *SNTSU* 9 (1984) 203–18.

Merk, Otto. "Glaube und Tat in den Pastoralbriefen," *ZNW* 66 (1975) 91–102.

5. *Travel Notices; Letter Closing* (3:12-15)

12. When I get to send Artemas to you or Tychicus, make every effort to come to me at Nicopolis, for I have chosen to spend the winter there. 13. Diligently arrange for the travels of Zenas the lawyer and Apollos, so

that there be no shortage for them. 14. And as for our colleagues, too, let them learn to engage in good deeds to meet compelling needs that are lacking, so that they not be unproductive. 15. All who are with me greet you. Greet those who love us in faith. Grace be with you all.

Notes

12. *When I get to send Artemas to you or Tychicus:* This conjunction should require a subjunctive verb and not the future indicative (and see Rev 4:9). In this Hellenistic anomaly (Zerwick, 233–34) the moods in the text retain their original nuances. Artemas is known only here in the NT. Tychicus is a fellow Asian with Timothy (Acts 20:4); he is mentioned as an emissary in Asia Minor in 2 Tim 4:12; Col 4:7; Eph 6:21.

    make every effort to come . . . Nicopolis . . . to spend the winter: As in 2 Timothy, the apostolic *parousia* is reversed (2 Tim 4:9), for Paul summons his associates to join him. Nicopolis is mentioned only here in the NT. Presumably it is a location on the Adriatic coast in Epirus (contemporary Albania). See 2 Tim 4:21 for winter travel concerns. Travel on the Mediterranean was ordinarily suspended in winter. Hence there is a call to hurry. Acts 27:12-44 records the failed attempt to reach a winter haven on Crete during Paul's journey to Rome for trial. The winter stop at Nicopolis here cannot be fit into Paul's journeys in the letters and Acts. A mission tour to western Macedonia or even Illyricum seems to be in view (see Rom 15:19 for a reference to Illyricum).

13. *arrange for the travels of Zenas the lawyer and Apollos:* In the context of the Christian practice of hospitality, "arrange for the travels" denotes supplying the wherewithal for the journey (see 1 Cor 16:6-7, 11; 2 Cor 1:16; Rom 15:23-24, and also Acts 15:3; 3 John 6). In fulfilling the order Titus will offer an example of hospitality to the overseers (see 1:8) and for the church generally (compare 1 Tim 5:10). Zenas is mentioned only here in the NT. *Nomikos* ("lawyer") most likely denotes a secular lawyer or notary (Epictetus, *Diatr.* 2.13.6; *P. Oxy.* 237.8.2-4) rather than an expert in Jewish Law, given the PE's low opinion of the latter (1:14; 1 Tim 1:6-7). A person named Apollos was lionized by some at Corinth (1 Cor 1:12), where he worked following Paul's initial efforts there (1 Cor 3:6). After that he spent a good deal of time at Ephesus (1 Cor 16:12), where he had originally been introduced to Christianity by Prisca and Aquila (Acts 18:24).

14. *let them learn to engage in good deeds to meet compelling needs:* Despite the intellectual focus on matters of doctrine and faith, learning also involves action in these letters (see 3:5, 8, and compare 1 Tim 5:4; contrast 1 Tim 5:13; 2 Tim 3:7). Such action, as well as neutralizing the effects of the opponent teachers in the community would encourage the community as it confronts these changes and challenges.

    The compelling needs receive no specific clarification. The sentiment resembles that at 1 Tim 5:16, which looks to stretching the thin resources of the church to come to the support of "real" and needy widows. It also recalls the work of those widows who exercise hospitality, serve the faithful, assist the afflicted, and pursue every good deed (1 Tim 5:4, 10) and the call to the wealthy to be rich in the good works of sharing their bounty (1 Tim 6:17-19, and compare Eph 4:28; see also 2:14).

that they not be unproductive: The fruitfulness of the Christian life is the issue in the parable of the sower (Mark 4:19 *parr.*). Paul often speaks of fruit as a spiritual benefit (see Gal 5:22, and compare Rom 1:13; 6:21, 22; Phil 1:11; 4:17). However, he also expresses a concern for fruitfulness in terms of valuable accomplishments (1 Cor 14:14 and Phil 1:22). This resembles the usage here. Like Titus, 2 Pet 1:8 also sees fruitfulness as connected with actions that proceed from virtue. Ephesians 5:9-11 contrasts these with the fruitless works of evil.

In general this concluding exhortation, with its appeal to avoid disruption, the corrective warning to and even ostracism of the divisive person, and the call to be busy in doing good resemble the end of 2 Thessalonians (3:6-15). It depicts an ideal of an energetic community, responding to needs, working in unanimity, under the broad expectation of the return of Christ Jesus.

15. *Grace be with you all:* The final greeting is like that of 2 Tim 4:22b. The salutation here closely resembles that at the end of 1 Corinthians, containing as it does: (1) a reference to wintering location; (2) a concern for travel needs; (3) the mention of Apollos.

Interpretation

The final greeting begins with some references to mission personnel and community generosity (vv. 12-14) and ends with Paul's passing on the greeting of his companions (v. 15). The salutation comes to a quick close.

The summons to Titus to join Paul (3:12) suggests that Titus' work on Crete is not to be drawn out in time. The obvious optimism about setting in place the presbyter-overseers and rectifying the other matters, as well as neutralizing the effects of the opponent teachers in the community, would encourage the community as it confronts these changes and challenges.

Sending Zenas and Apollos on, outfitted for their trip, suggests ongoing mission to other areas that links the Cretan church to other Pauline church centers. The call to the community to distinguish themselves by good deeds to meet necessities reiterates both the group's consciousness of the church (*hoi hēmeteroi*, "our colleagues") and the importance of good works for the community to be fruitful. Both themes are mentioned together at 2:14.

For Reference and Further Study

Borse, Udo. *1. und 2. Timotheusbrief*, 130–31.

Duncan, George S. "Paul's Ministry in Asia—The Last Phase," *NTS* 3 (1957) 211–18.

________. "Chronological Table to Illustrate Paul's Ministry in Asia," *NTS* 5 (1958) 43–45.

Malherbe, Abraham J. *Social Aspects of Early Christianity*. Baton Rouge and London: Louisiana State University Press, 1977, 67–68.

Metzger, Wolfgang. *Die letzte Reise des Apostels Paulus: Beobachtungen und Erwägungen zu seinem Itinerar nach den Pastoralbriefen*. Stuttgart: Calwer, 1976.

INDEXES

SCRIPTURE AND OTHER ANCIENT WRITINGS

Christian Scriptures

Early Jewish Writings

Early Christian Writings

Greco-Roman Writings

AUTHORS

SUBJECTS